Get Writing

Sentences and Paragraphs

Mark Connelly
Milwaukee Area Technical College

WADSWORTH
CENGAGE Learning™

Australia • Brazil • Japan • Korea • Mexico • Singapore • Spain • United Kingdom • United States

WADSWORTH
CENGAGE Learning

Get Writing: Sentences and Paragraphs
Mark Connelly

Publisher: Michael Rosenberg

Acquisitions Editor: Stephen Dalphin

Development Editor: Michell Phifer

Editorial Assistant: Dawn Giovanniello

Technology Project Manager: Joe Gallagher

Marketing Manager: Mary Jo Southern

Advertising Project Manager: Brian Chaffee

Project Manager, Editorial Production:
Brett Palana-Shanahan

Senior Print Buyer: Mary Beth Hennebury

Permissions Editor: Sarah Harkrader

Composition: Newgen

Text Designer: Brian Salisbury

Photo Manager: Sheri Blaney

Photo Researcher: Jill Engerbretson

Cover Designer: Linda Beaupre

For product information and technology assistance, contact us at
Cengage Learning Customer & Sales Support, 1-800-354-9706
For permission to use material from this text or product,
submit all requests online at **www.cengage.com/permissions**
Further permissions questions can be emailed to
permissionrequest@cengage.com

ExamView® and ExamView Pro® are registered trademarks of FSCreations, Inc. Windows is a registered trademark of the Microsoft Corporation used herein under license. Macintosh and Power Macintosh are registered trademarks of Apple Computer, Inc. Used herein under license.

© 2006 Cengage Learning, Inc. All rights reserved. Cengage Learning WebTutor™ is a trademark of Cengage Learning, Inc.

Library of Congress Control Number: 2004114403

Student Edition ISBN-13: 978-0-15-506316-7

Student Edition ISBN-10: 0-15-506316-2

Instructor's Edition ISBN-13: 978-1-4130-0262-1

Instructor's Edition ISBN-10: 1-4130-0262-5

Credits appear on page 487, which constitutes a continuation of the copyright page.

Wadsworth
25 Thomson Place
Boston, MA 02210-1202
USA

Cengage Learning is a leading provider of customized learning solutions with office locations around the globe, including Singapore, the United Kingdom, Australia, Mexico, Brazil, and Japan. Locate your local office at:
international.cengage.com/region

Cengage Learning products are represented in Canada by Nelson Education, Ltd.

For your course and learning solutions, visit **academic.cengage.com**

Purchase any of our products at your local college store or at our preferred online store **www.ichapters.com**

Printed in China
5   6   7   12   11   10   09   08

Brief Contents

Contents

v

Part 3   WRITING SENTENCES   167

Chapter 12   Recognizing the Power of Words   168

Chapter 13   Writing Sentences   182

HANDBOOK   425

Preface

The Goals of *Get Writing*

Get Writing helps students acquire skills and develop confidence as writers by engaging them in their own writing. *Get Writing* assumes that students have things to say about their goals, families, jobs, college, personal interests, and the world around them. Throughout the book students are given opportunities to express themselves on a range of topics and to then examine and improve their words, sentences, and paragraphs. Above all, *Get Writing* connects critical thinking (what students are trying to say about a topic) with grammar and mechanics (what they have written about the topic).

Approach

Get Writing guides students to improve their writing by asking two questions.

1. **What are you trying to say?**
   Why did you choose this topic?
   What do you want readers to know about it?
   What details are important?
   What is the best way to organize your ideas?

2. **What have you written?**
   Are your words effective?
   Do your sentences clearly express what you wanted to say?
   Can readers follow your train of thought?
   What mechanical errors detract from your message?

Get Writing is designed to serve a variety of students, including recent high school graduates, working adults returning to school, and those for whom English is a second language. Writing exercises and sample paragraphs cover a range of interests—sports, history, politics, science, the media, popular culture, minority issues, and world events.

Get Writing does not teach writing in isolation. It assists students with the writing tasks they will encounter in other courses and in their jobs. Writing assignments ask students to comment on their progress in college, identify challenges, and consider strategies for improving their writing skills, study habits, and time management.

Focus on Writing

Get Writing offers students a variety of writing opportunities.

What Are You Trying to Say?/What Have You Written? Chapters begin by asking students to express their thoughts in sentences and paragraphs on a range of topics. After writing a draft, they are asked to examine what they have written. By examining their word choices, use of details, and critical thinking skills, they learn to improve their writing and to link what they are studying with their own work.

Responding to Images Visual prompts open and close chapters, encouraging students to use critical thinking to write about images that depict jobs, family, school life, and social issues. Photos are often paired to encourage analysis and comparison.

Critical Thinking Students are prompted to write about personal experiences and world issues ranging from terrorism to favorite television shows.

Real World Writing Throughout *Get Writing,* students write, revise, and edit documents they will encounter beyond the classroom: announcements, e-mail, resumes, and letters.

Working Together Collaborative writing and editing exercises demonstrate the value of peer review and provide practice working in groups.

Organization

Get Writing consists of five parts, which can be taught in different sequences to meet the needs of instructors.

Part 1: Getting Started introduces students to the importance of writing and provides strategies for succeeding in writing courses. The writing process, from prewriting to final editing, is explained in practical steps.

Part 2: Developing Paragraphs shows students how to build paragraphs by creating clear topic sentences supported by details. Chapters cover five patterns of development: description, narration, example, comparison and contrast, and cause and effect.

Unlike other textbooks, *Get Writing* integrates student and professional readings into each chapter.

Exam skills demonstrate how students use different patterns of development to answer essay questions.

Student paragraphs illustrate how students use a particular pattern of development to build paragraphs for personal essays, college assignments, and examinations.

Putting Paragraphs Together show how separate paragraphs work together to create a short essay.

Short professional essays demonstrate how writers use patterns of development. Readings include pieces by Jose Antonio Burciaga, Yi-Fu Tuan, Ellen Goodman, Suzanne Britt, and Stephen King.

Part 3: Writing Sentences explains the parts of sentences and how they work together to express thoughts. Students are given practical tips for detecting and repairing common sentence errors.

What Do You Know? opens each chapter, offering a short quiz with answers so students can test themselves to see how much they know about each unit.

Sequenced exercises direct students to identify and repair individual sentences, then detect and repair errors in context.

Writing exercises guide students to develop their own sentences and paragraphs, then to identify and correct errors in their writing.

What Have You Learned? concludes each chapter, offering a short quiz with answers so students can test themselves, identifying areas that need review.

Points to Remember end each chapter, providing main points for quick review and easy reference.

Parts 4 and 5: Understanding Grammar and Using Punctuation and Mechanics demonstrate that grammar is not a set of arbitrary rules but a tool to express ideas and prevent confusion. *Get Writing* connects grammar with critical thinking, so students understand that decisions about sentence structure depend on what they are trying to say. As in Part 3, these chapters open and close with self-graded quizzes. Visual writing prompts, critical thinking exercises, and What Are You Trying to Say?/ What Have You Written? offer students a variety of writing opportunities to connect what they learn about grammar with what they write. Cumulative exercises contain errors based on lessons in previous chapters, providing students with realistic editing and revising challenges.

Other Features

The **Handbook** summarizes rules and guidelines for easy reference.

Writing at Work offers practical advice on the most common writing tasks students face outside the classroom—writing e-mail, letters, and résumés.

Writing on the Web guides students to use the Internet to locate online writing resources.

ESL boxes provide help with specific writing problems encountered by students still mastering English.

Ancillaries

The *Annotated Instructor's Edition* provides answers to all exercises found in the student version of the textbook.

The *Instructor's Manual/Test Bank* is an inclusive supplement written by Luis Nazario of Pueblo Community College. The *Instructor's Manual* section includes a variety of teaching aids, including directions on how to use the integrated features of *Get Writing,* such as the Working Together activities, visual writing prompts, Critical Thinking assignments, and What Are You Trying to Say?/ What Have You Written? assignments. The manual also discusses how to incorporate the professional and student model paragraphs in class and provides additional writing assignments, collaborative activities, and teaching tips for every chapter. The *Instructor's Manual* offers additional ESL information for many chapters as well as suggestions for teaching to various learning styles.

The *Test Bank* consists of almost 600 testing items: one test for each writing chapter (Chapters 1–11) and three tests—one diagnostic test and two mastery tests—each for Chapters 12–27. These tests are a combination of generative testing items, which ask students to write their own sentences within guided parameters, and objective questions that cover the skills and concepts presented in the textbook.

Acknowledgments

All books are a collaborative effort. My special thanks goes to Michael Rosenberg, publisher; Stephen Dalphin, acquisitions editor; and Michell Phifer, development editor, for their support, vision, and enthusiasm for *Get Writing*. I would also like to thank the talented Wadsworth production and marketing team: Brett Palana-Shanahan, production project manager; Mary Jo Southern, marketing manager; Katrina Byrd, marketing manager; and Joe Gallagher, technology project manager.

Get Writing: Sentences and Paragraphs benefited greatly from comments and suggestions made by a dedicated group of reviewers:

Jeanette Adkins, *Tarrant County College*

Cassandra Bagley, *Kentucky State University*

Elaine Bassett, *Troy University*

Jessica Carroll, *Miami-Dade Community College*

Henry Castillo, *Temple Junior College*

Sujata Chohan, *Heald College*

Judy Covington, *Trident Technical College*

Sara Cushing, *Piedmont Technical College*

Deborah Davis, *Richland College*

Roberta Eisel, *Citrus College*

Ruth Ellis, *North Central Texas College*

Jason Evans, *Prairie State College*

Eric Fish, *Northeast State Technical Community College*

Todd Fox, *California State University, Long Beach*

Virginia Gibbons, *Oakton Community College*

Suzanne Gitonga, *North Lake College*

Elaine Herrick, *Temple College*

Vicki Houser, *Northeast Tennessee State College*

Christine Hubbard, *Tarrant County College*

Christy Hughes, *Orangeburg-Calhoun Technical College*

Jane Johnson, *Kilgore College*

Jerry Kane, *TESST College of Technology*

Patricia Malinowski, *Finger Lakes Community College*

Mimi Markus, *Broward Community College*

Gretchen McCroskey, *Northeast State Technical Community College*

Julie Nichols, *Okaloosa-Walton Community College*

Virginia Nugent, *Miami-Dade Community College*

Laura Ore, *Austin Community College*

Valerie Russell, *Valencia Community College*

Joseph Smigelski, *Diablo Community College*

Pamela Tackabury, *Fullerton College*

Linda Marianne Taylor, *Tri-County Technical College*

Kendra Vaglienti, *Brookhaven College*

Carolyn Varvel, *Art Institute of Colorado, Denver*

Wendy Jo Ward, *Miami-Dade Community College*

Benjamin Worth, *Lexington Community College*

Gary Zacharias, *Palomar College*

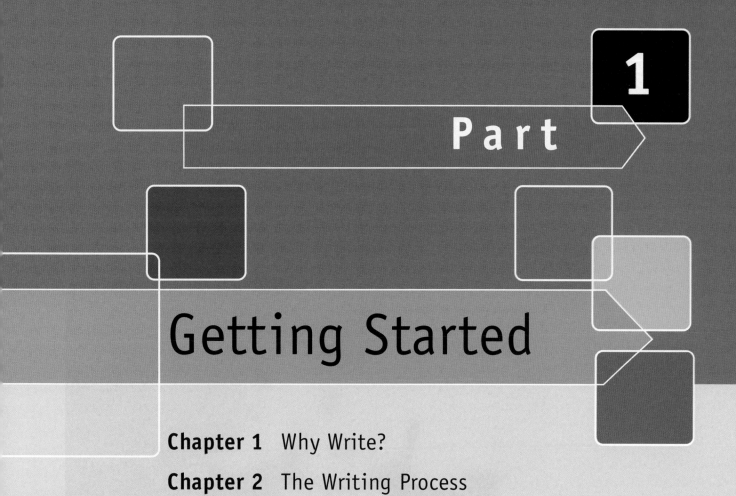

Part 1

Getting Started

Why Write?

GET WRITING

How do you write? Do you make plans first or just start writing? Do you consider how readers will respond to your ideas? Does what you write express what you are trying to say?

Write three or four sentences describing your method of writing and how you would like to improve it.

You probably did not enroll in college to study writing. Most of us think of writers as people who write for a living—novelists, reporters, biographers, and screenwriters. But writing is an important part of almost anyone's job.

Thinking of your future career, you probably imagine yourself in action—a nurse treating patients, a police officer investigating a crime scene, or a contractor walking through a construction site. All these professionals are writers. They may not publish books or articles, but they depend on writing to achieve their goals. Nurses and police officers record their daily actions and observations in charts and reports that may become evidence in court. Contractors write letters, plans, proposals, and streams of e-mail to architects, suppliers, clients, and inspectors. Whatever field you enter, your success will depend on your ability to communicate ideas in writing.

WRITING ACTIVITY   GET WRITING

Describe your future career. What job do you want after graduation?
In what situations do people in that field write to others?

_____

_____

_____

_____

_____

_____

_____

_____

_____

_____

_____

_____

_____

_____

_____

Read what you have written and list the most important ways writing will shape
your future.

_____

_____

_____

GOALS OF THIS BOOK

Get Writing has been created to

- increase your awareness of the importance of writing
- improve your knowledge of the writing process
- increase your understanding of sentences and paragraphs
- overcome common writing problems
- prepare you for writing challenges in college and your future career

Using *Get Writing*

At first glance any textbook can be intimidating. Look through *Get Writing* to become comfortable with it. Mark useful passages with bookmarks or Post-Its for quick reference. Remember to use *Get Writing* as a resource not only in English courses, but in any writing you do in or out of school.

WORKING TOGETHER

Discuss writing with three or four other students and ask them to list problems and questions they have—from getting started writing to using commas. List your own top five problems:

1. _____

2. _____

3. _____

4. _____

5. _____

Look at the table of contents and index in *Get Writing* to locate pages that address these problems.

What Is Good Writing?

Many students are confused about what is considered "good writing." Comments by teachers and professors can be confusing and contradictory. What is considered "good writing" in high school is often unacceptable in college. English teachers urge you to use colorful words and creative language to express yourself, while business and technical instructors insist that you avoid personal insights and use standard terminology. Writing that is effective in one situation is inappropriate in another.

The Writing Context

Although spelling, capitalization, and punctuation have standard rules, many elements of what makes writing "good" are shaped by the context. Writing does not take place in a vacuum. Writing occurs in a context shaped by four things:

1. the writer's goal
2. the readers' needs, expectations, beliefs, and knowledge
3. the situation, discipline, occupation, or event in which the writing takes place
4. the nature of the document

Context explains why a newspaper article about a plane crash differs from a government accident report or a lawyer's letter to an injured passenger. Written in simple language and printed in narrow columns for quick skimming, a newspaper article summarizes events for general readers. A government report written by engineers might run to hundreds of pages and contain technical terms most people would not understand. A lawyer writing to victims would use persuasive language to urge them to take legal action.

When you write, ask yourself four key questions about context:

What Is Your Goal?

Are you writing to share an idea, complete an assignment, answer a question, or apply for a job? Do you want readers to change their minds or take action?

Who Is the Reader?

Who are you writing to—a single person or a group? Is your reader likely to agree or disagree with your ideas? What information do you have to include to convince readers to accept your views?

What Is the Discipline or Situation?

Each discipline, profession, business, or community has unique traditions, standards, expectations, values, and culture. Humanities professors encourage students to present individual interpretations of novels, films, or paintings. Science instructors, however, expect students to follow rigid rules of objective research and avoid personal comments. An advertising agency depends on creativity, whereas an accounting firm demands accuracy. One city council might stress industrial development, whereas another values historical preservation. The writing situation greatly shapes the way you present ideas and format the document.

What Is Expected in the Document?

When you write, make sure your message matches the nature of the document. Don't expect people to read a ten-page e-mail or assume a professor will accept a two-page term paper.

WRITING ACTIVITY

GET WRITING

A group of high school students are suspended for sharing prescription cold pills during a recent flu epidemic. Although no money changed hands and students followed the recommended dosage, they violated the school's zero tolerance policy on drug use.

Briefly describe the context of the following documents:

A suspended student explaining what happened to an online friend in an Instant Message:

the writer's goal _____

the reader _____

the discipline _____

the document _____

A parent's e-mail to the school board demanding her daughter be readmitted to school:

the writer's goal _____

the reader _____

the discipline _____

the document _____

A newspaper editorial supporting or criticizing the principal's actions:

the writer's goal _____

the reader _____

the discipline _____

the document _____

The school board's statement to local, state, and national media that have requested information about the incident:

the writer's goal _____

the reader _____

the discipline _____

the document _____

To learn more about writing contexts, look at websites, newspapers, and magazines. Notice how the style of articles in *Seventeen, People,* and *Cosmopolitan* differs from that of the *New York Times, Newsweek,* and *Foreign Affairs.*

STRATEGIES FOR SUCCEEDING IN WRITING COURSES

1. *Review your syllabus and textbooks carefully.* Make sure you know the policies for missed classes, late papers, and incompletes. Note due dates on your calendar.

(continued)

2. *As soon as possible, read descriptions of all assignments listed in the syllabus.* Reviewing assignments in advance allows you to think ahead and make notes for upcoming papers.

3. *Make sure you fully know what your instructor expects on each assignment.* Study your syllabus, sample papers, and handouts for guidance. If you have any questions about an upcoming paper, ask your instructor.

4. *Locate support services.* Many colleges have computer labs, tutoring facilities, and writing centers to assist students.

5. *Talk to other students about writing.* Bounce ideas off other students. Ask them to comment on your choice of topic, main idea, or support. Share rough drafts with others.

6. *Experiment by writing at different times and places.* If you are new on campus, you may find some places easier to work in than others. The casual atmosphere of a student union may be a better writing environment than a computer lab or the library. You may find it easier to write early in the morning or after working out.

7. *If you don't already write on a computer, learn.* Most colleges offer short courses in word processing. Once you graduate you will be expected to work on a computer. Though a bit cumbersome at first, writing on a computer makes your job as a student much easier.

8. *Read your papers aloud before turning them in.* The fastest and easiest way to edit papers is to read them aloud. It is easier to "hear" than "see" missing and misspelled words, awkward phrases, fragments, and illogical statements.

9. *Keep copies of all assignments.*

10. *Study returned papers, especially ones with poor grades.* When you get an F or D− on an assignment, you might want to throw it away or bury it under some books. Although they are painful to look at, these papers hold the key to success. Note the instructor's comments and suggestions. List mechanical errors and note sections in *Get Writing* that can help you overcome these problems in future assignments.

11. *Never copy or use the work of others in your writing without informing your readers.*

12. *Write as often as you can.* Writing, like anything else, takes practice. Keep a journal or an online blog, e-mail friends, and take notes in class. Record your thoughts while you watch television. Any kind writing will help you get used to thinking in sentences and paragraphs.

CRITICAL THINKING

GET THINKING
AND WRITING

Describe your writing experiences in high school or in a recent job. What assignments were the most difficult? What comments did teachers make about your writing? What letters or reports gave you the most trouble at work?

Read your comments and identify the most important ideas you discovered. Summarize your most important point in one sentence:

_____

_____

_____

What two or three things do you want to change about your writing?

1. _____

2. _____

3. _____

WHAT HAVE YOU WRITTEN?

Read your comments out loud. What changes would you make if you had to turn it in for a grade?

- Are there sentences that are off the topic and should be deleted?
- Could you add more details and examples?
- Could you choose more effective words?
- Would a teacher or other readers understand your main point?

GET WRITING

What challenges do you face this semester? Review your syllabi and course outlines for upcoming assignments. Write three or four sentences describing the biggest challenge you face this semester. How can you increase your chances of success? Do you need to organize your time better? Do some assignments require outside help?

© Eric Kamp/Index Stock Imagery

WRITING ON THE WEB

Exploring Writing Resources Online

The Internet contains a constantly expanding variety of resources for student writers: dictionaries, encyclopedias, grammar exercises, databases, library catalogs, editing tips, and research strategies.

1. Review your library's electronic databases, links, and search engines. Locate online dictionaries and encyclopedias that can assist you with upcoming assignments.

2. Using a search engine such as AltaVista, Yahoo!, or Google, enter key words such as *prewriting, proofreading, narration, capitalization, thesis statement, comma exercises, editing strategies,* and other terms that appear throughout the book, the index, or your course syllabus. In addition to providing formal databases, many schools and instructors have constructed online tutorials that can help you improve your writing, overcome grammar problems, and help in specific assignments.

POINTS TO REMEMBER

1. Writing is important not only in college but in any career you enter.
2. Writing takes place in a context formed by the writer's goal, the reader, the discipline or situation, and the nature of the document.
3. You can improve your writing by studying past efforts.
4. Writing improves with practice. Write as often as you can.

2

The Writing Process

© David Chen /Index Stock Imagery

GET WRITING

Where do you get your ideas? Are you a careful consumer of information? Do you ask yourself questions before you write?

Write a short statement explaining why it is important to think before simply repeating what you see and hear.

This book concentrates on the building blocks of writing—words, sentences, and paragraphs. To fully understand them, however, you need to see how they work together to create whole documents—essays, letters, and e-mails. You have to get the big picture.

This chapter explains the writing process: how to select a topic, explore ideas, organize details, and create a document that expresses what you want to say. Experienced writers work in many different ways, but most follow a step-by-step method to save time and improve their writing. Follow these steps in your first writing assignments, then feel free to make changes to create your own composing style, a way of writing that works with the way you think and the task you face.

THE WRITING PROCESS

Step 1   Prewrite: Use critical thinking to explore ideas.
Step 2   Plan: Establish context, develop a thesis, outline ideas.
Step 3   Write: Get your ideas on paper.
Step 4   Cool: Put your writing aside.
Step 5   Revise: Review and rewrite your paper.
Step 6   Edit: Check the final version for mechanical errors.

POINT TO REMEMBER

You can improve your writing by asking yourself two questions:

What am I trying to say?
What have I written?

Although writing can be broken into separate stages, it is often a *recursive,* or repeated, process. Writers don't always work in fixed steps but write, revise, and edit as they go along. They may edit and polish the first paragraph before starting the rest of the paper. On another assignment, they may write the conclusion first. Writing on a computer allows you to move from writing to editing, coming up with new ideas and fixing errors as you work.

Step 1: Prewrite

It is part of the business of the writer . . . to examine attitudes, to go beneath the surface, to tap the source.
JAMES BALDWIN

To be a successful writer, you need to see things with a "writer's eye." Good writers are not passive. They don't simply repeat what they have heard or seen on television, and they don't just jot down everything they "feel." Good writers use *critical thinking.* They observe their subject closely, ask questions, collect facts, test commonly held beliefs, and avoid making snap decisions. Good writing is never "about" a topic—it has a purpose and makes a point. A good paper shares more than facts and dates, first impressions, or immediate reactions. Good writing goes beyond the obvious to explore ideas and events, to analyze people and ideas.

STRATEGIES FOR INCREASING CRITICAL THINKING

1. *Study subjects carefully—don't rely on first impressions or make snap judgments.* If your car is stolen and your neighbor's house is broken into, you may quickly assume that crime is increasing in your community. But until you study police reports, you really only know that you are one of two victims. It could be that crime is actually dropping but that you and your neighbor happen to fall into the shrinking pool of victims.

2. *Distinguish between facts and opinions.* Don't mistake people's opinions, attitudes, or feelings as facts. Opinions express a point of view. They can be valid—but they are not evidence. You can factually report that your sister sleeps until ten, doesn't make her bed, and won't look for a summer job. But calling her "lazy" states an opinion, not a fact.

3. *Don't rely on limited evidence.* Isolated events and personal experiences may be interesting but lack the authority of extensive objective research. The fact that your great-grandfather smoked three packs of cigarettes a day and lived past ninety does not prove that tobacco is harmless.

4. *Avoid basing judgments on weak comparisons.* No two situations are ever identical. Because a policy works in Japan does not mean it will work in the United States. Strategies that worked in the Gulf War might not be effective in another conflict. Comparisons can be compelling arguments but only if supported by facts.

5. *Don't confuse a time relationship with cause and effect.* Events take place over time. If you develop headaches after a car crash, you might assume they were caused by the accident. But the headaches could be caused by lack of sleep or a food allergy and have nothing to do with your recent accident.

6. *Judge ideas, not personalities.* Don't be impressed by celebrity endorsements or reject an idea because the person supporting it is controversial. Judge ideas on their own merits. Unpopular people often have good ideas, and popular people can be wrong.

7. *Avoid making absolute statements.* If you make absolute statements such as "all politicians are corrupt" or "people always regret buying a used car," your argument can be dismissed if a reader can provide a single exception.

8. *Examine quotations and statistics offered as support.* People often try to influence us by offering quotations by famous people or impressive statistics. But until you know the full context of someone's statement or the origin of the statistics, they have little value. Statistics may be based on biased research and easily distorted. Even accurate numbers can be misinterpreted.

9. *Above all, think before you write.*

TIPS FOR BRAINSTORMING

1. **Focus brainstorming by keeping the final paper in mind.** Review the assignment instructions.

2. **Use full sentences to write out important ideas you may forget.**

3. **Use key words for a quick Internet search.** Glancing at a list of websites may stimulate new ideas.

4. **Think of the list as a funnel leading from broad subjects to defined topics.** Avoid creating a list of random ideas.

Prewriting Techniques

Prewriting puts critical thinking into action. Experiment with one or all of these methods to see which helps you the most.

Brainstorming lists ideas. A student brainstorming for an upcoming psychology paper starts with the title of a chapter in a textbook, then lists ideas to discover a topic:

"Depressive Disorders"
Depression

Effects of depression
Suicide
SAD — Seasonal Affective Disorder
Postpartum depression
Postpartum depression and child neglect/abuse/murder (Houston case)
Topic: *Postpartum depression as basis for insanity plea*

In **freewriting,** you record your thoughts, feelings, attitudes, and impressions by writing as quickly as possible. When you freewrite, you are not trying to create a rough draft but discover ideas. Many students find that writing one idea triggers another. Freewriting is like talking into a tape recorder to capture everything you know about a topic. When you freewrite, don't stop to check spelling, think about writing in complete sentences, or worry about going off topic. Remember, you are not writing an essay but exploring ideas.

To freewrite, sit with a blank page or computer screen and write as fast as you can about a topic:

> Last week big campus demonstration against oil companies protesting drilling in artic wildlife preserves. Students left the demonstration in gas guzzling SUVS. Problem of the environment is that consumers dont want to change their lifestyles. People don't want oil drilling or refineries or oil tankers damaging the environment but they want to drive big cars, have big air-condition houses, power boats, lawnmowers, and they want all that energy cheap. People want to blame the government and corporate leaders for global warming and pollution. But can we save the environment without making sacrifices. Driving small cars, living in smaller houses. Paying $5 a gallon for gas like Europe. . . . Using less electricity. Buying less and recycling more and consuming less. We want some kind of magic solution, its like people who want to be slim and attractive but not have to diet or exercise. Or people who want the money and prestige of being doctors and lawyers but don't want to study or work hard. Maybe TV with it's instant solutions where every problem is solved in sixty minutes is to blame for our immature attitudes toward everything in society today.

The paragraph is filled with confusing sentences and spelling errors. It trails off into a series of unrelated observations. But the student has identified the heart of a good paper—people's unrealistic desire to save the environment without changing their lifestyle.

Asking questions about a topic can identify your existing knowledge, reveal terms or ideas that need to be defined, and indicate what research might have to be conducted. Asking questions is a good way of putting critical thinking into action because questions leave room for doubt and further reflection. A student planning to describe her first apartment can improve her paper by asking questions:

Why did I choose this topic?
Why did I think of describing my apartment and not my car or favorite restaurant?
What did it mean to me?
What made it significant to me?
What is the most important thing I want people to know about it?
What do I remember most about that apartment?
How do I feel about it now?

TIPS FOR FREEWRITING

1. **Use freewriting for personal essays and open-topic assignments.** Freewriting allows you to explore your existing knowledge and beliefs. This method, however, may not help you respond to highly structured assignments or develop business documents.
2. **Use a question to focus freewriting.** Asking yourself "Why do kids drop out of school?" is a better starting point than a general idea of "writing a paper about public schools."
3. **Don't feel obligated to write in complete sentences.** Making lists or jotting down key words can save time.
4. **Save your freewriting for future assignments.**
5. **Highlight important ideas by underlining or circling them.**

TIPS FOR ASKING QUESTIONS

1. **Keep the assignment in mind as you pose questions.**
2. **Avoid questions that call for simple yes or no answers.** Use questions that ask "why?" or "how?"
3. **Remember that the goal of asking questions is to identify a topic and prompt critical thinking.**

Was it a good or bad place to live?
How did my apartment help me grow as a person?
What problems did I have?
Would I want to move back?
What is the best/worst thing that happened to me there?
How did that apartment change my life? Did I learn any lessons from it?

Questions like these can spark insights and help the student write an interesting description that does more than list details about rooms and furniture.

Clustering (also called **diagramming, mapping,** and **webbing**) uses markers like circles, columns, boxes, and arrows to discover and organize ideas. If you are visually minded, this method may be easier to use than freewriting or asking questions. It can be very useful if you are writing about a group of topics or comparing two subjects.

Here a student explores the influence of television on children:

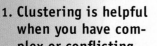

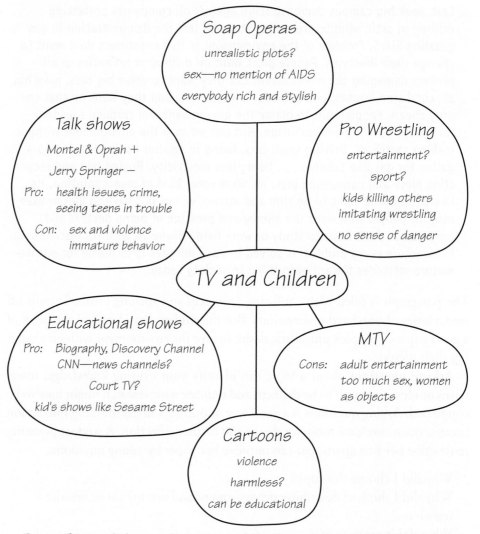

TIPS FOR CLUSTERING

1. **Clustering is helpful when you have complex or conflicting ideas.** You can group related items and place pro and con items in separate columns.
2. **Keep the artwork simple.** Don't spend too much time on the appearance of your notes. Remember, you are not creating a visual aid for a formal presentation, just a rough diagram.

Points: TV gives kids unrealistic views of life. Soap and rock stars have casual sex but no one gets AIDS. TV cops and wrestlers engage in fights but never end up in a wheelchair. Maybe the solution is for parents to comment as they watch or get kids to see more responsible and realistic news and educational programs.

By mapping out ideas and balancing positive and negative aspects of television, the student has been able to focus on a main topic.

> ### POINTS TO REMEMBER
>
> 1. The goal of prewriting is to explore ideas, develop a topic, and organize points—not write a rough draft.
> 2. Don't feel obligated to use a single prewriting technique—blend as many methods as you need.
> 3. Save prewriting notes. Ideas that may not be appropriate for one assignment could be useful for future papers.
> 4. Keep prewriting simple. Elaborate notes may be difficult to follow.

WRITING ACTIVITY

Select one of the topics below or from the list on pages 459–460 and prewrite for ten minutes. You may use one or more techniques. If you have an upcoming assignment in any of your classes, use this opportunity to get started.

Topics

financial aid	talk show hosts	stem cell research
your worst job	qualities of a good parent	Ecstasy
campus daycare	singles bars	MTV
your first car	favorite celebrity	campus fashion

Step 2: Plan

Moving from Topic to Thesis

Narrowing Your Topic

Once you develop a topic through prewriting, you may have to narrow it to a subject you can handle. There is little new you can say about crime in five hundred words, but you could write something interesting about boot camps for first offenders, racial profiling, or DNA evidence.

Developing a Thesis

After narrowing the topic, the next step is developing a **thesis,** or main point. If you want to write about lie detectors, you might concentrate on their scientific reliability, moral implications, or influence on juries. As you think and write about your topic, you should develop a controlling idea or point of view. A good paper is not "about" a subject; it makes a statement, expresses an opinion. The thesis states your opinion or explains your intent, what you want your readers to know:

Topic	lie detectors
Narrowed topic	scientific accuracy of polygraph examinations
Controlling idea	admissibility into courtrooms
Thesis	*Polygraph examinations should be admitted in court only when judges carefully explain to juries that lie detectors are not 100 percent accurate.*

Topic	my hometown
Narrowed topic	housing pattern in my hometown
Controlling idea	housing pattern's effect on young people growing up
Thesis	*The sprawling subdivisions of my hometown isolated young people from friends, school activities, and jobs, making them prone to loneliness and drug abuse.*

POINT TO REMEMBER

Don't confuse a *thesis* with a narrowed topic. A thesis does more than focus the subject of a paper—it has to express an opinion, make a statement.

WORKING TOGETHER

Select one of the general topics below or from the previous exercise and develop a narrowed topic, a controlling idea, and a thesis. When you are finished, share your work with other students. Make sure each person in the group develops a thesis and not just a narrowed topic.

General Topics

student housing	NFL and NBA salaries	reality television
sexual harassment	campus jobs	school loans
computer viruses	minimum wage	poverty
online dating	immigration laws	terrorism
used cars	annoying customers	police officers

General topic: _____

Narrowed topic: _____

Controlling idea: _____

_____

Thesis: _____

_____

Organizing Support

Once you have developed a thesis, you are ready to organize the paper, outlining the introduction, body, and conclusion. A few minutes of careful thought at the start of the process can save you time later on. In planning your paper, consider your goal, your reader, the discipline, and the nature of the paper.

Your goal	What do you want the paper to accomplish? What details, facts, or observations do you need to support your thesis?
Your reader	What information do your readers need? What support will they find most convincing?

Do readers have any biases or misconceptions you must address?

The discipline Will your paper follow the standards used in this discipline or profession?

The paper What is the appropriate format for this paper?

Creating an Outline

An outline does not have to be elaborate or use roman numerals and capital letters. Even a rough sketch can organize ideas and save time. Your plan works like a road map to guide your writing—listing your paper's beginning, middle, and end. But it is subject to change. New thoughts will come to mind, and you may expand or narrow your paper as you write.

The type of outline you develop depends on your topic. In planning a narrative, a simple timeline can organize ideas. In other papers, a more complex plan can serve to balance conflicting ideas, organize complicated evidence, or place confusing events in a logical order. Most outlines cover three basic parts of a document: introduction, body, and conclusion.

Introduction grabs attention
announces the topic
addresses reader concerns
prepares readers for what follows

Body organizes supporting details in a logical pattern

Conclusion ends with a brief summary, a final thought or observation, question, call for action, or prediction

---

POINT TO REMEMBER

You can place your thesis at the beginning, middle, or end of the paper. If your audience is opposed to your opinion, you may wish to present facts or tell a story before expressing your point of view.

WRITING ACTIVITY

Develop an outline for a topic and thesis you created in the previous exercise. You may also use this opportunity to organize your next assignment.

Topic: _____

Introduction: _____

_____

Body: _____

_____

_____

_____

_____

Conclusion: _____

Step 3: Write

After reviewing your plan, write as much as you can. Your goal is not to produce a final draft but to get your ideas on paper. Don't feel obligated to write in complete sentences—to save time, list ideas. Don't worry about spelling or grammar at this point. If you stop to look up a word in a dictionary, you will break your train of thought. Instead, highlight errors for future reference as you write:

> *Last year _____ people (get figures from Time article) lost their most valuable possession—there ? <u>identity.</u> Computer hackers got their social security #'s, bank account, even passwords and empited their checking accounts, billed their credit cards, took out loans, bought cars, even used there ID's to post <u>bale</u>. According to Jim <u>Hogobian</u> (sp?) it can take two to three years for a <u>victum</u> to get there (?) records straight. In the meantime these people will have loans denied, be harassed by creditors, and find that most law enforcement authorities are of little help.*

GET WRITING ▶ **WRITING ACTIVITY**

Write a draft of the paper you planned in the previous exercise or for an upcoming assignment.

Step 4: Cool

This is an easy—but important—step. After you finish writing, put your work aside and let it "cool." When you complete a draft, your first thought might be to quickly go over your work. Because your ideas are fresh in your mind, it is difficult to be objective about what you have produced on paper. Set the work aside. Take a walk, do an errand, or study another assignment. Then return to your work. If you have an e-mail to send today, try to write a draft in the morning, then set it aside so you can read and revise it in the afternoon.

Step 5: Revise

Revising means "to see again." It means much more than simply correcting spelling mistakes and adding missing details.

Revising Checklist
1. Print a copy of your draft. You may find revising on a computer difficult because the screen prevents you from seeing the whole paper.
2. Review your assignment and your goal. Does your draft meet the requirements and express what you want to say?

3. Examine the thesis—is it clearly expressed? Should it be located in another part of the essay for better effect?

4. Does the introduction gain readers' attention and prepare them for the body of the essay?

5. Does the body present enough details to support your thesis? Is the information clearly organized? Can readers follow your train of thought?

6. Are there any lapses in critical thinking? Should you present additional evidence or restate your opinions?

7. Are there missing details needed to support your thesis? Are there unrelated ideas that should be deleted?

8. Does the conclusion leave readers with a fact, comment, or question they will remember, or does it only repeat the introduction?

Having revised your work, you are ready to write additional drafts. Your work may need only minor changes. In other instances, it is easier to start a new version using a different approach.

Using Peer Review

Teachers often convince students that getting help with assignments is cheating. But it is not cheating to have other people read your work, make suggestions, and answer questions you ask them. You should not let others *write* the paper for you, but you can benefit from hearing their criticisms and suggestions.

PEER REVIEW GUIDELINES

1. Make sure reviewers understand the writing task. They will find the writing hard to evaluate if they don't know who is supposed to read it or what it has to accomplish. Explain your assignment and any instructor's directions before showing people your writing.

2. Let the writing speak for itself. Don't coach people by telling them what you are trying to say. Explain the assignment, then let people read your draft so they can objectively examine the words on the page. After hearing their initial comments, you might explain what you want to say, then ask if they think you accomplish your goals.

3. Ask specific questions. If you just ask, "Is this any good?" or "What do you think?" you may only get vague responses. Instead, ask readers if they understand your thesis, if the introduction is clear, if you present enough details, if your arguments make sense.

4. Encourage readers to be critical. Too often friends and other students want to be polite and positive and may be reluctant to sound negative.

5. When reviewing other people's writing, be objective and make constructive criticisms. Don't just point out errors. Try to suggest changes.

REVISING ACTIVITY

Revise the draft you have written. You may wish to share your work with other students and ask them to suggest ways of improving it.

Step 6: Edit

The final step in the writing process is editing the final form of the document. In editing, you want to make sure you not only correct spelling and capitalization errors but eliminate wordy phrases and rewrite confusing or weak sentences.

Editing Checklist

1. Read your paper out loud. It is often easier to "hear" than see errors such as misspelled or missing words, awkward phrases, clumsy sentences, and fragments. (See Chapters 14 and 27.)

2. Make sure your sentence structure is appropriate to the type of document. An e-mail should be written in short, easy-to-read sentences. A long essay or research paper, however, can include long and complex sentences. (See Chapter 13.)

3. Delete wordy phrases, such as "at this point in time" for "now" or "blue in color" for "blue." (See Chapter 12.)

4. Make sure your final document meets the required format. Should it be single or double spaced? Do you need documentation such as endnotes and a works cited page?

EDITING ACTIVITY

Edit the paper you have written and revised. Share your paper with other students. Refer to the index or table of contents of this book to find help with grammar problems.

AVOID PLAGIARISM

Never copy or use the work of others in your writing without informing your readers. Plagiarism is cheating. Faced with a tough assignment, you may be tempted to download an article from the Internet, copy a friend's paper, or take paragraphs from a magazine to put into your paper. Students caught copying papers are often flunked or expelled. If you use an outside source like a website or magazine, just changing a few words does not make your writing original. You can quote important statements or use statistics and facts if you tell readers where they came from. You don't always need detailed footnotes to prove you are not stealing. Just make sure you mention sources as you use them:

> *Newsweek* recently reported that a bioterrorism attack could kill 10 million people. The CIA, according to CNN, prevented the sale of anthrax stolen from a Swedish research lab last year.

Use quotation marks when you copy word for word what someone has said or written:

> Sandy Rodriguez called *The Great Gatsby* "an American fable about love, obsession, corruption, and loneliness."

Mention the author when you use your own words to express the same idea, called *paraphrasing*:

> According to Sandy Rodriguez, *The Great Gatsby* is an American tale about passion, corruption, and isolation.

CRITICAL THINKING

How effectively do our leaders inform us? Do you feel that presidents, members of Congress, governors, and mayors speak honestly and directly to the public? Do they provide valid reasons for their actions? Write a short paragraph stating your view about how a particular leader or political figures in general communicate to us.

© Jim Starr/Index Stock Imagery

What skills does it take to present ideas to others? Why is it important to consider how others will evaluate a message? How can writing make a good impression on others? In three or four sentences state what you believe are the most important things for making writing effective.

WRITING ON THE WEB

1. Using a search engine like AltaVista, Yahoo!, or Google, enter terms such as *writing process, writing strategies, prewriting techniques, revising papers, improving college writing,* and *proofreading skills* to locate sites that might assist you in this course.
2. Write an e-mail to a friend. Notice the writing process you use to create an informal document. How many times do you revise, edit, and rewrite a simple message?

POINTS TO REMEMBER

1. Writing is a process—it does not occur in a single burst of inspiration.
2. Good writing has a purpose, a *thesis* or controlling idea. It is not a collection of random thoughts, first impressions, or feelings. Good writing reflects *critical thinking*—close observation, research, and analysis.
3. Prewriting techniques help explore ideas. Brainstorming, freewriting, and asking questions can identify topics, discover new ideas, narrow a topic, and develop a thesis.
4. Outlines, whether formal or informal, organize ideas and identify missing information or unnecessary details.
5. First drafts serve to get ideas on paper—they are not expected to be flawless.
6. Reading papers out loud while revising and editing can help detect missing details, awkward sentences, misspelled words, and grammar errors.
7. Avoid plagiarism. Never use the work of others without informing readers.

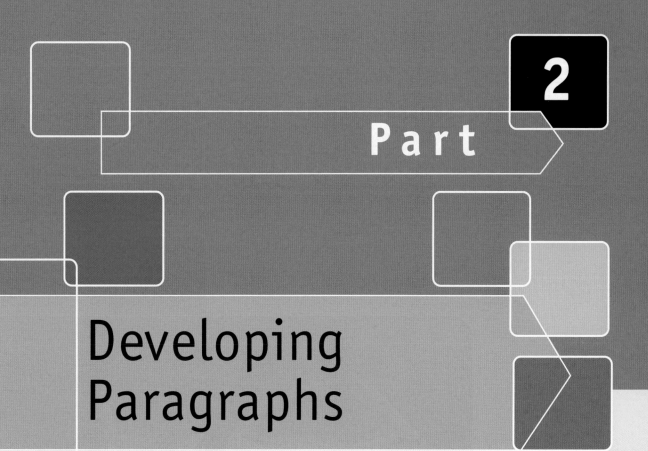

Part **2**

Developing Paragraphs

Developing Topic Sentences and Controlling Ideas

© Ed Lallo/Index Stock Imagery

What do you consider success? What kind of career do you want? Are money and status important to you?

Write a paragraph describing the job you would like to have in ten years.

24

What Is a Paragraph?

Paragraphs are the building blocks of anything you write. They play important roles in expressing your ideas and helping readers follow your train of thought.

A paragraph is a group of related sentences that express a main idea.

Written without paragraphs, even a short paper can be hard to read:

```
              Only Diabetes
I am not much of an athlete. I hate sports. I never
work out. But every October I take part in the annual
Run for Diabetes. I do it to help my sister. Ann was a
bright, funny, energetic fourteen year old until dia-
betes changed her life. When she lost weight, became
tired, and collapsed on her way home from school, I
was afraid she had leukemia. Ann was diagnosed with
diabetes, and I was relieved. It was only diabetes. I
thought all she would have to do was give up candy and
take a few shots to be OK. But diabetes is far more
devastating than most people realize. Insulin keeps
diabetics alive, but it is no cure. Diabetes remains a
leading cause of death. It is also a leading cause of
blindness. Diabetics can develop ulcers and infections
that require amputation. Ann had to do more than give
up candy. She must test her blood six times a day,
take painful injections, and monitor everything she
eats and drinks. Twice she has gone into diabetic
shock and been rushed by paramedics to the emergency
room. Ann's physical, emotional, and social life has
been radically changed by a disease too many people
think is easily managed. I have seen a bright, fun-
filled kid become a somber and often depressed girl
who faces early heart disease and failing eyesight.
More research is needed to find better treatments and
maybe even a cure. This October I will be running for
Ann. Maybe you should join me.
```

The same paper written in paragraphs is easier to understand. Paragraphs highlight main ideas and the writer's train of thought. Each paragraph serves a specific purpose.

```
              Only Diabetes
    I am not much of an athlete. I hate sports. I          introduction
never work out. But every October I take part in the
annual Run for Diabetes. I do it to help my sister.
Ann was a bright, funny, energetic fourteen year old
until diabetes changed her life. When she lost weight,
```

became tired, and collapsed on her way home from school, I was afraid she had leukemia. Ann was diagnosed with diabetes, and I was relieved. It was only diabetes. I thought all she would have to do was give up candy and take a few shots to be OK.

transition and support

But diabetes is far more devastating than most people realize. Insulin keeps diabetics alive, but it is no cure. Diabetes remains a leading cause of death. It is also a leading cause of blindness. Diabetics can develop ulcers and infections that require amputation. Ann had to do more than give up candy. She must test her blood six times a day, take painful injections, and monitor everything she eats and drinks. Twice she has gone into diabetic shock and been rushed by paramedics to the emergency room.

transition and conclusion

Ann's physical, emotional, and social life has been radically changed by a disease too many people think is easily managed. I have seen a bright, fun-filled kid become a somber and often depressed girl who faces early heart disease and failing eyesight. More research is needed to find better treatments and maybe even a cure. This October I will be running for Ann. Maybe you should join me.

Paragraphs play key roles in organization:

- Paragraphs serve as building blocks.
- Paragraphs generally develop a single main idea expressed in a *topic sentence.*
- Paragraph breaks signal transitions, moving readers from one main idea to another.
- Like chapters in a book, paragraph breaks provide pauses, allowing readers to digest ideas before moving to new material.
- Paragraph breaks in dialogue indicate shifts between speakers.

WHAT DO YOU KNOW?

Answer each question about paragraphs True or False.

1. _____ Paragraphs organize ideas.

2. _____ Paragraphs make essays easier to read.

3. _____ Paragraphs must consist of at least five sentences.

4. _____ Long essays about complex topics must have long paragraphs.

5. _____ Introductions and conclusions should always be placed in separate paragraphs.

Answers appear on the following page.

WHAT ARE YOU TRYING TO SAY?

Write about one of the following topics:

- Compare your attitudes about music, jobs, or money with those of your parents.
- Explain your plans for this semester.
- Summarize the plot of your favorite book or movie.
- Describe your worst job interview, day at work, or school experience.
- Give your reasons for the success or failure of a sports team.
- Explain the need for better daycare, more parking, or improved tutoring at your school.

_____

_____

_____

_____

_____

_____

_____

_____

_____

_____

_____

_____

_____

_____

_____

_____

_____

_____

_____

ANSWERS TO WHAT DO YOU KNOW? ON PAGE 26:
1. true, 2. true, 3. false (paragraphs can be of any length), 4. false (complex essays often have short paragraphs to show transition or dramatize an idea), 5. false (short essays may not require whole paragraphs to introduce or end an essay)

WHAT HAVE YOU WRITTEN?

Read your text carefully. Is it well organized? Did you use more than one paragraph? If you wrote a single paragraph, would breaks make your comments easier to follow? Are there short, choppy paragraphs that could be combined to join related ideas?

Topic Sentences and Controlling Ideas

Most paragraphs contain a topic sentence that states what the paragraph is about and conveys a **controlling idea** that expresses a main point or opinion. The other sentences in the paragraph relate to the topic sentence, supporting it with facts, details, comments, and observations. Topic sentences often open paragraphs to introduce the main idea and indicate the support to follow:

The Pelham Bay Inn is the best site for the alumni fund-raiser. Located on the bay, the hotel ballroom and patio offer guests a sweeping view of the harbor. Unlike the major hotels downtown, the Pelham Bay Inn has free parking. Since most alumni will arrive from out of town, the harbor location will spare guests from having to contend with downtown traffic and the current construction on College Avenue. People flying in can take the hotel shuttle van from the airport, saving them the cost of renting cars or taking taxis.

But topic sentences can appear anywhere in a paragraph:

The neighborhood youth center has been in operation for almost thirty years but only recently began offering girls' basketball. Almost fifty girls now spend Saturdays and two weekday afternoons running and drilling in the gym. But the girls learn a lot more than athletics. Their coach, Judy Sanchez, has become a source of insight, support, and guidance many girls are missing at home or school. Judy talks to her players frankly about school, boys, fashion, dieting, and sex. She answers questions honestly and maintains a sense of humor that often does more to change a teenager's mind than threats or lectures. She encourages girls to stay in school, delay sexual activity, and make plans for college and careers. *Judy Sanchez is a role model who helps confused girls become thinking women.*

Topic sentences serve key roles in a paragraph:

- Topic sentences tell readers what the paragraph is about.
- Topic sentences make a general statement supported by the rest of the paragraph.
- Topic sentences indicate the kind of detail readers should expect in the paragraph.
- Topic sentences signal shifts in the writer's train of thought.
- Topic sentences dramatize a writer's main points, making writing easier to read and remember.

EXERCISE 1 Identifying Topic Sentences in Paragraphs

Underline the topic sentences in each paragraph.

1   Home is where the heart is. There's no place like it. I love my home with a ferocity totally out of proportion to its appearance or location. I love dumb things about it: the hot-water heater, the plastic rack you drain dishes in, the roof over my head, which occasionally leaks. And yet it is precisely those dumb things that make it what it is—a

place of certainty, stability, predictability, privacy, for me and for my family. It is where I live. What more can you say about a place than that? That is everything.

ANNA QUINDLEN, "HOMELESS"

2 The computer hacker is not a social animal. He struggles with small talk and has difficulty communicating with technically uninformed people, and his introversion confines him to a tightly knit circle of friends. Arriving unescorted at a party, he will drift about making perfunctory conversation before gravitating to the basement (or garage) to happily chat away in technobabble with two or three like-minded people. At the party's breakup, he will offer genuine thanks to the host, not so much for the Chivas, but for the chance to meet a fellow developer of self-propagating autonomous computer programs. A sporadic user of alcohol, the computer hacker breaks his prolonged dry spells with feverish bouts of whisky drinking with other hackers, who invariably spend the evening contriving a plot to destabilize the currency market.

JONATHAN RITTER, "THE WORLD VIEW OF THE COMPUTER HACKER"

3 Change comes hard in America, but it comes constantly. The butcher whose old shop is now an antiques store sits day after day outside the pizzeria here like a lost child. The old people across the street cluster together and discuss what kind of money they might be offered if the person who bought their building wants to turn it into condominiums. The greengrocer stocks yellow peppers and fresh rosemary for the gourmands, plum tomatoes and broad-leaf parsley for the older Italians, mangoes for the Indians. He doesn't carry plantains, he says, because you can buy them in the bodega.

ANNA QUINDLEN, "MELTING POT"

4 During her remarkable 44-year career, Mrs. Bessie Taylor Gwynn taught hundreds of economically deprived black youngsters—including my mother, my brother, my sisters and me. I remember her now with gratitude and affection—especially in this era when Americans are so wrought-up about a "rising tide of mediocrity" in public education and the problems of finding competent, caring teachers. Miss Bessie was an example of an informed, dedicated teacher, a blessing to children and an asset to the nation.

CARL T. ROWAN, "UNFORGETTABLE MISS BESSIE"

READING TOPIC SENTENCES

No doubt by this point in the semester you have read textbooks in this and other courses. If you have underlined or highlighted as you studied, look at your textbooks.

1. Examine the sentences you highlighted. How many of them are topic sentences? Do they state a controlling idea supported by the rest of paragraph?
2. Skim through a few pages in your textbooks. How important are topic sentences in communicating ideas? Would it be harder to read and remember information if authors did not use topic sentences?

As you read, notice how writers use topic sentences to emphasize important ideas.

Writing Topic Sentences

To be effective, topic sentences have to be clearly and precisely worded. An abstract or general statement might express a controlling idea but give little direction to the paragraph. The more defined a topic sentence is, the easier it is for readers to grasp what you are trying to say.

EXERCISE 2 Identifying Topic Sentences and Controlling Ideas

Select the best topic sentence in each group.

1. a. _____ Denver is the largest city in Colorado.

   b. _____ I spent my freshman year in Denver.

   c. _____ I loved going to college in Denver.

   d. _____ My freshman year in Denver taught me lessons that shaped the rest of my life.

2. a. _____ Terrorism is a problem in our lives today.

   b. _____ Terrorism threatens to destroy the profitability of domestic airlines.

   c. _____ Terrorists have threatened the airlines.

   d. _____ The airlines face a major problem with terrorism.

3. a. _____ Car insurance should be mandatory in this state.

   b. _____ Last year over 15,000 uninsured drivers were involved in accidents.

   c. _____ My cousin was hit by a drunk driver who had no insurance.

   d. _____ Uninsured drivers pose a threat.

4. a. _____ Cyberstalking, which takes advantage of the anonymity of the Internet, has ruined lives, destroyed reputations, and led to at least six deaths.

   b. _____ Cyberstalking is a new kind of crime.

   c. _____ People have used the Internet to post threatening messages, spread rumors, or send counterfeit e-mails.

   d. _____ A disgruntled student sent official-looking e-mails identifying his teacher as a registered sex offender to dozens of citizens and government agencies.

5. a. _____ My high school football coach taught me discipline.

   b. _____ Playing basketball taught me the importance of teamwork.

   c. _____ I played on a tennis team that toured six states.

   d. _____ High school sports helped me make friends, learn the importance of teamwork, and appreciate the need for discipline.

EXERCISE 3 Developing Topic Sentences

Write a topic sentence for each subject, inventing details or opinions to express a controlling idea.

EX: Subject   **Binge drinking**

   Topic sentence   *Binge drinking introduces students to a life-threatening set of habits.*

1. **Subject**   **Your favorite sports team**

   Topic sentence   _____

   _____

2. **Subject**   **Balancing work and school**

   Topic sentence   _____

   _____

3. **Subject**   **Teenagers and AIDS**

   Topic sentence   _____

   _____

4. **Subject**   **Shopping online**

   Topic sentence   _____

   _____

5. **Subject**   **High school gossip**

   Topic sentence   _____

   _____

Paragraphs without Topic Sentences

Some paragraphs may not have a topic sentence you can underline. But all have a controlling idea, a main point:

> The following morning the mayor and Red Cross officials, accompanied by a news crew, examined the damage left by Hurricane Hugo. More than a dozen beach homes had been swept out to sea, leaving only bent pilings. A quarter-mile section of the boardwalk, Margate's main street, was shattered. The beach was covered with shingles from nearby houses, toppled lifeguard towers, and thousands of cans and bottles blown from recycling bins. Wrecked sailboats were stacked like firewood alongside the main pier. The Margate Inn, a century-old bed and breakfast hotel popular with New York tourists, was ripped off its foundation and listed to one side like a sinking ocean liner.

The details about the storm are so clear that they can stand alone and do not need a topic sentence such as "Hurricane Hugo devastated Margate."

POINT TO REMEMBER

A paragraph may not have a topic sentence, but it must have unity and purpose. All the ideas in a paragraph should relate to a clear point readers will easily understand. *All paragraphs should have a controlling idea.*

EXERCISE 4 **Identifying Controlling Ideas and Creating Topic Sentences**

Read each paragraph and describe in your own words its controlling idea—
its main idea. Then supply a possible topic sentence.

1   Holcomb, too, can be seen from great distances. Not that there is much to see—simply an aimless congregation of buildings, divided in the center by the main-line tracks of the Santa Fe Railroad, a haphazard hamlet bounded on the south by a brown stretch of the Arkansas (pronounced "Ar-kan-sas") River, on the north by a highway, Route 50, and on the east and west by prairie lands and wheat fields. After rain, or when snowfalls thaw, the streets, unnamed, unshaded, unpaved, turn from the thickest dust into the direst mud. At one end of the town stands a stark old stucco structure, the roof of which supports an electric sign—DANCE—but the dancing has ceased and the advertisement has been dark for several years. Nearby is another building with an irrelevant sign, this one in flaking gold on a dirty window—HOLCOMB BANK. The bank closed in 1933, and its former counting rooms have been converted into apartments. It is one of the town's two "apartment houses," the second being a ramshackle mansion known, because a good part of the local school's faculty lives there, as the Teacherage. But the majority of Holcomb's homes are one-story frame affairs, with front porches.

TRUMAN CAPOTE, IN COLD BLOOD

Controlling idea: _____

_____

Possible topic sentence: _____

_____

2   Capone was a late riser, having customarily stayed up past dawn, eating, drinking, and nightclubbing, and visitors who called before noon would find him in dressing gown and silk pajamas, which, like the silk sheets he slept on, were monogrammed. He ordered the pajamas, so-called French models, from Sulka in lots of a dozen at $25 each. He preferred royal blue with gold piping. He also fancied colored shorts of Italian glove silk, costing $12. His suits, custom-made by Marshall Field at $135 each, with right-hand pockets reinforced to support the weight of a revolver, ran to light hues—pea green, powder blue, lemon yellow—and he affected matching ties and socks, a fedora, and pearl-gray spats. A marquise diamond sparkled in his tiepin, across his bulging abdomen stretched a platinum watch chain encrusted with diamonds, and on his middle finger he wore a flawless, 11 carat, blue-white diamond that had cost him $50,000.

JOHN KOBLER, CAPONE

Controlling idea: _____

_____

Possible topic sentence: _____

_____

3   At eight o'clock in the evening the house-doors will be locked. The children are having supper. The shops are shut. The electric-sign is switched on over the night-bell of the little hotel on the corner, where you can hire a room by the hour. And soon the whistling will begin. Young men are calling their girls. Standing down there in the cold, they whistle up at the lighted windows of warm rooms where the beds are already turned down for the night. They want to be let in. Their signals echo down the deep

hollow street, lascivious and private and sad. Because of the whistling, I do not care to stay here in the evenings. It reminds me that I am in a foreign city, alone, far from home. Sometimes I determine not to listen to it, pick up a book, try to read. But soon a call is sure to sound, so piercing, so insistent, so despairingly human, that at last I have to get up and peep through the slats of the Venetian blind to make quite sure that it is not—as I know very well it could not possibly be—for me.

CHRISTOPHER ISHERWOOD, "BERLIN DIARY"

Controlling idea: _____

_____

Possible topic sentence: _____

_____

4   Al Smith rolled heavy barrels of fish in and out of the market, put the fish on ice, cleaned them and wrapped them. He worked from four o'clock in the morning until five in the afternoon, except on Friday. On Friday, he started work at three. Returning home at night tired and dirty and reeking of fish, he scrubbed off the odor and went downstairs to the store. But in the 1890's twelve dollars a week was almost enough to support a mother and a sister. He stayed at the market for four years. Then, to increase his pay to fifteen dollars, he became a laborer, carrying heavy pipes at a pump works. It wasn't until 1896, when he was twenty-two years old, that he got his first political job.

ROBERT CARO, *THE POWERBROKER*

Controlling idea: _____

_____

Possible topic sentence: _____

_____

Revising Paragraphs

Even when you have an outline with clearly stated topic sentences, you may have difficulty making paragraph breaks as you write the first draft. New ideas will come to you as you write. Out of habit, you may produce a draft without paragraph breaks. In reading over paragraphs, look at your notes. What are your main ideas? Paragraphs should isolate main points and demonstrate transitions.

WORKING TOGETHER

Working with a group of students, read over this student essay and indicate where you would make paragraph breaks. What breaks will make the essay easier to read?

    Television addiction is a compulsive disorder that affects the health and social development of many children. Although some experts dispute the accuracy of using the term *addiction* to describe excessive TV viewing, observers like Marie Winn insist the term applies. Like other addictive substances, television lets people blot out the real world and passively absorb rather than think or act. And like smokers or drinkers who want to quit, addicted TV viewers find it difficult to break the habit. Today television threatens the health of our children, who too often consume fattening junk food while they view television. Coming home from school, they watch cartoons, talk shows, soap operas, or the myriad of cable offerings. Instead of playing games or engaging in sports, they spend their free hours viewing television. Obesity is becoming a serious problem for adolescents, and many doctors confirm that excessive television watching plays a key role in promoting overeating and inactivity. In addition, excessive TV viewing has detrimental effects on a child's social development. The child who isolates himself or herself to watch TV does not interact with others by talking or playing games. He or she may feel more connected to sitcom families and soap opera characters than to brothers and sisters. Too often "family time" consists of people watching television together. Isolated and lonely children fall into a vicious circle of passive viewing rather than interacting with other people or exploring the world outside. Parents, accustomed to protecting children from the dangers of the outside world—crime, drugs, bad companions—often fail to see the damage TV poses.

_____

_____

_____

_____

_____

_____

_____

_____

_____

_____

_____

_____

_____

_____

_____

_____

_____

_____

_____

_____

_____

_____

In trying to get your thoughts on paper, you may find yourself listing ideas in two- or three-sentence paragraphs. In revising, identify your controlling ideas and organize supporting details to create fully developed paragraphs.

EXERCISE 5 Revising Paragraphs

Examine this draft of a student essay. Identify its main ideas and then rewrite the essay in no more than four paragraphs.

I loved Toms River, New Jersey. We lived only a few miles from the shore, and I often spent summer afternoons sailing in the bay or walking on the beach.

I enjoyed my high school because I had a lot of friends and participated in a lot of activities. I played softball and football.

My father was transferred to Minneapolis my junior year.

I hated leaving my school and friends but thought I would be able to adjust.

I found the move harder to deal with than I thought.

Instead of living in a colonial house on a half-acre lot, we moved into a downtown loft. It was spacious, offered a wonderful view, and had both a swimming pool and a health club.

As big as our two-floor loft was, it began to feel like a submarine. I missed the feel of wind and fresh air.

After two years in a city loft, I could not wait to go to college in Madison, Wisconsin.

The first thing I did when I got my acceptance letter was to get my sailboat out of storage. I am never going to live far from grass and water again.

_____

_____

_____

_____

_____

_____

_____

_____

_____

_____

_____

_____

_____

_____

_____

_____

_____

Using Paragraph Breaks in Dialogue

Dialogue, direct quotations from a conversation, is hard to follow unless paragraphs show the transitions between speakers. Paragraph breaks show the back and forth nature of a conversation, clearly indicating when one person stops talking and another begins:

> I get out of the car. The white man comes over and stands right in front of me. He's almost two feet taller.
>
> "If you're going to drive, why don't you carry your license?" he asks in an accusatory tone.
>
> "I didn't bring it," I say, for lack of any other defense.
>
> I look at the damage to his car. It's minor, only a scratch on the paint and a pimple-sized dent.
>
> "I'm sorry," I say. "Tell me how much it will cost to fix, and I'll pay for it; that's no problem." I'm talking to him in English, and he seems to understand.
>
> "This car isn't mine," he says. "It belongs to the company I work for. I'm sorry, but I've got to report this to the police, so that I don't have to pay for the damage."
>
> "That's no problem," I tell him again. "I can pay for it."
>
> RAMÓN "TIANGUIS" PÉREZ, *Diary of an Undocumented Immigrant*

EXERCISE 6 Using Paragraph Breaks in Dialogue

Rewrite this paragraph to separate the direct quotations of the two speakers.

I love my sister, but often Sharon drives me crazy. Just last week I faced a crisis. I had to drive to school to take a makeup exam before my math teacher had to file her midterm grades. I got dressed, packed up my books, and raced downstairs to my car only to discover I had a flat tire. I raced upstairs and woke Sharon, who was still sleeping. "Sharon, I need to borrow your car," I blurted out. "Why," she asked, upset that I disturbed her. "My car has a flat." "So, this is your day off." "I know, but I have to make up an exam today." "Go tomorrow after work," she said. "No way," I told her. "I have to take the exam today. It's the last possible day for makeups," I argued. "I don't want anyone driving my new car," Sharon mumbled. "New car? It's five years old," I told her. "Well, it is new to me. Take the bus." At that moment the phone rang. Mom was on her way to drop off some clothes. She was only too glad to drop me off at school.

CRITICAL THINKING

GET THINKING AND WRITING

In two or more paragraphs describe the courses you are taking this semester. Which classes are the most interesting? What is the hardest course? Which course poses the greatest challenge?

WHAT HAVE YOU WRITTEN?

Write out the topic sentence or controlling idea for each paragraph. Is each one clearly stated? Could they be made more precise or more effective with different wording? Do the details in each paragraph support the controlling idea?

Do paragraphs help organize your thoughts and make logical transitions between main points?

Review your sentences for spelling errors (see Chapter 27), fragments (see Chapter 14), run-ons and comma splices (see Chapter 16), and errors in agreement (see Chapter 19 and page 314).

WHAT HAVE YOU LEARNED?

Answer each question about paragraphs True or False.

1. _____ Every paragraph must have a topic sentence.

2. _____ Paragraphs usually consist of three or more sentences.

3. _____ Paragraph breaks are essential when you present dialogue.

4. _____ Topic sentences always open a paragraph.

5. _____ An essay must always have five paragraphs.

Answers appear on the following page.

GET WRITING

Is creativity and personal expression important to you? Would you rather own your own business than work for a large corporation? Does a career mean more to you than money? Contrast the image of a potter in a studio with that of the executive on page 24.

Write a few sentences describing which photograph better expresses your idea of success.

WRITING ON THE WEB

Using a search engine such as AltaVista, Yahoo!, or Google, enter terms such as *paragraphs, topic sentences, controlling ideas,* and *writing paragraphs* to locate current sites of interest.

1. Review recent articles in online journals and note how writers use topic sentences to state main ideas and paragraphs to organize articles.
2. Write an e-mail to a friend, then review your use of paragraphs. How can paragraphs make even a short e-mail easier to read?

POINTS TO REMEMBER

1. Paragraphs are the building blocks of an essay.
2. Every paragraph must have a controlling idea supported by details.
3. Paragraph breaks signal transitions between main points.
4. Paragraph breaks are used to separate direct quotations in dialogue.
5. Precisely worded topic sentences guide writing, helping you decide what details to include in paragraphs and which details to leave out.

ANSWERS TO WHAT HAVE YOU LEARNED? ON PAGE 38
1. false (see pages 28 and 31), **2.** true, **3.** true (see pages 26 and 36), **4.** false (see page 28), **5.** false

Supporting Topic Sentences with Details

GET WRITING

Write a paragraph describing your reaction to this photograph. Do you find it playful or disturbing? Are children influenced by the toys they play with? Should weapons be used as playthings?

What Are Supporting Details?

Paragraphs need a topic sentence and a clear controlling idea. For the controlling idea to be effectively expressed, it must be supported by details—observations, experiences, facts, testimony, statistics, or examples. Without enough support, a topic sentence remains unproven. Irrelevant details can distract readers and weaken the controlling idea.

WHAT DO YOU KNOW?

Read the following paragraph carefully and underline the topic sentence, then cross out the sentences that do not support the controlling idea.

The college must improve its computer system. This semester almost five hundred students did not receive their final grades because of a programming error. The college e-mail system, which is critical to the distance learning department, was down for two weeks, preventing students from turning in assignments. The ten-year-old computer system lacks the speed, capacity, and sophistication our college needs. It's the same with the dorms. They are so old, more students are moving off campus. The school does not have enough parking lots to serve the growing number of adult students who want to come to class directly from work to take night classes. To attract students and expand services, the college must provide cutting-edge information technology the current system cannot support.

Answers appear on the following page.

WHAT ARE YOU TRYING TO SAY?

GET WRITING
AND REVISING

Select one of the topics below or develop one of your own and make a few notes before writing:

gas prices	soap operas	college sports
the evening news	AM radio	planning weddings
party crashers	campaign commercials	campus social life
fast food	car repairs	health insurance

Write a clear topic sentence and develop a paragraph that supports it with relevant details:

_____

_____

_____

_____

_____

_____

_____

_____

_____

_____

_____

_____

WHAT HAVE YOU WRITTEN?

Read your paragraph carefully:

1. Underline the topic sentence. Is it clearly stated? Does it express a focused controlling idea?
2. Do the other sentences support the controlling idea, or do they introduce unrelated information?

Steps to Building Effective Paragraphs

1. Start with a Clear Topic Sentence and Focused Controlling Idea

In Chapter 3 you learned the importance of developing a topic sentence. When you revise something you have written, examine your topic sentences to make sure they state a clear controlling idea.

Weak Topic Sentence	Improved Topic Sentence
My uncle taught me a lot.	My uncle taught me respect and discipline.
The Internet helps poor schools.	The Internet helps poor schools provide online resources their libraries cannot afford.

EXERCISE 1 Improving Topic Sentences

Revise each of the weak topic sentences, adding details to create a more focused controlling idea.

EX: College is harder than high school.

College demands more work and provides students with less support than high school.

1. Advertising can hurt impressionable teens.

_____

2. **Online dating can be dangerous.**

_____

_____

3. **Americans should study foreign languages to help our country.**

_____

_____

4. **Balancing school and work is hard.**

_____

_____

5. **Exercise is beneficial.**

_____

_____

2. Distinguish between Supporting Detail and Restating the Topic Sentence

Support does not just repeat ideas. A topic sentence makes a statement or expresses a point of view. The sentences that follow should provide additional information, observations, facts, examples, or quotations. In a rough draft you may find yourself repeating ideas rather than introducing support:

> Professional athletes are getting paid too much. Their salaries are out of hand. Teams are spending too much just to pay their players. These outrageous salaries are alienating fans, eroding the ability of teams in smaller markets to attract players, and making the game as a whole less interesting. Players should be compensated, but their salaries should not destroy the game that supports them— especially when they can make millions in lucrative endorsements.

The first sentence states the controlling idea. But the next two sentences simply repeat it and weaken the essay. In addition, there is little factual support for the writer's position. Deleting repetitions and adding facts can strengthen the paragraph:

> Professional athletes are getting paid too much. Mickey Mantle's top salary in the 1960s was $100,000, or about twelve times the average teacher's income. Today the Yankees pay midlevel players millions of dollars, often 160 times what a teacher earns. These outrageous salaries are alienating fans, eroding the ability of teams in smaller markets to attract players, and making the game as a whole less interesting. Players should be compensated, but their salaries should not destroy the game that supports them— especially when they can make millions in lucrative endorsements.

3. Support Topic Sentences with Adequate and Relevant Details

Topic sentences state an opinion or observation that requires adequate and relevant support. The other sentences should contain details that directly support the topic sentence—not simply list everything you know or can remember about the topic.

A topic sentence is not a writing prompt to inspire you to write everything you can think of, but a clear statement requiring specific evidence.

Vague

We must stop illegal immigration. We have to keep people from entering America by breaking the rules. All over the world people are waiting in refugee camps to enter this country. They take classes and learn English and wait their turn. But every year millions of illegal immigrants jump over fences, swim ashore, or hide in shipping containers and ignore the law. People in this country feel they can break whatever law they please. Half the cars going down my street break the speed limit. The high school lawns are scattered with beer bottles. Students nowadays have to go through metal detectors to keep them from bringing guns to school. The liquor store on the corner bricked up its windows to stop the break-ins. We don't need more people to add to this. People who break one law are going to break others. Illegal immigration poses a special threat to our security these days.

This paragraph has a clear topic sentence. But the second sentence simply restates the topic sentence. The sentences about speeders, metal detectors, and store security relate to general lawlessness and have little to do with illegal immigration. The last sentence mentions a "special threat" but provides no detailed support. Eliminating repetition and adding more specific detail can create a more effective paragraph:

Improved

We must stop illegal immigration. All over the world people are waiting in refugee camps to enter this country. They take classes preparing them to find jobs and housing and understand our banking system. They learn English. They follow the rules and pass through security screening before being granted visas. But each year millions of illegal immigrants jump over fences, swim ashore, or hide in shipping containers and ignore the law. They enter the country ill-equipped to fit into our society. Many become criminals or the victims of criminals. These days illegal immigration poses a special threat to our national security. It is too easy for terrorists to slip into this country across our unprotected borders. The routes illegal aliens and drug smugglers use today can be used tomorrow by terrorists to bring in weapons of mass destruction.

EXERCISE 2 Recognizing Relevant Supporting Details

Read each topic sentence carefully and check those sentences that provide relevant support. Ignore sentences that simply restate the topic sentence or contain irrelevant details.

1. Public schools should not ignore the importance of physical education.

a. _____ Many school officials ignore the value of physical education.

b. _____ Physical education provides young people with supervised activities that burn off stress in productive games and sports.

c. _____ Physical education teaches students the need for proper exercise and nutrition to maintain health and avoid disease.

d. _____ Public schools face dwindling resources and more children needing special assistance.

   e. _____ Nearly 40 percent of today's children are overweight because they do
      not get enough exercise.

2. Las Vegas is the fastest-growing city in America.

   a. _____ Retirees find the warm, dry climate of the city appealing.

   b. _____ Families with young children move to Las Vegas to take advantage
      of the city's highly regarded school system.

   c. _____ Las Vegas builds more hotel rooms each year than any other city in
      the world.

   d. _____ Las Vegas has been featured in many motion pictures.

   e. _____ Because the city earns so much revenue from gambling, residents pay
      very low property taxes, making homes more affordable.

3. Cable television provides filmmakers with the chance to make movies
   traditional producers and distributors would reject.

   a. _____ Cable channels like HBO earn revenue from millions of subscribers,
      unlike movie studios that have to sell tickets.

   b. _____ An art film that might sell only a handful of tickets in one city could
      attract a significant national audience that makes a cable channel
      profitable.

   c. _____ Cable television fees keep rising.

   d. _____ Cable television is noted for showing daring programs.

   e. _____ Unlike movie houses, which have limited hours, cable channels
      screen movies around the clock, so art films can serve as late-night
      filler if needed.

4. Immigration changed the face of America's cities in the early 1900s.

   a. _____ Urban neighborhoods revealed the influence of new arrivals.

   b. _____ Immigrants introduced new cuisine, new customs, and new fashions.

   c. _____ Streets in Cleveland, Chattanooga, and Chicago now featured Jewish
      delis, Irish pubs, German bakeries, and Italian restaurants.

   d. _____ The automobiles began to replace the horse, and soon every major
      city was building an airport.

   e. _____ Catholic schools and synagogues sprouted up among the long-
      established Protestant churches.

5. We must stop the destruction of rain forests.

   a. _____ Rain forests produce much of the planet's oxygen.

   b. _____ Rain forests must be saved from eradication.

   c. _____ Each day thousands of acres of precious rain forest are cut for timber
      or to provide pastureland for farm animals.

   d. _____ Rain forests have rare plants that may contain cures for many deadly
      human diseases.

   e. _____ People take the environment for granted.

Types of Support

Observations and Personal Experiences

Personal observations include details and impressions about a person, place, thing, or situation. If you write an essay about your high school football team, much of the supporting detail would include your memories of the coach, the players, key games, and other teams. A topic sentence stating that high school football builds character could include your observations of friends who developed discipline and became more mature by playing on the team. An essay about urban renewal could contain your observations of new buildings in your neighborhood.

Like personal observations, accounts from your own life can supply rich details to support a topic sentence. As a college student, you are an authority on higher education. Your experiences as a parent, a car buyer, or a veteran can provide insights unavailable in facts and figures.

Personal accounts can humanize an issue and provide gripping evidence. Nathan McCall uses his own childhood experience to demonstrate the extent of racism in newly integrated schools:

> My harshest introduction to the world of white folks came in September 1966, when my parents sent me to Alford J. Mapp, a white school across town. It was the beginning of my sixth-grade school year, and I was walking down the hall, searching for my new class, when a white boy timed my steps, extended his foot and tripped me. The boy and his friends nudged each other and laughed as I stumbled into a locker, spilling books and papers everywhere. "Hey, n*****," the boy said. "You dropped something."
>
> *MAKES ME WANNA HOLLER*

TIPS FOR USING PERSONAL OBSERVATIONS AND EXPERIENCES AS SUPPORT

1. **Personal observations and experiences are best suited for personal essays.** They may not be appropriate in objective research papers or business reports.
2. **Make sure your observations and experiences directly support the topic sentence.** Your goal is not to tell a story but provide support. Avoid including unnecessary detail or unrelated events.
3. **Because personal experiences and observations are only one person's opinion or story, balance this support with facts, statistics, or other people's experiences.** Understand the limits of personal experiences as evidence. You may have to prove that your observations or experiences are not isolated events.
4. **Use personal observations and experiences to humanize impersonal data such as numbers and statistics.**

Examples

Examples are specific events, people, objects, or situations that represent a general trend. Although they are individual items, they are not isolated. If you want to support a topic sentence that asserts the need for better campus daycare, you might tell the story of one single parent to demonstrate the problem. To support her view that reading is an especially difficult challenge for children with dyslexia, Eileen Simpson uses specific letters of the alphabet to show how easily they can be confused by readers with dyslexia:

> Reading is the most complex skill a child entering school is asked to develop. What makes it complex, in part, is that letters are less constant than objects. A car seen from a distance, close to, from above, or below, or in a mirror still looks like a car even though the optical image changes. The letters of the alphabet are more whimsical. Take the letter *b*. Turned upside down it becomes a *p*. Looked at in a mirror, it becomes a *d*. Capitalized, it becomes something quite different, a *B*. The *M* upside down is a *W*. The *E* flipped over becomes an Ǝ. The reversed *E* is familiar to mothers of normal children who have just begun to go to school. The earliest examples of art work they bring home often have I LOVƎ written on them.

> *Reversals*

TIPS FOR USING EXAMPLES AS SUPPORT

1. **Make sure your examples are representative — not exceptions.** Listing a half dozen celebrities who are high school dropouts does not adequately support the idea that staying in school is a waste of time.
2. **Use examples people recognize.** Avoid using obscure events or people as examples that require lengthy explanations.
3. **Provide more than one example if you can.**
4. **Blend examples with factual support.** To prove that your example is not an isolated case, provide statistics or expert testimony.

Facts

Facts are observable and objective details that can be checked, examined, and documented by others. A personal observation might state, "Tom has an old car." The term "old" is a personal impression that some people could debate. "Tom has a 1984 Mustang" is a factual statement that anyone can easily verify. Facts are not opinions, but they can be used to support opinions. Opinions are statements that express a personal interpretation or point of view. Opinions can be used as support (see page 50), but they should not be confused with facts:

Opinions	Facts
The building is too tall for the neighborhood.	The building is twenty-two stories high.
Sarah is too young to live alone.	Sarah is seventeen years old.
This computer is very affordable.	This computer costs $799.95.

Because facts are objective, they can provide powerful support for a topic sentence. In some cases writers choose to let facts speak for themselves and present them without a topic sentence. Although there is no topic sentence, Robert Caro's description about Robert Moses's playgrounds has a clear controlling idea:

> When Robert Moses began building playgrounds in New York City, there were 119. When he stopped, there were 777. Under his direction, an army of men that at times during the Depression included 84,000 laborers reshaped every park in the city and then filled the parks with zoos and skating rinks, boathouses and tennis houses, bridle paths and golf courses, 288 tennis

courts and 673 baseball diamonds. Under his direction, endless convoys of trucks hauled the city's garbage into its marshes, and the garbage filled the marshes, was covered with earth and lawn, and became more parks. Long strings of barges brought to the city white sand dredged from the ocean floor and the sand was piled on mud flats to create beaches.

THE POWERBROKER

TIPS FOR USING FACTS AS SUPPORT

1. **Facts should directly support the topic sentence or controlling idea, not bring up other issues.**
2. **Use facts from reliable sources readers will recognize and respect.** Facts taken from government publications, encyclopedias, and mainstream magazines will be more convincing than facts from someone's home page or an advertisement.
3. **Use facts to balance personal observations and examples to add credibility to your opinions.**
4. **Make sure you use representative facts.** Don't just pick facts that support your opinion. Try to get the big picture and use facts fairly. Don't take facts out of context.

Statistics

Statistics are facts expressed in numbers. Statistics can make dramatic statements readers can easily understand and remember:

Over 15 percent of Americans do not have health insurance.
One in nine women will develop breast cancer.
This year 85 percent of our graduates will go on to college.

Used properly, statistics are convincing evidence to support a topic sentence. Tony Brown uses numbers to prove his point that African American spending habits need to change to make blacks more competitive:

The key to making Black America competitive with White America is really quite simple. Black Americans now earn nearly $500 billion annually, according to the economist Andrew F. Brommer. This is roughly equivalent to the gross domestic product of Canada or Australia. And yet Blacks spend only 3 percent of their income with a Black business or Black professional. By spending 97 percent of their money outside their racial community, they exacerbate their own social and economic problems.

BLACK LIES, WHITE LIES

TIPS FOR USING STATISTICS AS SUPPORT

1. **Make sure the items being counted are clearly defined.** Statistics about juvenile delinquents, for example, are not accurate if people use different definitions of delinquency.
2. **Use statistics from reliable government sources, academic institutions, respected writers, or mainline magazines.**
3. **Make sure you present enough statistics.** Stating that "Over 80 percent of Acme workers own stock in the company" makes the firm sound employee owned— until you learn the average worker only has a dozen

(continued)

shares. Ninety percent of the stock could be held by outsiders or even a single investor.

4. **Consider alternative interpretations of statistics.** Often numbers can be interpreted differently. If reports of child abuse have risen 50 percent in two years, does this mean more children are being abused or just that more cases are being reported?

Testimony (Quotations)

Testimony includes the words, experiences, opinions, and observations of others. They can be participants in an event, witnesses, or outside experts. Testimony can be stated in direct quotations that repeat word for word what someone wrote or said or in indirect summaries. The words or observations of a single real person can add life to a paragraph.

Louis Mizell uses the words of a victim to dramatize the problems caused by professionals who discuss sensitive issues on cell phones, which can be easily intercepted:

Doctors and lawyers frequently discuss everyday business on cellular phones. In one case, a doctor was notified that a VIP patient had tested positive for AIDS. The information was intercepted, and before long the VIP's medical status was common knowledge. In another case, a lawyer from Ohio reviewed a client's prenuptial agreement with a second lawyer who was using a cellular telephone. A teenage neighbor of the second lawyer intercepted the conversation. "Before long, the whole damn neighborhood knew about our secret wedding and my financial situation," said the angry groom.

"WHO'S LISTENING TO YOUR CELL PHONE CALLS?"

TIPS FOR USING TESTIMONY AS SUPPORT

1. **Avoid using quotations from famous people unless they directly support your topic sentence.** Adding quotations by Shakespeare or Martin Luther King, no matter how impressive, will only distract readers unless the words clearly support your controlling idea.
2. **Make sure you quote people accurately.** Don't rely on your memory of what someone said. Try to locate the original source and copy it accurately.
3. **Place direct quotations in quotation marks.** Remember to use quotation marks when you copy word for word what someone else has said or written. (See page 20.)
4. **Do not take quotations out of context.** Make sure that the quotations you use reflect someone's overall attitudes and experiences, not isolated outbursts.
5. **If needed, explain who you are quoting.** Testimony will only be effective if readers understand the speaker's knowledge or value. Just adding quotations to a paragraph will not impress readers:

The rising crime rate is ruining the South Side. Joe Long said, "I can't take it anymore, so I am moving."

Improved

The rising crime rate is ruining the South Side. Joe Long, who has lived here for thirty-eight years, said, "I can't take it anymore, so I am moving."

(continued)

6. Verify the accuracy and validity of opinions. Opinions can be powerful evidence, as long as the person you are quoting is a respected expert or authority. Avoid biased opinions or those based on little factual support.

Blending Support

Because each type of support has limitations, writers often use more than one to provide evidence for a topic sentence:

topic sentence

facts

statistics

expert testimony

example with testimony

facts

    Credit card debt is crippling American consumers. Credit card debt has doubled in the last five years. The average American now carries a balance of $8,000. According to the National Council of Bankers and Lenders, the number of households declaring personal bankruptcy rose 15 percent just last year. Roberta Loren, president of Chicago's Consumer Union states, "More Americans are using credit cards to pay for necessities like gas and groceries. They are making it week to week, but amassing debts they may never pay off." With some cards charging 21 percent interest, many people are spending thousands each year just to pay interest. Casey Stevens, a twenty-five-year-old paralegal, began using credit cards in college to buy CDs, pizzas, books, and clothes. By the time she graduated, she owed almost seven thousand dollars on three credit cards. "Once I got a good job," Casey admitted, "I thought I'd pay off my cards the first year. But I needed clothes to wear to court, a new computer, tires for my car, plane tickets to visit my parents. Before I knew it, my debts soared to $23,000. I am making good money, but I am still driving the car I had in college because after rent, everything goes to pay my cards." Casey may soon join the 24,000 Americans with good jobs who declare bankruptcy each month.

POINT TO REMEMBER

In selecting support, ask this question: Does this support my controlling idea? In writing the first draft you may remember facts or experiences. New ideas about your subject may come to mind. But unless these details directly support the topic sentence, they do not belong in this paragraph.

EXERCISE 3 Developing Supporting Details

Supply supporting details for each topic sentence. Make sure the details directly support the controlling idea expressed by the topic sentence.

1. Coach Wilson gets the most from his players.

    a. Testimony _____

    b. Example _____

    c. Fact _____

    d. Personal observation _____

2. Single parents face special problems when they attend college.

   a. Statistics _____

   b. Testimony _____

   c. Example _____

   d. Fact _____

3. Hollywood gives young people misleading ideas about adult life.

   a. Testimony _____

   b. Fact _____

   c. Personal observation _____

   d. Example _____

4. Good jobs are almost impossible to find without higher education.

   a. Statistics _____

   b. Fact _____

   c. Example _____

   d. Personal experience _____

5. Young people take their health for granted.

   a. Example _____

   b. Fact _____

   c. Statistics _____

   d. Personal observations _____

EXERCISE 4 Revising the Paragraph

Revise this paragraph, deleting repetitive and irrelevant details and adding your own ideas that support the topic sentence.

Peer pressure can overwhelm teenagers. The need to feel "in" can consume a teen's life. Without the right clothes, the right makeup, the right shoes, the right palm pilot or cell phone, young people are exiled, ridiculed, and mocked. Children have been known to drop out of school because their families cannot afford the stylish clothes that seem mandatory to win acceptance. This kind of behavior reinforces the worst kind of values. Societies often have unhealthy values. Not that long ago blacks were barred from certain clubs, schools, and restaurants. The Chinese were once not allowed to own certain businesses. Many Ivy League universities limited the number of Jewish students who could attend. Today young people learn that style is more important than character and that material possessions are the measure of success. No wonder we are a nation of consumers who can barely pay our credit card bills. We learn too early that things are supposed to make us happy.

EXERCISE 5 Writing Organized Paragraphs

Write a well-organized paragraph that builds on one or more of the following topic sentences.

   1. First-year students need discipline to avoid distractions that might jeopardize their academic performance.

2. Men and women have different attitudes about dating.

3. Parents must monitor their children's use of the Internet.

4. Americans must learn more about the Arab world.

5. The fashion industry gives girls unrealistic images of women's bodies.

WORKING TOGETHER

Working with a group of students, edit this paragraph from a student paper to eliminate repetition and irrelevant details. Review sentences for fragments (see Chapter 14), comma splices (see pages 231–232), and misspelled words (see Chapter 27).

```
     For the first time in my life. I could not wait
for school to start. I could not wait for summer vaca-
tion to end. Normally I love summer. Throughout high
school, I spent most summers at my parents' beach
house, working on the boardwalk with two of my cousins
and their friends. But this past summer I worked third
shift at a convenience store. The job payed minimun
wage. I got the lowest pay the law allows. I had to
stand behind a registor, handle drunks demanding beer
after hours, and endure hours of endless boredom
waiting for seven a.m. By three a.m. my eyes felt like
sandpaper, my legs ached, and my head ached. When my
shift was over I went home but was unable to sleep
during the day. I was always tired. I never got enough
rest. I was a like a zombie all summer. I may not know
what job I want after I finish college, I certainly
know what I don't want.
```

_____

_____

_____

_____

_____

_____

_____

_____

_____

_____

_____

CRITICAL THINKING

In recent years a number of trials have been broadcast on television. Do you think that cameras in the courtroom distort justice and turn trials into theater? Or do they teach people about our criminal justice system? Write one or more paragraphs stating an opinion supported by details.

WHAT HAVE YOU WRITTEN?

Read your paragraphs out loud. Is there a clear controlling idea? Have you stated it in a topic sentence? Do you provide enough supporting detail? Are there irrelevant details that should be deleted? Edit your sentences for run-ons and comma splices (see Chapter 16), agreement errors (see Chapter 19), and misplaced modifiers (see Chapter 17).

© Mary Ellen Mark

Compare this image with the one on page 40. Is your reaction to this one different? Do you see a connection between these two photographs? Does our culture glorify guns and violence? How can we prevent juvenile crime? What motivates young people to turn to violence?

Write a paragraph describing what this image symbolizes to you. If you see it as evidence of a social problem, you may wish to outline one or more possible solutions.

WHAT HAVE YOU LEARNED?

Read the following paragraph carefully and underline the topic sentence, then cross out the sentences that do not support the controlling idea.

Obesity is a major problem in the twenty-first century because our bodies were designed to store calories. The human body was designed to store excess food for future times of need. For thousands of years humans lived on what they could hunt, fish, or gather. Even early farmers were forced to go without food until their crops were ready to harvest. The ability to store excess calories helped them survive days or weeks of hunger. But today people have access to food twenty-four hours a day. We eat many more calories than we use and store the rest as fat. We eat a lot more food than we need to. We put on weight because we don't have the sporadic food supply our ancestors faced. The biological feature that helped humans survive centuries ago now causes us to die early of heart disease and diabetes unless we change our lifestyles.

Answers appear below.

WRITING ON THE WEB

Using a search engine such as AltaVista, Yahoo!, or Google, enter terms such as *paragraph design, modes of development, revising paragraphs,* and *topic sentences* to locate current sites of interest.

1. Review recent online articles and notice how writers select and organize details to support a topic sentence and express a controlling idea.
2. Note how authors use the modes of development to organize paragraphs.

POINTS TO REMEMBER

1. Paragraphs must have clearly stated controlling ideas.
2. Topic sentences must be supported with facts, statistics, personal observations and experiences, or testimony.
3. Avoid simply restating the topic sentence.
4. Details should directly support the topic sentence, not introduce new or irrelevant ideas.
5. Each type of support has limitations, so use more than one.

ANSWERS TO WHAT HAVE YOU LEARNED? ON PAGE 53
Obesity is a major problem in the twenty-first century because our bodies were designed to store calories.
Cross out the following: *The human body was designed to store excess food for future times of need. We eat a lot more food than we need to.*

5

Developing Paragraphs Using Description

© Reuters/CORBIS

GET WRITING

What were your first reactions to the events of September 11, 2001? Where were you? How did you find out about the attacks? How did people around you respond?

Select details and choose words carefully to develop a paragraph that describes what you thought and felt that day.

55

What Is Description?

Description presents facts, images, and impressions of people, places, things, and events. It records what we see, hear, feel, taste, touch, and smell. Good description not only presents information but brings subjects to life:

Saudi Arabia is a striking blend of shopping malls and mosques, camels and BMWs, vast deserts and palatial fountains.

Exhausted by the six-week trial, Ted Mendoza tapped the phone nervously, unsure how to tell his boss about the jury's verdict.

To maintain its reputation for objective reporting, the *Star Ledger,* the largest and most influential newspaper in the state, never endorses political candidates.

GET WRITING
AND REVISING

WHAT ARE YOU TRYING TO SAY?

Write a paragraph describing one of the following:

- your first car
- your favorite store
- people found at a local store, club, concert, or coffee shop
- your favorite television show
- the best or worst neighborhood in your town
- the greatest or most disappointing party, vacation, or restaurant you have experienced

_____

_____

_____

_____

_____

_____

_____

_____

_____

_____

_____

_____

_____

_____

_____

_____

_____

_____

_____

_____

WHAT HAVE YOU WRITTEN?

Read your paragraph carefully. Underline those words that provide details about your subject. Does your description give readers a clear impression? Could minor details be deleted? Could your word choices be more precise?

Creating Dominant Impressions

The goal in writing description is not to list every detail you can think of but to highlight a major point by creating dominant impressions readers will remember. If you attempt to provide readers with everything you can remember about your first apartment, your description can become a jumble of obvious and trivial details:

> On August 23, 2001, I moved into my first apartment, an upper flat at 2634 North Newhall. The living room had a sofa and a coffee table. On the right side of the room was a series of wall units containing books and CDs. On the left side of the room was a small desk and the stereo. The TV was opposite the sofa. Behind the sofa were three large windows and a door, which opened onto a small porch. There were two small bedrooms. They did not have closets but did have built-in wardrobes. The dining room was large with built-in buffets and large windows. The kitchen was a small L-shaped room. It contained a stove, refrigerator, and a large sink. Next to the kitchen was a small bathroom with a tub but no shower. Although awkward, the flat had plenty of space for my friends when they came over. I only lived there a year, but I remember it fondly.

The paragraph provides a lot of details but tells us very little. The writer states he or she recalls the apartment fondly but gives no reasons why. Much of the paragraph is cluttered with unimportant details—the date, the address, and furniture arrangements. It also is filled with obvious details like the living room having a sofa and the kitchen having a stove.

A more effective description deletes minor and obvious details to create a dominant impression:

> My first apartment was a large, ill-designed flat. The spacious living and dining rooms featured large French windows, built-in buffets, palatial moldings, and ornate door knobs. In contrast, the L-shaped kitchen was so narrow only one person could squeeze past the refrigerator at a time. The child-sized bedrooms looked like crew quarters on a battleship. Both were 9x9, made smaller by large built-in wardrobes. But the large living room was

perfect for my friends. I lived only a block from campus, and almost every afternoon friends dropped by to crash, eat takeout, watch soaps, play video games, or surf the Internet to conduct research for Econ 101. That oddly shaped flat became a collective crash pad, student union, and library. We worked, partied, dated, and tutored each other through our toughest year of college. I've moved to a better apartment, but I will always think of that odd flat as the best place to have spent my first year away from home.

By creating a dominant impression, adding brief narratives to include action, and showing rather than telling why the flat holds fond memories, the description becomes lively and effective.

POINT TO REMEMBER

The dominant impression is the controlling idea of a description paragraph.

EXAM SKILLS

Many examination questions call for writing one or more description paragraphs. As with any exam, read the question carefully and make sure your paragraph directly responds to it.

From Introduction to Abnormal Psychology

What are the principal characteristics of paranoid schizophrenia?

general description
Paranoid schizophrenia is one of four main types of schizophrenia, one of the common and most devastating mental illnesses. The main characteristics include delusions of per-

details
secution, racing thoughts, delusions of grandeur, illogical and unrealistic thoughts, and hallucinations. Patients may believe they are being spied upon or conspired against. They often are suspicious of doctors, friends, and family members. Social withdrawal and hostile outbursts make it difficult for them to retain relationships or hold down jobs. The disease can be

general description
disabling, even life-threatening. Drugs can control symptoms, but many patients do not take their medication because of the side-effects.

The paragraph opens with a general description of the disease, noting that it is one of several types of schizophrenia. The student then provides a list of specific characteristics. The student brings the paragraph to a close by describing current treatment.

EXERCISE 1 Recognizing Dominant Impressions and Supporting Details

Read the following descriptive paragraph and identify the dominant impression and controlling idea and list the supporting details.

State Street, that "great street," is a dirty, desolate, and depressing street for most of its length. It runs straight and potholed from the Chicago city line, up through the black ghettos of the South Side, an aching wasteland of derelict factories pitted with broken windows, instant slum apartment blocks, vandalized playgrounds encased in chain-link fencing, and vacant lots where weeds sprout gamely from the rubble and from the rusting hulks of abandoned automobiles. Those shops that remain open are protected by barricades of steel mesh. One or two men occupy every doorway, staring sullenly onto the street, heedless of the taunting clusters of skyscrapers to the north.

RUSSELL MILLER, *BUNNY: THE REAL STORY OF "PLAYBOY"*

Dominant impression:

_____

_____

Supporting details:

1. _____

2. _____

3. _____

4. _____

Key words:

1. _____   2. _____

3. _____   4. _____

5. _____   6. _____

7. _____   8. _____

9. _____   10. _____

EXERCISE 2 Creating Dominant Impressions

Create a dominant impression for each subject.

1. **Your elementary school**

_____

_____

2. **A talk show host**

_____

_____

3. **People waiting at an airport gate for a late plane**

_____

_____

4. Favorite childhood game or pastime

_____

_____

5. Your boss on a very bad day

_____

_____

EXERCISE 3 Supporting Dominant Impressions

Select a topic from Exercise 2 and list examples of details that would support the dominant impression.

Dominant impression:

_____

_____

Supporting details:

1. _____

2. _____

3. _____

4. _____

Improving Dominant Impressions and Supporting Detail

To be effective, dominant impressions and supporting details have to be precisely stated. The words you choose and the way readers react to them are critical in developing a description paragraph.

EXERCISE 4 Revising Dominant Impressions and Supporting Details

Revise the following descriptions by inventing details and adding more precise and effective word choices (see pages 172–178 about word choice and connotations).

1 The restaurant was wonderful. We were seated at a good table with an excellent view. The music was perfect. After a nice glass of wine, we enjoyed a great Italian meal. Everything about the food was great. The evening ended with coffee and dessert, which was very good.

2 The movie was terrible. The plot made no sense. The action scenes were confusing and too violent. The lead actress did not act well. Her scenes were so fake. The musical score did not suit the mood of the movie. The ending was very bad.

3 The old college library was great. The furniture and paintings made you feel you were in a historic place. The books were easy to find. The old lamps on the book tables were interesting. You really felt you were in college when you walked in.

4 The year's football team is the best ever. The coach is smart. The quarterback repeatedly shows a lot of skill. The defense has great ability. All the players work so well.

5 I learned a lot delivering papers after school in junior high. The job made me responsible. I had to change my habits. I learned the importance of being organized. Problems forced me to think for myself.

Student Paragraphs

Description of a person:

I'm part of a growing group of people I call "invisible Hispanics." Because of intermarriage, many Hispanics have last names like O'Brien, Edelman, and Kowalski. My father is third-generation Irish. He met my mom when he was working on a road project in Mexico. I was born in Juárez but grew up in Atlanta. I speak and write Spanish. I visit my aunt in Cancún two or three times a year. I belong to several Hispanic organizations. But because of my blonde hair, my Georgia accent, and my last name, Callaghan, I am frequently seen as an outsider by Hispanics who don't speak Spanish and have never been to Mexico.

Description of a place:

Ground Zero now looks very innocent. From the viewing stand you can see a vast square pit the size of a strip mine. Trucks move back and forth down below like tiny toys. It looks like a construction site on a grand scale. Men in yellow hard hats signal each other with flags. Forklifts carry building materials. The place almost looks hopeful, like the foundation of the world's biggest building. The looks on the faces of tourists who come every day from Japan, Germany, Italy, and Kansas, however, remind you what happened here.

Description of an event:

Last Saturday I went to Jamie O'Donoghue's third annual "Festa Polyesta"—a seventies theme party. For one night the usual Irish décor of the pub was masked by posters of Burt Reynolds and Farrah Fawcett. Men in white suits and girls in disco dresses bounced to the whining voices of the Bee Gees and the heated moans of Donna Summer. Winners of the "Saturday Night Fever" dance competition won timely prizes—lava lamps, mood rings, and Studio 54 T-shirts. The grand prize was grabbing all the eight-track tapes you could carry.

PUTTING PARAGRAPHS TOGETHER

The First Internet

introduction

topic sentence

supporting details

Over a hundred and fifty years ago, Morse invented the telegraph. <u>Within a few years this invention changed the nineteenth century the way the Internet changed the late twentieth.</u> The telegraph revolution- ized how people communicated, how nations fought wars, and how companies conducted business.

> **1.** How does this paragraph introduce readers to the topic?
> **2.** How does the student describe the impact of the telegraph?

description of communications before and after telegraph

Before the telegraph, people had to rely on hand- delivered messages or flag signals that could be seen for only a few miles in good weather. The telegraph now made it possible to send a message hundreds or thousands of miles in a few minutes. Now investors in Cleveland or Chattanooga could get instant stock reports direct from Wall Street. In the past, armies often fought battles days or weeks after a war ended because there was no way to inform them. During the Civil War news was telegraphed nationwide, so even the public could follow battles on a daily basis. <u>The telegraph erased distances, sped up the pace of life, and unified the country.</u>

topic sentence

> **1.** How does this paragraph build on the first one?
> **2.** What details does the student include to describe how the telegraph changed people's lives and historical events?
> **3.** The student places the topic sentence last. Is this effective? Why or why not?

topic sentence

<u>The telegraph, like the Internet, empowered av- erage citizens.</u> People could now send telegrams and instantly communicate with friends, family, and clients. A small entrepreneur in Kenosha could now do business in New York, Chicago, New Orleans, and Boston without opening expensive offices. Average citizens could flash telegrams to the White House, letting the president know what they thought of his actions. The telegraph captured people's imagination. One couple living in different cities actually were married by telegraph.

descriptive details

> **1.** How does this paragraph follow the previous ones?
> **2.** How do the details support the topic sentence?
> **3.** What impact does the last line have?

Readings

As you read these descriptions, notice how writers use details to create dominant impressions.

GAZA DIARY

CHRIS HEDGES

No doubt you have seen images of the Palestinian refugee camps on television. Chris Hedges, a New York Times *reporter, visited Khan Younis, a refugee camp in Gaza, a strip of desert occupied by Israel after the 1967 war. Khan Younis was the setting for ongoing conflicts between Arabs and Israelis. In 2005 Israel began dismantling its settlements and withdrawing from Gaza.*

AS YOU READ:

Notice how Hedges organizes and selects details, mixing objective facts with personal observations.

Friday afternoon, June 15, Khan Younis

Words to Know

shantytown slum of poorly built dwellings

rivulets streams or gullies

falafel Arab dish

1   Khan Younis is a dense, gray, concrete <u>shantytown</u>, the black waters from sewers running in thin <u>rivulets</u> down the middle of alleys. There are no gardens or trees. There is no place for children to play, other than the dunes in front of the neighboring Israeli settlements. Vendors in small, dingy stalls sell roasted corn on the cob or <u>falafel</u>. Hunks of meat hang on giant hooks, alongside wooden tables piled with tomatoes, potatoes, green peppers, and green beans. During the rains the camp floods with wastewater. Crude septic tanks, called percolating pits, lie outside homes, covered only by a thin layer of sand. When the pits overflow, the dirty water may slosh into the dwellings. The drinking water, which often does not flow for more than a couple of hours each day, is brackish and brown. It has left many in the camp with kidney problems. Only the lonely <u>minarets</u>, poking up out of the clutter, lend a bit of dignity to the slum.

minarets thin round towers of a mosque

intifada literally "shaking off" in Arabic; term for Palestinian uprising against Israeli authorities

2   The latest <u>intifada</u> erupted in September 2000, when Ariel Sharon, then the Israeli opposition leader and now the prime minister, visited the al-Aqsa Mosque, one of the holiest sites in Islam, with about 1,000 Israeli police. Arafat pleaded with then prime minister Ehud Barak to help stop the visit, fearing the violence that would surely erupt, but Barak could do nothing. Since then nearly 500 Palestinians have been killed, along with 100 Israelis and a dozen Israeli Arabs.

3   Khan Younis is one of eight refugee camps in Gaza. It is surrounded on three sides, like a horseshoe, by Israeli military positions. The soldiers there fire down on the roofs of the concrete shacks— asbestos mostly, held down by piles of rocks, cement blocks, and old tires. Bands of Palestinian gunmen, who often initiate the shooting, fire back.

4   A blistering white sun beats down on the camp. Our shirts become damp. Our shoes are soon covered with dust. We walk in single file

behemoths large beasts or
monsters

through the concrete maze, jostling our way past groups of Palestinians.
Finally we are afforded a look at the dunes hugging the camp. They are
dotted on top with Israeli gun emplacements, sandbagged bunkers, large
concrete slabs, and a snaking electric fence. Armored green jeeps and
tanks roar and clank along the fence's perimeter, throwing up clouds of
dust. Knots of nervous Palestinians stand gazing in the direction of the
behemoths until they pass out of sight.

Balkans war-torn nations:
Serbia, Bosnia, Croatia

    The walls of the houses facing the settlements, especially in the El
Katadwa neighborhood, on the western edge of the camp, are pock-
marked with bullet holes. Jagged chunks of masonry have been ripped
away by tank fire. Barrels filled with sand and stacked one on top of the
other— for me, an eerie reminder of the Balkans— deny Israeli snipers
a view of the streets.

    Beyond the fence we can see a mobile crane, from which dangles a
yellow metal box draped with camouflage. It lumbers inside the Israeli
compound like a jerky robot. I am told that the snipers fire down from
the box while suspended over the camp.

backgammon board game
played with dice and
counters
perimeter edge or border

    We turn down a crowded alley and come upon a group of older men
seated on chairs in a patch of sand, playing backgammon. A black plastic water tank and a TV antenna loom over them. A radio, perched on a
window ledge behind metal bars, plays Arabic music. At dusk these men,
and the families that live along the perimeter, will move deeper into the
camp to seek safety with relatives and friends. Bands of Palestinian gunmen will creep up to shoot at the Israeli positions, and the crackle of au-
tomatic fire will punctuate the night air. ■

5

6

7

GET THINKING AND WRITING

CRITICAL THINKING AND DISCUSSION

Understanding Meaning: What Is the Writer Trying to Say?

1. What is the dominant image that Hedges creates?
2. Does the description of gun emplacement, tanks, and fences make the
   refugee camp seem more like a prison?
3. Does this description help you understand why many people see these
   camps as breeding grounds for terrorism?

Evaluating Strategy: How Does the Writer Say It?

1. How important are specific details in describing the refugee camps? Underline facts and details you find significant.
2. How does Hedges use paragraphs to organize his description?

Appreciating Language: What Words Does the Writer Use?

1. What does the term "refugee camp" suggest to you? Does it imply that the
   residents will eventually be moved to other places? Are people expected to
   live their entire lives in "refugee camps"?
2. Underline words that create the dominant impressions in each paragraph.

Writing Suggestions

1. Write a paragraph describing a poor neighborhood you have seen. Avoid using general words like "bad" or "crowded." Select specific details and avoid including unimportant facts like dates and addresses.
2. *Collaborative writing:* Work with a group of students and write a paragraph describing the social problems that refugee camps might produce.

MY ECUMENICAL FATHER

JOSE ANTONIO BURCIAGA

Jose Antonio Burciaga (1940–1996) grew up in an El Paso synagogue, where his father worked as a custodian. After serving in the U.S. Air Force, Burciaga attended the University of Texas, where he received a fine arts degree. Burciaga became both an artist and a writer. In this part of his book Drink Cultura, *he describes his father.*

AS YOU READ:

Notice that Burciaga never tells readers what his father looked like. The dominant impression is of his father's values, not his appearance.

Words to Know

Feliz Navidad "Merry Christmas" in Spanish

Hanukkah Jewish holiday, also called Festival of Lights

orthodox Jews who strictly observe religious laws and customs

menorah eight-branched candleholder used to celebrate the eight nights of Hanukkah

pagan idols symbols of non-Jewish faith

1 ¡Feliz Navidad! Merry Christmas! Happy Hanukkah! As a child, my season's greetings were tricultural— Mexicano, Anglo and Jewish.

2 Our devoutly Catholic parents raised three sons and three daughters in the basement of a Jewish synagogue, Congregation B'nai Zion in El Paso, Texas. José Cruz Burciaga was the custodian and *shabbat goy*. A shabbat goy is Yiddish for a Gentile who, on the Sabbath, performs certain tasks forbidden to Jews under orthodox law.

3 Every year around Christmas time, my father would take the menorah out and polish it. The eight-branched candleholder symbolizes Hanukkah, the commemoration of the first recorded war of liberation in that part of the world.

4 In 164 B.C., the Jewish nation rebelled against Antiochus IV Epiphanes, who had attempted to introduce pagan idols into the temples. When the temple was reconquered by the Jews, there was only one day's supply of oil for the Eternal Light in the temple. By a miracle, the oil lasted eight days.

5 My father was not only in charge of the menorah but for 10 years he also made sure the Eternal Light remained lit.

6 As children we were made aware of the differences and joys of Hanukkah, Christmas and Navidad. We were taught to respect each celebration, even if they conflicted. For example, the Christmas carols taught in school. We learned the song about the twelve days of Christmas, though I never understood what the hell a partridge was doing in a pear tree in the middle of December.

We also learned a German song about a boy named Tom and a bomb—*O Tannenbaum*. We even learned a song in the obscure language of Latin, called "Adeste Fideles," which reminded me of, *Ahh! d'este deo*, a Mexican pasta soup. Though 75% of our class was Mexican-American, we never sang a Christmas song in *Español*. Spanish was forbidden. [7]

So our mother—a former teacher—taught us "Silent Night" in Spanish: *Noche de paz, noche de amor:* It was so much more poetic and inspirational. [8]

While the rest of El Paso celebrated Christmas, Congregation B'nai Zion celebrated Hanukkah. We picked up Yiddish and learned a Hebrew prayer of thanksgiving. My brothers and I would help my father hang the Hanukkah decorations. [9]

At night, after the services, the whole family would rush across the border to Juarez and celebrate the *posadas,* which takes place for nine days before Christmas. They are a communal re-enactment of Joseph and Mary's search for shelter, just before Jesus was born. [10]

To the posadas we took candles and candy left over from the Hanukkah celebrations. The next day we'd be back at St. Patrick's School singing, "I'm dreaming of a white Christmas." [11]

One day I stopped dreaming of the white Christmases depicted on greeting cards. An old immigrant from Israel taught me Jesus was born in desert country just like that of the West Texas town of El Paso. [12]

On Christmas Eve, my father would dress like Santa Claus and deliver gifts to his children, nephews, godchildren and the little kids in orphanages. The next day, minus his disguise, he would take us to Juarez, where we delivered gifts to the poor in the streets. [13]

My father never forgot his childhood poverty and forever sought to help the less fortunate. He taught us to measure wealth not in money but in terms of love, spirit, charity and culture. [14]

We were taught to respect the Jewish faith and culture. On the Day of Atonement, when the whole congregation fasted, my mother did not cook, lest the food odors distract. The respect was mutual. No one ever complained about the large picture of Jesus in our living room. [15]

Through my father, leftover food from B'nai B'rith luncheons, Bar Mitzvahs and Bat Mitzvahs, found its way to Catholic or Baptist churches or orphanages. Floral arrangements in the temple that surrounded a Jewish wedding *huppah* canopy many times found a second home at the altar of St. Patrick's Cathedral or San Juan Convent School. Surplus furniture, including old temple pews, found their way to a missionary Baptist Church in *El Segundo Barrio*. [16]

It was not uncommon to come home from school at lunch time and find an uncle priest, an aunt nun and a Baptist minister visiting our home at the same time that the Rabbi would knock on our door. It was just as natural to find the president of B'nai Zion eating beans and tortillas in our kitchen. [17]

My father literally risked his life for the Jewish faith. Twice he was assaulted by burglars who broke in at night. Once he was stabbed in the hand. Another time he stayed up all night guarding the sacred [18]

Juarez Mexican city across the river from El Paso

B'nai B'rith Jewish organization

Bar Mitzvahs Celebration of a Jewish boy's thirteenth birthday and entrance into manhood

Bat Mitzvahs Celebration of a Jewish girl's thirteenth birthday and entrance into womanhood

Torahs after anti-Semites threatened the congregation. He never philosophized about his *ecumenism,* he just lived it.

19   Cruz, as most called him, was a man of great humor, a hot temper and a passion for dance. He lived the Mexican Revolution and rode the rails during the Depression. One of his proudest moments came when he became a U.S. citizen.

20   September 23, 1985, sixteen months after my mother passed away, my father followed. Like his life, his death was also ecumenical. The funeral was held at Our Lady of Peace, where a priest said the mass in English. My cousins played mandolin and sang in Spanish. The president of B'nai Zion Congregation said a prayer in Hebrew. Members of the congregation sat with Catholics and Baptists.

21   Observing Jewish custom, the cortege passed by the synagogue one last time. Fittingly, father was laid to rest on the Sabbath. At the cemetery, in a very Mexican tradition, my brothers, sisters and I each kissed a handful of dirt and threw it on the casket.

22   I once had the opportunity to describe father's life to the late, great Jewish American writer Bernard Malamud. His only comment was, "Only in America!" ■

Torahs elaborate scrolls of Hebrew scripture

anti-Semites people who hate Jews

ecumenical showing respect for other people's religions

CRITICAL THINKING AND DISCUSSION

GET THINKING AND WRITING

Understanding Meaning: What Is the Writer Trying to Say?

1. What is the dominant image that Burciaga creates?
2. What values does Burciaga's father represent?
3. What is the point of Burciaga's description? Does he imply that readers can learn from his example?

Evaluating Strategy: How Does the Writer Say It?

1. What details does Burciaga use to support his thesis? Which do you find the most significant?
2. Why are the details of his father's funeral important?
3. Does Malamud's comment make an effective conclusion? Why or why not?

Appreciating Language: What Words Does the Writer Use?

1. Underline words that create the dominant impressions in each paragraph.
2. What words does Burciaga use to describe his father? Are they effective?

Writing Suggestions

1. Write a paragraph describing a person you feel represents beliefs or attitudes you value. Describe a coach who taught you the real meaning of sportsmanship or a relative who overcame a difficult challenge. Establish a clear controlling idea to guide what details you include.
2. *Collaborative writing:* Work with a group of students and write a paragraph describing why a country like the United States needs more people like Cruz Burciaga.

STEPS TO WRITING A DESCRIPTIVE PARAGRAPH

1. Study your subject and apply critical thinking by asking key questions:
   - Why did I choose this subject?
   - What does it mean to me?
   - What is important about it?
   - What do I want other people to know about?
2. List as many details as you can, keeping your main idea in mind.
3. Review your list of details, highlighting the most important ones, especially those that create a dominant impression.
4. State a controlling idea or topic sentence for your paragraph.
5. Write a first draft of your paragraph.
6. Read your paragraph out loud and consider these questions:
   - Is my subject clearly described?
   - Do I provide enough details?
   - Are there minor or irrelevant ideas that can be deleted?
   - Do I use clear, concrete words that create an accurate picture of my subject?
   - Do I create a clear dominant impression?
   - Does my paragraph tell readers what I want them to know about my topic?

Selecting Topics

Consider these topics for writing descriptive paragraphs:

People
a person who taught you a lesson
a celebrity you admire
a clique in high school or a campus group
the crowd at a local club, spa, coffee house, or student union
a type of employee or customer you encounter at work
the best or worst boss, teacher, or coach you have
your generation's attitude toward a subject like AIDS, sex, terrorism, marriage, or work

Places
your ideal home
campus housing
best club, restaurant, gym, or bookstore you know
a place where you worked
your neighborhood
a place that exposed you to something new
a place you hope you never have to see again

Things
your first car
your computer

a favorite childhood toy and what it represented
a prized possession
something you lost and why you still miss it
a time of day at school, your home, or job
a season of the year
a local newspaper, television show, or website

EXERCISE 5 Planning and Writing Paragraphs

Select a topic from the above lists or choose one of your own and develop details and a topic sentence.

Topic: _____

Possible supporting details:

1. _____

2. _____

3. _____

4. _____

5. _____

Circle the most important details to create a dominant impression.
State your controlling idea and write a topic sentence:

_____

_____

First sentence: topic sentence, first detail, or introductory statement

_____

_____

Supporting details:

1. _____

2. _____

3. _____

4. _____

5. _____

Last sentence: final detail, concluding statement, or topic sentence:

_____

_____

Write out your paragraph and review it by reading it out loud.

WORKING TOGETHER

Working with a group of students, revise this description from a student paper to delete irrelevant or obvious details that do not support the dominant impression and controlling idea. Edit the paragraph for fragments (see Chapter 14), run-ons and comma splices (see Chapter 16), and spelling errors (see Chapter 27).

Growing up in a Chicago high rise, I enjoyed spending weekends at my uncle's cottage in Lake Geneva. Located a little over an hour from the Loop. My uncle built the cottage ten years ago as a gift to his family. He was accountant for General Motors and he later worked for several law firms that handled tax cases. The A-frame cabin has striking views because of its floor to roof windows overlooking the lake. Sitting on the porch I would watch the sunsets over the lake, hearing only the gentle rustle of leaves and the soft slap of water against the dock. Other people go jogging, or mediate, or play chess to get rid of stress—but none of those things appeal to me. Jogging is to physical and meditation and chess take too much concentration when I am stressed. Away from the city, from traffic, from school, from work I would sit transfixed until the sun went down. Although I loved the swimming, the games, the horseplay with my cousins, those quiet afternoons on the porch were memomorable. Without them I would never have been able to find the peace of mind I needed to juggle work, school, and family. Next year I hope to be better orgainized.

_____

_____

_____

_____

_____

_____

_____

_____

_____

_____

_____

_____

_____

CRITICAL THINKING

Describe the college course you think will be the most important to your future life or career. Explain what you learned and how you hope to apply it in the future.

WHAT HAVE YOU WRITTEN?

Read your paragraphs carefully. Do you clearly describe the course's significance to your future? Do you include specific details? Are the supporting details clearly organized?

Write out the topic sentence or implied controlling idea:

_____

_____

_____

List the main supporting details in your paragraphs:

_____

_____

_____

Do they support your controlling idea and create a dominant impression? Could you improve your description by adding more details? Are there minor facts or trivial details that could be deleted?

© Gabe Palmer/CORBIS

Write a paragraph describing a childhood friend. Select key details to create a dominant impression of your friend's personality. Consider what made this person so special. Why do you still remember him or her? How did he or she change or influence your life? Consider the most important thing you want people to know about your friend.

WRITING ON THE WEB

Using a search engine such as AltaVista, Yahoo!, or Google, enter terms such as *description, writing description,* or *rhetorical mode description* to locate current sites of interest.

1. Review online articles that describe a recent event, person, or situation. Notice how the writers develop controlling ideas, create dominant impressions, use supporting details, and choose particular words.
2. Write an e-mail to a friend describing a recent event on campus, at work, or in your life. Revise your paragraphs to create controlling ideas, build dominant impressions, and organize supporting details.

POINTS TO REMEMBER

1. Description paragraphs present images and impressions of places, people, things, and events.
2. Effective descriptive paragraphs create dominant impressions that state the writer's most important points.
3. Dominant impressions and controlling ideas are supported with specific details.
4. Many description paragraphs do not contain a topic sentence but have a clear controlling idea.

Developing Paragraphs Using Narration

© Images.com /CORBIS

GET WRITING

Have you ever been in a situation where you had to hide your feelings? Did you have to mask your fear to appear strong for others, "keep a straight face" to avoid offending people, or act in a professional role different from your personality?

Write a paragraph that tells the story of one of these incidents. Carefully select and organize details that support your main point.

What Is Narration?

The goal of narration is to tell a story or relate a chain of events. History books, newspaper articles, biographies, accident reports, the Bible, Greek myths, and fairy tales are examples of narration. Many of the papers you will write in college will use narration. Narratives explain events:

> After my flight was canceled, I had to rent a car and drive through the snowstorm at twenty miles an hour.

> Desperate to stop the flow of skilled workers to the West, East Germany erected the Berlin Wall in 1961.

> After a disappointing start, the team won eight straight games, stunning both fans and sportswriters.

GET WRITING
AND REVISING

WHAT ARE YOU TRYING TO SAY?

Write a paragraph that relates one of the following events:

- a job interview
- an encounter with a stranger you found unforgettable
- a humorous event
- an incident at work you feel most proud or ashamed of
- a childhood event that scared you

WHAT HAVE YOU WRITTEN?

Read your paragraph carefully. Does your narrative highlight the most important events, or is it cluttered with minor details? Is your paragraph clearly and logically organized?

Writing Narration: Making a Point

Effective narratives focus on a main point, teaching readers something about the event. In writing a narrative, your job is not to record every single detail but to focus on the most important ones. Narrative paragraphs do not always have a topic sentence, but they should have a controlling idea and dramatize a clearly focused point:

Narrative Lacking Focus

It was June 4, 2003. Eager to start my new job, I woke early and dressed in my brand new suit and tie. I bought them the week before at Marshall Field's with money I got for my birthday. I polished my shoes. I fiddled with my hair to get it just right. I wanted to make a good impression. I left early so I could run my car through the car wash on Elm Street just in case my new boss saw me pull up. It is an eight-year-old Volvo with over 125,000 miles on it. But when it is washed and waxed, it looks quite impressive. I took the freeway downtown and got off on Wells Street. I pulled up to the Boynton Building at 608 West State Street and parked right in front where Mrs. Smith had told me to and walked in the main entrance. I showed the receptionist my letter, and she directed me to the second-floor sales office. Anxious to do well, I took a deep breath and went in and introduced myself to Sarah Graham. She smiled and directed me to a tiny cubicle with a computer screen and a telephone headset. That is when I discovered that as an "account representative" my job consisted of cold calling businesses in the Yellow Pages.

The paragraph recounts someone's first day at work but makes little impact. The writer's main point—the contrast between his expectations and the reality of the job—is lost amid minor details such as the date, addresses, where he purchased his suit, and comments about his car. Deleting these details and highlighting his anticipation emphasizes his final disappointment:

Eager to start my new job, I woke early and dressed in my brand new suit and tie. I polished my shoes. I fiddled with my hair to get it just right. I wanted to make a good impression. Advertising is about image, and I wanted to prove to everyone at Douglass, Lancaster, and MacArthur that I was executive material. I had visions of making presentations in polished boardrooms in New York and LA. I even left early, so I could run my car through the car wash just in case my new boss saw me pull up. Entering the spacious lobby of the Boynton Building, I felt thrilled. I could not wait to start. I introduced myself to Sarah Graham, who directed me to a dim, low-ceilinged room filled with tiny cubicles. Two dozen men and women in sweat shirts, T-shirts, and tattered blue jeans sat hunched over telephones, their tiny desks cluttered with candy wrappers, Coke cans, and rumpled newspapers. That is when I discovered that as an "account representative" my job consisted of cold calling businesses in the Yellow Pages.

Tips for Making Points

1. **In writing a narration paragraph, keep this question in mind: What is the most important thing I want my reader to know?**
2. **Delete minor details that do not help create your main point.**
3. **Focus on conflict or contrast to create tension or drama.**
4. **Organize details to create strong impressions.**
5. **Use concrete words rather than general or abstract terms to provide dramatic but accurate depictions of events:**

Abstract

The snowstorm affected the campus and made life difficult for the students who had been preparing for midterm examinations.

Concrete

The blizzard paralyzed the campus, knocking out power in classrooms, frustrating students cramming for midterm examinations.

6. **Avoid shifting point of view (from "I" to "you" or "they") unless there is a clear change in focus:**

Awkward Shift

When *I* drive over those train tracks *your* teeth rattle.

Improved

When *I* drive over those train tracks *my* teeth rattle.

or

When *you* drive over those train tracks *your* teeth rattle.

Acceptable Change in Point of View

When *I* was in school ten years ago *I* never had the opportunities *you* have.

7. **Use tense shifts to show logical changes between past and ongoing or current events:**

I *walked* to Elm Street where the city *is constructing* a new bridge.

I *was born* in Trenton, which *is* the capital of New Jersey.

We *sing* songs Cole Porter *wrote* sixty years ago.

EXERCISE 1 Making a Point

GET WRITING *Select one of the following subjects, narrow the topic, and establish a controlling idea.*

your reaction to an accident you witnessed
an encounter with someone in distress
an argument or confrontation between two people you observed
the plot of your favorite story, book, or movie
an event, situation, or rumor that affected your high school
an event that shaped your attitudes or values
a dispute with a landlord, neighbor, customer, or fellow employee

Narrowed topic: _____

Point or controlling idea: _____

*Now develop a narrative paragraph that uses details to support the controlling idea.
After completing your paragraph, review your subject and your main point.
Does your paragraph tell readers what you want them to know? Are there minor
details to delete and important details to emphasize?*

EXAM SKILLS

Many examination questions call for writing one or more narrative paragraphs. As with any exam, read the question carefully and make sure your paragraph directly responds to it. In writing a narrative, remember your goal is not to tell everything that happened or every detail you can remember but to concentrate on an important point. Your narrative should have a clearly stated goal and topic sentence to guide the events you select.

From Modern American History

What was the significance of the Triangle Shirtwaist Fire?

introduction
and summary
of events

details

controlling
idea

In March 1911 a fire broke out in the Triangle Shirtwaist Factory in New York. Hundreds of workers, most of them young women, were trapped on the top floors. Crowds of New Yorkers watched as girls jumped from the tenth floor to escape the fire and others screamed unable to escape the flames. The fire killed 141 workers. An investigation revealed the building did not have enough exits and that many doors had been locked. Public outrage fueled reformers' demands for safer working conditions, better wages, and improved building codes. The Triangle Shirtwaist Fire demonstrated the need for political reform and forced state and city governments to assume more responsibility in regulating businesses and protecting workers.

Writing Narration: Using Transitions

A narrative paragraph explains events that occur in time—whether measured in seconds, minutes, hours, days, weeks, or years. To prevent confusion and help readers follow events, it is important to use transitions to signal shifts in time:

In June 2000 I began working as a cab driver. The training had been brief, but I thought I was fully prepared. *The first few days* were hectic, but the manager assigned new drivers to shuttle runs. I did not have to answer calls but simply travel back and forth between the airport and downtown hotels. *The next week* I collected my cab and headed out, working on my own. I found it difficult to answer the radio calls. Before I figured out the address, another driver had snatched the call. The dispatcher was rude and cut me off when I tried to ask a question. After paying for the cab rental, gas, and insurance I made only eleven dollars the first week. *By the end of the month* I learned how to handle radio calls and check the paper for downtown events. I got several good fares by hitting theaters as soon as plays let out. *In the next several months* I learned other tricks of the trade, such as having frequent fliers e-mail me to set up airport runs and bypassing the dispatcher. *By the end of the year* I became a seasoned veteran.

KEY TRANSITION WORDS

before	now	then
after	later	first
after a while	following	finally
next	immediately	suddenly
following	the following day	hours, hours, weeks later
while	in the meantime	that morning, afternoon, etc.

EXERCISE 2 Identifying Transitions

Underline transitional statements in the following paragraph.

When I first arrived in Bellingham, I rented a car at the airport and followed my sister's direction to the hotel. After checking in, I grabbed a quick lunch and made a few calls. No one was home. I tried my sister's cell phone but could not get through. I took a shower, changed, and unpacked. I plugged in my laptop and checked my e-mail. I tried calling at three o'clock and again at four. I assumed everyone was running errands, getting things ready for the wedding. It was not until after dinner that I finally tracked down my cousin, who offered to drive me to the rehearsal.

Writing Narration: Using Dialogue

Narratives often involve interactions between people. If you are telling a story about an event that involved another person, dialogue—direct quotations—can advance the the story better than a summary of a conversation:

Summary

A good boss has to be a good teacher. My manager Al Basak is a nice person, very polite, and often funny. But he never gives people enough information to act on their own when he is out of the office. Last month he left to attend a two-day conference, telling me that if any sales reps called to remind them that their expense reports were due on Monday. I asked what to do if they asked for advances. He told me I could send them something if they needed it. Before I could ask anything else, he was out the door. An hour later the phone rang. A sales rep in Cleveland wanted a thousand-dollar advance. I panicked. Was a thousand too much? I told the sales rep I did not know if I could do that. I promised to call Al and check. I hung up and tried to call Al, but before I could get through to him another sales rep called asking if he could e-mail his expense report. All I could tell him was that the report was due Monday, but that Al did not tell me whether it could be e-mailed. I promised to call Al and check. I hung up and knew this was going to be a long, long day.

Narrative with Dialogue

A good boss has to be a good teacher. My manager Al Basak is a nice person, very polite, and often funny. But he never gives people enough information to act on their own when he is out of the office. Last month he left to attend a two-day conference, telling me, "If any of the sales reps call, remind them their expense reports are due on Monday."

"What if they need advances?" I asked him.

"Well, you can send them something if they need it."

Before I could ask anything else, he was out the door. An hour later the phone rang. A sales rep in Cleveland wanted an advance. "Can you send me a thousand dollars?" she asked.

I panicked. Was a thousand too much? "I don't know if I can send you that much."

"Well, call Al."

"I will."

I hung up and tried to call Al, but before I could get through to him another sales rep called asking if he could e-mail his expense report. "They are due Monday, but Al never told me if you could e-mail them."

"Are you sure? Call Al and find out."

"OK, I will," I sighed. I hung up and knew this was going to be a long, long day.

- Dialogue brings people to life by letting them speak their own words. Their tone, attitude, and lifestyle can be demonstrated by the words they choose.

- Because dialogue is formatted in short paragraphs, it is faster and easier to read than a long block of text. In addition, direct quotations can reduce the need for statements like "he said" or "she told me."

POINT TO REMEMBER

In writing dialogue, start a new paragraph each time a new person speaks. Because dialogue may include many short paragraphs, including one-word responses such as "No," your essay may appear to be longer than the assigned length. Use a computer word count. A three-page essay with dialogue is often no longer than a page and a half of description.

EXERCISE 3 Writing Narration Using Dialogue

Write a narrative paragraph that uses dialogue—direct quotations—to relate an event: like a confrontation between two people, an argument, a job interview, or a conversation.

Student Paragraphs

Personal narrative:

On my first day in Toronto I went to the CN Tower to have lunch and get a sweeping view of the city. Using my map, I checked off the sights I wanted to cover on my two-day layover. I visited the York Hotel, then explored the vast underground complex of shops, offices, and tunnels that allow people to travel throughout downtown without having to face bad weather. I ended my first day by taking a cab to Casa Loma, the huge castlelike mansion on a hill that features stables, a secret passage, towers, and suits of armor.

Narrative in a history paper:

In the 1920s abundant rain led many small Midwestern farmers to acquire lands in regions previously considered too dry for cultivation. Many went into debt to buy land to pursue the dream of owning their own farms. In the 1930s, however, the above-average rainfalls ceased, followed by years of severe drought. Farmers saw their thin layers of topsoil blow away in whirling clouds of dust. Millions of acres of cropland became hard-baked desert. Unable to meet their mortgages, thousands of families found themselves facing hunger and eviction.

Narrative in psychology midterm:

The reason that many mentally ill people are now homeless is because public policy failed to supply enough outpatient clinics and group homes. Throughout much of the twentieth century mental patients were housed in large state-run institutions. Many were merely warehouses offering little treatment. Patients were often victims of abuse and neglect. By the late 1960s advocates for the mentally ill argued that many patients would be better served by being mainstreamed rather than isolated. States eager to save money closed aging and costly mental hospitals. Mentally ill people were reintroduced to society, but few had coping skills to find employment or housing. The group homes and outpatient clinics advocates envisioned never opened. As a result today we see schizophrenics panhandling and living on the streets.

PUTTING PARAGRAPHS TOGETHER

Dumb and Dumber

introduction

background to event

Sometimes we are so ashamed of something dumb we have done we have to lie. We just can't let anyone know how stupid we have been. Last Fourth of July I was getting ready for a picnic with my friends. I was supposed to bring paper plates and plastic cups. I got the supplies ready, then put on a new pair of cream slacks and a white shirt. The boxes were not heavy but bulky, so I carried my car keys so I would not have to try to dig them out of my pocket when I got to the garage. I left my apartment and headed down the hall to the elevator. Just as the elevator reached the lobby and the doors slid open, the boxes shifted and I dropped my car keys. The keys bounced twice and dropped right down the narrow slot between the floor and the elevator. They were gone! I could not believe it! Kneeling, I could see my keys resting two or three feet below.

climax
mistake #1

1. What is the controlling idea of this paragraph? Does it have a topic sentence?
2. How does the student organize the details?
3. How effective is the end of the paragraph? Is it a good place to make a break in the narrative? Why or why not?

Cursing myself, I punched the button and went back up to the third floor. I was running late and had to get my car keys. I dumped the boxes in the hall and ran to my apartment to get a flashlight and a clothes hanger. I was convinced I could hook my key ring with a hanger and be on my way. The elevator floor was dirty, so to be smart I quickly changed into jeans so I would not ruin my new cream slacks. I bent the hanger into the perfect key ring grabber and raced down the hall, letting the apartment door slam behind me.

focus on action

details to emphasize being in a rush

mistake #2

1. How does this paragraph advance the narrative?
2. How does it build on the first paragraph?
3. The student ends the first and second paragraphs by describing mistakes he made. Is this effective? Do the paragraphs highlight the "dumb" things mentioned in the first sentence?

My coat hanger worked perfectly. I snagged the keys on the third try and had them just inches from the floor when the wire slipped and the keys vanished out of sight. Oh well, I thought, I would make a few calls and get them later. <u>When I reached my apartment I dug into my jeans and realized I had left my apartment keys in the new cream slacks I had carefully folded and laid on the bed.</u>

initial good luck

bad luck

topic sentence
realizes mistake #2

1. How does this paragraph follow the preceding one?
2. How does the student organize details?
3. Does the last sentence seem like a good place to end a paragraph? Why or why not?

<u>I was now locked out of my car and my apartment.</u> For a moment I thought I would just walk to the drugstore and call a cab; then I realized I had no money. My wallet was in the cream slacks along with my cell phone. I was trapped. I raced back to the lobby and spent an hour and a half fishing for my car keys. I

topic sentence

thinks of plan

realizes plan won't work

managed to finally grab them just as my roommate came
through the lobby.

> **1.** How does this paragraph advance the narrative?
> **2.** What are the important details in this paragraph? How do they relate to the idea of doing "something dumb"?

roommate's question

He looked at my smudged clothes and dirty hands
and asked, "Hey, I thought you were going to a
picnic?"

Playing innocent, I pocketed my car keys and
followed him to the elevator. <u>"I had a flat tire,"
I lied, letting him go ahead so he could open the
apartment door.</u>

conclusion

> **1.** How effective is this final paragraph? Does it bring the narrative to a logical close?
> **2.** How does the last line relate to the opening line?
> **3.** How important are final paragraphs in a narrative? How can writers highlight or demonstrate an idea or detail they want readers to remember?

Readings

As you study the readings, notice how each paragraph works and how the paragraphs work together to create a narrative.

TICKETS TO NOWHERE

ANDY ROONEY

Andy Rooney is best known for his humorous commentaries on Sixty Minutes. *A longtime CBS reporter, Rooney began his career writing for* Stars and Stripes *during World War II. In this column Rooney describes the fate of a typical lottery player.*

AS YOU READ:
Notice how Rooney uses different ways to organize his paragraphs in this narration. Some paragraphs use narration to tell a story about Jim Oakland's past. Others use comparison to contrast his dreams of wealth and the reality of his situation.

Things never went very well for Jim Oakland. He dropped out of high
school because he was impatient to get rich but after dropping out he
lived at home with his parents for two years and didn't earn a dime. 1

He finally got a summer job working for the highway department
holding up a sign telling oncoming drivers to be careful of the workers 2

ahead. Later that same year, he picked up some extra money putting flyers under the windshield wipers of parked cars.

3   Things just never went very well for Jim and he was 23 before he left home and went to Florida hoping his ship would come in down there. He never lost his desire to get rich but first he needed money for the rent so he took a job near Fort Lauderdale for $4.50 an hour servicing the goldfish aquariums kept by the cashier's counter in a lot of restaurants.

4   Jim was paid in cash once a week by the owner of the goldfish business and the first thing he did was go to the little convenience store near where he lived and buy $20 worth of lottery tickets. He was really determined to get rich.

5   A week ago, the lottery jackpot in Florida reached $54 million. Jim woke up nights thinking what he could do with $54 million. During the days, he daydreamed about it. One morning he was driving along the main street in the boss's old pickup truck with six tanks of goldfish in back. As he drove past a BMW dealer, he looked at the new models in the window.

6   He saw the car he wanted in the showroom window but unfortunately he didn't see the light change. The car in front of him stopped short and Jim slammed on his brakes. The fish tanks slid forward. The tanks broke, the water gushed out and the goldfish slithered and flopped all over the back of the truck. Some fell off into the road.

7   It wasn't a good day for the goldfish or for Jim, of course. He knew he'd have to pay for the tanks and 75 cents each for the fish and if it weren't for the $54 million lottery, he wouldn't have known which way to turn. He had that lucky feeling.

8   For the tanks and the dead goldfish, the boss deducted $114 of Jim's $180 weekly pay. Even though he didn't have enough left for the rent and food, Jim doubled the amount he was going to spend on lottery tickets. He never needed $54 million more.

9   Jim had this system. He took his age and added the last four digits of the telephone number of the last girl he dated. He called it his lucky number . . . even though the last four digits changed quite often and he'd never won with his system. Everyone laughed at Jim and said he'd never win the lottery.

10   Jim put down $40 on the counter that week and the man punched out his tickets. Jim stowed them safely away in his wallet with last week's tickets. He never threw away his lottery tickets until at least a month after the drawing just in case there was some mistake. He'd heard of mistakes.

11   Jim listened to the radio all afternoon the day of the drawing. The people at the radio station he was listening to waited for news of the winning numbers to come over the wires and, even then, the announcers didn't rush to get them on. The station manager thought the people running the lottery ought to pay to have the winning numbers broadcast, just like any other commercial announcement.

12   Jim fidgeted while they gave the weather and the traffic and the news. Then they played more music. All he wanted to hear were those numbers.

13   "Well," the radio announced said finally, "we have the lottery num-

bers some of you have been waiting for. You ready?" Jim was ready. He clutched his ticket with the number 274802.

"The winning number," the announcer said, "is 860539. I'll repeat that. 860539." Jim was still a loser.   14

I thought that, with all the human interest stories about lottery winners, we ought to have a story about one of the several million losers. ■   15

GET THINKING
AND WRITING

CRITICAL THINKING AND DISCUSSION

Understanding Meaning: What Is the Writer Trying to Say?

1. How significant is the title? Does it work to shape readers' attitudes even before they read the column?
2. What is the most important thing Rooney wants you to know about Jim Oakland?
3. How does Rooney describe Jim's life? What details stand out? Write one sentence in your own words that describes your view of Jim.
4. What values does Jim have? Are they realistic?
5. What is Rooney's thesis—can you state it in your own words?
6. *Critical thinking:* What seems to have motivated Rooney to write this piece? Are the last lines necessary to get his meaning across, or does his description of Jim Oakland prove his point?

Evaluating Strategy: How Does the Writer Say It?

1. Rooney does not tell readers what Jim looked like. Do you think this is deliberate? Why or why not?
2. What details and examples does Rooney use to demonstrate Jim's values?
3. How does Rooney use paragraph breaks to organize details and show shifts in his train of thought?
4. *Critical thinking:* Rooney notes that the last four digits of the phone number of Jim's last date changed often. What does this detail suggest about Jim's lifestyle?

Appreciating Language: What Words Does the Writer Use?

1. Rooney refers to Jim Oakland by his first name. What impression does this create? Would calling him Oakland throughout the column create a different effect? Why or why not?
2. Rooney notes that "Jim was still a loser" when his number did not come up in the lottery. Does the word "loser" apply to Jim's entire life? What makes a person a "loser"? Would you define Jim as a loser?

Writing Suggestions

1. Write one or more paragraphs that describe your idea of a loser. You may describe the life of a single person or use several examples.
2. *Collaborative writing:* Working with a group of students, write a short paragraph stating whether or not you consider Rooney's column an effective argument against lotteries.

THE FENDER BENDER

Ramón "Tianguis" Pérez

Ramón "Tianguis" Pérez is an undocumented worker and does not release personal information.

AS YOU READ:

Consider attitudes many Americans have toward "illegals," or undocumented workers. In this narrative Ramón Pérez relates a minor incident that reveals how fragile life is for immigrant workers who lack legal status.

1   One night after work, I drive Rolando's old car to visit some friends, and then head towards home. At a light, I come to a stop too late, leaving the front end of the car poking into the crosswalk. I shift into reverse, but as I am backing up, I strike the van behind me. Its driver immediately gets out to inspect the damage to his vehicle. He's a tall Anglo-Saxon, dressed in a deep blue work uniform. After looking at his car, he walks up to the window of the car I'm driving.

2   "Your driver's license," he says, a little enraged.

3   "I didn't bring it," I tell him.

4   He scratches his head. He is breathing heavily with fury.

5   "Okay," he says. "You park up ahead while I call a patrolman."

6   The idea of calling the police doesn't sound good to me, but the accident is my fault. So I drive around the corner and park at the curb. I turn off the motor and hit the steering wheel with one fist. I don't have a driver's license. I've never applied for one. Nor do I have with me the identification card that I bought in San Antonio. Without immigration papers, without a driving permit, and having hit another car, I feel as if I'm just one step away from Mexico.

7   I get out of the car. The white man comes over and stands right in front of me. He's almost two feet taller.

8   "If you're going to drive, why don't you carry your license?" he asks in an accusatory tone.

9   "I didn't bring it," I say, for lack of any other defense.

10   I look at the damage to his car. It's minor, only a scratch on the paint and a pimple-sized dent.

11   "I'm sorry," I say. "Tell me how much it will cost to fix, and I'll pay for it; that's no problem." I'm talking to him in English, and he seems to understand.

12   "This car isn't mine," he says. "It belongs to the company I work for. I'm sorry, but I've got to report this to the police, so that I don't have to pay for the damage."

13   "That's no problem," I tell him again. "I can pay for it."

14   After we've exchanged these words, he seems less irritated. But he

says he'd prefer for the police to come, so that they can report that the dent wasn't his fault.

While we wait, he walks from one side to the other, looking down the avenue this way and that, hoping that the police will appear.   15

Then he goes over to the van to look at the dent.   16

"It's not much," he says. "If it was my car, there wouldn't be any problems, and you could go on."   17

After a few minutes, the long-awaited police car arrives. Only one officer is inside. He's a Chicano, short and of medium complexion, with short, curly hair. On getting out of the car, he walks straight towards the Anglo.   18

The two exchange a few words.   19

"Is that him?" he asks, pointing at me.   20

The Anglo nods his head.   21

Speaking in English, the policeman orders me to stand in front of the car and to put my hands on the hood. He searches me and finds only the car keys and my billfold with a few dollars in it. He asks for my driver's license.   22

"I don't have it," I answered in Spanish.   23

He wrinkles his face into a frown, and casting a glance at the Anglo, shakes his head in disapproval of me.   24

"That's the way these Mexicans are," he says.   25

He turns back towards me, asking for identification. I tell him I don't have that, either.   26

"You're an illegal, eh?" he says.   27

I won't answer.   28

"An illegal," he says to himself.   29

"Where do you live?" he continues. He's still speaking in English.   30

I tell him my address.   31

"Do you have anything with you to prove that you live at that address?" he asks.   32

I think for a minute, then realize that in the glove compartment is a letter that my parents sent to me several weeks earlier.   33

I show him the envelope and he immediately begins to write something in a little book that he carries in his back pocket. He walks to the back of my car and copies the license plate number. Then he goes over to his car and talks into his radio. After he talks, someone answers. Then he asks me for the name of the car's owner.   34

He goes over to where the Anglo is standing. I can't quite hear what they're saying. But when the two of them go over to look at the dent in the van, I hear the cop tell the Anglo that if he wants, he can file charges against me. The Anglo shakes his head and explains what he had earlier explained to me, about only needing for the police to certify that he wasn't responsible for the accident. The Anglo says that he doesn't want to accuse me of anything because the damage is light.   35

"If you want, I can take him to jail," the cop insists.   36

The Anglo turns him down again.   37

38   "If you'd rather, we can report him to Immigration," the cop continues.

39   Just as at the first, I am now almost sure that I'll be making a forced trip to Tijuana. I find myself searching my memory for my uncle's telephone number, and to my relief, I remember it. I am waiting for the Anglo to say yes, confirming my expectations of the trip. But instead, he says no, and though I remain silent, I feel appreciation for him. I ask myself why the Chicano is determined to harm me. I didn't really expect him to favor me, just because we're of the same ancestry, but on the other hand, once I had admitted my guilt, I expected him to treat me at least fairly. But even against the white man's wishes, he's trying to make matters worse for me. I've known several Chicanos with whom, joking around, I've reminded them that their roots are in Mexico. But very few of them see it that way. Several have told me how when they were children, their parents would take them to vacation in different states of Mexico, but their own feeling, they've said, is, "I am an American citizen!" Finally, the Anglo, with the justifying paper in his hands, says goodbye to the cop, thanks him for his services, gets into his van and drives away.

40   The cop stands in the street in a pensive mood. I imagine that he's trying to think of a way to punish me.

41   "Put the key in the ignition," he orders me.

42   I do as he says.

43   Then he orders me to roll up the windows and lock the doors.

44   "Now, go on, walking," he says.

45   I go off taking slow steps. The cop gets in his patrol car and stays there, waiting. I turn the corner after two blocks and look out for my car, but the cop is still parked beside it. I begin looking for a coat hanger, and after a good while, find one by a curb of the street. I keep walking, keeping about two blocks away from the car. While I walk, I bend the coat hanger into the form I'll need. As if I'd called for it, a speeding car goes past. When it comes to the avenue where my car is parked, it makes a turn. It is going so fast that its wheels screech as it rounds the corner. The cop turns on the blinking lights of his patrol car and leaving black marks on the pavement beneath it, shoots out to chase the speeder. I go up to my car and with my palms force a window open a crack. Then I insert the clothes hanger in the crack and raise the lock lever. It's a simple task, one that I'd already performed. This wasn't the first time that I'd been locked out of a car, though always before, it was because I'd forgotten to remove my keys. ∎

CRITICAL THINKING AND DISCUSSION

Understanding Meaning: What Is the Writer Trying to Say?

1. What is the point of the story? What does the writer want his readers to understand?
2. Why did the van driver insist on calling the police?

3. Why is such a minor accident a threat to the writer?
4. How does the police officer treat the writer? Why?

Evaluating Strategy: How Does the Writer Say It?

1. Why is a minor incident like this a better example to illustrate the plight of undocumented workers than a major accident?
2. How does Pérez use dialogue to tell his story? Is this effective?

Appreciating Language: What Words Does the Writer Use?

1. Underline the words that dramatize Pérez's attempts to resolve the incident without calling the police.
2. Consider the tone, style, and word choice of this essay. Was it easy to read? Why or why not? What does this suggest about the audience Pérez was trying to reach?

Writing Suggestions

1. Write a paragraph that describes an accident you have witnessed. How did you react? Did you try to help? What lesson did you learn? Avoid including minor details like dates or addresses and focus on details that support the point you are trying to make.
2. *Collaborative Writing:* Discuss this essay with a number of students and write a paragraph describing the way they feel undocumented workers should be treated.

STEPS TO WRITING A NARRATIVE PARAGRAPH

1. Study your topic and use critical thinking by asking key questions:
   Why did I choose this event to write about?
   What did it mean to me?
   Why do I remember it?
   What is significant about it?
   What do I want other people to know about it?
   What is my most important point?
2. List your point or message as a topic statement to guide your writing (the topic sentence does not have to appear in the finished paragraph).
3. List supporting details that establish your point.
4. Review your list of supporting details, deleting minor ones and highlighting significant ones.
5. If people appear in your narrative, consider using dialogue rather than indirect summaries of conversations. Remember to use paragraph breaks to indicate a shift in speakers. (See pages 28 and 31.)
6. Write a first draft of your paragraph.
7. Read your paragraph aloud and consider these questions:
   Does my paragraph make a clear point?
   Does it tell readers what I want them to know?
   Do I provide sufficient details?
   Are there unimportant details that could be deleted?

(continued)

Do I use concrete words, especially verbs, to describe action?

Do I avoid illogical shifts in point of view or tense?

Do I provide clear transitions to advance the narrative and explain the passage of time?

Selecting Topics

Consider these topics for writing narrative paragraphs:

an encounter with a stranger that taught you something

a situation in which you had to give someone bad news

a telephone call that changed your life

taking an exam you were unprepared for

a childhood experience that shaped your values or attitudes

buying a car

voting for the first time

a sporting event you participated in

an argument between two people you witnessed

a favorite family story

an event that changed a friend's life

a brief history of your college or employer

an event that occurred in your high school

how your parents or grandparents came to America or moved to your city

a sporting event you watched

the plot of your favorite book or movie

a brief biography of a person you admire

EXERCISE 4 Planning and Writing Paragraphs

Select a topic from the above lists or choose one of your own and develop details and a topic sentence that states the point of your narrative.

Topic: _____

Possible supporting details:

1. _____

2. _____

3. _____

4. _____

5. _____

Circle the most important details that explain the event.

State the point of your narrative and write a topic sentence:

_____

_____

Organize your supporting details chronologically using transitional statements to advance the narrative.

First sentence: topic sentence, first detail, or introductory statement:

_____

_____

Supporting Details:

1. _____

2. _____

3. _____

4. _____

5. _____

Last sentence: final detail, concluding statement, or topic sentence:

_____

_____

Write out your paragraph and review it by reading it out loud.

WORKING TOGETHER

Working with a group of students, revise this paragraph from a student paper to delete irrelevant details, illogical shifts in tense and person, and awkward transitions. Edit the paper for fragments (see Chapter 14), run-ons (see Chapter 16), and misspelled words (see Chapter 27).

Like most days after work, I stop at a Starbucks for coffee and a change to read the paper and unwind from the day. It was a wonderfully sunny spring day. I happen to glance over at a nearly table and notice a familiar face. Nancy Sims was older of course and heavier than she was in high school. She wears torn jeans and a sweatshirt with no makeup. In high school she always wearing stylish clothes. You could see her scuffed shoes, broken nails, and matted hair. I returned to reading my paper, not wanting her to see me staring at her. Suddenly, I sense someone standing next to my table. I look up and saw her. I smiled, thinking she is going to ask if I went to Washington High. She bent over my table. Her breath is sour and her teeth chipped and stained. "Excuse me, she said, "can you give me your change?" I looked up into her spaced-out eyes and realize she has no idea who I am and push my small pile of coins toward her. She scoops them up greedily and put them in the paper bag she used as a purse and headed to the door. I remembered the last time I saw her at graduation and wondered,

what happened to this girl from a nice family who was
heading to college with so much hope?

_____

_____

_____

_____

_____

_____

_____

_____

_____

_____

_____

_____

CRITICAL THINKING

GET THINKING
AND WRITING

_Have you ever learned a lesson "the hard way"? Did a poor decision ever teach you
something? Select an event and summarize what happened and explain the lesson
you learned. Develop a strong topic sentence to guide your paragraph._

WHAT HAVE YOU WRITTEN?

Read your paragraph carefully. Do you clearly state your opinion?

Write out the topic sentence or implied controlling idea:

_____

_____

List the main supporting details in your paragraph:

_____

_____

_____

_Do they support your controlling idea and provide evidence for your point of view?
Could you improve your paragraph by adding more details? Are there minor facts or
trivial details that could be deleted?_

GET WRITING

Have you ever witnessed an event that changed your life? Did you witness an accident, see a celebrity, watch an athletic triumph, or see a performance you cannot forget?

Write a paragraph that tells the story of this event. Focus on creating a strong controlling idea that is supported by relevant details.

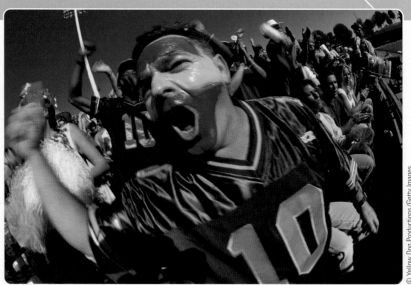

© Yellow Dog Productions/Getty Images

WRITING ON THE WEB

Using a search engine such as AltaVista, Yahoo!, or Google, enter terms such as *narration, writing narration, narrative techniques,* and *first-person narratives* to locate current sites of interest.

1. Review news articles in online versions of magazines like *Time* and *Newsweek* and notice how writers explain events. How do they organize paragraphs, use dialogue, and signal transitions?
2. Write an e-mail to a friend describing something you saw or experienced. Revise your paragraphs to delete minor details and highlight important points.

POINTS TO REMEMBER

1. Narration paragraphs should make a clear point, not simply summarize events.
2. Narratives can be written in first person ("I"), second person ("you"), or third person ("he," "she," or "they"). Avoid illogical shifts:

   I climbed to the top of the hill where *you* can see for miles.

3. Narration can be stated in past or present tense. Avoid illogical shifts:

   I *drove* to the library where I *study* all night.

4. Paragraphs should have clear transition statements to advance the narrative, indicate the passage of time, and prevent confusion.
5. Dialogue—direct quotations—can be more effective than summaries of conversations. Remember to use quotation marks and begin a new paragraph to indicate a shift in speakers.

Developing Paragraphs Using Example

© Ed Andrieski-Pool/Getty Images

Kobe Bryant on his way to court

GET WRITING

Athletes were once expected to be role models who inspired young people by example. In recent years several sports figures have been involved in crimes and scandals.

Write a paragraph stating whether or not you think professional athletes should be seen as role models.

What Is an Example?

Examples illustrate an idea, issue, event, theory, or characteristic. Examples serve to explain something or support a point of view. You can explain that a verb is "a word that expresses action" by giving readers examples—*run, sell, buy, create*. To argue that your street needs a stop sign, you can list examples of recent accidents to prove the intersection is not safe. Examples are specific items that represent something more general:

> Dorm residents may use small appliances like *hair dryers, electric razors, and box fans.*

> *Biff Henderson, Mike Mendoza, and Sean Regan* are examples of high school coaches who stress academic achievement as well as athletic performance.

> Community property, *like city parks and national landmarks*, require public support.

POINT TO REMEMBER

Descriptions provide details about one subject. Examples provide details about a subject that represents a general type.

GET WRITING AND REVISING

WHAT ARE YOU TRYING TO SAY?

Write a paragraph that uses one or more examples to explain an idea or support a point of view about one of the following topics:

- a best friend
- problems single parents face
- TV shows you like or dislike
- campus security
- ideal jobs
- good or bad qualities of a sports player or team

_____

_____

_____

_____

_____

_____

_____

_____

_____

_____

_____

_____

_____

_____

_____

WHAT HAVE YOU WRITTEN?

Read your paragraph carefully. Underline the topic sentence. Does it clearly state what your subject is about? Do the examples relate to your main idea or support your point of view? Do some examples need too much explaining? Will readers be able to understand them? Could you think of better examples?

Writing Example Paragraphs

Example paragraphs illustrate ideas or give readers evidence to support an opinion. Readers may be confused by complex concepts or abstract terms. Specific examples can make ideas easier to understand:

> Although they dressed like gang members and flashed hand signals to each other in the halls, <u>the Iron Kings were responsible only for acts of childish vandalism.</u> They spray painted graffiti on abandoned cars. One night they knocked over every trashcan on 34th Street and later rolled a dumpster in front of the art museum steps. Their most serious offense consisted of stuffing mailboxes with snow. The Iron Kings were never a serious threat to the community.

The examples about knocking over trashcans and putting snow in mailboxes illustrate what the writer means by "acts of childish vandalism."

Writers also use examples as evidence, giving readers specific facts or incidents to support a point of view:

> <u>The computer lab is too small.</u> Last week I had to wait over an hour just to print a copy of my English paper. Every Monday there are at least ten or fifteen students waiting in line to use one of the sixteen computers. At the end of the semester when students are working on research papers, you can wait four hours to use a computer. Last night I went to the computer lab thinking that at nine o'clock there might be room. Four students were waiting to use a computer. Two of them told me they had been there for over an hour.

All these examples of having to wait to get a computer provide support for the student's point that the computer lab is too small.

Types of Examples

You can develop a paragraph using a single or multiple examples. A **single extended example** provides in-depth details about a person, place, or thing that illustrates something more general. The fact that some suburban shopping malls are now losing business because of downtown redevelopment can be demonstrated by the fate of one shopping center:

topic sentence stating a
point of view

single example

Many of the suburban shopping malls that once threatened to destroy downtown businesses are now in trouble. For example, Northridge Mall became an instant hit when it opened in 1976. Suburban families loved the free parking, its hundred stores, five restaurants, and movie theater. For twenty years it was a shopping mecca, but as more people moved downtown to live in refurbished lofts and new condos, the suburban mall lost business. Young professionals preferred to live and shop downtown. Few wanted to drive ten miles to Northridge. One by one merchants left the mall. The mall owners had less money to spend on maintenance and improvements, and by 2000 the 1970s-style mall looked shabby and old-fashioned. In 2004, Northridge, once the state's largest mall, was bulldozed to the ground.

You can also develop a paragraph using **multiple examples:**

> <u>_Tracker_ is a terrible movie.</u> The story of a a med student saving his girl-friend from terrorists makes no sense. Some scenes are absolutely ridiculous. Jeff Jones is supposed to be a first-year medical student, yet is shown performing a complex brain operation when his girlfriend is kidnapped. The FBI claims they can't find the terrorists, but Jones somehow turns his cell phone into a tracking device and follows them to an abandoned oil rig. In the course of the film he flies a plane, steals a one-man sub, uses scuba gear, and fires an AK-47 with deadly accuracy. Moviegoers will wonder when a medical student had time to learn all these James Bond skills. But most will probably be too busy trying to figure out why international terrorists would kidnap a Brooklyn kindergarten teacher in the first place.

topic sentence stating general idea

example 1

example 2

example 3

example 4
example 5

TIPS FOR USING MULTIPLE EXAMPLES

1. **Choose a range of examples.** A list of specific examples can simply offer a number of exceptions rather than provide significant evidence. Use examples that include facts, statistics, or expert testimony to create a broad base of support.
2. **Avoid examples that require extensive explanations.**
3. **Choose examples readers will recognize and understand.**
4. **Place the examples in a logical order— by time or by importance.**
5. **Make sure your examples directly support your topic sentence or controlling idea.**

Using Hypothetical Examples

Most writers use real examples to illustrate an idea. In some cases, however, you can invent **hypothetical examples** to explain a subject:

> <u>Before you offer to volunteer, make sure you are covered by insurance.</u> For example, you offer to help watch children at a church-sponsored daycare center. While you are there, a child falls down and breaks a leg. You call 911 and attend to the child until paramedics arrive. Three weeks later the child's mother files a lawsuit against you for failing to prevent the injury. You discover that the church and daycare center have insurance that covers only employees. To avoid the cost of a trial, your lawyer suggests paying the mother the $10,000 she demands.

topic sentence

hypothetical example

TIPS FOR USING HYPOTHETICAL EXAMPLES

1. **Hypothetical examples are useful to illustrate ideas, but because they are not real they are not effective support for an argument.**
2. **Use hypothetical examples that are simple and easy to understand.**
3. **Add facts or statistics to demonstrate the significance of hypothetical examples:**

Last year over two thousand volunteers were sued in this state.
Nearly eight hundred were ordered to pay a total of $12,500,000 to plaintiffs.

EXERCISE 1 Identifying Examples

Read the paragraph carefully and answer the questions that follow it.

Gentrification, the process of turning slums into upscale neighborhoods, is changing cities across America. This is not new. Forty years ago investors began buying rundown rooming houses in shabby neighborhoods in Philadelphia for thirty or forty thousand dollars. Today these refurbished townhouses in Society Hill sell for up to a million dollars. In Milwaukee the abandoned Blatz Brewery has been turned into a luxury apartment building featuring a health club and swimming pool. In San Francisco an old Del Monte factory became the Cannery, an upscale shopping center. Gentrification brings new life to old buildings, draws consumers and renters to downtown neighborhoods, and increases downtown property values. But not everyone is happy to see a neighborhood change. For example, many low-income residents fear that gentrification will only increase their rent or property taxes and drive out affordable businesses. A neighborhood that once consisted of fast-food restaurants and corner groceries could be turned into one dominated by exclusive restaurants and pricey gourmet shops.

1. **What is the topic sentence?** _____

_____

2. **How many examples are given?** _____

_____

3. **Are any examples hypothetical?** _____

_____

4. **What facts or statistics could be added to create additional support?** _____

_____

Writing Examples: Using Transitions

A paragraph that includes examples needs clear transitions to prevent it from becoming a list of unrelated items. It is important to link examples and show how they support your topic sentence or controlling idea:

My neighborhood has deteriorated in the last year. In June, *for example,* three stores on Elm Street went out of business.

KEY TRANSITION WORDS

It is helpful to introduce examples and link them to your topic sentence with transition words or phrases:

For example, . . .	For instance, . . .
Consider the case of . . .	To illustrate, . . .
To demonstrate, . . .	Another example is . . .

(continued)

> Recent experiences reveal . . .   A case in point is . . .
> An example is . . .   Examples could include . . .
> The best example is . . .   One of the worst cases is . . .

EXERCISE 2 Creating Examples to Explain an Idea

Select one of the following ideas and write a paragraph that uses one or more real or hypothetical examples to illustrate your controlling idea:

> GET WRITING

a best friend
a boss's good or bad behavior
the status of campus housing
problems single parents face
the way drugs or alcohol can affect someone's personality
the effects of being downsized
prejudice
reality television shows

After completing your paragraph, review the controlling idea and the example or examples you developed. Do the examples clearly illustrate your ideas, or do they simply relate stories or offer descriptions?

EXAM SKILLS

Many examination questions call for writing one or more example paragraphs. As with any exam, read the question carefully and make sure your paragraph directly responds to it. Create a clear topic sentence and develop one or more examples that illustrate or provide proof.

From Business Management

Explain the concept of eminent domain.

<table>
<tr><td>topic
sentence
giving
explanaion

examples</td><td>*Eminent domain is the government's right to take private property for public use. The federal government possesses the right of eminent domain, as do states, and many railroads and other public utility companies. For example, eminent domain gives a city the right to condemn houses in order to build a freeway or expand an airport. States can take private land to create parks. During World War II, for instance, the federal government used eminent domain to acquire private property needed to expand army bases. In the 1960s urban planners used eminent domain to condemn whole neighborhoods in major cities to sweep away slums and create new housing, highways, and airports. Although the government has eminent domain, citizen and consumer groups have increasingly filed lawsuits to prevent*</td></tr>
<tr><td>conclusion</td><td>*the loss of their property or to demand more compensation.*</td></tr>
</table>

EXERCISE 3 Creating Examples to Support a Point of View

GET WRITING ▶ *Select one of the following ideas and write a paragraph that uses one or more factual or hypothetical examples to support your point of view:*

why citizens don't vote
why people immigrate to the United States
why so many Americans are overweight
why or why not marijuana should be legalized for medical use
why or why not states should recognize gay marriage
why you chose your major
why or why not you want to own your own business

After completing your paragraph, review your controlling idea and the example or examples you developed. Do the examples support your point of view, or do they simply relate stories or offer descriptions?

Student Paragraphs

Single, extended example:

Sid Greenberg was the best boss I ever had. He made me feel like I was part of his family. When my father was hit by a car while at a convention in Atlanta, Sid got me a plane ticket and paid for my hotel. Even though he was in the middle of a major project, Sid called me every day to ask how my father was. I stayed in Atlanta for five days until my father was discharged, then drove him home. Although I did not have any sick days left, Sid issued me a full paycheck when I got back. When I suggested I could use my bonus money to pay him back, he just smiled and told me to forget it. "Your Dad's OK," he told me. "That's the important thing."

Multiple examples:

The women's dorm needs better security. Last month three first-floor rooms were broken into and vandalized. A week later two cars were stolen from the parking lot. Several women have reported suspicious-looking men loitering in the basement laundry. Purses, books, jackets, backpacks, and a notebook computer have been taken from the first-floor lounge. Bicycles have been stolen from the club room. Over seventy-five students have left the dorms to live in more expensive but safer apartments.

Hypothetical example:

When we think of addiction we think of drugs and alcohol. But even positive things like exercise, dieting, and saving money can be addictive when people become obsessed and compulsive. For example, people can become addicted to a diet. Without developing a true eating disorder, they become so fearful of snacking that they stop seeing friends, dating, going to social functions, or even watching TV with family members if food is present. They may eat healthy meals, but the fear of going off their rigid diet cripples them socially. They constantly fear temptation, so avoid people and isolate themselves. If they do eat something forbidden, they become depressed and punish themselves by skipping meals or exercising until exhaustion. Although they are not ruining their health with drugs, alcohol, or starvation diets, these addicts suffer withdrawal, depression, and low self-esteem. Anything taken to extreme can become dangerously addictive.

PUTTING PARAGRAPHS TOGETHER

Networking

Networking has proven to be the most effective way of getting a job, especially a job you really want. Networking creates a personal database of people who can help you get the job you want or know those who can. There are several networking strategies students should begin using long before they graduate and start looking for jobs.

topic sentence

introduction

explanation

1. What is the controlling idea of this paragraph?
2. How does the student explain "networking"?

Students can begin networking by contacting places they would like to work to ask about the company or organization rather than a job. People are often reluctant to talk to callers looking for a job, but many are willing to help students expressing an interest in their company or industry. Students can ask which courses they should take, which companies are growing, and who to contact for jobs when they graduate. Active professionals have current insights and can provide practical advice you may not learn in the classroom.

example 1 topic sentence

1. What is the controlling idea of this paragraph?
2. How does it connect to the first paragraph?

example 2 topic sentence

<u>Students can also network by joining professional organizations.</u> Almost every career, from nursing to long-haul trucking, has an organization. Many of these offer student discounts for subscriptions and convention fees. Reading professional journals can help you learn more about the field, build a list of names, and identify organizations that are hiring. By attending conventions you can meet people face to face, ask questions, get your name known, and collect business cards. Being a member of an organization can distinguish you from the field of recent graduates looking for a job who have no connection to the profession or industry.

conclusion

1. What is the controlling idea of this paragraph?
2. How does joining a professional organization benefit a student?
3. How does this paragraph build upon the preceding one?
4. What is the writer's final point?

Readings

As you study the readings, notice how writers use paragraphs to highlight main points and signal transitions.

THE COMPANY MAN

ELLEN GOODMAN

Ellen Goodman worked for Newsweek *and the* Detroit Free Press *before joining the* Boston Globe *in 1967. Her columns, widely syndicated since 1976, have discussed feminism, sexual harassment, and family relationships.*

AS YOU READ:

Goodman uses a single hypothetical example to develop an essay about a workaholic. Notice how she uses paragraphs to organize main ideas. Notice also how Goodman repeats the word "work" to make her point.

He worked himself to death, finally and precisely, at 3:00 a.m. Sunday morning.   1

    The obituary didn't say that, of course. It said that he died of a coronary thrombosis—I think that was it—but everyone among his friends and acquaintances knew it instantly. He was a perfect Type A, a workaholic, a classic, they said to each other and shook their heads—and thought for five or ten minutes about the way they lived.   2

3   This man who worked himself to death finally and precisely at 3:00 a.m. Sunday morning— on his day off— was fifty-one years old and a vice-president. He was, however, one of six vice-presidents, and one of three who might conceivably— if the president died or retired soon enough— have moved to the top spot. Phil knew that.

4   He worked six days a week, five of them until eight or nine at night, during a time when his own company had begun the four-day week for everyone but the executives. He worked like the Important People. He had no outside "extracurricular interests," unless, of course, you think about a monthly golf game that way. To Phil, it was work. He always ate egg salad sandwiches at his desk. He was, of course, overweight, by 20 or 25 pounds. He thought it was okay, though, because he didn't smoke.

5   On Saturdays, Phil wore a sports jacket to the office instead of a suit, because it was the weekend.

6   He had a lot of people working for him, maybe sixty, and most of them liked him most of the time. Three of them will be seriously considered for his job. The obituary didn't mention that.

7   But it did list his "survivors" quite accurately. He is survived by his wife, Helen, forty-eight years old, a good woman of no particular marketable skills, who worked in an office before marrying and mothering. She had, according to her daughter, given up trying to compete with his work years ago, when the children were small. A company friend said, "I know how much you will miss him." And she answered, "I already have."

8   "Missing him all these years," she must have given up part of herself which had cared too much for the man. She would be "well taken care of."

9   His "dearly beloved" eldest of the "dearly beloved" children is a hardworking executive in a manufacturing firm down South. In the day and a half before the funeral, he went around the neighborhood researching his father, asking the neighbors what he was like. They were embarrassed.

10   His second child is a girl, who is twenty-four and newly married. She lives near her mother and they are close, but whenever she was alone with her father, in a car driving somewhere, they had nothing to say to each other.

11   The youngest is twenty, a boy, a high-school graduate who has spent the last couple of years, like a lot of his friends, doing enough odd jobs to stay in grass and food. He was the one who tried to grab at his father, and tried to mean enough to him to keep the man at home. He was his father's favorite. Over the last two years, Phil stayed up nights worrying about the boy.

12   The boy once said, "My father and I only board here."

13   At the funeral, the sixty-year-old company president told the forty-eight-year-old widow that the fifty-one-year-old deceased had meant much to the company and would be missed and would be hard to replace. The widow didn't look him in the eye. She was afraid he would read her bitterness and, after all, she would need him to straighten out the finances— the stock options and all that.

Phil was overweight and nervous and worked too hard. If he wasn't at the office, he was worried about it. Phil was a Type A, a heart-attack natural. You could have picked him out in a minute from a lineup.

14

So when he finally worked himself to death, at precisely 3:00 a.m. Sunday morning, no one was really surprised.

15

By 5:00 p.m. the afternoon of the funeral, the company president had begun, discreetly of course, with care and taste, to make inquiries about his replacement. One of the three men. He asked around: "Who's been working the hardest?" ■

16

GET THINKING AND WRITING

CRITICAL THINKING AND DISCUSSION

Understanding Meaning: What Is the Writer Trying to Say?

1. How significant is the title? What is a "company man"?
2. What does Phil represent? Do you know people like him?
3. What seems to drive Phil to work so hard?
4. *Critical thinking:* If a woman, African American, or Hispanic had Phil's job and worked hard, would he or she be seen as a "role model"? Why or why not?

Evaluating Strategy: How Does the Writer Say It?

1. Would Goodman's essay be stronger if she included more than one example?
2. What impact does the final paragraph have?
3. What details about Phil's life suggest that something was missing?

Appreciating Language: What Words Does the Writer Use?

1. Goodman puts certain phrases in quotation marks, such as "well taken care of" and "dearly beloved." What is the effect of highlighting these terms?
2. What is a Type A personality?

Writing Suggestions

1. Write one or more paragraphs that use the example of a single student, neighbor, employee, boss, or friend who illustrates a personality type. Is someone you know a perfect example of a shopaholic, a cheapskate, a grind, a party animal, an ideal parent?
2. *Collaborative writing:* Working with a group of students, write a short statement that answers the question, "What do we owe to our jobs?"

ODD ENDERS

LARRY ORENSTEIN

Larry Orenstein is an assistant foreign editor at the Toronto newspaper the Globe and Mail. *He is a member of the Crime Writers of Canada.*

AS YOU READ:
Orenstein published this humorous piece in a Canadian newspaper. Because he is writing for readers who skim rather than read articles, he uses brief paragraphs. Orenstein provides multiple examples to entertain his readers and illustrate his concept of Odd Enders, people who die in unusual circumstances.

1   Death is never funny. It is cancer, heart failure, stroke, clogged arteries, pneumonia, emphysema, asthma, bronchitis, choking, drowning, car accident. It is mostly quiet, conventional and inevitable.

2   But, in the twilight area between Dryden's "Death in itself is nothing" and Kojak's "Death is dumb," there are "other causes." A man who stumbles during his morning <u>constitutional</u>, bites his tongue and dies of gangrene— as Allan Pinkerton, head of the U.S. detective agency bearing his name, did in 1884— is a man who is checking out with a drum roll, a man who, in short, is joining the Club of Odd Ends.

3   Membership in the club sometimes requires the assistance of a sponsor. In 1977, a 36-year-old San Diego woman decided to murder her 23-year-old husband, a U.S. Marine drill instructor, to collect his $20,000 in life insurance. First, she baked him a blackberry pie containing the venom sac of a tarantula. But he ate only a few pieces. She then tried to (1) electrocute him in the shower, (2) poison him with lye, (3) run him over with a car, (4) make him hallucinate while driving by putting amphetamines in his beer, and (5) inject an air bubble into his veins with a hypodermic needle. Finally, dispensing with subtlety, she and an accomplice, a 26-year-old woman, beat him over the head with a metal weight while he slept. This worked.

4   In 1978, a Parisian grocer stabbed his wife to death with a wedge of parmesan cheese. In 1984, a New Zealand man killed his wife by jabbing her repeatedly in the stomach with a frozen sausage.

5   In April, 1984, a 41-year-old Pennsylvania man was asphyxiated after his 280-pound wife sat on his chest during an argument. Nine months later, a 41-year-old Indiana woman beat her male companion to death by repeatedly dropping a bowling ball on his head while he lay on the floor in front of a television set.

6   Last summer, a man in Sao Paulo, Brazil, caught his wife in bed with her lover, and glued her hands to the man's penis. Doctors separated the two, but the man died from toxic chemicals absorbed through his skin. In Prague, a woman jumped out of a third-story window after learning her husband had been unfaithful. She landed on the husband, who was entering the building at that moment. He died instantly; she survived.

Words to Know

constitutional brisk walk

despondent hopeless
ricocheted bounced off

angina heart disease

recluse one who leads a secluded life

severed cut
dialysis machine kidney machine

septicemic poisoning blood infection

A <u>despondent</u> Los Angeles man put a gun to his head and pulled the trigger. The bullet passed through his head, <u>ricocheted</u> off a water heater and struck his female companion between the eyes.

Some people, of course, discover the Club of Odd Ends on their own and sign their membership cards with a flourish. An Italian man set himself on fire, apparently had second thoughts and died falling off a cliff trying the beat out the flames. Last fall, a 26-year-old computer specialist died near Bristol apparently after tying one end of a rope to a tree and the other around his neck, getting into his car and driving off.

In 1971, a Shrewsbury man killed himself by drilling into his skull eight times with an electric power drill. Sixteen years later, a Chichester man who could no longer bear the pain from <u>angina</u> killed himself by drilling a hole in his heart.

Some people become Odd Enders by accident. In 1947, an eccentric U.S. <u>recluse</u>, while carrying food to his equally reclusive brother, tripped a burglar trap in his house and was crushed to death under bundles of old newspapers, three breadboxes, a sewing machine and a suitcase filled with metal. His brother starved to death.

In 1982, a 27-year-old man fired two shotgun blasts at a giant saguaro cactus in the desert near Phoenix. The shots caused a 23-foot section of the cactus to fall and crush him to death. That same year, an elderly Louisiana man with ailing kidneys was waving a gun at quarrelling relatives when it went off. The bullet <u>severed</u> a tube from his <u>dialysis machine</u>, and he bled to death.

In 1983, the assistant manager of a topless night club in San Francisco was crushed to death between the ceiling and a trick piano rigged to rise 12 feet above the club's stage. When the club was opened in the morning, the man's 240-pound body was found draped over his naked, intoxicated girl friend, who survived apparently by kicking a switch to stop the cables hoisting the piano.

In November, 1985, a flight attendant with three months of experience survived the hijacking of an Egyptian airliner that left 60 people dead in Malta. She was killed seven months later when her plane crashed in a sandstorm near Cairo.

In April, an award-winning astronomer at the University of Arizona was crushed to death between a door and a 150-ton revolving telescope dome. In June, a man demonstrating electrical currents to his children in Orillia, Ont., was electrocuted when an experiment backfired. A California woman taking pictures of a glacier in Alaska was killed when a 1,000-pound chunk of ice broke free and fell on her.

A 22-year-old Peruvian woman died of <u>septicemic poisoning</u> in June after the rusty padlock on the leather chastity belt that her jealous husband forced her to wear dug into her flesh and caused an infection.

In 1980, the 70-year-old mayor of a Maryland town who was checking a sewage-treatment plant slipped on a catwalk, fell into a tank of human waste and drowned. In July, a retired barman in Northern Ireland was buried alive when he fell into a grave being dug for his brother.

7

8

9

10

11

12

13

14

15

16

17   The Club of Odd Ends, however, does not accept all applicants. A Brazilian public servant lost an arm last summer when he stuck it into a lion's cage "to test God's power." One night in 1982, an Ohio bachelor awoke, thought he saw a prowler at the foot of his bed, reached for his gun, fired into the darkness and shot himself in the penis.

18   Some people, of course, are destined to become Odd Enders no matter what they do. In May, a Louisiana lawyer stood in the stern of his new boat, raised his hands skyward and said: "Here I am." He was killed by a bolt of lightning. ■

CRITICAL THINKING AND DISCUSSION

GET THINKING AND WRITING

Understanding Meaning: What Is the Writer Trying to Say?

1. How significant is the title? What is an Odd Ender?
2. What is Orenstein's goal? What does he want to achieve by telling all these stories to his newspaper readers?
3. *Critical thinking:* Orenstein opens his article saying "Death is never funny," then provides a list of strange, odd, and witty stories about people dying. What is Orenstein trying to say? Is death ever funny?

Evaluating Strategy: How Does the Writer Say It?

1. Would a long single example be as effective? Why or why not?
2. Which example is the best illustration of an Odd Ender?
3. Some of Orenstein's paragraphs contain only one or two sentences. Why is this common in newspaper articles?

Appreciating Language: What Words Does the Writer Use?

1. Consider Orenstein's term "Odd Ender"? What impact do those words have?
2. How easy is Orenstein's piece to read? Could you skim this article over coffee or on the bus and get Orenstein's point?

Writing Suggestions

1. Invent your own term to describe a personality or situation, then illustrate it with a list of short examples.
2. *Collaborative writing:* Working with a group of students, write your own examples of Odd Enders.

STEPS TO WRITING AN EXAMPLE PARAGRAPH

1. Clearly establish your topic and describe it accurately. Examples will work only if they illustrate a precisely defined topic or provide evidence for a clearly stated point of view.
2. Consider your readers when you choose examples. Will they recognize the people, events, or situations you provide as support?

(continued)

3. Avoid examples that are too complicated or require too much explanation.
4. Organize examples in a clear pattern. You might arrange events by time, or group people by their age or profession. Avoid creating a jumble of examples that will confuse readers.
5. If you use a single example, delete minor details and focus on those that clearly support your main point.
6. Write a draft of your paragraph.
7. Read your paragraph out loud and ask yourself these questions:
   Do I have a clear topic sentence that defines my subject?
   Do the examples illustrate or represent my subject?
   Will readers make the connection between my examples and the larger topic they are supposed to represent?
   Can you think of better examples?

Selecting Topics

There are two ways to develop topics for an example paragraph. First, select a specific person, place, thing, or idea you think represents something more general:

A friend overreacts to a minor event, providing the perfect example of a "drama queen" or an "overreactor."

A fraudulent charge appears on your credit card, giving you a personal example of a new kind of consumer scam.

A request from your boss provides a perfect example of a "no-win situation."

Second, select a topic or state an opinion, then think of examples that best illustrate your idea or provide evidence for your point of view.

Describe a "dead-end job," then provide examples.

Outline your definition of a good relationship, then illustrate it with one or more examples.

Argue for a change in the law and use examples to support your opinion.

EXERCISE 4 Planning and Writing Paragraphs

GET WRITING

Establish a topic and define it carefully. Determine what you want readers to understand about it by listing the most important points you want to dramatize.

Topic: _____

Details, things readers should know:

1. _____

2. _____

3. _____

4. _____

Example or examples that represent the topic:

1. _____

2. _____

3. _____

4. _____

First sentence: topic sentence, first example, or introductory statement:

_____

_____

Examples

1. _____

2. _____

3. _____

4. _____

Last sentence: final example, concluding statement, or topic sentence:

_____

_____

WORKING TOGETHER

Working with a group of students, revise the following student paragraph about mentors. Add new sentences to supply missing information. Delete minor or unrelated details.

```
      Everyone needs a mentor. When I first was hired at
Harrison, Ford, and Gray, I was overwhelmed by the size
of the firm. I felt lost. I knew my job but was lost
outside my cubicle. Then Sara Hojaty took me under her
wing. She introduced me to people and explained office
procedures. We went to lunch at Sardi's that first
week. The next week we had dinner at Twenty-One. The
company had an endless list of rules, but she showed me
which were the most important. Whenever I had a problem
Sara was there to coach me through it. Because of her I
began to feel part of the team and developed the confi-
dence I needed to succeed. Another thing I liked about
her was the way she found the greatest shopping bar-
gains in town.
```

CRITICAL THINKING

GET THINKING AND WRITING

Maybe you have seen the bumper sticker that reads "Practice Acts of Random Charity." Can you think of any examples? Did a friend do something for a stranger in trouble that surprised you?

WHAT HAVE YOU WRITTEN?

Read your paragraph carefully. Write out your topic sentence:

_____

Is it clearly worded? Could it be revised to better state your controlling idea?
Do your examples illustrate the topic sentence? Are there unrelated details that could be deleted? Can you supply better examples?

GET WRITING

Were previous generations of athletes better role models? Did they behave better, or did the media avoid reporting about problems in their private lives? Are today's players corrupted by multimillion-dollar contracts and corporate endorsements? Do athletes still play for the love of the game?

Write a paragraph comparing today's sports figures with those of the past. What, if anything, has changed?

© Elwin Williamson / Index Stock Imagery

WRITING ON THE WEB

Using a search engine such as AltaVista, Yahoo!, or Google, enter terms such as *example, writing example paragraphs,* and *example techniques* to locate current sites of interest.

1. Review news articles in online versions of magazines like *Time* and *Newsweek* and notice how writers use examples to illustrate ideas.
2. Write an e-mail to a friend and use examples to explain your ideas. If you are having problems at school, provide specific examples.

POINTS TO REMEMBER

1. Examples are not descriptions. Descriptions provide details about one person, place, or thing. Examples provide details about a person, place, or thing that represents a general type or supports a point of view.
2. Example paragraphs need strong, clearly worded topic sentences that identify the main idea the examples represent or support.
3. Because examples can be dismissed as exceptions, it is important to provide facts, statistics, and other evidence to support a point of view.

8

Developing Paragraphs Using Comparison and Contrast

© Jon Feingersh /CORBIS

GET WRITING

Do you think men and women bring different qualities to the workplace? Do men and women use different strategies to manage employees, motivate workers, resolve problems, or seek advancement?

Write a paragraph that answers these questions by comparing men and women you have met at work or school.

What Are Comparison and Contrast?

Comparison and contrast measure similarities and differences. Comparison focuses on how two things are alike. Contrast highlights how they are different. Textbooks use comparison and contrast to explain two methods of accounting, two historical figures, two types of poetry, two machines, or two economic philosophies. Your jobs may require you to use comparison to make decisions. As consumers we often use contrast to determine which product to buy, which apartment to rent, or whether we should buy or lease a car. Much of the writing you will do in college or in your job will use comparison and contrast:

> Antibiotics are effective in treating most bacterial infections, but they have little or no effect on viral infections.

> Coach Wilson always stressed teamwork, but Coach Harris concentrates on two or three key players.

> I strongly recommend you consider buying rather than leasing your next car.

WHAT ARE YOU TRYING TO SAY?

AND REVISING

Write a paragraph that compares one of the following pairs:

- high school and college instructors
- college and NFL football
- two popular talk shows, soap operas, or sitcoms
- male and female attitudes about dating, marriage, or careers
- two jobs you have had
- two cities or neighborhoods you have lived in

_____

_____

_____

_____

_____

_____

_____

_____

_____

_____

_____

_____

WHAT HAVE YOU WRITTEN?

Read your paragraph carefully. Underline your topic sentence. Does it clearly state the two topics? What are the important details you listed for the first topic?

a. _____

b. _____

c. _____

What are the important details you listed for the second topic?

a. _____

b. _____

c. _____

Can you think of better details to add? Are there any unrelated details that could be deleted? How could you revise this paragraph to improve its impact?

The Purposes of Comparison and Contrast

TIPS FOR WRITING COMPARISON PARAGRAPHS TO EXPLAIN

1. **Create direct, clearly worded sentences that describe both items.**
2. **Use details and examples to illustrate each type.**
3. **Point out key similarities and key differences.**
4. **Use concrete words rather than general or abstract words.**
5. **Avoid details that require too much explanation or background.**

Comparison and contrast paragraphs are used for two reasons—to explain and to convince.

Writing to Explain

Comparisons can be used to explain similar topics, showing the differences between air-cooled and water-cooled engines, between state and federal laws, or between African and Indian elephants. You can think of comparisons as two descriptions. The goal of these paragraphs is to teach readers something and to clear up any confusion they may have:

Many people use the words "jail" and "prison" interchangeably. It is not uncommon, for example, to hear someone say, "He robbed a bank and served ten years in jail." But jails and prisons are very different institutions. City and county jails are short-term facilities. People who are arrested are detained in jail until they are charged or until they go to trial. People convicted of crimes and given short sentences are sent to jail. Jails generally offer minimal services beyond meals and showers. People convicted of serious crimes and sentenced to terms of several months to life are sent to a variety of state and federal prisons. Prisons range from minimal facilities to maximum security institutions. Unlike jails, which are designed to detain people for short terms, prisons provide drug counseling, literacy programs, and vocational training designed to help convicts start a new life.

EXERCISE 1 Using Comparison and Contrast to Explain

Write a paragraph using comparison or contrast to explain the similarities and differences of one of the following topics:

GET WRITING

two television shows	two cities or	two bands
AM vs. FM radio	neighborhoods	PC vs. Macintosh
hybrid vs. gas-powered cars	college vs. professional teams	two cell phone plans two airlines

Writing to Convince

In other paragraphs you may use comparison to convince, to prove to readers that one idea is better than another. You might recommend that customers buy one kind of insurance over another or to vote for one candidate rather than an opponent. Comparison paragraphs that are used to convince readers require a clearly stated topic sentence:

> At this point newspaper polls suggest Angel Cortez has a slight margin over Alderman Federmann in the race for mayor. Cortez, a popular ad executive and radio station owner, has excited a lot of interest and energized young voters. He is young, bright, energetic, and articulate. He promises to transform a stodgy city hall machine into a twenty-first-century engine for social change. But anyone who really cares about this city will vote for sixty-two-year-old Sy Federmann. Federmann has been working in city government for thirty-six years. He has been part of every reform movement in the city's history, helping integrate the schools in the 1970s, save the downtown business district, expand the airport, and attract developers to revitalize the riverfront. He knows how to motivate the slow-to-move city council and has a record of securing funds from the federal government. Cortez is a great business leader who is good for the city. But having no experience working in government, he will unlikely be able to do more than give speeches and do public appearances. Real change will come with Federmann. He has the record to prove it. As mayor, Federmann will finally have the power to make use of almost forty years of experience.

TIPS FOR WRITING COMPARISON PARAGRAPHS TO CONVINCE

1. **Create a strong topic sentence clearly stating your choice.**
2. **Provide readers with concrete evidence and examples to support your topic sentence, not just negative comments:**

Ineffective
Cortez does not know what he is talking about. He is unrealistic, ignorant, and egotistical.

Improved
Cortez has never served in government. He has no practical knowledge of the city bidding process, has never worked with council members, and has a leadership style that works in business but not in politics.

3. **Support your topic sentence with examples, facts, quotes, and statistics.**

EXERCISE 2 Using Comparison and Contrast to Convince

GET WRITING ▸ *Choose one of the following topics and write a paragraph that uses comparison or contrast to convince readers that one item in a pair is better than the other.*

talk show hosts	types of parents	new cars
diets	healthcare plans	stores, cafés, or clubs
political candidates	cable news programs	actors, singers, or other performers

Organizing Comparison and Contrast Paragraphs

Because they deal with two topics, comparison and contrast paragraphs can be a challenge to organize clearly:

Confusing

Southwest Community College is a two-year college in El Paso. It is fully accredited and offers associate degrees as well as diplomas in business, liberal arts, medical technology, and industrial design. It has 7,600 students. El Paso Business Institute is a two-year college in El Paso. It offers diplomas in business and medical technology. Southwest Community College charges roughly $2,000 a year for books, fees, and tuition. El Paso Business Institute costs almost $8,000 a year. Southwest Community College is a public institution and receives state aid. El Paso Business Institute is a private school. El Paso Business Institute has about 1,500 students. General Motors and Delco Medical Systems have exclusive training contracts with El Paso Business Institute, so that almost 90 percent of the school's graduates get jobs with those two companies. Southwest Community College graduates get jobs throughout the state, and about half its students transfer to four-year schools. Both schools have a lot to offer El Paso high school graduates. It depends on their goals.

The paragraph contains a number of details, but it shifts back and forth between the two schools and so is hard to follow.

There are basically two methods of organizing comparison paragraphs—*subject-by-subject* or *point-by-point.*

Subject-by-Subject

The **subject-by-subject method** divides the paragraph into two parts. The opening line usually introduces the two topics and states the controlling idea. The paragraph describes the first subject, then the second. Most of the actual comparison occurs in the second part of the paragraph:

Southwest Community College and El Paso Business Institute are two-year colleges offering a range of opportunities to local high school graduates. Southwest Community College is a fully accredited public institution that offers associate degrees and diploma programs in business, liberal arts, medical technology, and industrial design. Funded in part by state aid, it charges its 7,600 students roughly $2,000 a year for books, fees, and tuition. Southwest graduates get jobs throughout the state, and about half transfer to four-year schools. El Paso Business Institute, which has about 1,500 students, is a private school that costs almost $8,000 a year. It offers diplomas in business and medical technology. General Motors and Delco Medical Systems have exclusive training contracts with the school, so almost 90 percent of its graduates get jobs with those two companies.

- Subject-by-subject paragraphs may be the simplest to organize because they divide the paragraph into two parts.
- You can avoid repetition by mentioning facts and details found in both subjects in a single statement:

    Karla Benz and Tamika Johnson are recent college graduates and single mothers who used the Internet to find jobs.

Point-by-Point

The **point-by-point method** creates a series of comparisons, showing similarities and differences in specific points:

    Southwest Community College and El Paso Business Institute are two-year colleges offering a range of opportunities to local high school graduates. Southwest Community College is a fully accredited public institution that

EXAM SKILLS

Many examination questions call for writing one or more comparison and contrast paragraphs. As with any exam, read the question carefully and make sure your paragraph directly responds to it. Determine whether your goal is to use comparison and contrast to explain similarities and differences between two subjects or convince that one is better than the other. Make sure your paragraph has a strong, clear topic sentence and organizes details using the subject-by-subject or point-by-point method.

From Mechanical Engineering

What are the main differences between a gasoline and a diesel engine?

general
description — *Gasoline and diesel engines, both developed in Germany in the late nineteenth century, are internal combustion engines used to power motor vehicles. Nickolaus Otto developed the*
first subject — *four-stroke engine in 1876, which was used with Daimler's carburetor to create the first automobile engines. Most cars and light trucks use gasoline engines because of their light weight. Gas engines are only 20–25 percent efficient. Rudolf Diesel*
second subject — *developed the diesel engine in 1892, which uses a heavier fuel and achieves efficiencies ranging from 25 to 42 percent. Diesel engines are heavy, so they are impractical for airplanes and most passenger cars. Diesel engines are used in trains, trucks, and stationary power plants.*

The paragraph states the common details shared by the two engines, then uses the subject-by-subject method to organize a comparison of the engines' development, fuel, weight, efficiency, and current uses.

offers associate degrees and diploma programs in business, liberal arts, medical technology, and industrial design. El Paso Business Institute offers diplomas in business and medical technology. Southwest Community College has 7,600 students and charges roughly $2,000 a year for books, fees, and tuition. El Paso Business Institute has about 1,500 students and costs almost $8,000 a year. Southwest graduates get jobs throughout the state, and about half transfer to four-year schools. El Paso Business Institute has exclusive training contracts with General Motors and Delco Medical Systems, so almost 90 percent of its graduates get jobs with those two companies.

- Point-by-point comparisons allow you to place specific facts, numbers, dates, or prices side by side for easier reading.
- Point-by-point comparisons can be useful when writing to convince because you can prove detail by detail how one subject is better than the other.

Student Paragraphs

Comparison and contrast of two jobs:

For two years I worked nine to five in a claims office. It required a forty-five-minute commute, a six-dollar-a-day parking fee, and wearing a suit and tie. I was jammed into a tight cubicle and could take only two five-minute breaks. When the system was down, which happened often, my time was wasted, and all I could do was read the paper and wait. When the accounting department needed our office space, we were given the option of working from home. My current job allows me to work from home much of the time, so I can now sleep an hour later because my commute takes a few seconds. I can wear jeans and a T-shirt and have my whole apartment to work from. I can take breaks when I want. When the system is down, I can run errands, do my wash, work on a school assignment, or take a nap. My neighbors might think I'm unemployed, but I am often working overtime every week.

Comparison and contrast of two television shows:

Sitcoms break down into two types—the family sitcom and the workplace sitcom. In the family sitcom the action takes place in a living room. It is the oldest kind of show, dating back to the days of *Ozzie and Harriet* and *Father Knows Best*. *The Cosby Show* and *Everybody Loves Raymond* are updates but really much the same. The focus is on family life and the interactions between husbands and wives and parents and children. Cosby was a doctor who rarely had to leave dinner to see a patient. Raymond is a sportswriter who seems to spend every night at home. In contrast, the characters in *M.A.S.H.* and *Taxi* seemed to live at work. These shows explore the relationships between bosses and employees, between office rivals and office pals. These shows focus on the two places we spend most of our lives and encounter most of our problems. A few shows like *King of Queens* and *Will and Grace* are the most realistic because they blend both worlds.

Comparison and contrast of two countries:

Iraq and Iran are two Middle Eastern nations that are often in the news, but few Americans realize how different these neighbors are. Iran, called Persia until 1935, is an ancient nation that goes back thousands of years to biblical times. The people are Persians, not Arabs. They speak Farsi, not Arabic. The population is predominantly Shiite. Under the Shah, Iran was closely linked to Europe and the United States. Today Iran is an Islamic republic seeking to create a new identity. Iraq, on the other hand, is a relatively new country, created by the British after World War I. The people have strong tribal and ethnic ties. The Kurds in the north have a long history of regional independence. Still in turmoil since the fall of Saddam, Iraq's future is unsettled.

PUTTING PARAGRAPHS TOGETHER

The Civil War lasted longer than many expected and cost more lives than anyone feared because both sides had strong advantages.

introduction

topic sentence

1. What is the goal of this paragraph?
2. Is a one-sentence introduction helpful or distracting?

The North had a larger population, better transportation, and a more advanced industrial base than the South. The North had the capital and factories to produce the materials of war: weapons, uniforms, and ammunition. Its extensive merchant fleet and strong navy meant Union forces could import needed supplies. The North had all the resources to build a powerful modern army to crush the weaker Confederate forces.

topic sentence
Northern advantages

supporting details

1. What are the main ideas in this paragraph?
2. How does the student organize this paragraph?

topic sentence
Southern advantages

supporting details

<u>In contrast, the South, though less populated and less industrial, had clear strengths.</u> First, the South basically achieved all its goals by seceding and creating the Confederacy. It only had to protect its borders from attack. Its armies fought on familiar territory and could use this knowledge to wage guerrilla raids against Union forces. Defending armies throughout history have often been able to hold off much larger invading armies. The South hoped recognition and possible support from Great Britain would tip the balance in its favor if it could keep Union forces at bay.

1. How does this paragraph contrast with the previous one?
2. How does the student organize the details?
3. How does this paragraph build on the ideas mentioned in the first one?

conclusion

details

topic sentence

Although Southern armies fought hard and inflicted heavy losses on Union forces, they were steadily ground down. They had no resources for a long war, and without outside support, the Confederacy slowly crumbled. <u>Despite its inferior position, the South was able to inflict high casualties on the North in America's most costly conflict.</u>

1. How does this paragraph serve to end the comparison?
2. Does the topic sentence relate to the ideas in the opening paragraph?

Readings

As you study these readings, notice how writers use paragraphs to organize comparisons and make transitions between subjects.

CHINESE SPACE, AMERICAN SPACE

YI-FU TUAN

Yi-Fu Tuan was born in China and later moved to the United States. Now a geography professor in Madison, Wisconsin, he studies cultural differences between America and his native country.

AS YOU READ:
To explain the difference between American and Chinese culture, Tuan focuses on the contrast between traditional American and Chinese houses. Notice how Tuan uses paragraphs to organize his ideas.

1 Americans have a sense of space, not of place. Go to an American home in <u>exurbia</u>, and almost the first thing you do is drift toward the picture window. How curious that the first compliment you pay your host inside his house is to say how lovely it is outside his house! He is pleased that you should admire his vistas. The distant horizon is not merely a line separating earth from sky, it is a symbol of the future. The American is not rooted in his place, however lovely: his eyes are drawn by the expanding space to a point on the horizon, which is his future.

2 By contrast, consider the traditional Chinese home. Blank walls enclose it. Step behind the spirit wall and you are in a courtyard with perhaps a miniature garden around a corner. Once inside his private compound you are wrapped in an <u>ambiance</u> of calm beauty, an ordered world of buildings, pavement, rock, and decorative vegetation. But you have no distant view: nowhere does space open out before you. Raw nature in such a home is experienced only as weather, and the only open space is the sky above. The Chinese is rooted in his place. When he has to leave, it is not for the promised land on the <u>terrestrial</u> horizon, but for another world altogether along the vertical, religious axis of his imagination.

3 The Chinese tie to place is deeply felt. <u>Wanderlust</u> is an alien sentiment. The Taoist classic *Tao Te Ching* captures the ideal of rootedness in place with these words: "Though there may be another country in the neighborhood so close that they are within sight of each other and the crowing of cocks and barking of dogs in one place can be heard in the other, yet there is no traffic between them; and throughout their lives the two peoples have nothing to do with each other." In theory if not in practice, farmers have ranked high in Chinese society. The reason is not only that they are engaged in a "root" industry of producing food but that, unlike <u>pecuniary</u> merchants, they are tied to the land and do not abandon their country when it is in danger.

4 <u>Nostalgia</u> is a recurrent theme in Chinese poetry. An American reader of translated Chinese poems may well be taken aback— even put off— by the frequency, as well as the sentimentality, of the lament for home. To understand the strength of this sentiment, we need to know that the Chinese desire for stability and rootedness in place is prompted by the constant threat of war, exile, and the natural disasters of flood and drought. Forcible removal makes the Chinese keenly aware of their loss. By contrast, Americans move, for the most part, voluntarily. Their nostalgia for home town is really longing for a childhood to which they cannot return: in the meantime the future beckons and the future is "out there," in open space. When we criticize American rootlessness, we tend to forget that it is a result of ideals we admire, namely, social mobility and optimism about the future. When we admire Chinese rootedness, we forget that the word "place" means both a location in space and position in society: to be tied to place is also to be bound to one's station in life, with little hope of betterment. Space symbolizes hope, place, achievement and stability. ∎

Words to Know

exurbia suburbs

ambiance atmosphere, mood

terrestrial earthly

wanderlust desire to travel

pecuniary financial

nostalgia longing for the past

CRITICAL THINKING AND DISCUSSION

Understanding Meaning: What Is the Writer Trying to Say?

1. How does the author see a difference between "space" and "place"?
2. What do houses reveal about American and Chinese values and culture?
3. How has history influenced the way Americans and Chinese live? What events shaped the Chinese desire to be "rooted" in one place?
4. What negative aspects does Tuan see in the Chinese sense of place?

Evaluating Strategy: How Does the Writer Say It?

1. Tuan spends most of his essay describing China rather than the United States. Does this make sense? Should a comparison and contrast essay always devote equal space to both subjects? Why or why not?
2. Tuan uses one item to focus his comparison. Is this an effective device? Why or why not?
3. What impact does the final paragraph have?

Appreciating Language: What Words Does the Writer Use?

1. Tuan uses the word "rootlessness." Does this seem like something negative to many people? Does being "rootless" suggest a lack of values?
2. Tuan uses the German-derived word "wanderlust" in an article about America and China. Does this make sense?

Writing Suggestions

1. If you are familiar with a different culture or a different part of the country, use a single point of reference to show differences. You might compare New York and Los Angeles cab drivers, Northern and Southern restaurants, or Mexican and American soap operas.
2. *Collaborative writing:* Discuss the differences between high school and college with a group of students, then select a single point and develop a short comparison paragraph.

NEAT PEOPLE vs. SLOPPY PEOPLE

SUZANNE BRITT

Suzanne Britt has written articles for the New York Times, *the* Boston Globe, Newsweek, *and the* Cleveland Plain Dealer. *Her books include* Show and Tell *and* Images: A Centennial Journey.

AS YOU READ:

Suzanne Britt uses the subject-by-subject method to organize her observations about neat and sloppy people. Think of people you know who fit in these categories.

1   I've finally figured out the difference between neat people and sloppy people. The distinction is, as always, moral. Neat people are lazier and meaner than sloppy people.

2   Sloppy people, you see, are not really sloppy. Their sloppiness is merely the unfortunate consequence of their extreme moral <u>rectitude</u>. Sloppy people carry in their mind's eye a heavenly vision, a precise plan, that is so stupendous, so perfect, it can't be achieved in this world or the next.

3   Sloppy people live in Never-Never Land. Someday is their <u>métier</u>. Someday they are planning to alphabetize all their books and set up home catalogues. Someday they will go through their wardrobes and mark certain items for <u>tentative</u> mending and certain items for passing on to relatives of similar shape and size. Someday sloppy people will make family scrapbooks into which they will put newspaper clippings, postcards, locks of hair, and the fried corsage from their senior prom. Someday they will file everything on the surface of their desks, including the cash receipts from coffee purchases at the snack shop. Someday they will sit down and read all the back issues of *The New Yorker*.

4   For all these noble reasons and more, sloppy people never get neat. They aim too high and wide. They save everything, planning someday to file, order, and straighten out the world. But while these ambitious plans take clearer and clearer shape in their heads, the books spill from the shelves onto the floor, the clothes pile up in the hamper and closet, the family mementos <u>accumulate</u> in every drawer, the surface of the desk is buried under mounds of paper and the unread magazines threaten to reach the ceiling.

5   Sloppy people can't bear to part with anything. They give loving attention to every detail. When sloppy people say they're going to tackle the surface of the desk, they really mean it. Not a paper will go unturned; not a rubber band will go unboxed. Four hours or two weeks into the <u>excavation</u>, the desk looks exactly the same, primarily because the sloppy person is <u>meticulously</u> creating new piles of papers with new headings and <u>scrupulously</u> stopping to read all the old book catalogs before he throws them away. A neat person would just bulldoze the desk.

6   Neat people are bums and clods at heart. They have <u>cavalier</u> attitudes toward possessions, including family heirlooms. Everything is just another dust-catcher to them. If anything collects dust, it's got to go and that's that. Neat people will toy with the idea of throwing the children out of the house just to cut down on the clutter.

7   Neat people don't care about process. They like results. What they want to do is get the whole thing over with so they can sit down and watch the rasslin' on TV. Neat people operate on two unvarying principles: Never handle any item twice, and throw everything away.

8   The only thing messy in a neat person's house is the trash can. The minute something comes to a neat person's hand, he will look at it, try to decide if it has immediate use and, finding none, throw it in the trash.

9   Neat people are especially vicious with mail. They never go through

Words to Know

rectitude correctness

métier vocation, specialty

tentative hesitant, unsure

accumulate gather

excavation digging

meticulously careful

scrupulously conscientious, exacting

cavalier casual, inconsiderate

their mail unless they are standing directly over a trash can. If the trash can is beside the mailbox, even better. All ads, catalogs, pleas for charitable contributions, church bulletins and money-saving coupons go straight into the trash can without being opened. All letters from home, postcards from Europe, bills and paychecks are opened, immediately responded to, then dropped in the trash can. Neat people keep their receipts only for tax purposes. That's it. No sentimental salvaging of birthday cards or the last letter a dying relative ever wrote. Into the trash it goes.

Neat people place neatness above everything, even economics. They are incredibly wasteful. Neat people throw away several toys every time they walk through the den. I knew a neat person once who threw away a perfectly good dish drainer because it had mold on it. The drainer was too much trouble to wash. And neat people sell their furniture when they move. They will sell a La-Z-Boy recliner while you are reclining in it.   10

Neat people are no good to borrow from. Neat people buy everything in expensive little single portions. They get their flour and sugar in two-pound bags. They wouldn't consider clipping a coupon, saving a leftover, reusing plastic non-dairy whipped cream containers or rinsing off tin foil and draping it over the unmoldy dish drainer. You can never borrow a neat person's newspaper to see what's playing at the movies. Neat people have the paper all wadded up and in the trash by 7:05 a.m.   11

Neat people cut a clean swath through the organic as well as the inorganic world. People, animals, and things are all one to them. They are so insensitive. After they've finished with the pantry, the medicine cabinet, and the attic, they will throw out the red geranium (too many leaves), sell the dog (too many fleas), and send the children off to boarding school (too many scuffmarks on the hardwood floors). ∎   12

GET THINKING AND WRITING

CRITICAL THINKING AND DISCUSSION

Understanding Meaning: What Is the Writer Trying to Say?

1. What are the main differences Britt sees between neat and sloppy people?
2. What does the author mean when she says sloppy people "are not really sloppy"?
3. What motivates sloppy people to keep from organizing things or throwing things out?
4. What does Britt mean when she says sloppy people live in "Never-Never Land"?
5. *Critical thinking:* Britt suggests that neat people are not sentimental. Can you think of exceptions? Do you know people who lovingly organize and catalog their books, pictures, and videos because they want to preserve and protect them?

Evaluating Strategy: How Does the Writer Say It?

1. How does Britt use topic sentences to develop her paragraphs? Why do comparisons require clearly stated controlling ideas?
2. How does Britt use specific examples like cleaning a desk to make her point?

Appreciating Language: What Words Does the Writer Use?

1. Make a list of the words Britt uses to describe neat and sloppy people. Which list contains more positive terms? Which list contains words that suggest aggression or coldness?
2. How could you change the impact of Britt's essay by replacing the words she uses to describe neat and sloppy people?

Writing Suggestions

1. Building upon Britt's observations, write a paragraph stating whether you would rather have a neat or a sloppy person as a roommate.
2. *Collaborative writing:* Discuss Britt's essay with a group of other students, then work together to create one or more paragraphs that contrast spenders vs. savers, dieters vs. eaters, smokers vs. nonsmokers, joggers vs. drivers, those who swear and those who don't, or another pair of opposites.

STEPS TO WRITING A COMPARISON AND CONTRAST PARAGRAPH

1. Narrow your topic and identify key points by creating two lists of details.
2. Determine the goal of your paragraph. Do you plan to explain differences or argue that one subject is better or more desirable than the other?
3. Develop a topic sentence that clearly expresses your main point.
4. Determine whether to use subject-by-subject or point-by-point to organize your details, then make a rough outline.
5. Write a draft of your paragraph, then consider these questions:
   Is my topic sentence clearly stated?
   Are there minor details that should be deleted or replaced?
   Is my paragraph clearly organized?
   Do I provide enough information for readers to understand my comparison or accept my point of view?

Selecting Topics

Consider these topics for developing comparison and contrast paragraphs:

two places you have lived

high school and college instructors

traditional and Internet courses

attending college full-time vs. working and attending part-time

living on campus or at home

best and worst jobs

satellite vs. cable TV

the way a person, neighborhood, job, or company has changed

a friend vs. a best friend

your parents' attitudes and your own

two ways of meeting people

two methods of looking for a job

two campus organizations

EXERCISE 3 Planning and Writing Comparison and Contrast Paragraphs

GET WRITING

Select a topic from the above list or choose one of your own and develop details and a topic sentence that states the goal of your paragraph.

Topic: _____

Possible supporting details:

Subject 1	**Subject 2**
1. _____	1. _____
2. _____	2. _____
3. _____	3. _____
4. _____	4. _____

Topic sentence:

_____

_____

Organization (subject-by-subject or point-by-point): _____

First sentence: topic sentence, first detail, or introductory statement:

_____

_____

Supporting details in order:

1. _____

2. _____

3. _____

4. _____

Last sentence: final detail, concluding statement, or topic sentence:

_____

_____

Write your paragraph and review it by reading it out loud.

WORKING TOGETHER

Working with a group of students, revise this rough draft of an e-mail to make it easier to read by organizing it in a subject-by-subject or point-by-point pattern. Consider why comparison and contrast writing depends on clear organization to be effective.

```
Dear Sales Staff:

Until our systems upgrade is complete, we will be
using both Federated Express and Air National for
shipping. Make sure you use blue labels for Federated
Express and yellow labels for Air National packages.
When you have documents to ship, use Federated Ex-
press. Bulk packages should go Air National unless
going to the New York office. Make sure you register
all shipments in the log book. Remember that Air Na-
```

tional packages have to have a red stamp before being shipped. The best way to reach Federated Express is at 1-800-555-1500. If you have any questions about Air National, check their website at www.airnational .com. Use Federated for anything going to the New York office.

© Bettmann /CORBIS

How have the roles of men and women changed in the last fifty years?

Write one or more paragraphs comparing and contrasting male and female relationships then and now. What has changed? What has remained the same? You may use either subject-by-subject or point-by-point to organize your ideas.

WRITING ON THE WEB

Using a search engine such as AltaVista, Yahoo!, or Google, enter terms such as *writing comparison, comparison and contrast essays, organizing comparison essays, subject-by-subject comparison,* and *comparison point by point* to locate current sites of interest.

1. Search for news articles that use comparison and contrast and review how writers organized their ideas.
2. Write an e-mail to a friend using comparison and contrast to discuss how something has changed or the difference between two classes, two concerts you attended, or two jobs you are considering.

POINTS TO REMEMBER

1. Comparison points out similarities; contrast points out differences.
2. Comparison can be used to explain differences or argue that one subject is superior to another.
3. Comparison paragraphs should have a clear topic sentence expressing your goal.
4. Comparison paragraphs can be organized subject-by-subject to discuss one topic, then the other; or point by point to discuss both topics in a series of comparisons.
5. Comparison paragraphs depend on clear transitions to prevent confusion.

Developing Paragraphs Using Cause and Effect

© Zefa Visual Media/Index Stock Imagery

Is downloading music without paying for it stealing? What causes some people to see a difference between robbing CDs from a store and using a computer to get them for free?

Write a paragraph stating your view about illegal downloading. Do you consider it a crime? Why or why not?

What Is Cause and Effect?

Why did terrorists attack the World Trade Center? What led to the collapse of Enron? Why was a popular television show canceled? How will the invasion of Iraq change the Middle East? Will gas be cheaper next year? The answers to all these questions call for cause and effect writing that explains why things happen and examines or predicts results:

Airlines are losing money because of rising fuel costs, decreased business travel, and costly security requirements.

I quit my job at the department store because my hours were cut.

People who stay on this diet for more than a month can develop high blood pressure.

WHAT ARE YOU TRYING TO SAY?

GET WRITING AND REVISING

Write a paragraph that explains the causes or effects of one of the following topics:

Causes why

- students drop out of high school
- companies send jobs overseas
- teenagers become overweight
- digital cameras are popular

Effects of

- being downsized
- taking too many courses
- having children as a teenager
- becoming a citizen

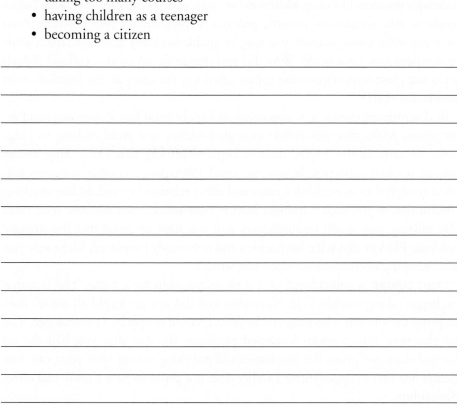

_____

_____

_____

_____

_____

_____

WHAT HAVE YOU WRITTEN?

Read your paragraph carefully. Underline the topic sentence. List the main causes or effects in your paragraph:

1. _____

2. _____

3. _____

Do these causes or effects logically relate to your topic sentence? Can you think of better causes or effects? To revise this paragraph, what changes would you make?

Cause and Effect: Critical Thinking

Cause and effect writing calls for careful observation and critical thinking. After studying a problem like drug addiction for years, experts disagree as to what causes people to take narcotics—poverty, genetics, depression, or peer pressure. Even when you write about yourself, you may be unable to clearly determine the reasons for decisions you have made. Why did you decide to attend this college? Which factor was most important—the course offerings, the campus, the location, your parents, the cost?

In determining causes, it is important to look beyond first impressions and assumptions. Make sure you collect enough evidence and avoid rushing to judgment. As early as the 1920s, doctors began reporting that many lung cancer patients smoked cigarettes. It was not until 1964, however, that scientists collected enough data to establish a cause and effect relationship and declare smoking a health risk. If you spot a stranger leaving your office, then discover your Palm Pilot missing, you might be suspicious. But you have no proof that the stranger took your PDA or that it has been stolen and not simply misplaced. Make sure you avoid jumping to conclusions when you write.

Don't confuse a coincidence or a time relationship for a cause. The fact that you began taking vitamin C in November and did not get a cold all winter does not prove the vitamin is keeping you healthy. It could simply be a coincidence. The fact that your transmission developed problems the day after you had the oil changed does not prove the mechanics did anything wrong with your car. Just because one event happens after another does not prove there is a cause and effect relationship.

EXERCISE 1 Critical Thinking and Cause and Effect

Read each statement and evaluate how effectively the writer uses critical thinking to identify a cause and effect relationship. Write C *for a clear cause,* X *for a time relationship or coincidence, and* P *for a possible cause and effect relationship.*

1. _____ Every time I wash my car it rains. I washed my car this morning; therefore it will rain today.

2. _____ Teenagers are consuming 35 percent more fast food than their parents' generation, and less than half report doing any regular exercise. No wonder many young people are overweight.

3. _____ Last year aviation fuel prices soared and ticket sales dropped, causing airline profits to shrink dramatically.

4. _____ Lengthened tours of duty in combat zones explain the rising number of stress-related disorders in military personnel.

5. _____ Bill's kids are always in trouble. It's because he is always away from home on business.

6. _____ Sarah speaks Spanish. She would be great working in our bilingual program.

7. _____ Last week a freshman died of a heart attack during training. On Monday a player passed out in the weight room. Coach Wilson is driving his team too hard.

8. _____ KXTL switched from rock to a pure hip-hop format last year and increased its market share 32 percent. Americans love hip-hop more than rock music.

9. _____ Ever since the president took office Internet stocks have lost money. His policies are bad for business.

10. _____ I did data entry for fifteen years, and now I need glasses. Looking at a computer screen eight hours a day ruined my eyes.

EXERCISE 2 Identifying Causes

Read the following paragraph, then answer the questions that follow.

Atlas Industries closed its National Avenue plant in 1999. The hundred-year-old eight-story factory was costly to maintain and harder to retool than modern single-story plants. Robotic and computerized technology could not be installed without rewiring the entire building, which would have cost nearly $2 million. Inspectors determined the factory's eighteen freight elevators would have to be replaced in 2000, at a cost of $12 million. The loss of elevator capacity during these repairs would slow production and require expensive employee overtime to meet deadlines. In addition, the unionized workforce was being paid up to $26 an hour, much more than the workers in the Alabama facility. Despite tax breaks offered by both the state and the city, Atlas closed its doors, laying off five thousand employees.

1. **What is the topic sentence?** _____

2. **What are the causes? Restate them in your own words:**

   a. _____

   b. _____

   c. _____

   d. _____

   e. _____

EXERCISE 3 Identifying Effects

Read the following paragraph, then answer the questions that follow.

The closing of the Atlas plant crippled the local economy, especially on the city's south side. The loss of five thousand high-paying jobs nearly eliminated the middle class in the industrial suburbs. Workers who once made $20 or $30 an hour now struggled to find jobs paying $8 or $10. Personal bankruptcy soared 22 percent on the south side in 2001. Local car dealers saw new car sales drop by 38 percent and used car sales fall 22 percent. Restaurants, bowling alleys, movie theaters, and nearly every retail store on National Avenue reported a dramatic loss in sales. Almost five hundred Atlas employees put their houses up for sale in 2002, and property values suffered as many of these houses became rental properties. Rex Jewelers, Capitol Motors, and Colosimo's Restaurant closed, citing the loss of local business. According to the mayor, this part of the city may take years to readjust.

1. **What is the topic sentence?** _____

2. **What are the effects? Restate them in your own words:**

EXAM SKILLS

Examination questions often call for cause and effect answers. Given the time limit of most exams, it is important to identify key causes or effects. Because any answer you give will likely be incomplete, you can qualify your answer with a strong introduction or conclusion.

From Earth Science

What are the causes of global warming?

topic sentence	*Global warming is caused by human activity. Factories, cars,*
cause #1	*power plants, and cities generate heat and pollution that rise into the atmosphere. Greenhouse gases form a barrier that*
cause #2	*traps the heat and prevents it from leaving the atmosphere. Carbon dioxide is believed to be a primary greenhouse gas. The destruction of the rain forests has reduced the vegetation that can absorb carbon dioxide. In some parts of the world farmers*
cause #3	*use fire to clear forests, destroying plants and producing a great deal of pollution. The rapid industrialization and booming*
cause #4	*consumer economy of China , which has a billion people, will only intensify these causes.*

a. _____

b. _____

c. _____

d. _____

e. _____

Student Paragraphs

Cause paragraph:

When I look back at my high school friends who dropped out, I suppose I could list half a dozen reasons why they decided to leave school. Most of them claimed school bored them. They could not wait to get out. Others hated the teachers. They resented being picked on by the seniors. Some resented the rich kids who could afford designer clothes and drove new cars. A few of my friends even said they hated school because they missed their favorite soap operas. But the over-all reason they dropped out was that they never looked ahead. None of them ever had a plan for what they wanted to do after they dropped out of school.

Effect paragraph:

The city's anti-cruising policy has been success-ful in keeping teenage drivers from dragging up and down Mayfair Road. The number of high-speed accidents has dropped 50 percent. Residents report less noise, less litter, and safer streets. But the policy has had unexpected results. Business at Mayfair Mall's food court and movie complex has dropped off 25 percent. The young people who used to pack the food court on weekends are staying away. High school students are now gathering at Westwood Mall, because dragging and cruising on Highway 10 brings few complaints from rural residents and little police response.

Cause and effect paragraph:

Last semester I moved off-campus because I found dorm life impossible. Maybe because I am twenty-three, I found it hard to live with freshmen right out of high school. They were noisy, rude, and disruptive. Working twenty hours a week, I need my sleep. The TVs and stereos in the dorm blast well past midnight, even on weekdays. Getting a studio apartment cost more and required a longer commute, but the results have been worth it. I can get to sleep early and take naps when I need to. I have no distractions when I study. I find myself more relaxed, less irritated, and more focused. I now work twenty-five hours a week, get better grades, and experience less stress because I am living alone.

PUTTING PARAGRAPHS TOGETHER

Moving On

introduction

topic sentence

    Late last year I decided to quit the best job I ever had. I gave up a fun, high-paying job and went back to school because I wanted a future. I was a cocktail waitress at one of the hottest clubs in town for over two years. Some weekends I made $500 in tips. I had great friends. We worked hard but had fun. We met celebrities. We worked parties, weddings, and conventions. It was never boring. I became friends with all my coworkers. On our days off we went shopping, swimming, and dating. It was like one endless party, and for the first year I hoped it would never change.

supporting details

causes

> 1. How effective is the first sentence? Does it grab your attention?
> 2. Why are the details about the job important?
> 3. What is the purpose of this paragraph?

topic sentence
showing transition

supporting details
causes

effects

    After some time passed, my attitudes changed because I began to see this job as a dead end. I noticed that all my friends had money but no savings. They had plenty of dates but no relationships. They made a lot of money in cash and spent it all on clothes and trips. They were always broke. I had seen them at first as glamorous and fun. But I saw they were really very shallow, dating one guy after another, going to one party after another. As time passed, the gossip and games became empty and tired. The result was I began to hate going to work and putting up with late hours.

> 1. How do the details in this paragraph show a change from the first?
> 2. How does this paragraph use cause and effect?
> 3. How does the student show how something fun became something boring?

topic sentence

effects

    I started business college in September and feel like I am building a real future. My self-esteem went up because I took courses, read books, learned computers. The tests and projects gave me something to focus on and plan for. I began to feel like someone

living in the adult world. Having to pay for books and
tuition forced me to save money and give up partying
and shopping. I still work three nights a week and
enjoy my friends' company now and then. Right now
I have less spending money but am a lot more happy
because I know I am accomplishing something genuine.

1. How does this paragraph build on the one before?
2. How does the student use effect to show change?
3. How does the student end the paragraph? Does it serve to end the entire writing?

Readings

As you study the readings, notice how writers use paragraphs to highlight main points and signal transitions in writing cause and effect.

WHY WE CRAVE HORROR MOVIES

STEPHEN KING

Stephen King is best known as a writer of horror novels, many of which have been made into motion pictures. His books include The Shining, The Dead Zone, Christine, Misery, *and* The Green Mile.

AS YOU READ:

King uses cause and effect to explain why people love horror films. Notice that King uses examples and narratives to demonstrate reasons for the popularity of scary movies. He uses paragraphs, including one-sentence paragraphs, to organize ideas and highlight transitions.

1 I think that we're all mentally ill; those of us outside the asylums only hide it a little better— and maybe not all that much better, after all. We've all known people who talk to themselves, people who sometimes squinch their faces into horrible grimaces when they believe no one is watching, people who have some hysterical fear— of snakes, the dark, the tight place, the long drop . . . and, of course, those final worms and grubs that are waiting so patiently underground.

2 When we pay our four or five bucks and seat ourselves at tenth-row center in a theater showing a horror movie, we are daring the nightmare.

3 Why? Some of the reasons are simple and obvious. To show that we can, that we are not afraid, that we can ride this roller coaster. Which is not to say that a really good horror movie may not surprise a scream out of us at some point, the way we may scream when the roller coaster twists through a complete 360 or plows through a lake at the bottom of

Words to Know

innately naturally

reactionary backward looking,
    conservative

voyeur one who enjoys
    watching others

penchant fondness, liking

exalted glorious

couplets two consecutive
    rhyming lines in a poem

coveted popular, highly
    desirable

sanctions punishments

the drop. And horror movies, like roller coasters, have always been the special province of the young; by the time one turns 40 or 50, one's appetite for double twists or 360-degree loops may be considerably depleted.

We also go to reestablish our feelings of essential normality; the horror movie is <u>innately</u> conservative, even <u>reactionary</u>. Freda Jackson as the horrible melting woman in *Die, Monster, Die!* confirms for us that no matter how far we may be removed from the beauty of a Robert Redford or a Diana Ross, we are still light-years from true ugliness.

And we go to have fun.

Ah, but this is where the ground starts to slope away, isn't it? Because this is a very peculiar sort of fun, indeed. The fun comes from seeing others menaced— sometimes killed. One critic has suggested that if pro football has become the <u>voyeur's</u> version of combat, then the horror film has become the modern version of the public lynching.

It is true that the mythic, "fairy-tale" horror film intends to take away the shades of gray. . . . It urges us to put away our more civilized and adult <u>penchant</u> for analysis and to become children again, seeing things in pure blacks and whites. It may be that horror movies provide psychic relief on this level because this invitation to lapse into simplicity, irrationality, and even outright madness is extended so rarely. We are told we may allow our emotions a free rein . . . or no rein at all.

If we are all insane, then sanity becomes a matter of degree. If your insanity leads you to carve up women, like Jack the Ripper or the Cleveland Torso Murderer, we clap you away in the funny farm (but neither of those two amateur-night surgeons was ever caught, heh-heh-heh); if, on the other hand, your insanity leads you only to talk to yourself when you're under stress or to pick your nose on your morning bus, then you are left alone to go about your business . . . though it is doubtful that you will ever be invited to the best parties.

The potential lyncher is in almost all of us (excluding saints, past and present; but then, most saints have been crazy in their own ways), and every now and then, he has to be let loose to scream and roll around in the grass. Our emotions and our fears form their own body, and we recognize that it demands its own exercise to maintain proper muscle tone. Certain of these emotional muscles are accepted— even <u>exalted</u>— in civilized society; they are, of course, the emotions that tend to maintain the status quo of civilization itself. Love, friendship, loyalty, kindness— these are all the emotions that we applaud, emotions that have been immortalized in the <u>couplets</u> of Hallmark cards and in the verses (I don't dare call it poetry) of Leonard Nimoy.

When we exhibit these emotions, society showers us with positive reinforcement; we learn this even before we get out of diapers. When, as children, we hug our rotten little puke of a sister and give her a kiss, all the aunts and uncles smile and twit and cry, "Isn't he the sweetest little thing?" Such <u>coveted</u> treats as chocolate-covered graham crackers often follow. But if we deliberately slam the rotten little puke of a sister's fingers in the door, <u>sanctions</u> follow— angry <u>remonstrance</u> from parents, aunts and uncles; instead of a chocolate-covered graham cracker, a spanking.

11   But anticivilization emotions don't go away, and they demand periodic exercise. We have such "sick" jokes as, "What's the difference between a truckload of bowling balls and a truckload of dead babies?" (You can't unload a truckload of bowling balls with a pitchfork . . . a joke, by the way, that I heard originally from a ten-year-old.) Such a joke may surprise a laugh or a grin out of us even as we recoil, a possibility that confirms the thesis: If we share a brotherhood of man, then we also share an insanity of man. None of which is intended as a defense of either the sick joke or insanity but merely as an explanation of why the best horror films, like the best fairy tales, manage to be reactionary, anarchistic, and revolutionary all at the same time.

12   The mythic horror movie, like the sick joke, has a dirty job to do. It deliberately appeals to all that is worst in us. It is <u>morbidity</u> unchained, our most base instincts let free, our nastiest fantasies realized . . . , and it all happens, fittingly enough, in the dark. For those reasons, good liberals often shy away from horror films. For myself, I like to see the most aggressive of them— *Dawn of the Dead,* for instance— as lifting a trap door in the civilized forebrain and throwing a basket of raw meat to the hungry alligators swimming around in that subterranean river beneath.

13   Why bother? Because it keeps them from getting out, man. It keeps them down there and me up here. It was Lennon and McCartney who said that all you need is love, and I would agree with that.

14   As long as you keep the gators fed. ∎

remonstrance reprimand, scolding

morbidity disease, something unhealthy

CRITICAL THINKING AND DISCUSSION

GET THINKING AND WRITING

Understanding Meaning: What Is the Writer Trying to Say?

1. King opens his essay with the line, "I think that we're all mentally ill." Is this an effective introduction? Why or why not? What does he mean by saying we are a little crazy?
2. What reasons does King give for the popularity of horror movies?
3. How does the fascination of horror films relate to sick jokes in King's view?
4. *Critical thinking:* King suggests that something deeply human draws people to horror films. Do you think this also explains why in the past children loved legends about werewolves, witches, vampires, and haunted houses?

Evaluating Strategy: How Does the Writer Say It?

1. In explaining causes, where does King use narration, description, comparison, and example?
2. How effective is the last line? Does this bring King's essay to a logical conclusion?
3. King uses one-sentence paragraphs in two places. Are they effective? Why or why not? When are short paragraphs like these useful?

Appreciating Language: What Words Does the Writer Use?

1. What do the "hungry alligators" represent? Is this an effective image? Why or why not?
2. What does King mean by his term "psychic relief"?

Writing Suggestions

1. Write several sentences that give reasons why people also enjoy roller coasters and other amusement park rides.
2. *Collaborative writing:* Working with a group of students, provide reasons for the popularity of reality television shows.

I REFUSE TO LIVE IN FEAR

DIANA BLETTER

Diana Bletter was born in New York City but now lives in Israel. She has written articles for Newsday *and the* International Herald Tribune. *Bletter and Samia Zina helped organize Dove of Peace, a friendship organization for Arab and Jewish women.*

AS YOU READ:

In this article Bletter outlines the effects of terrorism in Israel. Her article was written before the terrorist attacks of September 11, 2001. Consider how her comments relate to the way Americans are living in an era of terrorism and security measures.

For most of my life, I thought a shoe box was just a shoe box. Until the afternoon I discovered that it could also be considered a lethal weapon.   1

This is what happened: I had just gone shopping for shoes—one of my favorite pastimes—in the small Mediterranean town of Nahariyya in northern Israel, where I've lived for the last five years. I sat down on a bench to change into my new purchase. I was so busy admiring my feet that I left the shoe box (with my old shoes) on the bench. Fifteen minutes later, I suddenly remembered it and turned back. When I approached the street, I saw crowds of people, barricades and at least five policemen.   2

"What happened?" I asked.   3

"Everyone's been evacuated. Someone reported a suspicious object on a bench down the street."   4

"Oh, no!" I shouted. "My shoes!"   5

Had I arrived even a few seconds later, a special bomb squad—complete with robot—would have imploded my shoe box to deactivate what could have been a bomb hidden inside. The policeman shook his finger at me. "This is the Middle East!" he said angrily. "You can't be careless like that!"   6

Reality Bites, Hard

7 Moving to Israel from America's tranquil suburbia has taught me about living with the threat of terrorism, something we Americans— after the bomb at Atlanta's Olympic Games and the explosion of TWA Flight 800 — are finally being forced to think about on our own turf. The brutal fact of a terrorist attack is that it shatters the innocent peace of our days, the happy logic of our lives. It inalterably changes the way we live.

8 I can no longer daydream as I walk down a street— now I know that, to stay alive, I have to remain aware of who and what surrounds me. As my fiancé always tells me, "Your eyes are your best friends!" and I use them to keep track of emergency exits, the closest windows, the nearest heavy object that could be used in self-defense.

9 I used to be a reflexive litter-grabber— in my hometown, I never hesitated to pick up a coffee cup from the sidewalk and toss it in a nearby garbage can. In Israel, I've learned not to touch litter and to stay away from garbage cans— on several occasions, bombs have been placed in them. If I see a knapsack, shopping bag or— yes— a shoe box left unattended, I now do three things: One, ask passersby if they forgot the package; two, get away from it as fast as I can; and three, report it to the police.

Necessary Inconveniences

10 Living in a country where terrorism is always a possibility means that at every entrance to a public place, guards search every bag. I forgot this the first time I walked into Nahariyya's lone department store; a guard stopped me to look through my pocketbook. "How could I have shoplifted?" I asked. "I haven't set foot in the store." Then I remembered that in America, people worry about what someone might sneak *out* of a store; in Israel, people worry what weapons or bombs someone might sneak *in* to a store.

11 The first few days after a terrorist attack seem very quiet. Since all of Israel is only the size of New Jersey, everybody usually knows someone who was hurt or killed. The nation slips into mourning: People avoid going out, attending parties, sitting in cafés.

12 Gradually, though, daily life returns to normal. Israelis (and now, Americans) have to prove again and again to potential terrorists that we're not giving in to our fears. If we voluntarily restrict our movements and our lives, terrorists have vanquished us.

13 During the latest hostilities in Lebanon (whose border is about seven miles from Nahariyya), Samia Zina, my dear friend— and a Muslim Arab— dreamed about me, one of those vivid dreams that seems prophetic when you wake. She dreamed that the fighting had forced her to flee her home, and that I'd hidden her and her children in my house (and I certainly would have, had the nightmare been a reality). The next day, Samia popped by to tell me her dream and give me the two stuffed chickens she'd been moved to cook for me.

"Thank you," I said, astonished by the food and the dream. "But I know you would have hidden me, too." 14

Terrorists attempt to divide people by fear, but in our community they've brought so-called enemies together: Even Arabs and Jews watch out for each other in public places, knowing that terrorists target everyone. By resisting the temptation to become paranoid and isolated, by sticking up for one another, we remain undefeated. ■ 15

GET THINKING
AND WRITING

CRITICAL THINKING AND DISCUSSION

Understanding Meaning: What Is the Writer Trying to Say?

1. What is the point of Bletter's opening story about the shoe box?
2. How has living in Israel changed the way Bletter walks down a street?
3. What three things does she do if she spots an unattended shopping bag or a knapsack on the street? Do you think Americans will have to learn to live like this?
4. *Critical thinking:* Terrorists in the Middle East plant bombs to create terror and sharpen the divide between Jewish and Arab Israelis. How have these attacks had the opposite effect? What causes Jews and Arabs to depend on each other?

Evaluating Strategy: How Does the Writer Say It?

1. How does Bletter use comparison to develop her point? How is life in the United States different from life in Israel?
2. How effective is the last line? Is this Bletter's thesis?
3. What examples does Bletter use to show the effect terrorism has had on her behavior?

Appreciating Language: What Words Does the Writer Use?

1. Bletter never defines "terrorism" in her essay. How do you define the word? What is a terrorist in your view?
2. Bletter uses a simple style of language to describe a very complex political situation. Is this effective?

Writing Suggestions

1. Write a paragraph describing the effects terrorism has had on your life since September 11, 2001. Have you encountered more security in airports, known friends who had greater difficulty getting jobs or dealing with immigration authorities?
2. *Collaborative writing:* Discuss Bletter's article with a group of students. In Israel terrorists plant bombs in small packages. In the United States we fear terrorists will use biological, chemical, and radioactive weapons. Does the size and mysterious nature of these weapons make the average citizen feel helpless and vulnerable? Work together and develop a short paragraph about how terrorism affects the way Americans feel about their personal

safety. Do you think people in New York or Washington have more fear than those living in Racine or San Antonio?

STEPS TO WRITING A CAUSE AND EFFECT PARAGRAPH

1. Study your topic and use critical thinking by asking key questions:
    Am I going to explain causes or effects or both?
    What is the most important cause or effect I want readers to know?
    Are there any terms I need to define?
    Do readers need any background information?
    What evidence such as facts, examples, or quotations can support my ideas?
2. Develop a topic sentence that clearly states your controlling idea.
3. Review your list of causes or effects and delete minor or confusing details. Organize your ideas by time or by order of importance.
4. Write a draft of your paragraph.
5. Read your paragraph out loud and consider these questions:
    Does the paragraph have a clear topic sentence?
    Are the causes or effects clearly stated and supported by facts, examples, and other evidence?
    Is the paragraph clearly organized?

Selecting Topics

Consider these topics for cause and effect paragraphs:

Explain the causes of one of the following topics:

teenage pregnancy
domestic violence
terrorism
a recent scandal
current attitudes about the homeless, an ethnic group, or a political figure
gangs
your choice of major or career
success or failure of a business or sports team

Write a paper measuring the effects of one of the following topics:

the Internet
immigration
welfare reform
gas prices
cell phones
airport security
single-parent families

EXERCISE 4 Planning and Writing Cause and Effect Paragraphs

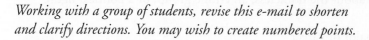

Select a topic from one of the lists on page 141 or choose one of your own. Develop a topic sentence that states your point of view.

Topic: _____

Causes or effects:

1. _____

2. _____

3. _____

4. _____

First sentence: topic sentence, first cause or effect, or introductory statement:

_____

_____

Causes or effects:

1. _____

2. _____

3. _____

4. _____

Last sentence: final cause or effect, concluding statement, or topic sentence:

_____

_____

Write out your paragraph and review it by reading it out loud.

WORKING TOGETHER

Working with a group of students, revise this e-mail to shorten and clarify directions. You may wish to create numbered points.

Dear Service Staff:

Customers often ask why they can't come behind the counter or enter the garage to look at their cars being serviced. Remember under no circumstances let anyone behind the counter who is not employed by the dealership. People have to understand we have a problem here. Our insurance company will not cover injuries of any customers in the service areas. We work with valuable equipment and it is too easy for people to walk off with electronic components if they are allowed to walk around the shop area. You have to re-

member, too, that people get in the way when mechanics
are trying to work.

Sid Matthews

CRITICAL THINKING

*What effect have twenty-four-hour cable news networks had on the way we see events?
Are minor events like car chases exaggerated because they make good television? Are
important issues overlooked because they are hard to show on television or because
they take place in remote areas? Write a paragraph stating your views.*

WHAT HAVE YOU WRITTEN?

Read your paragraph carefully. Write out your topic sentence or controlling idea:

_____

_____

List the effects you identify:

_____

_____

_____

*Are they significant effects? Can you think of more significant ones? Could you place
them in a different order to make your paragraph stronger and easier to read?*

© Najlah Feanny/CORBIS SABA

In some states convicts work
in chain gangs, picking up trash and
pulling weeds along highways. Supporters of this policy say it teaches
prisoners discipline. Critics argue it
only humiliates them.

Write a paragraph listing the positive or negative effects of chain
gangs. Do you think this experience teaches criminals a lesson or
just degrades them?

WRITING ON THE WEB

Using a search engine such as AltaVista, Yahoo!, or Google, enter terms such as *writing cause and effect, cause and effect essays, organizing cause and effect essays,* and *critical thinking and cause and effect.*

1. Search for news articles using cause and effect and review how writers organized their ideas.
2. Write an e-mail to a friend using cause and effect to explain a decision you have made or to give reasons for a problem.

POINTS TO REMEMBER

1. Cause and effect paragraphs need clear topic sentences.
2. Cause and effect paragraphs depend on critical thinking and evidence. Readers will expect you to prove your points.
3. Qualify your comments and acknowledge alternative interpretations.
4. Peer review can help detect mistakes in critical thinking like hasty generalizations or confusing time relationships for cause and effect.

10

Toward the Essay

© Julie Dennis/Index Stock Imagery

What does it take to communicate effectively? Why is it important to consider your reader? If you had to write a charity fund-raising letter, what would you want to know about the readers?

Write a list of questions you would ask about them before writing.

So far in this book you have studied and written different types of paragraphs. Most college assignments, however, demand more than one-paragraph responses. Instructors usually require students to write essays.

What Is an Essay?

An essay is a group of related paragraphs that develops a *thesis,* or main idea. An essay may be written to inform, entertain, or persuade. Essays may consist of facts and statistics or personal thoughts and feelings. Essays can be written about global warming, the death penalty, or your summer vacation. Although written in a variety of styles and lengths, essays generally consist of three main parts:

introduction
body
conclusion

Each part plays an important role in stating the thesis and supporting it with details. Knowing how the parts of an essay work will improve your writing and give you the organizational skills needed to create research papers and business reports in the future.

The Introduction

Introductions should

- grab attention,
- announce the topic,
- address reader concerns, and
- prepare readers for what follows.

Introductions should make strong statements that arouse interest and prepare readers for what follows. Avoid making general statements that simply serve as weak titles that just tell people what you are writing about:

Weak

This paper is about property taxes. People and businesses are leaving this state because they are too high. This is bad for Wisconsin.

You can use a number of techniques to create effective introductions:

Open with a Thesis Statement

Wisconsin must lower property taxes to prevent a massive loss of revenue needed to improve education and pay for welfare reform.

Begin with a Fact or Statistic

In 2004 more than two hundred small businesses left Wisconsin and moved to other states to escape high property taxes.

Use a Quotation

Testifying before the state senate last month, Janet Sanchez announced, "After thirty-six years in Milwaukee, our company is moving to Texas because of property taxes."

Open with a Short Example

In 1919 there were few jobs for black army veterans. Frank Washington opened a small repair job that grew into a major company that employed over a hundred people until his grandson was forced to close because of high property taxes.

The Body

The body of an essay should

- organize supporting details in a logical pattern.

The main part of your paper should be clearly organized so readers can understand the details you present and follow your train of thought.

Weak

States have to raise taxes to pay for roads, schools, police, and other services. Over two hundred businesses left our state last year because of high property taxes. Governments use a number of taxes and fees to raise money. People think taxes in this state are too high though.

To prevent your paper from becoming a confusing jumble of facts and ideas, create a clear pattern people can follow.

- *Organize details by time* and explain them as a chain of events. Tell readers the history of your subject or the way things have changed.
- *Organize details spatially* by dividing them into types. A paper about property taxes could discuss how taxes affect homeowners, business owners, and developers. A report about drug addiction could be organized by discussing different drugs, different reasons people use drugs, or different treatments. Patients could be discussed by their age, the drug they abuse, or by their income level.
- *Organize ideas by importance* so the paper opens or closes with your most significant points.

The Conclusion

The conclusion of an essay should

- end with a brief summary, a final thought or observation, question, call for action, or prediction.

A short paper or narrative may not require a separate conclusion, but the paper should have a meaningful ending that will make an impression on readers. Avoid summarizing or repeating what you have just written:

Weak

```
    In conclusion, property taxes are too high. People
and businesses are leaving this state. This is hurting
Wisconsin.
```

A conclusion can make people remember and think about your ideas, if you end on a strong point.

End with a Meaningful Quotation

```
    Edwin Sador, director of the state budget, warns
that our state "must cut property taxes or face a loss
of 10,000 jobs in the next two years."
```

End with a Call to Action

```
    If you care about the future of our state, vote
Yes on referendum 12 next month.
```

Conclude with a Significant Fact or Statistic Readers Can Remember

```
    This time next year six of the state's largest em-
ployers will have left Wisconsin.
```

End with a Question

```
    If we want to create more jobs, can we continue to
chase businesses out of our state?
```

Developing Topic Sentences in Outlines

One way to develop a well-organized essay is to use a topic sentence outline. After writing your thesis, develop supporting ideas in complete sentences to form a topic sentence for each paragraph:

```
          Outline: Triton College Needs New Dorms

I     Our college needs new dorms to maintain
      enrollment.
II    The existing dorms are in poor condition and do
      not meet the needs of today's students.
III   Future students are expected to come from out of
      state, and desirable housing will be essential to
      secure needed enrollments.
IV    Although costly, new dorms are an investment we
      must make now.
```

Having established clear topic sentences, you can complete the essay by adding details to support each topic sentence:

Triton College Needs New Dorms

<u>Our college needs new dorms to maintain enroll-ment.</u> Triton College, like many other small colleges, requires a sufficient enrollment base to support its programs, generate tuition, and provide teaching opportunities for its tenured faculty. In the past almost half the students were local residents taking liberal arts degrees. The new high technology programs are so specialized they need to draw on out of state students to attain needed enrollments. Simply put, we need more student housing.

<u>The existing dorms are in poor condition and do not meet the needs of today's students.</u> Although the college has enough beds to meet the needs of current enrollments, the rooms are unattractive and out of date. The newest dorm was constructed in 1962. None of the dorms are air-conditioned. None offer Internet access or even have enough desk space for a computer, keyboard, and printer. The lobby, TV room, recreation area, and cafeterias are all shabby and unappealing.

<u>Future students are expected to come from out of state, and desirable housing will be essential to secure needed enrollments.</u> Students, especially those enrolling in high-tech programs, will expect dorms that are computer friendly. Triton's outdated facilities cannot compete with the state schools' dorms, which feature apartment-style units, state-of-the-art electronics, and retro coffee bars. Given our high tuition, students will expect their housing to be first class.

<u>Although costly, new dorms are an investment we must make now.</u> Without them Triton will face a loss of enrollments that could push the college into bank-ruptcy.

POINT TO REMEMBER

As when they create paragraphs, writers frequently use a method like example, comparison and contrast, or cause and effect to organize an entire essay. Although the overall goal may be to provide an example or make a comparison, the essay may contain paragraphs organized in different ways. Not all paragraphs in a comparison essay will include comparisons. Many will include narrations or descriptions. All the paragraphs, however, work together to support the writer's thesis.

EXERCISE 1 Examining the Essay

Read this student essay and note in the margin where the student uses narration, comparison and contrast, and cause and effect to develop this description of a neighborhood.

A Great Place

Tremont was a great place to grow up. My sisters and I loved our large apartment with its wide balconies, spacious living room, and big bedrooms. Our building did not have elevators, and we lived on the third floor. We did not care, because we enjoyed playing dolls on the wide, carpeted steps.

Living in Tremont was like living in a small town. We could walk to school and to Brucker Park where we played on the monkey bars and slides. After school we bought candy at the corner store or caught a matinee at the Knickerbocker, an elaborate old theater with crushed velvet seats and gold moldings. On summer evenings we played on the stoop while neighborhood dads played catch with their sons and nervous moms helped toddlers pedal their tricycles down the crooked pavement. Although we lived in New York City, it felt like a small town where people knew their neighbors, cared for friends, and watched out for each other's children.

All this changed when I was eight years old. Every family on our block, in fact every family in the neighborhood, got "the letter." We had to move. The city had condemned whole blocks of Tremont. Our spacious apartment buildings, cute stores, and candy shops were considered "blighted." Tremont was described as being "old," "decayed," "distressed," and "a slum."

After we moved to Long Island, my parents never went back to see what happened to Tremont because it would hurt too much. Only after moving to Chattanooga did I dare go back. In New York for Christmas one year, I took a cab to Tremont. My whole childhood neighborhood was gone. All the apartment buildings, the candy stores, the A&P, the Walgreens, even the ornate old Knickerbocker had been demolished. Block after block had been leveled. Now there was nothing but massive concrete pillars supporting the Bronx Expressway overhead.

The Tremont I knew is gone, but its memory stays with me as a great place to have grown up.

EXERCISE 2 Developing Essay Paragraphs

Select a topic from the following list or develop one of your own and prewrite for a few minutes to develop ideas.

> what you want high school students to know about college
> the best lesson your parents taught you
> the reasons you chose your major or career
> your opinion of the war on terrorism
> how to explain something difficult like death or divorce to a child
> the reason so many people complain of stress
> why men and women have problems understanding each other

Introduction and thesis: _____

_____

_____

Topic sentence for supporting paragraph: _____

_____

_____

Topic sentence for supporting paragraph: _____

_____

_____

Topic sentence for supporting paragraph: _____

_____

_____

Final topic sentence or conclusion: _____

_____

EXERCISE 3 Writing Essay Paragraphs

Using your outline as a guide, write the draft of your essay. When you complete the essay, review your outline and topic sentences. You may discard ideas and create new ones in the writing process. Make sure your final version, however, is clearly organized and that all the paragraphs support your thesis.

GET WRITING
AND REVISING

WORKING TOGETHER

Work with a small group of students and exchange papers. Make copies so each person can make corrections and comments. Discuss what you want to say and ask how what you have written could be improved.

GET THINKING AND WRITING

CRITICAL THINKING

Imagine your brother or sister returns from a late-night party claiming to have hit a mailbox on the way home. The next morning you hear about a hit-and-run accident a block from where the party was held. A witness has given police a description that matches the car your brother or sister was driving. Write three or four paragraphs describing the actions you would take. Would you do nothing, talk to your brother or sister, call the police, or try to find out more about the accident. How would you act if the hit-and-run driver simply sideswiped a car? If the accident involved a death or serious injury, would you behave differently? Why or why not?

WHAT HAVE YOU WRITTEN?

Read your paragraphs carefully. Do you clearly explain the actions you would take?

- How effective is your introduction? Does it engage readers or simply announce what your essay is about?
- How do you organize your main ideas? Do you use paragraphs to signal transitions or highlight main points? Could these paragraphs be better organized or more fully developed? Are there minor or distracting details that should be deleted?
- How do you end your essay? Does it make a final statement readers will remember, or does it just repeat what they have already read?

GET WRITING

How often do people fail to communicate clearly? Do you get letters from your bank or financial aid office that you find hard to read? Have you written papers that received poor grades because you did not explain your ideas clearly?

Write a paragraph describing ways peer review can improve your writing.

© Images.com /CORBIS

WRITING ON THE WEB

Using a search engine such as AltaVista, Yahoo!, or Google, enter terms such as *writing essays, types of essays,* and *composing essays* to locate current sites of interest.

1. Read news articles online and notice how writers develop introductions, create conclusions, and use paragraphs to organize their ideas.
2. Write a multi-paragraph e-mail to a friend. Make sure your message has a clear introduction and conclusion.

POINTS TO REMEMBER

1. An essay states a main idea supported by related paragraphs that provide details.
2. Essays consist of three parts:

   Introduction: grabs attention

   announces the topic

   addresses reader concerns

   prepares readers for what follows

   Body: organizes details in a clear, logical pattern

   Conclusion: ends with a brief summary, a final thought or observation, question, call for action, or prediction.
3. Essays often use different types of paragraphs—comparison, example, narration, cause and effect, and description—to support a thesis.
4. In writing essays, consider your readers in presenting ideas, selecting details, and choosing words.

11

Writing at Work

© Stephen Derr/Getty Images

How is writing at work different from writing at school? What do people expect in communications? Have you ever had to write anything for work? Do you expect writing will be important in your career?

Write a brief paragraph describing the writing challenges you expect to face.

Writing on the job is very different from writing in the classroom. Although memos, e-mail, letters, and résumés depend on the writing skills you learn in college, they are created in a very different environment, have different readers, and serve different purposes.

- *Business writing occurs in a specific context.* The tone, style, wording, and format of business writing is shaped by the history and standards of the profession, organization, readers, and topic.
- *Business writing is directed to specific readers.* In college you write to a general academic audience. In business you will address specific readers who will have special problems, questions, concerns, and values.
- *Business writing is action oriented.* In college you usually write papers that present ideas. At work you will more often direct people to take action—to buy a product, use a service, accept an explanation, or make an investment.
- *Business writing is sensitive to legal implications.* Letters, reports, and contracts are legal documents. You have to be careful not to make statements that can expose you to legal action.
- *Business writing represents the views of others.* In college your work expresses personal ideas and opinions. At work the e-mails, letters, and reports you write should reflect the values, attitudes, and positions of your employer. Avoid writing personal opinions that may bring you into conflict with your superiors.

This chapter focuses on two of the most common business writing assignments you will face: writing e-mail and creating résumés and cover letters to apply for a job.

E-mail

Today almost every job uses e-mail to communicate. Some people confuse e-mail with "instant messages" or chat room discussion. They write and answer e-mail without thinking, producing a stream of tangled ideas, missing details, grammar errors, and inappropriate comments. E-mail, like any kind of writing, takes thought and planning to be effective.

Strategies for Writing E-mail

1. **Realize that e-mail is <u>real mail.</u>** E-mail can be stored, distributed, and printed. Unlike a note or memo that can be retrieved or corrected, e-mail, once sent, becomes permanent. Never send e-mail when you are tired or angry. Avoid sending messages you will later regret.
2. **Think before you write.** E-mail should have a clear goal. Consider whom you are writing to, what they need to know, and how you can persuade them to accept your ideas.
3. **Follow the prewriting, drafting, revising, and editing strategies you would use in writing a paper document.** Don't let an e-mail message simply record whatever comes into your head. E-mail should have a clear purpose and an easy-to-follow organization. Plan before you write.
4. **Understand what messages <u>should not</u> be expressed in e-mail.** E-mail is considered appropriate for short, informative messages. Do not attempt

to send a fifteen-page report by e-mail, though it might be sent as an attachment. Do not send personal or sensitive information by e-mail. E-mail is seen as too informal and too public for confidential correspondence.

5. **Respond to e-mail carefully.** Often e-mail messages will have multiple readers listed. Before sending a reply, determine whether you want everyone or just a few people to see your response.

6. **Make sure you use the correct e-mail address.** E-mail addresses can be complicated and oddly spelled. Often names are shortened or reversed. Marsha Simpson might appear as "marsha.simpson," "msimpson," or "simpsonm." Double-check addresses.

7. **Clearly label your e-mail in the subject line.** Spam—unwanted e-mail messages—use misleading headings such as "Following up your call" or "This week's meeting" to grab attention. To prevent your e-mail from being overlooked or deleted before it is read, use specific identifying details in the subject such as "RE: Nov. 18th request for additional credit" or "Tredway Furniture Annual Budget Review Meeting."

8. **Include your reader's full name and the date in your inside address.**

9. **Keep e-mail direct and concise.** People expect e-mail to be direct and easy to read. Avoid complicated sentences and long paragraphs. Use short paragraphs, bulleted points, or numbered points to increase readability.

10. **End the e-mail with a clear summary, request, or direction.**

    - Summarize important points.
    - If you are asking for information or help, clearly state what you need, when you need it, and how you can be reached.
    - If you want readers to take action, provide clear directions.

11. **Ask readers for an acknowledgment if you want to make sure they received your message.**

12. **Review, edit, and double-check e-mail before sending.** Check your spelling, addresses, names, prices, or figures for accuracy. Read your e-mail out loud to catch missing words, illogical statements, confusing sentences, or awkward phrases.

13. **Print hard copies of important e-mail for future reference.**

EXERCISE 1 Revising E-mail

Revise this e-mail to create a clear, concise message.

```
Sid
This e-mail is a follow-up to our conversations last
week about the upcoming art exhibit we talked about.
I think we need to call Dean Andrews and discuss some
points before next week. I think we need to find out
if the school will provide any housing for visiting
artists. We also need to determine if Dean Andrews
plans to have a reception after the awards ceremony.
```

And I like I said, I think we have to get the school
to do more publicity.
Jill Dykstra

Résumés

Probably the first business documents you will write will be a résumé and cover letter. Before starting work on a résumé, it is important to know what a résumé is and what a résumé is not:

- *A résumé is <u>not</u> a biography or a list of jobs—it is a ten-second ad.* Research shows the average executive spends just ten seconds looking at each résumé before rejecting it or setting it aside for further reading. A résumé does not have to list every job you have had or every school you attended. It should not be cluttered with employer addresses or names of references. It should briefly but clearly present facts, experiences, skills, and training that relate to a specific job or profession.
- *The goal of a résumé is to get an interview, not a job.* Few people are hired based on a résumé. Résumés only show an employer that you are worth talking to. The goal of a résumé is to generate enough interest to prompt someone to call you for an interview.
- *You may need several résumés.* Companies create different ads for the same product to reach different people. You might need three or four résumés that target specific jobs. A nurse, for example, might create one résumé highlighting her intensive-care experience and another focusing on her work with abused children. Because résumés are quickly screened, they have to communicate at a glance. A résumé that tries to cover too many areas will be vague or confusing.

Strategies for Writing Résumés

1. **Understand that there are no absolute "rules" for writing résumés— only guidelines.** You may have heard people say that a résumé should only be one page or must never include your age. Because the world of work is so varied, there are exceptions.
2. **Develop your résumé by focusing on the job description or company.** Study the wording of want ads or job announcements and highlight skills and experiences that directly match those listed in the ad.
3. **Include your full name, address, telephone number with area code, and e-mail address:**

   Mary Skyler
   1492 Grandview Avenue
   Westfield, NJ 08070
   (201) 555-8989
   mskyler@njnet.com

4. **Provide a clear, objective statement describing the job you seek.** Avoid vague objectives like "a position making use of my skills and

abilities" or "sales, marketing, or public relations." If you have different interests, create separate résumés for each field or job:

```
Objective   Retail Sales Management
```

5. **Use a brief overview or summary to highlight key skills and experience:**

```
Overview    Five years' experience in retail sales
            management. Proven ability to hire,
            train, and motivate sales staff.
            Highly skilled in customer relations,
            point of purchase sales, and loss
            prevention.

Summary     Retail Sales Management

            • Sales manager, Walgreens 2002-2005
            • Loss prevention consultant, ABC,
              2001
            • Developed online sales associate
              program, lowering training costs 35%
            • Reduced turnover 65% first year
```

You may find it easier to write the overview last, after you have identified your key skills and accomplishments.

6. **List your most important credentials first.** If you are a college graduate with no professional experience, list education first. If a current or recent job relates to the job you seek, list experience first.

7. **Arrange education and job experience by time, beginning with the most recent.**

8. **Avoid general job descriptions:**

```
            Receptionist responsible for greet-
            ing visitors, maintaining schedules,
            logging incoming calls, scheduling
            appointments, and receiving and dis-
            tributing FAXs.
```

Focus on individual accomplishments and demonstrate the significance of your experience:

```
            Receptionist for 28 sales representa-
            tives generating $54 million in sales
            annually. Individually responsible for
            receiving and distributing FAXs used
            to expedite rush orders.
```

9. **List training seminars, volunteer work, hobbies, and military service only if they directly relate to the job you want.**

10. **Do not include addresses of employers, names of supervisors, or references.** These details can be supplied after you are called in for an interview.

Recent Graduate with Intern Experience

MARY SKYLER
1492 Grandview Avenue
Westfield, NJ 08070
(201) 555-8989
mskyler@njnet.com

GOAL	An entry-level position in nonprofit fund-raising.
OVERVIEW	Associate degree in marketing. Three years' experience in telemarketing, mass mailing, and Internet fund-raising. Demonstrated ability to work within budgets, maximize returns, and resolve problems.
EXPERIENCE Jan.–May 2006	*Intern* NEW JERSEY CENTER FOR THE PERFORMING ARTS Completed four-month internship, working directly with vice president in charge of fund-raising • Developed three direct-mail letters used in annual campaign that achieved a 15% return and $257,000 in pledges • Supervised 15 telemarketers during Pledge Week • Assisted vice president in press conferences, public appearances, and radio call-in program
EDUCATION	UNION COUNTY COMMUNITY COLLEGE, Plainfield, NJ Associate degree in marketing, May 2006 Completed courses in business management, accounting, sales and marketing, nonprofit financing, public relations, and communications skills • 3.5 GPA • One of six students selected to assist faculty in annual United Fund Drive
MILITARY 2000–2004	UNITED STATES ARMY *Sergeant* Military police, responsible for base patrol, crime-scene investigation, and preparation of evidence for legal staff • Selected to write, edit, and produce flyers and video presentations on sexual harassment, crime prevention, and terrorist security • Independently organized and managed mass mailings to service member families
LANGUAGES	Fluent Spanish

References and work samples available on request

Recent Graduate with Unrelated Experience

MARIA SANCHEZ
1732 St. Charles Avenue
New Orleans, LA 70130
(504) 555-1171
mariasanchez@earthlink.net

OBJECTIVE	Retail printing management
OVERVIEW	Five years' experience in retail sales management. Fully familiar with state-of-the-art printing equipment and techniques. Proven ability to lower overhead, increase sales, and build customer relations.
	• Certified to service and repair all Canon and Xerox copiers
EDUCATION	DELGADO COMMUNITY COLLEGE, New Orleans, LA Associate degree, printing and publishing, 2006 Completed courses in graphic design, editing, high-speed printing, and equipment repair
	• Attended Quadgraphics seminar • Assisted in design and production of college newspaper
	XEROX, New Orleans, LA Completed service training program, 2005
EXPERIENCE 2004–	FAST-PRINT, New Orleans, LA *Retail sales.* Work twenty hours a week assisting manager in counter sales, customer relations, printing, and inventory in downtown print shop.
1999–2004	CRESCENT CITY MUSIC, New Orleans, LA *Manager* of retail record outlet with annual gross sales of $2.5 million
	• Hired, trained, and supervised 30 employees • Reduced operating costs 15% first year • Developed special promotions with radio stations, increasing sales 32% • Prepared all financial statements
HONORS	Dean's list, 2005, 2006

References and transcripts available

Cover Letters

Cover letters can be as important as the résumés they introduce. Résumés submitted without letters are often discarded because employers assume that applicants who do not take the time to address them personally are not serious. Résumés tend to be rather cold lists of facts; cover letters allow applicants to present themselves in a more personalized way. The letter allows applicants to explain a job change, a period of unemployment, or a lack of formal education.

Strategies for Writing Cover Letters

In most instances, cover letters are short sales letters using standard business letter formats.

1. Avoid beginning a cover letter with a simple announcement:

   Dear Sir or Madam:

   This letter is to apply for the job of controller advertised in the San Francisco Chronicle last week. . .

2. Open letters on a strong point emphasizing skills or experiences:

   Dear Sir or Madam:

   In the last two years I opened fifty-eight new accounts, increasing sales by nearly $800,000.

3. Use the letter to include information not listed on the résumé. Volunteer work, high school experiences, or travel that might not be suited to a résumé can appear in the letter—if they are career related.

4. Refer to the résumé, indicating how it documents your skills and abilities.

5. End the letter with a brief summary of notable skills and experiences and a request for an interview. To be more assertive, state that you will call the employer in two or three days to schedule an appointment.

Cover Letter Responding to a Want Ad

MARY SKYLER
1492 Grandview Avenue
Westfield, NJ 08070
(201) 555-8989
mskyler@njnet.com

May 25, 2006

Vicki Spritzer
Foundation Management Services
45 West 54th Street
New York, NY 10017

RE: Fund-raising assistant position advertised in the *New York Times*, May 24, 2006

Dear Ms. Spritzer:

In 2005 the New Jersey Center for the Performing Arts raised $209,000 in its April direct-mail campaign. This year the letters I wrote, edited, and tested generated $257,000 — a 23% increase.

For the past four months I have worked directly with Deborah Mandel, vice president of the New Jersey Center for the Performing Arts in fund-raising and public relations. I assisted her in all phases of fund-raising, including direct mail, public appearances, telemarketing, and a radio pledge drive.

As my résumé shows, I have just received an associates degree in marketing. In addition to completing courses in business management and communications skills, I took special courses in fund-raising that included extensive research in online fund-raising.

Given my education in marketing and my experience in fund-raising, I believe I would be an effective fund-raising assistant for your firm. I look forward to the opportunity of discussing this position with you at your convenience. I can be reached at (201) 555-8989, or you can e-mail me at mskyler@njnet.com.

I can e-mail you samples of fund-raising letters, flyers, telemarketing scripts, and letters of recommendation if you wish.

Sincerely yours,

Mary Skyler

Cover Letter Responding to Personal Referral

MARIA SANCHEZ
1732 St. Charles Avenue
New Orleans, LA 70130
(504) 555-1171
mariasanchez@earthlink.net

May 25, 2006
Linda Chen
ABC Printing
1212 Canal Street
New Orleans, LA 70023

RE: Manager position for Canal Street ABC Print Shop

Dear Ms. Chen:

Tamika DuBois mentioned that ABC Printing is seeking a manager for its Canal Street print shop sometime this summer.

As my résumé shows, I have just completed my associates degree in printing and publishing and am fully familiar with all the equipment used by ABC Printing. During the past two years I have been working the counter at one of Fast-Print's busiest downtown locations.

Before deciding to go into printing and publishing, I managed one of New Orleans' major music stores. I supervised 30 employees, lowered operating costs, generated new accounts, and increased sales 32%.

Given my knowledge of printing and publishing techniques, practical experience in both print shop operations and retail management, I believe I could be an effective manager for ABC Printing. I would appreciate the opportunity to discuss this position with you at your convenience. I can be reached by phone at (504) 555-1171 or by e-mail at mariasanchez@earthlink.net.

Sincerely yours,

Maria Sanchez

WORKING TOGETHER

Working with a group of students, discuss the following résumé and cover letter and recommend changes. Delete needless information, reword awkward phrases, eliminate repetitions, and edit for spelling and other mechanical errors.

KARLA MESSER
1434 Douglas Avenue #456
Racine, WI 53453
(414) 555-7878

GOAL	To ultimately own my own business. In the meantime seeking a position in restaurant and or hotel management.
EDUCATION	Marshall High School, Racine, WI Graduated 2003 Was in band, school yearbook, tennis club
	Gateway Community College, Racine, WI Graduated 2006 Completed restaurant management progrom with courses in business law, hotel law, bookepping, food service management, and sales management.
EXPERIENCE 2002	Valentine's 1536 North Lincoln Avenue, Racine, WI 53245 Banquet waitress responsible for serving banquet dishes at banquets, weddings, and business lunches for up to 250 guests.
2003	Valentine's Assistant banquet manager responsible for assisting manager in organizing wait staff, menu organization, and working with clients setting up plans for upcoming events at the restaurant.
2004	Bruno's 756 Main Street, Racine, WI 53246 Assistant manager responsible for all lunch wait staff

serving up to 200 lunchtime customers in restaurant's pub and grill. Assisted owner in redesining menu offering to increase sales and reduce preparation time.

2005 · Holiday Inn-Airport
2700 South Howell Avenue, Milwaukee, WI 53206
Banquet operations assistant responsible for booking rooms, scheduling wait staff, ordering special supples, confirming reservations, etc.

| References | George Adello (262) 555-8989 | Francine Demarest (414) 555-9090 | Maria Valadez (261) 555-8987 |

KARLA MESSER
1434 Douglas Avenue #456
Racine, WI 53453
(262) 555-7878

May 25, 2006

Dear Ms. Mendoza:

This letter is to reply to the ad in the *Milwaukee Journal-Sentinel* that appeared May 22, 2006 last week.

This month I will complete my restaurant management program at Gateway Community College. I have studied food service administration, bookkeeping, office management, and business law. In addition, I have several years' experience working in restraurants and more recently the Holiday Inn. I have worked in banquet operations, restaurant operations, and convention planning.

I think I have a lot of good ideas that could benefit the Hyatt organization. I would be glad to be able to meet with you and discuss this job and my background. I can be reached at (262) 555-7878.

Thanking you for your attention,

Karla Messer

GET THINKING AND WRITING ▶ **CRITICAL THINKING**

Describe the most important aspects of the job you want when you graduate. What is more important to you: a high income or job security? Would you be willing to relocate? How will your first job fit into your life goals?

GET *WRITING*

How do you plan to look for a job when you graduate? Do you plan to use the college placement office, recruiters, employment agencies, want ads, or networking?

Write a paragraph outlining your plans. If you are unsure, consider learning more about the job search process by exploring the Internet and talking to friends and instructors.

WRITING ON THE WEB

Using a search engine like AltaVista, Yahoo!, or Google, enter terms such as *résumés, writing résumés, cover letters,* and *applying for jobs* to locate current sites of interest.

POINTS TO REMEMBER

1. Business writing occurs in a very different environment from college writing. Be sensitive to the tone, style, and format used in your field.
2. E-mail is real mail. Treat e-mail messages with the professionalism you would in writing a first-class letter.
3. E-mail should be clear, concise, and direct. Avoid long, rambling messages.
4. Realize the limits of e-mail. Longer documents should be sent as attachments.
5. Résumés should be written concisely so they can be scanned in seconds.
6. Résumés should stress important points in your career—avoid including hobbies, high school jobs, and other minor details.
7. Cover letters should emphasize skills and experience and link yourself to the job you want.
8. Cover letters give you the opportunity to explain unrelated experience and add information not suited for the résumé.

Part 3

Writing Sentences

Recognizing the Power of Words

© Canstock Images Inc./Index Stock Imagery

GET WRITING

How hard is it to choose the right word?

Write a few sentences describing a situation, such as applying for a job or writing a condolence card to a friend, when you had problems finding words to express what you were trying to say.

The Power of Words

Words are the building blocks of language. They have the power to inform, entertain, and persuade. When we talk, our word choices can be casual and haphazard because we also communicate through eye contact, tone of voice, and gestures. Speech is interactive. We can repeat sentences for emphasis and reword awkward phrases as we talk. If our listeners cannot understand what we are saying, they can ask questions:

> "Did you hear him tell us what to do about this thing today?"
> "What thing?"
> "That deal over there."
> "Oh, that thing, sure. We ship it Air."
> "Air Express?"
> "Right."

But when we write, our readers cannot ask questions or give us a chance to restate our ideas—we have to get things right the first time. Readers have to rely on the text to understand our meaning. We will not be there to correct false impressions, answer questions, or rephrase statements. Readers also assume our word choices will match the definitions they find in the dictionary.

WHAT DO YOU KNOW?

Choose the appropriate word in each sentence.

1. _____ The president's speech stirred the (conscience/conscious) of the nation.

2. _____ How will this project (effect/affect) my grade?

3. _____ (Its/It's) going to be difficult to repair your car.

4. _____ It is later (then/than) you think.

5. _____ The student (council/counsel) will meet at noon.

6. _____ Her remarks clearly (implied/inferred) that she would support us.

7. _____ Please remove keys and (lose/loose) change from your pockets.

8. _____ The cottage is (further/farther) down the road.

9. _____ Will you (except/accept) out-of-state checks?

10. _____ I am tired and need to (lay/lie) down.

Answers appear on the following page.

WHAT ARE YOU TRYING TO SAY?

Write a paragraph that describes a person you have strong feelings about. Provide details that explain why you like or dislike this person. What are his or her most noticeable characteristics? Choose words that reflect your point of view.

_____

_____

_____

_____

_____

_____

_____

_____

_____

_____

WHAT HAVE YOU WRITTEN?

Underline the key words in your paragraph. Do they give readers a strong impression? Could you improve your statement by choosing different words? Read your description out loud. What changes would you make to increase its impact?

GUIDELINES FOR USING WORDS

- _Use correct words._ Make sure you know a word's precise meaning.
- _Use effective words._ Use clear, concrete language your readers understand.
- _Use appropriate words._ Use words suited to your purpose, subject, audience, and document. Be aware of connotations.

Use Correct Words

English has a number of words that are easily confused or misunderstood:

elicit	to prompt or provoke	His threats failed to _elicit_ a response.
illicit	illegal	They found _illicit_ drugs.
than	used in comparisons	Leasing is cheaper _than_ buying.
then	used in time references	He worked all day, _then_ went home.
there	a place or direction	Put it over _there_.
their	possessive of "they"	Put it in _their_ mailbox.
they're	contraction of "they are"	_They're_ here!
_to_	preposition _or_ infinitive	She went _to_ college _to_ study law.
too	in excess _or_ also	It was _too_ cold to swim.
		Are they coming, _too_?
two	a number	We're a _two_-car family now.

ANSWERS TO WHAT DO YOU KNOW? ON PAGE 169
1. conscience, 2. affect, 3. It's, 4. than, 5. council, 6. implied, 7. loose, 8. farther, 9. accept, 10. lie.

(See pages 453–456 for other easily confused words.)

A NOTE ON SPELLING

An important part of using words is making sure you spell them correctly. Spelling errors confuse readers and make your work appear sloppy and unprofessional.

Tips for Improving Your Spelling

- *Pronounce new words.* Reading them out loud can help you recall letters you might overlook, like the *n* in "environment" or the *r* in "government."
- *Write out new words you learn in school and at your job.*
- *Make a list of words you repeatedly misspell and refer to it whenever you write.* Keep copies of this list in your notebook, by your desk, or in your purse or briefcase.

(See Chapter 27 for further help with spelling.)

EXERCISE 1 Using the Correct Word

Circle the correct word in each sentence.

1. The (principal / principle) asked the teacher to resign.
2. The lifeboat (foundered / floundered) in the heavy surf.
3. (Whether / weather) you go to college or get a job, you will need to learn how to use a computer.
4. We still don't (know / now) if she is going to speak next week.
5. Her speech will depend on (who's / whose) invited.
6. We toured the accident (site / sight).
7. Her parents (emigrated / immigrated) from Poland in the 1970s.
8. The mayor's speech cannot be (preceded / proceeded) by a comedic performance.
9. The president's speech made (allusions / illusions) to World War II.
10. We wondered if (anyone / any one) would call for help.

POINT TO REMEMBER

Words sometimes have special or specific meanings. One college might define a *full-time student* as someone who takes twelve credits, while another school requires students to take sixteen credits. The word *high-rise* means one thing in Manhattan and another in Kenosha. *Make sure your readers understand the exact meanings of the words you use. Define terms with footnotes or a glossary at the end of your document to prevent confusion.*

EXERCISE 2 Understanding Meaning

Define each of the words, then check your answers using a college dictionary.

archaic _____   lucrative _____

collateral _____   optician _____

discriminate _____   patron _____

fundamental _____   surrogate _____

homicide _____   topical _____

How many words have you heard but could not define? How many did you get wrong? Which words have additional meanings you were unaware of?

LEARNING MORE ABOUT WORDS

- Use a college dictionary to look up new or confusing words.
- Study the glossaries in your textbooks to learn special terms and definitions.

DICTIONARIES FOR ESL STUDENTS

If English is your second language, refer to dictionaries like the *Longman Dictionary of American English* and the *Collins Cobuild English Language Dictionary*. They give not only definitions but rules for combining words. If you look up *future*, for example, you learn that it often appears in phrases such as *predict the future, plan the future,* and *face the future*. These dictionaries include sample sentences to show how a word is used in context.

EXERCISE 3 Editing Your Writing

Select one or more writing responses you completed in a previous chapter or the draft of an upcoming assignment and review your use of words. Look for errors in usage. Have you confused there *and* their *or* its *and* it's? *Have you written* affect *for* effect *or* adapt *for* adopt? *List words you have confused in the back of this book or a notebook for future reference.*

Use Effective Words

To communicate effectively, you need to use words that are clear and concrete. Abstract and general terms lack impact:

> I hated my summer job at PizzaXpress. It was awful. I worked in the worst part of the business. It made me depressed. That place always made me feel bad, mentally and physically. I was uncomfortable and felt bad all the time. The whole experience was negative, and it took a toll on every part of me. It ruined my whole summer. Even my free days were like a waste. I was in no mood to do anything I normally liked. For the first time in my life I could not wait for school to start.

Words like *awful* and *negative experience* are vague. The statement simply announces that the writer hated his or her job but does not tell us why. Concrete language, however, creates stronger impressions:

> I hated my summer job at PizzaXpress. The kitchen was hot, noisy, and dangerous. The roar of the oven fans gave me headaches, and the sharp edges of the steel tables cut my arms and thighs. By the second night my hands were sore, swollen, and burned. The stress from demanding customers, rude drivers, and yelling managers ruined my whole summer. Even on free days, I never felt like seeing friends or going to the beach. For the first time in my life I could not wait for school to start.

Instead of *feeling bad mentally and physically,* this version offers specific details such as *sore, swollen, and burned hands.* Readers can understand why *demanding customers, rude drivers, and yelling managers* would ruin the student's summer.

Use Concrete Nouns

Concrete nouns create strong images readers can identify and remember.

Abstract	Concrete
residential rental unit	*apartment*
employment situation	*job*
individual	*boy*
educational facility	*junior high school*

Use Strong Verbs

Verbs should emphasize action. Avoid weak verb phrases that use several words to describe action that could be expressed with a single word.

Weak Verb Phrase	Strong Verb
make an examination	*examine*
effect a change	*change*
offer an apology	*apologize*
develop a plan	*plan*

Avoid Clichés

Clichés are worn-out phrases. They may have been colorful, striking, or entertaining at one time, but like jokes that have been told too often they are stale and meaningless:

Cliché	Improved
as white as snow	*pure white*
thin as a rail	*thin*
out like a light	*slept soundly*
selling like hotcakes	*popular*

EXERCISE 4 Improving Word Choices

Rewrite each of the following sentences, replacing abstract nouns, weak verb phrases, and clichés.

1. During the summer months of July 1976 an employee of a cotton storage facility in the Sudanese town of Nzara suddenly suffered a condition of shock and died from hemorrhages that proved to be uncontrollable.

   _____

   _____

   _____

2. Days later, two of the man's coworkers exhibited signs of ill health and quickly died of bleeding that was massive in scope.

   _____

   _____

3. The disease went through the village like a knife through butter, infecting and killing the resident population of Nzara.

   _____

   _____

4. People who were sick went to the nearby medical facility, which became as crowded as the subway at rush hour.

   _____

   _____

5. Not having knowledge about the deadly nature of the virus, doctors and nurses of the hospital facility contracted the disease as they made examinations of patients.

   _____

   _____

6. Soon the medical staff began to die, along with people who were family members of the patients.

   _____

   _____

7. Then suddenly the epidemic came to an end when the virus ran out of people who were healthy it could infect.

   _____

   _____

8. Scientific research personnel who made a study of this outbreak called the virus "Ebola," after the nearby Ebola River.

   _____

   _____

9. Medical experts saw the outbreak as having great significance because it made a suggestion that science had not conquered the problem of infectious disease.

   _____

   _____

   _____

10. Ebola never reached America, but within a few years another new virus, AIDS, would create a change in the way scientific research personnel addressed the study of infectious diseases.

_____

_____

_____

Use Appropriate Words

The words you choose should suit your purpose, your audience, and the document. Words, like clothing, can be formal or informal, traditional or trendy. Just as you dress differently for a job interview or a soccer game, you write differently to produce a research paper, a résumé, or an e-mail to your best friend. It is important to use the right level of diction or word choice.

LEVELS OF DICTION

formal / technical	terms used to communicate within a discipline or profession
standard	words commonly used in books, magazines, and newspapers intended for a general audience
informal	regional expressions, jargon used within specialized groups, slang, and text messaging (u for "you" or brb for "be right back")

Use the Appropriate Level of Diction

Doctors, lawyers, engineers, and stockbrokers use **formal** or **technical** terms that may be unfamiliar to most educated people. Many of your college textbooks include glossaries of technical terms. These terms must be understood for people to communicate without confusion. **Standard** words are widely known and used. They are the kind of words found in popular books, magazines, and on most websites. **Informal** English can include slang, jargon used on the job, and expressions spoken by an ethnic group or residents of a particular part of the country. Jazz artists, airline pilots, baseball fans, sailors, computer hackers, bankers, and people in show business all have their own words and phrases.

Formal / technical	Standard	Informal
taken into custody	_arrested_	_busted_
dissociative rage disorder	_violent outburst_	_going postal_
corrective lenses	_glasses_	_specs_

The level of diction writers use depends on their goal, their readers, and the document. Lawyers drafting motions to file in court use formal legal terminology. To communicate to their clients, they use standard terms anyone can understand. In sending e-mails to their office staff, they might use slang and jargon only a few people could understand.

It is important to make sure that you do not use inappropriate diction that may confuse readers or weaken the impact of your writing. Slang words in a research paper or business letter will make a writer seem insincere and unprofessional. Formal language can make a memo difficult to read at a glance.

EXERCISE 5 Selecting Appropriate Words

Revise each sentence to replace words that are inappropriate for a formal research paper.

1. Throughout World War II, Stalin pressured Churchill and Roosevelt to get on the ball and open the Second Front by invading Europe.

   _____

   _____

2. Industrial toxicologists discovered the presence of asbestosis in automobile workers was way bad.

   _____

   _____

3. Affirmative action policies that once fired up the administration to employ more minorities have been ignored in order to save a buck.

   _____

   _____

Revise each sentence to remove words that are inappropriate for an informal memo.

4. Tell the shipping department to immediately effectuate a transfer of all financial records to payroll.

   _____

   _____

5. Until our insurance problem is fixed, don't let any of the individuals from the sales department utilize company cars for transportation.

   _____

   _____

Use Appropriate Idioms

Idioms are expressions or combinations of words that are not always logical. For example, you *ride in a car* but *fly on a plane*. You *run into friends* when you meet them by accident and *run to friends* when you seek their help. Idioms can be a challenge to understand for two reasons. First, some idioms like *pay attention to* can't be easily understood by looking at the meaning of each word. Second, some idioms like *wrap your mind around* or *doesn't cut any ice* don't mean what they literally suggest. Idioms are often difficult or impossible to translate word for word into other languages.

In college and business writing you will be expected to use idioms accurately. If you are confused about the meaning of an idiom, refer to multilingual dictionaries like the *Longman Dictionary of American English* or the *Collins Cobuild English Language Dictionary.*

Commonly Misused Idioms

Incorrect	Correct
act *from* concern	act *out of* concern
bored *of* the idea	bored *with* the idea
different *than* the others	different *from* the others
in / with *regards* to	in / with *regard* to
irritated *with*	irritated *by*
on accident	*by* accident
relate *with*	relate *to*
satisfied *in*	satisfied *with*
superior *than*	superior *to*
type *of a*	type *of*
wait *on* line	wait *in* line

EXERCISE 6 Using the Appropriate Idioms

Write sentences using each of the following idioms correctly.

1. **get even with, get out of hand**

   _____

2. **take off, take on, take over**

   _____

3. **wait for, wait on**

   _____

4. **stand a chance, by chance**

   _____

5. **good at, good for, good with**

   _____

Be Aware of Connotations

All words have a **denotation,** or basic meaning. A *car* is a motor vehicle that transports people and goods. A *dwelling* is a place where people live. Some words also have **connotations,** or suggested meanings. A large automobile can be called a *luxury sedan* or a *gas guzzler.* A small vacation house can be called a *summer home,* a *cottage,* or a *shack.* Someone who spends money carefully can be termed *thrifty* or *cheap.* A person who blows up a government building can be denounced as a *terrorist* or praised as a *freedom fighter.* A private upscale college can be called *prestigious* or *elitist.* A discount motel can be *affordable* or *cheap.*

What we call things influences the way people respond to our ideas. Our connotations should match our attitudes. If you like a quiet little restaurant near campus, you are probably going to call it *softly lit, peaceful,* and *intimate* rather than *dark, boring,* and *cramped.* Advertisers use words with appealing connotations like *new, improved, natural,* and *free* to attract consumers. Politicians use connotations to influence voters. They might urge the public to support a project that will "*drain a swamp* to create *new homes* for *families,*" while their opponents argue the same project will "*destroy a wetland* to create *luxury condos* for *the rich.*"

Consider the different impact these words have:

casual	vs.	*sloppy*	*proud*	vs.	*vain*
young	vs.	*immature*	*brave*	vs.	*reckless*
the homeless	vs.	*bums*	*pre-owned*	vs.	*used*
cautious	vs.	*cowardly*	*simplistic*	vs.	*simple*

Connotations shape the way people perceive an event or situation:

In love with the young singer, the *passionate* fan *followed* his *idol* from concert to concert, *begging* to see her.

Obsessed with the young singer, the *deranged* fan *stalked* his *victim* from concert to concert, *demanding* to see her.

Constructed of *gleaming* steel, Federal Towers *soars* over the riverfront like a pair of *immense Greek columns.*

Constructed of *cold* steel, Federal Towers *looms* over the riverfront like a pair of *monstrous smokestacks.*

Asked to comment on the allegations, the mayor *declined* to answer.

Asked to comment on the allegations, the mayor *refused* to answer.

LEARNING CONNOTATIONS

To make sure you understand a new word's connotation, study how it is used in context. If the word is used in a phrase or sentence that seems negative, the word's connotation is probably negative. If the phrase or sentence seems positive, the word's connotation is probably positive. You can also use a thesaurus to find a word's synonyms and antonyms. If you look up *stubborn,* for example, you will find it means the same as *obstinate* and *pigheaded* and the opposite of *compliant* and *easygoing.*

WORKING TOGETHER

Working with a group of students, review the text of the following e-mail to eliminate negative connotations. Write a more positive version of this message.

```
We regret to inform employees that the bonus checks
we promised to distribute on March 1 will not be
available until March 30. Because many employees
failed to submit their pay forms on time, we were
unable to process them until last week. If you expect
to be paid on time, make sure you do not fail to
submit reports on time.
```

CRITICAL THINKING

In a paragraph, describe the way you talk—your favorite expressions, words you learned playing sports, working a job, or speaking with friends. What or who has influenced your vocabulary—your parents, friends, television, coworkers? Examine one or more of the greatest influences on your language. If English is not your native language, what English words were easiest for you to learn? Do you ever blend English and another language?

WHAT HAVE YOU LEARNED?

Choose the appropriate word in each sentence:

1. _____ The president's policy will (affect/effect) the way colleges charge tuition.

2. _____ We can't (accept/except) late assignments.

3. _____ (They're/There) coming here after the game.

4. _____ The mayor does not seem to be (conscious/conscience) of the budget problems.

5. _____ Hospitals require a (continual/continuous) supply of water.

Choose effective words and phrases in the following sentences:

6. _____ The city (conducted tests of/tested) the water supply for mercury.

7. _____ The heart sensor is (round/round in shape).

8. _____ She predicted that (hurricanes/hurricane activity) could ravage the coast.

9. _____ Scientists will have to (achieve purification of/purify) this substance to make it of medical use.

10. _____ The judge ordered that psychiatrists (render an examination of/examine) the defendant.

Choose the proper level of diction for a college research paper.

11. _____ (The mentally ill/head cases) require expensive treatment.

12. _____ Current juvenile justice policies fail to reform (gangbangers/gang members).

13. _____ The manager insisted he would (eighty-six/dismiss) anyone serving minors.

14. _____ The government wants to (weed out/eliminate) archaic regulations.

15. _____ The accountants will (dope out/assess) the cost of the new equipment.

Choose words with positive connotations:

16. _____ The committee met (secretly/privately) to discuss the lawsuit.

17. _____ The refugees were (expelled/relocated).

18. _____ The lumber mill (devours/processes) five thousand trees a day.

19. _____ The café was (dimly/softly) lit.

20. _____ This facility will store (toxic waste/industrial by-products).

Answers appear on the following page.

GET WRITING

© Piotr Powietrzynski/Index Stock Imagery

Study this photograph carefully. How would you describe its mood, what the man is thinking, the importance of the page in the typewriter?

Write a few sentences describing your reactions to this image. Then underline the key words you chose. What are their connotations? Do they express what you are trying to say?

WRITING ON THE WEB

1. Using a database or a search engine like AltaVista, Yahoo!, or Google, look up articles from a variety of magazines. What do you notice about the level of diction, the use of words? How do the styles of the *New Yorker,* the *Village Voice, People, Time,* and your local newspaper differ? What does this say about the writers, the publication, the intended readers?
2. Analyze the language used in chat rooms on America Online or other Internet services. Have these electronic communities produced their own slang or jargon? Do chat rooms of car enthusiasts differ from those dedicated to childcare or investments? Do people with special interests bring their particular terminology and culture into cyberspace?
3. Using a search engine like AltaVista, Yahoo!, or Google, enter the following search terms to locate current sites you might find helpful:

    diction   connotation   usage
    word choice   slang   vocabulary

    Write two or three sentences using new words you discover on the web. Determine which are technical, standard, or informal.
4. Ask your instructors for URLs of useful websites. Keep a list and update it when you find other sources.

POINTS TO REMEMBER

1. The words you choose shape the way readers will react to your writing.
2. *Choose correct words.* Check dictionaries to make sure you have selected the right words and spelled them correctly.
3. *Choose effective words.* Use words that are clear and concrete—avoid wordy phrases, clichés, and abstract terms.
4. *Consider connotations.* Be aware of the emotional or psychological impacts words may have. Choose words that reflect your message.
5. Review the lists of commonly confused and misspelled words on pages 453–457.
6. Study glossaries in your textbooks to master new terms you encounter in college.
7. Select a good college-level dictionary and get in the habit of referring to it several times a week. Use highlighters or Post-It notes to personalize your dictionary.
8. Practice using an online dictionary, especially if you write on a computer.

ANSWERS TO WHAT HAVE YOU LEARNED? ON PAGES 179–180
1. affect, 2. accept, 3. They're, 4. conscious, 5. continuous (see page 454), 6. tested, 7. round,
8. hurricanes, 9. purify, 10. examine (see page 173), 11. The mentally ill, 12. gang members, 13. dismiss,
14. eliminate, 15. assess (see pages 175–176), 16. privately, 17. relocated, 18. processes, 19. softly, 20.
industrial by-products (see pages 177–178)

Writing Sentences

© Mark Segal/Index Stock Imagery

Public telephones were once placed in booths so people could make calls behind closed doors. Have cell phones changed our concept of privacy? Have you heard people discuss personal or sensitive issues on cell phones in public places? Should you always let callers know where you are and who might be listening?

Write three or four sentences describing the way you think people should use cell phones in public.

What Is a Sentence?

Everything that happens in life—natural occurrences, historical events, conflicts, thoughts, feelings, opinions, ideas, and experiences—is explained in sentences. A main idea is connected to an action or linked with other words to express a thought. Long before they learn to read, children talk in sentences. Unwritten languages are spoken in sentences. The sentence is basic to all human communication:

This was the noblest Roman of them all.
SHAKESPEARE

Call me Ishmael.
HERMAN MELVILLE

The ballot is stronger than the bullet.
ABRAHAM LINCOLN

I have a dream.
MARTIN LUTHER KING

Things go better with Coke.
ADVERTISING SLOGAN

A **sentence** is a group of words that contains a subject and verb and states a complete thought.

WHAT DO YOU KNOW?

Underline the subjects (main idea) and circle the verbs (action words) in each sentence.

1. Children watch too much television.

2. The Senate debated the bill until midnight

3. We can't attend tonight's meeting.

4. Michael and Suzi work third shift.

5. Kim directs student plays and writes movie reviews for the college paper.

6. The faculty and the new administration rejected the budget and demanded a new audit.

7. Although suffering from flu and exhaustion, Ari won a silver medal.

8. Originally developed for use in military aircraft, this system will improve airline safety.

9. The coach, supported by angry players, demanded the referee call for a penalty.

10. France and Germany, once enemies in three wars, cooperate in industrial development.

Answers appear on the following page.

GET *WRITING*
AND *REVISING*

WHAT ARE YOU TRYING TO SAY?

Write a one-sentence response to each of the following questions:

1. What is the greatest challenge you face this semester?

_____

2. What was your favorite course in high school?

_____

3. Describe how you commute to school each day—do you walk, drive, or take the subway?

_____

4. Why did you enroll in college?

_____

5. What would you like to be doing in five years?

_____

WHAT HAVE YOU WRITTEN?

Read each sentence out loud. Have you expressed a complete thought? Does your sentence make sense? Does it state what you were thinking, what you were trying to say?

The Working Parts of a Sentence

This chapter explains the working parts of a basic sentence. By understanding how a sentence works, you not only avoid making mistakes but create writing that is fresh, interesting, and easy to read. To understand how sentences function, it is important to understand the parts of speech—words that have special functions.

PARTS OF SPEECH

Nouns	name persons, places, things, or ideas: *teacher, attic, Italy, book, liberty*
Pronouns	take the place of nouns: *he, she, they, it, this, that, what, which, hers, their*

(continued)

Verbs	express action:
	buy, sell, run, walk, create, think, feel, wonder, hope, dream
	link ideas:
	is, are, was, were
Adjectives	add information about nouns or pronouns:
	a *red* car, a *bright* idea, a *lost* cause
Adverbs	add information about verbs:
	drove *recklessly*, sell *quickly*, *angrily* denounced
	add information about adjectives:
	very old teacher, *sadly* dejected leader
	add information about other adverbs:
	rather hesitantly remarked
Prepositions	link nouns and pronouns, expressing relationships between related words:
	in the house, *around* the corner, *between* the acts, *through* the evening
Conjunctions	link related parts of a sentence:
	Coordinating conjunctions link parts of equal value:
	and, or, yet, but, so
	He went to college, *and* she got a job.
	Subordinating conjunctions link dependent or less important parts:
	When he went to college, she got a job.
Interjections	express emotion or feeling that is not part of the basic sentence and are set off with commas or used with exclamation points:
	Oh, he's leaving? *Wow!*

Words can function as different parts of speech:

I bought more *paint* [noun].
I am going to *paint* [verb] the bedroom.
Those supplies are stored in the *paint* [adjective] room.

Parts of speech can be single words or phrases, groups of related words that work together:

Tom and his entire staff [noun phrase]
wrote and edited [verb phrase]
throughout the night [prepositional phrase].

Subjects and Verbs

The two most important parts of any sentence are the subject and verb. The **subject** is the actor or main topic that explains what the sentence is about. Subjects, which generally appear at the beginning of the sentence, may be a single word, several words, or a phrase:

Tom works with toxic chemicals.
Tom and Ann work with toxic chemicals.
Working with toxic chemicals requires skill.

Subjects are usually **nouns** or **pronouns.**

What Are Nouns?

Nouns are names of people, places, ideas, or things:

People	Places	Ideas	Things
teacher	attic	freedom	pencil
children	mountain	tardiness	computer
banker	bank	wealth	penny
driver	car	speed	wheel

Count nouns may be singular or plural:

book	books
child	children

Spelling note: Most nouns become plural by adding an *s,* but some nouns have a plural spelling. See pages 412–414 for further information. Noncount nouns have only one form. Examples: *architecture, furniture.*

Nouns may be **common** or **proper.** Common nouns refer to general or abstract people, places, ideas, or things. Proper nouns refer to specific people, places, ideas, or things.

Common	Proper
high school	Washington High School
city	Chicago
teacher	Ms. Smith
supermarket	Safeway

Note: Proper nouns are always capitalized. See Chapter 26 for guidelines on capitalization.

ARTICLES

Indefinite articles *a* and *an* are used with singular nouns to indicate a type or kind of something:

Use *a* before a consonant sound— *a* car, *a* girl, *a* loft, *a* wagon.
Use *an* before a vowel sound— *an* apple, *an* error, *an* item, *an* oven.

The definite article *the* is used with singular or plural nouns to indicate something specific: *the* car, *the* apple, *the* girl, *the* girls.

The student borrowed *a* book.   (A specific student borrowed some book.)
A student borrowed *the* book.   (Some student borrowed a specific book.)

What Are Pronouns?

Pronouns take the place of a noun and can be the subject, object, or possessive of a sentence:

Noun	Pronoun
teacher	he *or* she
children	they
pencil	it

There are four types of pronouns: *personal, relative, demonstrative,* and *indefinite.*

Personal

Personal pronouns refer to people and have three forms, depending on how they are used in a sentence: *subjective, objective,* and *possessive.*

	Subjective		Objective		Possessive	
	Singular	**Plural**	**Singular**	**Plural**	**Singular**	**Plural**
1st person	I	we	me	us	my (mine)	our (ours)
2nd person	you	you	you	you	your (yours)	your (yours)
3rd person	he	they	him	them	his (his)	their (theirs)
	she		her		her (hers)	
	it		it		it (its)	

He drove *their* car to *our* house, so *we* paid *him.*
They rented a cottage because *it* was cheaper than *our* time-share.

Relative

Relative pronouns introduce noun and adjective clauses:

who, whoever, whom, whose   which, whichever   that, what, whatever

I will work with *whoever* volunteers.
Tom was levied a thousand dollar fine, *which* he refused to pay.

Demonstrative

Demonstrative pronouns indicate the noun (antecedent):

this, that, these, those

That car is a lemon.
These books are on sale.

Indefinite

Indefinite pronouns refer to abstract persons or things:

Singular				Plural	Singular or Plural		
everyone	someone	anyone	no one	both	all	more	none
everybody	somebody	anybody	nobody	many	any	most	some
everything	something	anything	nothing	few			
each	another	either	neither				

Everyone promised to come, but *no one* showed up.
Someone should do *something.*

Note: Pronouns must clearly refer to specific nouns called *antecedents* and agree or match their singular or plural form:

> *Incorrect*
> The neighborhood is desolate. Trash litters the street. Abandoned cars jam the alleys. The lawns are choked with weeds. The shabby houses have broken windows. Their front porches are cluttered with old furniture and rubbish. *They* just don't care.

[*Whom* does *they* refer to? Politicians, landlords, tenants, housing officials?]

> *Revised*
> The neighborhood is desolate. Trash litters the street. Abandoned cars jam the alleys. The lawns are choked with weeds. The shabby houses have broken windows. Their front porches are cluttered with old furniture and rubbish. *Slumlords* just don't care.

> *Incorrect*
> Every citizen should do *their* best.

Citizen is a singular noun.

> *Correct*
> Every citizen should do *his or her* best.
> Citizens should do *their* best.

(See Chapter 21 for further information about pronouns.)

CHOOSING SUBJECTS

In some languages, a noun and pronoun can be used together as a subject, but in English, you must choose one:

Incorrect: My *teacher she* wrote the book for our class.
Correct: My *teacher* wrote the book for our class.
or
She wrote the book for our class.

EXERCISE 1 Locating Singular and Plural Subjects

Underline the subject—the main idea—in each sentence. If the subject is plural, underline it twice. To identify the subject of the sentence, read the sentence carefully. What is the sentence about? What part is connected to an action or linked to other words?

1. The Chicago Fire was a major disaster.

2. The summer of 1871 was hot and dry.

3. By fall, Illinois was parched.

4. On October 8 brushfires erupted on the outskirts of Chicago.

5. The fires, fanned by strong winds, spread to the city.

6. The flames consumed the wooden buildings and timber sidewalks.

7. The firestorm leapt across the Chicago River and burned out the business district.

8. Four square miles of the city lay in smoking ruin and ashes.

9. Over 250 men, women, and children lost their lives in the fire, and nearly 100,000 were made homeless.

10. Damage to the nation's rail hub made the fire a national event.

EXERCISE 2 Locating Noun and Pronoun Subjects

Underline the subject in each sentence. Use two lines if the subject is a pronoun.

1. F. Scott Fitzgerald was born in St. Paul, Minnesota, in 1896 and attended Princeton University.

2. He left college before graduation to join the army during World War I.

3. Fitzgerald served in Alabama, where he met his future wife, Zelda Sayre.

4. He wanted to become a writer and enjoy literary and financial success.

5. Fitzgerald published his first novel in 1920.

6. While in France, Fitzgerald began work on *The Great Gatsby,* a book he considered to be his masterpiece.

7. The novel did not become a best-seller when first published.

8. Over the years critics and readers came to appreciate a book many originally dismissed as a superficial love story.

9. It inspired movie directors to create at least four film versions of Fitzgerald's novel.

10. Fitzgerald, who died in 1940, emerged as one of America's greatest literary figures.

Locating "Hidden Subjects"

Subjects are not always easy to spot. They don't always appear at the beginning of a sentence, and at first glance they may not look like important words. *Subjects are not possessive nouns, and they are not nouns in prepositional phrases.*

Inverted Sentences

In most sentences the subject comes before the verb:

I *bought* a new car.
Last night my father *fixed* the TV.
Every morning we *run* two miles.

In some sentences this pattern is inverted or reversed, so the subject follows the verb:

There *are* people waiting in the lobby.
At the bottom of steps *lies* a pile of used clothing.
Behind almost every successful comic *is* an unhappy childhood.

Possessives

Many sentences contain a subject that is the object of a possessive:

> Harrison's *career* suffered after being sued by her investors.
> Ted's *car* needs new tires.
> Last year's *models* were poorly received by the public.

The subject in each sentence appears after a possessive. The subject is not "Harrison" but "Harrison's *career*." One way to keep from being confused is to ask yourself who or what is doing the action or being linked to other ideas. What, for instance, "needs new tires"?—"Ted"? or "Ted's *car*"?

EXERCISE 3 Locating Subjects

Underline the subject in each sentence.

1. Behind expert predictions is pure guesswork.
2. The future is difficult to imagine.
3. In the nineteenth century experts feared that by 1900 America would be stripped of trees.
4. The nation's demand for wood to heat homes was growing faster than the ability of forests to regenerate themselves.
5. The experts' calculations may have been correct.
6. But they failed to anticipate that oil would replace wood as an energy source in the twentieth century.
7. As early as the 1920s, some scientists' studies suggested a coming "gasoline famine."
8. The world, they predicted, would soon run out of oil reserves.
9. Just a few years later, massive oil deposits were discovered in Texas.
10. Events, scientific research, and new inventions constantly disprove the wisest expert's past predictions.

Prepositional Phrases

Prepositions are words that express relationships between ideas, usually regarding time and place:

above	below	near	to
across	during	of	toward
after	except	off	under
against	for	outside	with
along	from	over	within
around	inside	past	without
before	like	since	

Prepositions can begin phrases: *before the rehearsal, during the night, after the election, up the chimney, under the stairs, around the corner, inside the factory, outside the campus.* Prepositional phrases appear frequently in English:

After the game we walked *around the corner. In the student union* I met everyone *on the winning team*. They walked *throughout the union* and signed autographs *during the celebration*.

The only thing you have to remember about prepositional phrases is that *the subject of a sentence will not be found in a prepositional phrase*. The subject of the first sentence is *we*, not *game*, which is part of the prepositional phrase *after the game*.

EXERCISE 4 Locating Subjects and Prepositional Phrases

Underline prepositional phrases in the following sentences. Underline the subject of the sentence twice.

1. Most people in the country think of thieves as men in black masks who rob banks or break into houses.

2. In the information age, however, many thieves use computers.

3. About five years ago a group of criminals in California developed a scheme to defraud consumers.

4. Dressed in conservative suits and presenting official-looking credentials, they convinced shopping mall owners to let them install ATMs.

5. The ATMs were dummies that were not connected to any banking network.

6. Customers who swiped their cards in the ATM and punched in their personal identification numbers received an error message.

7. The customers did not know that the rigged ATM had just recorded their account number and PIN.

8. In less than a week, the ATM collected data from fifty people.

9. After a month of complaints, the criminals apologized to the mall owners and removed their defective ATMs.

10. In a few days they stamped out plastic cards with the account numbers and used the PINs in real ATMs to loot bank accounts and max out credit cards held by the unsuspecting shoppers.

EXERCISE 5 Locating Subjects in Your Own Writing

Describe your favorite television program and explain why you like it. After you complete this description, underline the subject of each sentence.

GET WRITING

Verbs

Verbs express action, link ideas, or help other verbs.

Action verbs show what the subject is doing:

The teacher *distributed* the test booklets.
Canada *accepted* recommendations by the World Bank.
I *bought* a new computer.

Action verbs also express "invisible" behavior:

> The teacher *hoped* students would pass the test.
> Canada *contains* numerous mineral resources.
> I *believe* in being optimistic.

Linking verbs connect the subject to related ideas in the sentence. Linking verbs function much like an = sign. Instead of showing action, they express a relationship between ideas:

> The teacher *was* late.
> Canada *is* a major timber exporter.
> I *am* optimistic.

Helping verbs assist the main verb by adding information:

> The teacher *will* distribute the test booklets.
> Canada *should* win at least four gold medals in the Olympics.
> I *could* help next week.

Verbs also tell time, explaining when the action or relationship takes place:

Past	He *drove* home in the storm.	He *was* a driver.
Present	He *drives* home every night.	He *is* a driver.
Future	He *will drive* us home tonight.	He *will be* a driver.

(See pages 290–291 for further information on verb tense.)

Verbs are either singular or plural:

| Singular | He *drives* to school. | He *is* a driver. |
| Plural | They *drive* to school. | They *are* drivers. |

Verbs must "agree with," or match, their subjects. Many subjects that look like plurals are singular:

> *Six days* <u>is</u> not enough time.   The *jury* <u>is</u> deliberating until noon.
> The *United Nations* <u>is</u> sending aid.   The *price of books* <u>is</u> increasing.

(See Chapter 19 for further information on subject-verb agreement.)

EXERCISE 6 Locating Action Verbs

Underline the action verbs in each of the following sentences.

1. In the early morning hours of August 31, 1888, a London policeman discovered the stabbed and mutilated body of Polly Nichols.

2. A week later police found the slashed body of Annie Chapman.

3. These murders in London's impoverished East End gripped the public.

4. Radicals and reformers used the murders to demand social change.

5. When two more women were murdered in a single night, political pressure mounted against the government.

6. Someone claiming to be the killer sent the press a letter, signing it Jack the Ripper.

7. On November 9, authorities discovered the slashed remains of Mary Kelly, whose heart had been cut out.

8. Then the Ripper murders mysteriously stopped.

9. Four years later the police closed the case, leaving the murders unsolved.

10. Over a century later, "Ripperologists" debate the identity of the first-known serial killer.

EXERCISE 7 Locating Linking and Helping Verbs

Underline linking verbs once and helping verbs twice.

1. Airships are aircraft lifted by lighter-than-air gases rather than engines.

2. After World War I airships were the largest aircraft to carry passengers and freight.

3. Unlike existing airplanes, airships could carry passengers across continents and oceans.

4. Commercial airships were majestic aircraft with ornate staterooms and gourmet meal service.

5. Their reign, however, was brief.

6. By the 1930s commercial airplanes could carry passengers faster and cheaper than massive airships.

7. Airplanes could operate from smaller fields.

8. Photographs of the dramatic crash of the *Hindenburg* in 1937 would shock the public.

9. This single accident would change aviation history.

10. Airships, however, are sparking new interest as surveillance platforms to fight terrorism and direct traffic.

EXERCISE 8 Locating Action, Linking, and Helping Verbs

If you completed Exercise 5, read through your response and circle the action verbs. Underline linking verbs once and place two lines under helping verbs.

PHRASAL VERBS

Sometimes a verb consists of more than one word. This type of verb is called a *phrasal verb*. It consists of a verb and an *adverbial particle* such as *down*, *on*, or *up*. The adverbial particle may explain that something is completed, as in *finish up* or *close down*. Some phrasal verbs use idioms such as "She *ran up* a huge bill" or "That old building *cries out* for repairs." The literal meaning of *ran up* or *cries out* does not explain the verb's action.

(continued)

> **PHRASAL VERBS** *(continued)*
>
> Most phrasal verbs can be separated by pronouns or short noun phrases:
>
> I *picked* Joe's uncle *up* at noon.
> I *picked* him *up* at noon.
>
> Some phrasal verbs cannot be separated:
>
> We *went over* the paper together.
>
> Standard dictionaries may not include phrasal verbs. If you cannot understand a phrasal verb in context, refer to a dictionary like the *Longman Dictionary of American English* or the *Collins Cobuild English Language Dictionary.*

EXERCISE 9 Locating Subjects and Verbs

Circle the subject of each sentence and underline action and linking verbs. Underline helping verbs twice.

1. The word *laser* stands for **l**ight **a**mplification by **s**timulated **e**mission of **r**adiation.

2. Lasers emit an intense narrow beam of light.

3. The beam from a flashlight diffuses in a conelike pattern.

4. In contrast, a laser beam will appear like a glowing tube.

5. Geographers and mapmakers use lasers to accurately measure distances.

6. Industrial lasers are powerful enough to cut steel.

7. Powerful laser weapons in outer space could disable satellites and disrupt television broadcasts and telephone communications.

8. No one on the earth might be killed on a battlefield.

9. However, the loss of key satellites could ruin a nation's economy.

10. Whether used in peace or war, lasers are key instruments in the twenty-first century.

Building Sentences: Independent and Dependent Clauses

Sentences are made up of **clauses,** groups of related words that contain both a subject and a verb. There are two types of clauses: **dependent** and **independent.**

Dependent clauses contain a subject and verb but do *not* express a complete thought and are not sentences:

While I waited for the bus
Before we lost the game
After I moved to Chicago

Dependent clauses have to be joined to an independent clause to create a sentence that expresses a complete thought:

While I waited for the bus, it began to rain.
He thought highly of us before we lost the game.
After I moved to Chicago, I bought a new car.

Independent clauses are groups of related words with a subject and verb that express a complete thought. They are sentences:

I waited for the bus.
We lost the game.
The college canceled night school this semester.

Every sentence contains at least one independent clause.

Sentence Length

A sentence can consist of a single word—if it expresses a complete thought:

Run!
Stop!
Go!

In giving commands, the subject "you" is implied or understood, so it does not have to actually appear in print for a sentence to state a complete thought. A long train of words, however, is not necessarily a sentence:

Because the sophomore varsity team, which includes two all-state champions, practiced an additional six days this summer.

Although there is a subject ("team") and a verb ("practiced"), the words do not express a complete thought. If you read the sentence out loud, it sounds incomplete, like the introduction to an idea that does not appear. It leaves us wondering what happened because the team practiced six extra days. Incomplete sentences—phrases and dependent clauses—are called **fragments.**

A NOTE ON FRAGMENTS

Incomplete sentences that fail to express a complete thought are called *fragments*—a common writing error. Although sometimes written for emphasis, fragments should be avoided in college writing.

See Chapter 14 for help on avoiding fragments.

WORKING TOGETHER

Working with a group of students, revise the following paragraph to change linking verbs to action verbs.

```
The Student Union is the organizer of all campus
events. People who are interested in using the facili-
ties for parties, lectures, performances, or seminars
must contact Brenda Smith. As Student Union coordina-
tor, she is the person who approves all requests. She
is also the editor of the Student Union newsletter.
```

GET THINKING
AND **WRITING**

CRITICAL THINKING

People complain about crime, pollution, taxes, racial profiling, and poverty. But in many elections half the eligible voters do not vote. Why don't more Americans vote? What reasons do people give? Write a paragraph that explains why so many people fail to vote.

WHAT HAVE YOU WRITTEN?

Read your paragraph carefully. Circle the subjects and underline the verbs in each sentence. If you are unsure whether some of your sentences are complete, see Chapter 14.
   Choose one of your sentences and write it below:

_____

Does the sentence clearly express what you were trying to say? Is the subject clearly defined? Is the verb effective? Could more concrete words or stronger verbs (see pages 172–173) improve this sentence?
   Summarize your observations with one sentence. What is the main reason why many Americans don't vote?

_____

Read this sentence carefully. Circle the subject and underline the verb. How effective is your word choice (see Chapter 12)?
   Does this sentence fully express your ideas? Try writing a different version:

_____

Ask a fellow student to read and comment on both sentences. Can your reader understand what you are trying to say?

WHAT HAVE YOU LEARNED?

Circle the subjects (main idea) and underline the verbs (action and linking words) in each sentence. Underline helping verbs twice.

1. Parents should monitor their children's use of the Internet.

2. Woody Allen's movies are usually set in New York.

3. The price of gasoline varies across the country.

4. Many American stars were born in Canada.

5. The White House's security systems are continually updated.

6. My parents' house is being painted.

7. *Death of a Salesman* was written by Arthur Miller.

8. The printer's toner cartridge was replaced yesterday.

9. It was published last year.

10. Booker T. Washington was born in 1856.

Answers appear on the following page.

GET *WRITING*

How much privacy should high school students have? Should school authorities be able to search backpacks for weapons or let the police search lockers for drugs?

Write three or four sentences stating your views on student privacy.

WRITING ON THE WEB

The Internet offers resources on sentence structure and style.

1. Using a search engine like AltaVista, Yahoo!, or Google, enter terms such as *sentence structure, parts of speech,* and *independent clauses* to locate current sites of interest.
2. Review e-mails you have sent. What changes would you make in your writing? What would make your sentences more effective?

POINTS TO REMEMBER

1. The sentence is the basic unit of written English.
2. Sentences contain a subject and verb and express a complete thought.
3. Subjects explain what the sentence is about.
4. Verbs express action or link the subject to other words.
5. Phrases are groups of related words that form parts of sentences.
6. Dependent clauses are groups of related words with a subject and verb but do not state a complete thought.
7. Independent clauses are groups of related words that contain a subject and verb and express a complete thought.
8. All sentences contain at least one independent clause.

ANSWERS TO WHAT HAVE YOU LEARNED? ON PAGE 196

1. subject: *parents,* verb: *should monitor;* 2. subject: *movies,* verb: *are set;* 3. subject: *price,* verb: *varies;* 4. subject: *stars,* verb: *were born;* 5. subject: *security systems,* verb: *are updated;* 6. subject: *house,* verb: *is being painted;* 7. subject: *Death of a Salesman,* verb: *was written,* 8. subject: *cartridge,* verb: *was replaced;* 9. subject: *it,* verb: *was published;* 10. subject: *Booker T. Washington,* verb: *was born*

Avoiding Fragments

© Doug Mazell / Index Stock Imagery

Write three or four sentences describing your first impression of this picture. Does it represent traditional or outdated values? What does it suggest about the role of women in society? Do you see this as something desirable or irrelevant? Does it bring back happy memories?

In order to express yourself clearly, you have to write in sentences—groups of words that have a subject and a verb and express a complete thought:

I bought a new car.
Karen has to work tonight.
Should Tom and I drive you to the airport?

Each of these sentences states a complete thought and can stand on its own. They are **independent clauses.** They make sense all by themselves. Each sentence forms a pattern in which the subject—*I, Karen, Tom and I*—is connected to a verb expressing action—*bought, has to work, drive.* (See pages 185–194.)

In speaking we don't always express ourselves with complete sentences, especially when we are talking to people we know. In person, we communicate not only with words but with gestures, tone, and facial expressions. We may stop midsentence and move to the next idea when we see that people are following our train of thought. Because our communication is interactive, listeners can interrupt us with questions if they become confused:

"Going to the computer lab?"
"After lunch."
"Sure?"
"Got to."
"Really?"
"Forgot the econ project is due."
"See you later. Got to get my disks from the car."
"You drove?"
"Overslept. Missed the bus."
"Get a ride home?"
"Not leaving until four or five."
"No problem."

But when we write, our readers can rely only on the text we give them. If we don't write in complete sentences, we fail to express complete thoughts:

Bought a new car.   [Who bought the new car?]
Because Karen has to work tonight.   [Then what happens?]
Should Tom and I?   [Should Tom and I do what?]

Because we often think faster than we can write, it is easy to make mistakes in expressing ideas. We skip words, shift our train of thought midsentence, and break off phrases. Instead of creating a complete statement, we leave our readers with partial sentences called **fragments:**

Last night we saw a movie. Then we went to the new coffee house. *Located by the airport.* It was crowded. *Because all new places are popular. At least for a while.*

Revised
Last night we saw a movie. Then we went to the new coffee house located by the airport. It was crowded. All new places are popular, at least for a while.

WHAT DO YOU KNOW?

Label each sentence OK for a complete sentence and F for a sentence fragment.

1. _____ The university administration reporting they are unable to secure funds for additional construction projects.

2. _____ Take two aspirin and call me in the morning.

3. _____ Lowering automobile emissions has proven to be a challenge to scientists and engineers.

4. _____ The city council, which will fund the new playground.

5. _____ Available at any time for further consultation.

Answers appear on the following page.

What Are Fragments?

Fragments are incomplete sentences. They lack a subject, a complete verb, or fail to express a complete thought:

Subject Missing
Worked all night. [Who worked *all night*?]

Revised
He worked all night.

Verb Missing
Juan the new building. [What was Juan doing?]

Revised
Juan designed the new building.

Incomplete Verb
Juan designing the new building. [-*ing* verbs cannot stand alone.]

Revised
Juan is designing the new building.

Incomplete Thought
Although Juan designed the building. [It has a subject and verb but fails to express a whole idea.]

Revised
Juan designed the building.

or

Although Juan designed the building, he did not receive any recognition.

The term *fragment* is misleading because it suggests something small; length actually has nothing to do with writing complete sentences. A sentence can consist of a single word:

Run!

The subject "you" is understood. Commands express complete thoughts. A long trail of words, even those with subjects and verbs, can be a fragment if it fails to state a whole idea:

> Because physical activity, even moderate exercise such as walking, has been shown to lower blood pressure, reduce stress, and enhance a sense of well-being.

Although it looks like a long sentence, these words do not express a complete thought. Readers are left wondering: Because exercise is good . . . then what?

INCLUDING ALL VERBS

All parts of the verb phrase must be included to create a complete sentence. Be sure to include helping and linking verbs where needed:

> Sentence needing a helping verb: The popularity of basketball *is* growing.
> Sentence needing a linking verb: It *is* widespread in Latin America.

POINT TO REMEMBER

Reading out loud can help identify fragments. Ask yourself, "Does this statement express a complete thought?"

WHAT ARE YOU TRYING TO SAY?

AND **REVISING**

Write a brief response to each question.

1. What sport do you enjoy watching the most and why?

   _____

   _____

2. What can parents do to make their children appreciate the importance of nutrition and exercise?

   _____

   _____

ANSWERS TO WHAT DO YOU KNOW? ON PAGE 200
1. F (*-ing* verbs like *reporting* cannot stand alone), 2. OK, 3. OK, 4. F (verb missing), 5. F (subject and verb missing)

3. What is your opinion of reality television shows?

_____

_____

_____

4. What do you admire most about your best friend?

_____

_____

_____

5. Should women be required to register for the draft?

_____

_____

_____

WHAT HAVE YOU WRITTEN?

Read each of your responses out loud. Have you written complete sentences? Does each have a subject and verb? Can each sentence stand alone? Do any statements sound incomplete, like introductions to another idea? Rewrite any sentence fragments you discover.

EXERCISE 1 Identifying Fragments

Label each sentence OK *for a complete sentence and* F *for a sentence fragment.*

1. _____ After high school, James Dean moved to New York to study acting.

2. _____ His appearances in early television dramas and a stage play.

3. _____ Dean's good looks and emotionally charged performances made him an immediate star.

4. _____ Dean won further fame when he played a distraught teenager in *Rebel without a Cause.*

5. _____ The film *Giant* presenting him with the challenge of acting alongside Rock Hudson and Elizabeth Taylor.

6. _____ While *Giant* was being edited, Dean was killed in a car accident at twenty-four.

7. _____ When *Rebel without a Cause* was released after his death.

8. _____ Audiences were deeply moved by the film.

9. _____ Which included scenes of a fatal car crash.

10. _____ Although he made only three major films, Dean became a cult figure.

Correcting Fragments

There are two ways of correcting fragments:

1. Turn the fragment into a complete sentence by making sure it expresses a complete thought:

Fragments
Yale being the center for this research
Public opinion surveys
The mayor designated

Revised
Yale is the center for this research. [complete verb added]
The new study is based on public opinion surveys. [subject and verb added]
The mayor designated Sandy Gomez to head the commission. [words added to express a complete thought]

2. Attach the fragment to a sentence to state a complete thought. (Often fragments occur when you write quickly and break off part of a sentence.)

Fragments
He bought a car. *While living in Florida.*
Constructed in 1873. The old church needs major repairs.

Revised
He bought a car while living in Florida.
Constructed in 1873, the old church needs major repairs.

EXERCISE 2 Identifying and Correcting Fragments

Identify and correct the fragments by adding missing words or connecting them to another sentence. Some items may be correct.

1. **Few people realizing Harlem was originally designed to be an exclusive white community.**

_____

_____

2. **Developers clearing Harlem's pastures and small farms.**

_____

_____

3. **To build blocks of luxury townhouses featuring elevators and servants' quarters.**

_____

_____

4. Because real estate speculators were overly optimistic.

_____

5. They built too many houses.

_____

6. Facing terrible losses.

_____

7. Property owners divided houses into low-income apartments and rented to the city's growing black population.

_____

_____

_____

8. Who were traditionally forced to pay higher rents.

_____

9. Soon Harlem became a thriving black community.

_____

10. Featuring black-owned restaurants, theaters, and churches.

_____

_____

EXERCISE 3 Identifying and Correcting Fragments

Identify and correct the fragments by adding missing words or connecting them to another sentence. Some items may be correct.

1. Although computers have revolutionized writing and publishing. Some historians are concerned about the effect technology will have on written records.

_____

_____

2. For hundreds of years, historians, biographers, and journalists have relied on written records.

_____

_____

3. In addition, literary scholars have been able to view various drafts of a play or poem. Allowing them to see how a writer like Ibsen or Poe worked.

_____

_____

4. In the future many scholars fear they will have only final copies to work with. Writers having made revisions electronically so that earlier versions were erased.

_____

_____

5. Journalists also wondering if computers will make it easier for political and business leaders to alter records.

_____

_____

6. Because technology changes quickly. Future researchers being unable to access records stored on obsolete software.

_____

_____

7. For instance, records for the 1960 census are stored on reel-to-reel magnetic tapes that can be read only by a computer kept by the Smithsonian Museum.

_____

_____

8. Terrorists or hackers may be able to enter data banks and alter historical records.

_____

_____

9. On the other hand, computers and the Internet allowing today's researchers to examine documents held by libraries around the world.

_____

_____

10. No longer do students have to visit a library or museum to conduct research.

_____

_____

EXERCISE 4 Correcting Fragments

Revise the following paragraph to correct fragments.

Howard Hughes born in Texas in 1905, the son of a wealthy industrialist. At nineteen Hughes inherited his father's lucrative tool company. Fascinated with movies from an early age. Hughes moved to Hollywood. At first, the Hollywood establishment dismissed the young millionaire as a starstruck amateur. His first movie was so bad. Hughes refused to release it. But in 1927 his film _Wings_ won the Academy Award for Best Picture. Eager to pursue his passion for flying. Hughes wanted to make a film about World War I pilots. Sparing no expense. Hughes began filming _Hell's Angels._ He bought so many aircraft for battle scenes, his studio had more planes than many European air forces. Several stuntmen were killed in crashes. Hughes himself was nearly killed when he attempted a maneuver stunt pilots considered too dangerous. _Hell's Angels_ was made as a silent film. But by the time of its release. Sound movies had revolutionized the industry and captivated the public. Fearful the film would be considered obsolete. Hughes ordered much of the movie to be reshot. The lead actress, who spoke with a heavy Swedish accent. Was replaced by a starlet named Harlene Carpenter. Better known as Jean Harlow. The success of _Hell's Angels_ making her a major star.

_____

_____

_____

_____

_____

_____

_____

_____

_____

_____

_____

_____

_____

_____

_____

_____

_____

_____

_____

_____

EXERCISE 5 Correcting Fragments

Revise the following paragraph to correct fragments.

Long before people could communicate using the Internet, telephones, or the telegraph. They saw the need to relay information quickly. Without electricity all messages having to be delivered by coach or runner. During the French Revolution, a young engineer proposing a signaling system to connect Paris and Lille using semaphores. Claude Chappe, who received backing from the government. Working with his brother, Claude Chappe constructed a series of towers five to ten miles apart. The towers were equipped with two telescopes and two long wooden arms that could be set in forty-nine different positions, each signaling a letter or symbol. Letter by letter, the operator in one tower would set the wooden arms to send a message to the operator in the next tower who watched through a telescope. He would then copy the message, setting the arms on his tower to signal the next tower. Although expensive and cumbersome, the system could send a message across the countryside in hours instead of days. These windmill-like towers soon dotted the hills of Europe, connecting major cities.

In America, the Pony Express serving much the same purpose before the advent of the telegraph.

_____

_____

_____

_____

_____

_____

_____

_____

_____

_____

_____

_____

_____

_____

_____

_____

_____

WORKING TOGETHER

Working with a group of students, revise this e-mail to eliminate any fragments.

```
National Convention, March 24-27, San Diego, CA
This year's national convention held in San Diego at
the Del Coronado Hotel from March 24 to March 27. The
deadline for registration is March 1. Make sure to in-
clude both your business and home address on the at-
tached form. Reservations for flights and hotel rooms.
Must be arranged through the convention committee to
receive discounts. If you have any questions. Contact
the convention office at natconv@vica.org.
```

CRITICAL THINKING

GET THINKING
AND WRITING

Billions of people in other countries know the United States only from what they see in American movies and television shows. Do you think our popular culture gives *people a distorted view of our country, its citizens, and its values? Do Hollywood's images of sex and violence explain why many people from other cultures hate us? Write a short paragraph stating your opinion.*

WHAT HAVE YOU WRITTEN?

When you finish writing, identify and correct any fragments by adding missing elements or attaching the fragment to a related sentence.

1. Select one of your sentences and write it below:

   _____

   _____

2. Circle the subject and underline the verb.
3. Why does this sentence state a complete thought? What relationship is there between the subject and the verb?
4. Read the sentence out loud. Could you make the sentence more effective by replacing abstract words with concrete nouns and stronger verbs (see pages 172–173)? Try writing a different version of your sentence:

   _____

   _____

WHAT HAVE YOU LEARNED?

Label each sentence OK *for a complete sentence and* F *for a sentence fragment.*

1. _____ The computer has revolutionized the workplace.

2. _____ Move to the rear of the aircraft.

3. _____ While he was running for the Senate and condemning other candidates for being hypocrites.

4. _____ After the game, the defeated team was surprisingly upbeat.

5. _____ Caught in the glare of the headlights.

   Answers appear on the following page.

WHAT HAVE YOU WRITTEN?

Review writing exercises in this book, papers written for other courses, work you did in high school, and e-mails sent to friends for fragments. Do you have a tendency to forget words or break off phrases, creating incomplete sentences? If you discover fragments or continue to make them in upcoming assignments, review this chapter. When you write, refer to page 429 in the handbook.

© Carol Guenzi Agents/Index Stock Imagery

GET WRITING

Write a brief response to this photograph. How do your feelings about this image contrast with those about the picture on page 198? Do you find it humorous, acceptable, or offensive? Why?

Review what you have written. Could your sentences be improved by combining ideas into single sentences? Should some combined sentences be separated?

WRITING ON THE WEB

Using a search engine such as AltaVista, Yahoo!, or Google, enter the terms *sentence fragment, grammar,* and *sentence structure* to locate current sites of interest.

POINTS TO REMEMBER

1. Sentences contain a subject and verb and express a complete thought.
2. Sentence fragments are incomplete sentences—they lack a subject or verb or fail to express a complete thought.
3. Fragments can be used for special effect to dramatize words, recreate dialogue, or isolate a key phrase. They should be avoided in formal writing.
4. Reading a sentence out loud is the best way to detect a fragment. If a sentence sounds incomplete or like an introduction to something unstated, it is probably a fragment.
5. Fragments can be corrected in two ways:
   a. Create a complete sentence by adding missing elements.
   b. Attach the fragment to a sentence to state a complete thought.

ANSWERS TO WHAT HAVE YOU LEARNED? ON PAGE 208
1. OK, 2. OK, 3. F, 4. OK, 5. F

Building Sentences Using Coordination and Subordination

© Ewing Galloway/Index Stock Imagery

A century ago millions of immigrants passed through Ellis Island to enter the United States. Many were poor and did not speak English. Their children and grand-children became productive citizens, business leaders, celebrities, and major political figures.

Write a paragraph stating whether or not you think today's immigrants have the same opportunities.

We communicate in sentences—independent clauses that have a subject and verb and express a complete thought. Chapter 13 explains the working parts of a basic or *simple sentence,* a sentence with a single independent clause. But we do not always write in simple sentences. In telling a story, describing a person, making a comparison, or stating an argument, we often *coordinate* ideas, creating sentences with more than one complete thought. We place two or three independent clauses in a single sentence to demonstrate how one idea affects another:

I took History 101 in the summer, so I will take 102 this fall.
Vicki wanted to fly, but we insisted on taking the train.

In other cases we may *subordinate* a minor idea, reducing it to a dependent clause connected to an independent clause to create a sentence:

Because it started to rain, we canceled the hike.
Maria's grades improved after she began using a computer.

Without coordination and subordination, writing can become a list of choppy and repetitive simple sentences:

```
I attended Tulane University. I worked at Crescent
City Travel. It was only two years old. Crescent City
was one of the most successful travel agencies in New
Orleans. Crescent City offered a wide range of travel
services. It specialized in organizing business and
charity cruises. I worked with Cindy Skilling. She was
the daughter of the owner. She had a great personal-
ity. She was very helpful.
```

Joining ideas with coordination and subordination creates writing that is more interesting and easier to follow:

```
While I attended Tulane University, I worked at Cres-
cent City Travel. Although it was only two years old,
Crescent City was one of the most successful travel
agencies in New Orleans. Crescent City offered a wide
range of travel services, but it specialized in or-
ganizing business and charity cruises. I worked with
Cindy Skilling, who was the daughter of the owner. She
had a great personality, and she was very helpful.
```

What Do You Know?

Place a C *next to sentences that use coordination to join independent clauses and an* S *next to sentences that use subordination to join dependent clauses to independent clauses. Mark simple sentences—those with one independent clause—with an* X.

1. ____ Although the dealer slashed prices, the cars did not sell.

2. ____ Stock prices can be volatile, but bonds have fixed values.

3. ____ Trenton is the capital of New Jersey; Harrisburg is the capital of Pennsylvania.

4. _____ Haddonfield is one of the most picturesque and historical towns on the East Coast.

5. _____ José rented a loft apartment in Manhattan, but the rest of us stayed on Long Island.

6. _____ Don't delay; call 911 now!

7. _____ The Great Wall of China is mistakenly believed to be the only structure that can be seen from the moon.

8. _____ Children don't get enough exercise; they spend too much time watching television.

9. _____ Developing new methods of detecting computer viruses will be vital to protect our ability to communicate and process data.

10. _____ Because they cannot attract new accounts, these companies have to provide new products and services to existing customers.

Answers appear on the following page.

What Are Coordination and Subordination?

Coordination creates *compound sentences* that join independent clauses using semicolons or commas and coordinating conjunctions (*and, or, yet, but, so*):

Canada is America's greatest trading partner; Mexico is the second.
Canada is America's greatest trading partner, and Mexico is the second.

Subordination creates *complex sentences* that join an independent clause stating a complete thought with dependent clauses that add additional information or state a less important idea:

I took a cab because my car wouldn't start.
Because my car wouldn't start, I took a cab.

Note: When the dependent clause begins a sentence, it is set off with a comma

Note: Subordination is a way of avoiding *fragments* (Chapter 14), by connecting dependent clauses to independent ones.

CHOOSING THE RIGHT CONJUNCTION

You can connect clauses with either a subordinating or a coordinating conjunction—but not both. Use one or the other:

Incorrect
Although we returned to campus early, *but* there were long lines at the bookstore.

Correct
Although we returned to campus early, there were long lines at the bookstore.

We returned to campus early, *but* there were long lines at the bookstore.

WHAT ARE YOU TRYING TO SAY?

Write a paragraph that tells a story or relates the details of a recent decision you made. Why did you decide to enroll in college? What led you to buy a car, sell your home, select a daycare center, start or quit a job, or join a health club?

_____

_____

_____

_____

_____

_____

_____

_____

_____

_____

_____

_____

_____

_____

_____

_____

_____

WHAT HAVE YOU WRITTEN?

Underline the independent clauses in your paragraph—groups of words that have a subject and verb and express a complete thought. Do some sentences contain more than one complete thought? Did you create any sentences that contained a dependent clause (a group of words with a subject and verb that does not state a complete thought)?

If all the sentences are single independent clauses or simple sentences, read your paragraph out loud. Would your ideas be clearer if some of these sentences were combined into a single statement?

ANSWERS TO WHAT DO YOU
KNOW? ON PAGES 211–212
1. S, 2. C, 3. C, 4. X, 5. C, 6. C,
7. X, 8. C, 9. X, 10. S

Types of Sentences

Just as writers make choices about using different words to express an idea, they also use different types of sentences. Sentence types are determined by the number and kind of clauses they contain.

A **simple sentence** consists of a single independent clause. A simple sentence is not necessarily short or "simple" to read. Although it may contain multiple subjects and verbs and numerous phrases set off with commas, it expresses a single thought:

Jim sings.

Jim and Nancy sing and dance at the newly opened El Morocco.

Seeking to reenter show business, Jim and Nancy sing and dance at the newly opened El Morocco, located at 55th and Second Avenue.

A **compound sentence** contains two or more independent clauses but no dependent clauses. You can think of compound sentences as "double" or "triple" sentences because they express two or more complete thoughts:

Jim studied dance at Columbia; Nancy studied music at Julliard.
[*two independent clauses joined by a semicolon*]
Jim wants to stay in New York, but Nancy longs to move to California.
[two independent clauses joined with a comma and coordinating conjunction]

A **complex sentence** contains one independent clause and one or more dependent clauses:

Jim and Nancy are studying drama because they want to act on Broadway.
Because they want to act on Broadway, *Jim and Nancy are studying drama.*
[*When a dependent clause begins a complex sentence, it is set off with a comma.*]

A **compound-complex sentence** contains at least two independent clauses and one or more dependent clauses:

Jim and Nancy perform Sinatra classics, and they often dress in forties clothing *because the El Morocco draws an older crowd.*

Because the El Morocco draws an older crowd, Jim and Nancy perform Sinatra classics, and they often dress in forties clothing.

The type of sentence you write should reflect your thoughts. Important ideas should be stated in simple sentences to highlight their significance. Equally important ideas can be connected in compound sentences to show cause and effect, choice, or contrast. Minor ideas can be linked to complete thoughts in complex sentences as dependent clauses.

Coordination

Coordination creates *compound sentences* by linking two or more simple sentences (independent clauses). There are two methods of joining simple sentences:

1. Use a comma [**,**] and a coordinating conjunction (*and, or, nor, for, yet, but, so*).
2. Use a semicolon [**;**].

Coordinating Conjunctions

Coordinating conjunctions join simple sentences and show the relationship between the two complete thoughts:

and	adds an idea	We flew to Chicago, *and* we rented a hotel room.
or	shows choice	I will get a job, *or* I will sell the car.
nor	adds an idea when the first is negative	He was not a scholar, *nor* was he a gentleman.
but	shows contrast	He studied hard, *but* he failed the test.
yet		She never studied, *yet* she got an A.
for	shows a reason	He left town, *for* he had lost his job.
so	shows cause and effect	I had a headache, *so* I left work early.

A simple diagram can demonstrate the way to use coordinating conjunctions:

Independent clause, *and* independent clause.

or

nor

but

yet

for

so

Note: A comma always comes before the coordinating conjunction.

In some cases no coordinating conjunction is used. Parallel independent clauses can be linked with a semicolon:

Chicago handles our American accounts; Toronto handles our Canadian ones.

The Senate supports the budget; the House is undecided.

Semicolons are also used to join independent clauses with adverbial conjunctions (*however, meanwhile,* etc.), which are set off with commas:

Chicago handles our American accounts; however, Toronto handles our Canadian ones.

The Senate supports the budget; nevertheless, the House is undecided.

Adverbial Conjunctions

Adverbial conjunctions link independent clauses, but unlike coordinating conjunctions—*and, or, nor, for, yet, but, so*—they are set off with a comma and require a semicolon:

Independent clause; *adverbial conjunction,* independent clause.

Common Adverbial Conjunctions

To Add Ideas		
in addition	likewise	besides
moreover	furthermore	

She speaks French; *in addition,* she knows some Italian.
They refused to pay their bill; *furthermore,* they threatened to sue.

To Show Choice

instead   otherwise

He did not go to the library; *instead,* he used the Internet.
We sold the car; *otherwise,* we could not pay the rent.

To Show Contrast

however   nonetheless   nevertheless

We left early; *however,* we arrived two hours late.
He lost every game; *nevertheless,* he loved the tournament.

To Show Time

meanwhile   while   whenever

The company lowered prices; *meanwhile,* customers sought bargains.
He worked hard; *while* he was working, everyone else went shopping.

To Show Cause and Effect

thus   therefore   consequently
accordingly   hence

We lost our tickets; *hence,* we had to cancel our trip.
Our sales dropped; *therefore,* our profits are down.

To Show Emphasis

indeed   in fact

The housing market is tight; *indeed,* only four houses are on sale.
He was a gifted actor; *in fact,* he was nominated for a Tony Award.

Note: You don't have to memorize all the adverbial conjunctions. Just remember you need to use a semicolon unless independent clauses are joined with *and, or, for, nor, yet, but, so.*
Note: If you fail to join two independent clauses with a comma and a coordinating conjunction or a semicolon, you create errors called *run-ons* and *comma splices.*
See Chapter 16 for strategies to spot and repair run-ons and comma splices.

EXERCISE 1 Combining Simple Sentences (Independent Clauses) Using Coordinating Conjunctions and Commas

1. Write two simple sentences joined by *and*:

_____

_____

2. Write two simple sentences joined by *or*:

_____

_____

3. Write two simple sentences joined by *but*:

_____

_____

4. Write two simple sentences joined by *yet*:

_____

_____

5. Write two simple sentences joined by *so*:

_____

_____

EXERCISE 2 Combining Simple Sentences (Independent Clauses) Using Coordinating Conjunctions and Commas

Combine each pair of sentences using a comma and a coordinating conjunction.

**1. Lee De Forest developed the sound-on-film technique.
It revolutionized the film industry.**

_____

_____

**2. Now actors could talk and sing.
Sound created problems.**

_____

_____

3. Immigrant stars with heavy accents seemed laughable playing cowboys and cops. Their careers were ruined.

_____

_____

**4. A single studio orchestra now supplied the background score.
Thousands of musicians who had played in silent theaters were unemployed.**

_____

_____

5. Hollywood's English-language films lost foreign markets.

Dubbing techniques had to be created.

_____

_____

EXERCISE 3 Combining Simple Sentences (Independent Clauses) Using Coordinating Conjunctions

Add a second independent clause using the coordinating conjunction indicated. Read the sentence out loud to make sure it makes sense.

1. **The university purchased new computers,** *but* _____
   _____

2. **The blizzard swept up the East Coast,** *and* _____
   _____

3. **The company received a large government contract,** *so* _____
   _____

4. **You can take a bus,** *or* _____
   _____

5. **My uncle's store lost money for years,** *yet* _____
   _____

EXERCISE 4 Combining Simple Sentences (Independent Clauses) Using Semicolons

Write a sentence joining two independent clauses with a semicolon. Make sure the statement you add is a complete sentence.

1. _____ ;
   _____

2. _____ ;
   _____

3. _____ ; therefore
   _____

4. _____ ; however,
   _____

5. _____ ; in fact,
   _____

EXERCISE 5 Combining Simple Sentences (Independent Clauses) with Semicolons

Add a second independent clause to each sentence. Read each sentence out loud to make sure it makes sense.

1. **I love watching football at Mel's;** _____
   _____

2. The Mercedes was polished this morning; _____

_____

3. The Empire State Building is the tallest building in New York City; _____

_____

4. Brazil is the largest country in South America; _____

_____

WORKING TOGETHER

Working with a group of students, revise this paragraph to eliminate choppy sentences by creating compound sentences using coordination.

Few Americans have heard about the Fenian invasion. Canadians remember the group's ill-fated attack. The potato famine of the 1840s ravaged Ireland. Millions emigrated to escape hunger and disease. Hundreds of thousands of Irish arrived in America. They struggled to build new lives in the New World. Many harbored resentment against Great Britain. They blamed Great Britain for their suffering. Tens of thousands of Irishmen fought in the American Civil War. After the war some Irish veterans wanted to use their army training to attack Britain. They did not have any method of crossing the Atlantic. They decided to attack Canada. In 1866 about eight hundred Fenian soldiers crossed the border and captured Fort Erie. They were supported by a secondary force of five thousand men. American troops and Canadian forces frustrated their plans. They were forced to withdraw. The movement staged additional raids until the 1870s. All of them proved unsuccessful.

Subordination

Subordination creates *complex* sentences by joining an independent clause with one or more dependent clauses. Dependent clauses contain a subject and verb but cannot stand alone. They are incomplete thoughts and need to be joined to an independent clause to make sense:

Dependent Clause Stating an Incomplete Thought
Because I drive to school
After we went to the game

Dependent clauses are *fragments* and should not stand alone (see Chapter 14).

*Dependent Clause Linked to an Independent Clause Stating a
Complete Thought*
Because I drive to school, the bus strike did not affect me.
After we went to the game, we drove to Jane's for coffee.

POINT TO REMEMBER

Place a comma after a dependent clause when it comes before an independent clause.

> Because I missed the bus, I was late for school.
> I was late for school because I missed the bus. [no comma needed]

USING SUBORDINATING CONJUNCTIONS IN DEPENDENT CLAUSES

Begin clauses with a subordinating conjunction rather than a preposition.

Incorrect
My mother's family moved to the United States *because of* they wanted a better life.

Correct
My mother's family moved to the United States *because* they wanted a better life.

Because is a subordinating conjunction. *Because of* is a two-word preposition that must be followed by a noun or pronoun.

> The flight was delayed *because of* <u>fog</u>.
> We were delayed *because of* <u>him</u>.

Subordination helps distinguish between important ideas and minor details. Without subordination, writing can be awkward and hard to follow:

> I was born in Philadelphia. I grew up in San Francisco. My father was a stockbroker. He took a job in California. I was five. There was less competition on the West Coast. He retired last year. He started a consulting business.

Revised
> Although I was born in Philadelphia, I grew up in San Francisco. My father was a stockbroker. He took a job in California when I was five because there was less competition on the West Coast. After he retired last year, he started a consulting business.

Dependent clauses can be placed at the beginning, within, and at the end of an independent clause. When they come first or within an independent clause, they are set off with commas:

Primary Idea	*Secondary Idea*
I could not attend summer school.	*I could not get a loan.*
I met the mayor.	*I was working at city hall that summer.*
The house was sold.	*I rented it every summer.*

Complex Sentences
I could not attend summer school *because I could not get a loan.*
While I was working at city hall that summer, I met the mayor.
The house, *which I rented every summer,* was sold.

EXERCISE 6 Combining Ideas Using Subordination

Create complex sentences by joining the dependent and independent clauses. If the dependent clause comes first, set it off with a comma.

1. **I loved taking carriage rides in Central Park.**
   When I lived in New York.

   _____

   _____

2. **Even though it was constructed in 2001.**
   The bridge shows signs of wear and tear.

   _____

   _____

3. **Many children still delight in old-fashioned puppet shows.**
   Although people are accustomed to watching television.

   _____

   _____

   _____

4. **Bill avoided his favorite restaurants.**
   When he was on a diet.

   _____

   _____

5. **Although he completed only four major plays.**
   Chekhov is considered one of the world's greatest dramatists.

   _____

   _____

   _____

   _____

EXERCISE 7 Combining Ideas Using Subordination

Create complex sentences by turning one of the simple sentences into a dependent clause and connecting it with the more important idea. You may change the wording of the clauses, but do not alter their basic meaning. Remember that dependent clauses that open or come in the middle of a sentence are set off with commas.

EX: **Many people have never heard of Marcus Garvey. He was a significant figure in American history.**

Although many people have never heard of Marcus Garvey, he was a significant

figure in American history.

1. **Marcus Garvey was born in Jamaica. He became one of the most inspiring and controversial black leaders in the United States.**

   _____

   _____

2. **Garvey moved to America. He opened the New York Division of the United Negro Improvement Association, or UNIA, in 1917.**

   _____

   _____

3. **Garvey's philosophy stressed black nationalism, black pride, and black entrepreneurship. Many African Americans found his message uplifting.**

   _____

   _____

4. **Garvey believed American blacks should return to Africa. He was considered a radical.**

   _____

   _____

5. **The UNIA was unlike other black organizations at the time. It was international in scope.**

   _____

   _____

6. **Garvey distrusted working-class whites and labor unions. This alienated many liberals who believed in integration, class struggle, and social reform.**

   _____

   _____

7. **Garvey wore flashy uniforms and held marches. Many people saw him as a simple-minded buffoon leading ignorant people into wasted efforts and lost causes.**

   _____

   _____

8. **Civil rights leaders and socialists objected to Garvey's policies. They formed the Friends of Negro Freedom, which was dedicated to getting rid of Garvey "by any means necessary."**

   _____

   _____

   _____

9. Garvey's opponents supported the government's prosecution of Garvey for mail fraud. They also urged that the UNIA be disbanded.

   _____

   _____

10. Garvey was convicted, imprisoned, and later deported. Elements of his message still inspire people eighty years later.

    _____

    _____

WHAT ARE YOU TRYING TO SAY?

GET WRITING
AND REVISING

Write a simple sentence (an independent clause) that expresses a complete thought about a person, place, thing, event, or situation. Then write a dependent clause that adds additional information to the main idea. Join the two clauses to create a complex sentence. Remember to set off dependent clauses with commas when they are placed at the opening or within a sentence.

Example:

Simple sentence: <u>I missed the midterm exam.</u>

Dependent clause: <u>Because I had jury duty.</u>

Complex sentence: <u>I missed the midterm exam because I had jury duty.</u>

1. Simple sentence: _____

   Dependent clause: _____

   Complex sentence: _____

   _____

   _____

2. Simple sentence: _____

   Dependent clause: _____

   Complex sentence: _____

   _____

   _____

3. Simple sentence: _____

   Dependent clause: _____

   Complex sentence: _____

   _____

   _____

WHAT HAVE YOU WRITTEN?

Read the complex sentences. Do they make sense? Should the dependent clause be placed in another part of the sentence? Should the dependent clause be made into an independent clause that stands alone as its own sentence?

EXERCISE 8 Using Coordination and Subordination

The following passage is stated in simple sentences. Revise it and create compound and complex sentences to make it more interesting and easier to read.

> In 1933 the Federal Bureau of Prisons opened a new complex on Alcatraz. It is an island in San Francisco Bay. The prison was not like others. Alcatraz was designed to punish. It made no attempt to rehabilitate inmates. Prisoners were isolated in one-man cells. Mail was limited. Family visits were restricted. Newspapers were forbidden. Inmates received no news of the outside world. At first prisoners were not even allowed to speak during meals. The strict discipline proved stressful. Some inmates suffered nervous breakdowns. The prison soon got a reputation for severity. It was nicknamed "the Rock." The prison was very expensive to operate. There was no water supply on the island. Tons of water had to be shipped to Alcatraz each day. Visitors and employees had to be ferried back and forth. This was costly. By the 1960s the prison seemed outdated. In 1963 the federal government decided to close the facility.

After completing your draft, read it out loud. Have you reduced choppy and awkward sentences? Does your version make the essay easier to follow?

GET THINKING AND WRITING

CRITICAL THINKING

How well do high schools prepare students for college? Do courses and teachers provide the skills and knowledge needed to succeed in higher education? Do you have any suggestions to improve schools? Use simple, compound, and complex sentences to develop a paragraph stating your views.

WHAT HAVE YOU WRITTEN?

When you complete your paragraph, read over your work. Underline each independent clause once and each dependent clause twice. Did you create effective compound and complex sentences and punctuate them correctly? Read your sentences out loud. Are there missing words, awkward phrases, or confusing shifts that need revising?

1. Select one of the compound sentences and write it below:

_____

_____

_____

Are the independent clauses closely related? Do they belong in the same sentence? Could you subordinate one of the ideas to create a complex sentence? Try writing a complex sentence that logically reflects the relationship between the ideas:

_____

_____

_____

Does this complex sentence make sense—or does a compound sentence better express what you are trying to say?

Have you used the best method to join the two ideas? If you used a comma and coordinating conjunction, rewrite the sentence using a semicolon:

_____

_____

_____

How does this version affect meaning? Does it make sense? Why are coordinating conjunctions important?

2. Select one of your complex sentences and write it below:

_____

_____

_____

Underline the independent clause. Is it the more important idea? Does the dependent clause express only additional or less important information?

Turn the dependent clause into an independent one and create a compound sentence. Remember to use a semicolon or a comma with *and, or, yet, but,* or *so* to join the two clauses:

_____

_____

_____

Does the compound sentence better express what you are trying to say, or does it appear illogical or awkward?

Write the two independent clauses as separate simple sentences:

_____

_____

_____

How does stating these ideas in two sentences alter the impact of your ideas? Does it better express what you are trying to say or only create two choppy sentences?

When you are trying to express an important or complex idea, consider writing two or more versions using simple, compound, and complex sentences. Read them out loud and select the sentences that best reflect your ideas.

© Ed Kashi/IPN/AURORA

GET WRITING

How will today's immigrants change American society? What new values, cultures, insights will they represent? Do immigrants help America compete in a global economy? Without immigrants, could America become an isolated nation?

Write a paragraph on the influence of today's immigrants. Are they different from those immigrants depicted on page 210?

WHAT HAVE YOU LEARNED?

Place a C next to sentences that use coordination to join independent clauses and an S next to sentences that use subordination to join dependent clauses to independent clauses. Mark simple sentences—those with one independent clause—with an X.

1. _____ Contrary to popular belief, the Statue of Liberty is not located in New York; it stands in New Jersey territory.

2. _____ Most baseballs are manufactured in Haiti.

3. _____ Gasoline was rationed during World War II to conserve the nation's limited supply of rubber tires.

4. _____ The Rose Bowl is played in Pasadena, and the Sugar Bowl is played in New Orleans.

5. _____ The Yankees play in the Bronx, but the Giants play in New Jersey.

6. _____ Because new drugs can have dangerous side effects, they must be thoroughly tested.

7. ____ We moved our sales office to Austin after we won a major state construction contract.

8. ____ George Armstrong Custer graduated at the bottom of his class at West Point, but he became a general at the age of twenty-three.

9. ____ John Houseman began his acting career at seventy-one when he played a law professor in *The Paper Chase.*

10. ____ Vermont abolished slavery in 1777.

Answers appear below.

WRITING ON THE WEB

Using a search engine such as AltaVista, Yahoo!, or Google, enter terms such as *simple sentence, compound sentence, complex sentence, independent clause,* and *dependent clause* to locate current sites of interest.

POINTS TO REMEMBER

1. Simple sentences contain one independent clause and express a single complete thought.
2. Compound sentences link two or more independent clauses with a semi-colon (;) or a comma (,) and a coordinating conjunction (*and, or, yet, but, so, for, nor*).
3. Complex sentences link one or more dependent clauses with a single independent clause.
4. Compound-complex sentences link one or more dependent clauses to two or more independent clauses.
5. Use compound sentences to *coordinate* ideas of equal importance.
6. Use complex sentences to link an important idea with a dependent clause adding secondary information.
7. Use sentence structure to demonstrate the relationship between your ideas.

16

Repairing Run-ons and Comma Splices

© Tom Grill /CORBIS

How do you communicate with friends? How do tone, facial expressions, and gestures add meaning to your words? Do you depend on reading your friends' faces to tell if they understand what you are trying to say?

Think of an animated conversation you recently had with a friend and try to recapture it in a few sentences or a short paragraph. Do you find it hard to recreate the mood or feeling on paper? Why?

228

What Are Run-ons?

Run-ons are not wordy sentences that "run on" too long. **Run-ons** are incorrectly punctuated compound sentences. Chapter 15 explains how independent clauses are coordinated to create compound sentences that join two or more complete thoughts. You can think of them as "double" or "triple" sentences. Compound sentences demonstrate the relationship between closely related ideas that might be awkward or confusing if stated separately:

Omar speaks fluent Korean.   The army sent him to Germany.

Omar speaks fluent Korean, but the army sent him to Germany.
   [The coordinating conjunction *but* dramatizes the irony of a Korean
   speaker being sent to Germany.]

The city is responsible for road repairs.   The county is responsible for
                                             bridge repairs.

The city is responsible for road repairs; the county is responsible for
bridge repairs.
   [The semicolon links the two matching sentences as an equal pair.]

To be effective, compound sentences have to be accurately punctuated to avoid causing confusion. There are two methods of joining independent clauses:

Use a semicolon:
Independent clause; independent clause.
or
Use a comma with a coordinating conjunction:
Independent clause, *and* independent clause.

or	*so*
but	*for*
yet	*nor*

If you fail to use the right punctuation, you create a run-on. Run-on sentences—also called *fused sentences*—and a related error called *comma splices,* or *comma faults,* are some of the most common errors found in college writing. Because thoughts occur to us in a stream rather than a series of separate ideas, we can easily run them together in writing:

The college is facing a financial crisis but most students don't seem to be aware
of it. Unless the state legislature supports the new funding bill, the school
will have to make drastic cuts. *Faculty will be laid off student services will be*
cut. Construction of the new dorms will be halted. *I can't understand why no*
one seems concerned about two hundred classes may be canceled next semester.

Revised
The college is facing a financial crisis, but most students don't seem to be
aware of it. Unless the state legislature supports the new funding bill, the
school will have to make drastic cuts. Faculty will be laid off, and student
services will be cut. Construction of the new dorms will be halted. I can't

understand why no one seems concerned. About two hundred classes may be canceled next semester.

Run-ons can be of any length. Just as fragments can be long, run-ons can be very short:

I asked no one answered.   Let's drive Nancy knows the way.

Revised
I asked, but no one answered.   Let's drive; Nancy knows the way.

POINT TO REMEMBER

Unlike fragments, there are no acceptable run-ons. Run-ons are never written for special effect. We don't speak in run-ons. We usually pause between complete thoughts or connect them with words like *and* or *but*. In writing it is important to keep complete thoughts from being confused with others. Some teachers and editors, however, will use only a comma to connect independent clauses in sentences with no other punctuation:

She can help, that's her job.   Let's go, we'll be late.

WHAT DO YOU KNOW?

Label each sentence OK *for correct or* RO *for run-on.*

1. _____ Jazz originated in New Orleans but Chicago played an important part in its history.

2. _____ Hypertension is called a silent killer many people have no symptoms until they suffer a heart attack.

3. _____ Although he was born of French parents in a small village in Nigeria and spoke no English until he was eight years old, Alonzo felt right at home in midtown Manhattan.

4. _____ The car won't start the battery cables are corroded.

5. _____ The students were eager to help the flood victims, who needed food, shelter, and dry clothes.

Answers appear on the following page.

AND REVISING

WHAT ARE YOU TRYING TO SAY?

Write a brief narrative about something you did last weekend. Explain errands you ran, friends you saw, places you went, or chores you completed. Try to create compound sentences to show cause and effect, contrast, or choice.

Example:
I borrowed my sister's van, so I could pick up the lumber we needed. Atlantic Hardware is only four blocks away, but they don't carry the wood we need. I have to finish fixing the porch in two weeks, or my father will hire a contractor to complete the job.

_____

_____

_____

_____

_____

_____

_____

_____

_____

_____

WHAT HAVE YOU WRITTEN?

Read your draft carefully. Have you created any compound sentences—sentences that contain two independent clauses, two complete thoughts? Are the compound sentences properly punctuated? Do you join the independent clauses with semicolons or with commas and coordinating conjunctions (and, or, yet, but, so, for, nor)?

Run-ons: Fused Sentences and Comma Splices

Some writing teachers use the term _run-on_ to refer to all errors in compound sentences, while others break these errors into two types: fused sentences and comma splices.

Fused Sentences

Fused sentences lack the punctuation needed to join two independent clauses. The two independent clauses are _fused,_ or joined, without a comma or semicolon:

Travis entered the contest he won first prize

Revised

Travis entered the contest; he won first prize.

Nancy speaks Spanish but she has trouble reading it.

Revised

Nancy speaks Spanish, but she has trouble reading it.

Comma Splices

Comma splices are compound sentences where a comma is used instead of a semicolon:

My sister lives in Chicago, my brother lives in New York.

ANSWERS TO WHAT DO YOU KNOW? ON PAGE 230
1. RO (comma needed after _New Orleans_), 2. RO (semicolon needed after _killer_), 3. OK, 4. RO (comma + _and_ needed after _start_), 5. OK

Revised

My sister lives in Chicago; my brother lives in New York.

The lake is frozen solid, it is safe to drive on.

Revised

The lake is frozen solid; it is safe to drive on.

Identifying Run-ons

To identify run-ons, do two things:

1. Read the sentence carefully. Determine if it is a compound sentence. Ask yourself if you can divide the sentence into two or more independent clauses (simple sentences).

   Sam entered college but dropped out after six months.

   Sam entered college . . . [independent clause (simple sentence)] dropped out after six months . . . [not a sentence]

   [not a compound sentence]

   Nancy graduated in May but she signed up for summer courses.

   Nancy graduated in May . . . [independent clause (simple sentence)] she signed up for summer courses . . . [independent clause (simple sentence)]

   [compound sentence]

2. If you have two or more independent clauses, determine if they should be joined. Is there a logical relationship between them? What is the best way of connecting them? Independent clauses can be joined with a comma and *and, or, yet, but, so,* or with a semicolon.

   Nancy graduated in May, but she signed up for summer courses.

   But indicates a logical contrast between two ideas. Inserting the missing comma quickly repairs this run-on.

EXERCISE 1 Identifying Run-ons: Comma Splices and Fused Sentences

Label each item OK *for correct,* CS *for comma splice, or* F *for fused sentence. If your instructor prefers, you can label any error* RO *for run-on.*

1. _____ Tuberculosis, or TB, is a serious infectious disease that primarily affects the lungs, though other organs may be involved.

2. _____ Unlike AIDS, TB can be spread by indirect contact, a patient's sneeze can disperse infectious droplets to others.

3. _____ The TB bacillus is very hardy and can survive outside the body for months, a person's clothing and bedding can be sources for transmission.

4. _____ The first symptoms resemble those of a bad cold people suffer coughing, fever, and fatigue.

5. _____ TB patients may linger for years as the disease slowly robs them of breath eventually they die of exhaustion, lung hemorrhages, or secondary infections.

6. _____ Although the disease was known in the ancient world, it did not become a major killer until the nineteenth century.

7. _____ TB spread rapidly in the crowded industrial cities of Europe and America, millions became infected.

8. _____ For centuries doctors had no effective treatment; they could only prescribe bed rest and fresh air.

9. _____ In the 1940s new drugs were discovered they effectively treated TB and prevented it from spreading.

10. _____ By the 1980s TB seemed like a disease of the past but a new drug-resistant form has recently been discovered and it nearly always proves fatal.

EXERCISE 2 Identifying Run-ons: Comma Splices and Fused Sentences

Underline the comma splices and fused sentences in the following paragraph. If your instructor prefers, you can indicate fused sentences by underlining them twice.

Today's college students are accustomed to using notebook computers they are smaller and lighter than their parents' old portable typewriters. These slim models bear no relation to their ancestors. The first generation of computers were massive contraptions they filled entire rooms. They used thousands of vacuum tubes, which tended to burn out quickly. To keep the computers running people had to run up and down aisles, they pushed shopping carts full of replacement tubes. Because of their size, computers had limited military value. None could fit into an airplane, but during World War II some ships featured computers that weighed several tons. Early computers were expensive to operate only the government could afford to use them to make calculations. One expert thought that the United States would need only three computers. No one in the early 1950s could imagine that one day millions of Americans would own personal computers.

Repairing Run-ons: Minor Repairs

A fused sentence or comma splice may need only a minor repair. Sometimes in writing quickly we mistakenly use a comma when a semicolon is needed:

The Senate likes the president's budget, the House still has questions.

Revised

The Senate likes the president's budget; the House still has questions.

In other cases we may forget a comma or drop one of the coordinating conjunctions:

The Senate likes the president's budget but the House still has questions.

Senators approve of the budget, they want to meet with the president's staff.

Revised

The Senate likes the president's budget, but the House still has questions.

Senators approve of the budget, and they want to meet with the president's staff.

Critical Thinking: Run-ons Needing Major Repairs

In other cases run-ons require more extensive repairs. Sometimes we create run-ons when our ideas are not clearly stated or fully thought out:

Truman was president at the end of the war and the United States dropped the atomic bomb.

Adding the needed comma eliminates a mechanical error but leaves the sentence cumbersome and unclear:

Truman was president at the end of the war, and the United States dropped the atomic bomb.

Repairing this kind of run-on requires critical thinking. A compound sentence joins two complete thoughts, and there should be a clear relationship between them. It may be better to revise the entire sentence, changing it from a compound to a complex sentence:

Revised

Truman was president at the end of the war when the United States dropped the atomic bomb.

In some instances you may find it easier to break the run-on into two simple sentences, especially if there is no strong relationship between the main ideas:

Swansea is a port city in Wales that was severely bombed in World War II and Dylan Thomas was born there in 1914.

Revised

Swansea is a port city in Wales that was severely bombed in World War II. Dylan Thomas was born there in 1914.

POINT TO REMEMBER

A compound sentence should join independent clauses that state ideas of equal importance. Avoid using an independent clause to state a minor detail that could be contained in a dependent clause or a phrase:

Awkward

My brother lives in Boston, and he is an architect.

Revised

My brother, who lives in Boston, is an architect.

My brother in Boston is an architect.

Methods of Repairing Run-ons

There are a number of methods for repairing run-ons.

1. Put a period between the sentences.

   Sometimes in first drafts we connect ideas that have no logical relationship:

   John graduated in 2005, and the football team had a winning season.

   Revised

   John graduated in 2005. The football team had a winning season.

   Even if the two sentences are closely related, your thoughts might be clearer if they were stated in two simple sentences. Blending two sentences into one can weaken the impact of an idea you may want to stress:

   The alderman asked for emergency aid, and the mayor refused.

   Revised

   The alderman asked for emergency aid. The mayor refused.

2. Insert a semicolon between the sentences to show a balanced relationship between closely related statements:

   Trenton is the capital of New Jersey; Albany is the capital of New York.
   Employees want more benefits; shareholders want more dividends.

3. Connect the sentences with a comma and *and, or, yet, but,* or *so* to show a logical relationship between them:

I am tired, *so* I am going home.	[indicates one idea causes another]
I am tired, *but* I will work overtime.	[shows unexpected contrast between ideas]
I am tired, yet I will work harder.	
I am tired, *and* I feel very weak.	[adds two similar ideas]
I will take a nap, *or* I will go home early.	[indicates one of two alternatives]

4. Rewrite the run-on, making it a simple or complex sentence to reduce wordiness or show a clearer relationship between ideas:

   Kris developed a computer program and she later sold it to Microsoft.

   Paul moved to Chicago to live with his brother while he went to law school he wanted to save money.

   Revised

   Kris developed a computer program she later sold to Microsoft.
   [simple sentence]

   Paul moved to Chicago to live with his brother while he attended law school because he wanted to save money.

   [complex sentence]

POINTS TO REMEMBER

Often in revising a paper, you may wonder, "Should this comma be a semicolon?" To determine which mark of punctuation is correct, apply this simple test:

1. Read the sentence out loud. Ask yourself if you can divide the sentence into independent clauses (simple sentences that can stand alone).
2. Where the independent clauses are joined, you should see a semicolon or a comma with *and, or, yet, but,* or *so.*
3. If *and, or, yet, but,* or *so* are missing, the comma should be a semicolon.

Remember, a semicolon is a period over a comma—it signals that you are connecting two complete sentences.

WORKING TOGETHER

Working with a group of students, correct the fused sentences by using each method identified below. Have each member provide four solutions, then share your responses. Determine who came up with the most logical, easy-to-read sentence.

1. The community center is unable to maintain its current services the cost of a new roof demanded by state inspectors will bankrupt the organization.

   Two simple sentences:

   _____

   _____

   Two types of compound sentences:

   _____

   _____

   One complex sentence:

   _____

   _____

2. The FDA will license this new headache remedy doctors believe it will be a major breakthrough in treating migraines.

   Two simple sentences:

   _____

   _____

   Two types of compound sentences:

   _____

   _____

One complex sentence:

_____

_____

3. Computers and fax machines have increased demand for phone lines new area codes have been introduced in many states.

Two simple sentences:

_____

_____

Two types of compound sentences:

_____

_____

One complex sentence:

_____

_____

EXERCISE 3 Correcting Run-ons: Fused Sentences

Correct each fused sentence using each method. Notice the impact each correction has. When you finish each item, circle the revision you think is most effective.

1. Cyberspace has created virtual communities criminals lurk in these electronic neighborhoods.

a. Place a period between the two main ideas, making two sentences.

_____

_____

b. Connect the main ideas using a comma with _and, or, yet, but,_ or _so._

_____

_____

c. Connect the main ideas with a semicolon.

_____

_____

d. Revise the sentence, making it either simple or complex.

_____

_____

2. Her novel was a great success the movie was a major disappointment and financial disaster.

   a. Place a period between the two main ideas, making two sentences.

   _____

   _____

   b. Connect the main ideas using a comma with *and, or, yet, but,* or *so.*

   _____

   _____

   c. Connect the main ideas with a semicolon.

   _____

   _____

   d. Revise the sentence, making it either simple or complex.

   _____

   _____

3. Denver chefs have to be inventive their city's high altitude requires special cooking techniques.

   a. Place a period between the two main ideas, making two sentences.

   _____

   _____

   b. Connect the main ideas using a comma with *and, or, yet, but,* or, *so.*

   _____

   _____

   c. Connect the main ideas with a semicolon.

   _____

   _____

   d. Revise the sentence, making it either simple or complex.

   _____

   _____

EXERCISE 4 Revising Run-ons: Fused Sentences

Rewrite the fused sentences, creating correctly punctuated compound, complex, or simple sentences.

1. Television sets went on sale in the late 1930s they cost almost as much as new cars.

   _____

   _____

2. The picture tubes were long and they had to be placed vertically.

_____

_____

3. No one could see the screen facing the ceiling viewers used a tilted mirror.

_____

_____

4. Television stations broadcast only a few hours a week their programming was dull and unimaginative.

_____

_____

5. World War II began in 1941 and civilian broadcasting was terminated until 1945.

_____

_____

EXERCISE 5 Repairing Comma Splices and Fused Sentences with Commas and Semicolons

Revise each of the following sentences to correct run-ons by inserting commas and semicolons.

1. Recovering alcoholics sometimes call themselves Friends of Bill W. he was a founder of Alcoholics Anonymous.

2. Bill Wilson was not a doctor or a therapist he was a stockbroker and alcoholic.

3. He tried to remain sober and focus on rebuilding his career but the temptation to drink often overwhelmed him.

4. On a business trip in Ohio, Wilson had a sudden inspiration in later years it would change the lives of millions.

5. To keep himself from drinking he knew he needed to talk to someone and he began calling churches listed in a hotel directory.

6. He talked to several ministers he did not ask them for guidance but for the name of a local alcoholic.

7. Wilson was put in touch with Dr. Robert Smith he was a prominent physician whose life and career had been nearly destroyed by drinking.

8. As Wilson and Dr. Smith talked, they made an important discovery although they were strangers, they had much in common.

9. They shared the guilt about broken promises to their wives they knew how alcohol affected their judgment, their character, and their health.

10. Both men sensed they had learned something important only a drunk could help another drunk and this meeting led to the founding of Alcoholics Anonymous.

EXERCISE 6 Repairing Comma Splices and Fused Sentences

Edit the following passage for comma splices and fused sentences.

"Quota quickies" were some of the worst movies ever made but they served a purpose. In the 1930s members of Parliament became concerned about the number of American motion pictures playing in British cinemas. To combat the Americanization of British society and stimulate the lagging British film industry, the government imposed a quota it demanded that a certain percentage of films shown in Britain had to be made in Britain.

American studios did not want to limit the number of films they showed in England Hollywood executives hit on a plan it would maintain their share of the British market. Instead of lowering the number of American films they showed in Britain to meet the quota, they increased the number of British films. American studios hastily set up British film companies, hired British writers and directors, and made a series of low-budget English movies. They did not want to spend money on stars they hired London stage actors looking for extra pay. After their evening's performance, the actors were rushed to rented studios, given a script to study over a free dinner, and put to work with little rehearsal. To save money, most of the movies consisted of actors talking in a pub or living room. Rather than being filmed in expensive action scenes, a character would rush in and give a long-winded speech telling the others what had happened outside. To save time, directors rarely shot more than one take and they did not edit out mistakes. The movies were dull, awkward, and sometimes out of focus. The studios knew that no one would pay to see these awful films but that did not matter. The government quota only required that a percentage of films *shown* in Britain had to be British it did not require that anyone actually see them. London cinemas continued to show popular American movies during the day and early evening. Then late at night sleepy projectionists screened quota quickies to empty theatres. Often they were the only people, besides cleaning crews, who ever saw these films.

WORKING TOGETHER

Working with a group of students, revise this e-mail to eliminate fused sentences and comma splices.

```
Attention all students and faculty:

Recent environmental tests have revealed unacceptable
air quality in several buildings Statler Hall will
be closed March 1. Renovations are expected to take
one month classes will be relocated. English classes
meeting in Statler Hall will be held in the armory
building on 9th Street, all other liberal arts classes
will meet in the Women's Center. The college website
lists all room changes maps include new parking
instructions.
```

CRITICAL THINKING

*GET THINKING
AND WRITING*

*Many corporations use hidden surveillance cameras to monitor employees.
How would you feel if you learned that your workstation was being videotaped?
Do you think companies should be allowed to review their employees' behavior?
If you owned a business, would you feel you had the right to see if your employees
were doing their jobs, treating customers with respect, and following government
regulations? Select one of these questions and write a response that clearly states
your views.*

WHAT HAVE YOU WRITTEN?

*Read your response carefully and underline the compound sentences—those
containing two or more independent clauses. Did you avoid run-ons? Did you join
the independent clauses with a semicolon or a comma with* and, or, yet, but, so?

Select one of your compound sentences and write it out below:

_____

_____

1. Why did you place more than one complete idea in this sentence? Are the
    independent clauses logically related? Does your compound sentence link
    ideas of equal importance, show cause and effect, demonstrate a choice, or
    highlight a contrast? Could you improve the impact of your sentence by
    using a different coordinating conjunction?

2. If the ideas are not of equal importance, would it be better to subordinate
    one of them?

    Unequal
    My cousin lives in Austin, and he won a Pulitzer Prize.

    Revised
    My cousin, who lives in Austin, won a Pulitzer Prize.

    Select a simple sentence—a single independent clause—and write it out below:

_____

    *Think about the main idea you were trying to express, and write another sentence
about the same topic:*

_____

3. Read the two sentences. Should these ideas remain in separate sentences, or
    would it be more effective to join them in a compound sentence to dem-
    onstrate their relationship?

    When you are trying to express an important or complex idea, consider writ-
    ing two or more versions using simple, compound, and complex sentences. Read
    them out loud and select the sentences that best reflect your ideas.

© Bill Keefrey/Index Stock Imagery

GET WRITING

Do you find writing different from talking? Have you found it harder to write an e-mail to a friend than talking on the phone? Why is choosing the right word more important in writing than speaking?

Write a paragraph describing the main differences between speaking and writing a message.

WHAT HAVE YOU LEARNED?

Label each sentence OK *for correct or* RO *for run-on.*

1. _____ After serving in the Gulf War, many veterans reported experiencing unexplained health problems.

2. _____ Saudi Arabia is rich in oil but it lacks water.

3. _____ Shari completed law school and is prepared to take the bar exam this month.

4. _____ Frank St. John bought a boat in Miami and began a charter service.

5. _____ Parents rushed to see the coach they wanted to congratulate her for winning the championship.

Answers appear on the following page.

WRITING ON THE WEB

Using a search engine such as AltaVista, Yahoo!, or Google, enter terms such as *run-on, comma splice, comma fault, compound sentence, complex sentence,* and *sentence types* to locate current sites of interest.

POINTS TO REMEMBER

1. Run-ons are common writing errors.
2. A run-on is an incorrectly punctuated compound sentence.
3. Compound sentences join two or more related independent clauses using semicolons or commas with *and, or, yet, but,* or *so.*
4. Run-ons can be corrected in two ways:
   a. If the sentence makes sense when you read it out loud, and the independent clauses are related, add the missing words or punctuation:

   Independent clause; *independent clause.*

   or

   Independent clause, and *independent clause.*
   or
   yet
   but
   so

   b. If the sentence does not make sense, reword it or break it into separate simple or complex sentences.

ANSWERS TO WHAT HAVE YOU LEARNED? ON PAGE 242
1. OK, 2. RO (see page 231), 3. OK, 4. OK, 5. RO (see page 231).

Correcting Dangling and Misplaced Modifiers

© Aneal Vohra/Index Stock Imagery

How hard is it for people to work together, to keep a common goal and stay motivated? Have you ever been part of a group at work or a team that failed to keep its goal in mind? Have you noticed that some people can compromise and work with others and other people can't?

Write a paragraph about an experience you had working with others. Why did your group succeed or fail in your opinion?

What Are Modifiers?

Modifiers describe words and phrases. Whether they are adjectives (*hot, green, new, stolen, creative*), adverbs (*hotly, creatively, slightly, deeply*), or participial phrases (*driving to school, leading the team to victory, playing his mother's violin*), they must be clearly linked to what they modify. Changing the position of a modifier in a sentence alters the meaning:

Sentence	*Meaning*
Only Tom ordered tea for lunch.	Tom was the one person to order tea.
Tom ordered *only* tea for lunch.	Tom ordered tea and nothing else.
Tom ordered tea *only* for lunch.	Tom ordered tea for lunch but not for other meals.

Dangling Modifiers

A **dangling modifier** is a modifier attached to the beginning or end of a sentence that is not clearly linked to what it is supposed to describe:

Dangling Modifier
Running a red light, two children were hit by a cab.   [Who ran the red light—two children?]

Correct
Running a red light, a cab hit two children.

Dangling Modifier
I canceled my trip, having caught a bad cold.   [Who caught a bad cold—my trip?]

Correct
Having caught a bad cold, I canceled my trip.

What Do You Know?

Put an X next to each sentence with a dangling or misplaced modifier and OK next to each correct sentence.

1. _____ Rowing across the lake, a pale moon rose over the mountains.

2. _____ First sold in the late 1930s, televisions did not become popular until the 1950s.

3. _____ John F. Kennedy became the first Roman Catholic president elected in 1960.

4. _____ Basing his film on the life of William Randolph Hearst, Orson Welles's *Citizen Kane* became a classic.

5. _____ Faced with declining sales, many car companies in the 1970s laid off workers, closed plants, and borrowed heavily.

6. _____ Last night I sat up looking at my old yearbooks and drinking tea, which filled me with nostalgia.

7. _____ I saw the man who won the Boston Marathon in the airport last week.

8. _____ We missed the bus so we had to take the car to the game with bad tires.

9. _____ She stayed at the Mark Hopkins, one of the most famous hotels in San Francisco.

10. _____ Painted by Picasso in the 1920s, the auctioneer was disappointed so few people bid on the portrait.

Answers appear on the following page.

GET WRITING
AND REVISING

WHAT ARE YOU TRYING TO SAY?

Write a paragraph describing someone who influenced your values or shaped your direction in life—a family member, a friend, a boss, a teacher, a coach. Provide adjectives that describe this person's characteristics and adverbs to describe this person's actions.

_____

_____

_____

_____

_____

_____

_____

_____

_____

_____

_____

_____

_____

_____

_____

_____

_____

_____

_____

_____

Circle each modifying word or phrase and underline the word or words it describes. Are they clearly linked? Are any sentences confusing? Could any sentences be interpreted in different ways? Could your modifiers be located closer to what they describe?

Avoiding Dangling Modifiers

We frequently start or end sentences with modifying words, phrases, or clauses:

> Constructed entirely of plastic . . .
> First described by Italian explorers . . .
> Available in three colors . . .

These modifiers make sense only if they are correctly linked with what they are supposed to modify:

> *Constructed entirely of plastic,* the valve we use weighs less than six ounces.
> Tourists are amazed by the volcano, *first described by Italian explorers.*
> *Available in three colors,* these raincoats are popular with children.

In writing, however, it is easy to create sentences that are confusing or illogical:

> *Constructed entirely of plastic,* we use a valve that weighs less than six ounces.
> The volcano amazes tourists, *first described by Italian explorers.*
> *Available in three colors,* children love these raincoats.

Because the ideas are clear in your mind, even reading your sentences out loud may not help you spot a dangling modifier. Keep this simple diagram in mind:

Modifier, main sentence

Think of the comma as a hook or hinge that links the modifier with what it describes:

> One of the most popular sports cars is the Corvette, *introduced in 1953.*
> *Located near the airport,* the hotel is convenient for conventioneers.

The comma links *introduced in 1953* and *Corvette* and *located near the airport* with *the hotel.*

ANSWERS TO WHAT DO YOU KNOW? ON PAGES 245–246
1. X (the moon did not row), 2. OK, 3. X (*elected in 1960* modifies *Kennedy*, not *Roman Catholic president*), 4. X (*Basing his film* has to modify Welles, not *Citizen Kane*), 5. OK, 6. X (yearbooks, not tea, caused nostalgia), 7. X (the runner did not win a marathon *in the airport*), 8. X (the car, not the game, had *bad tires*), 9. OK, 10. X (the auctioneer was not *painted by Picasso*)

TESTING FOR DANGLING MODIFIERS

Dangling modifiers can be easily missed in routine editing. When you find a sentence that opens or ends with a modifier, apply this simple test:

1. Read the sentence, then turn the modifier into a question, asking who or what is being described?

    <u>Question, Answer</u>

2. The answer to the question follows the comma. If the answer makes sense, the sentence is probably correct. If the answer does not make sense, the sentence likely contains a dangling modifier and requires revision.

Examples:

Running across the street, I was almost hit by a car.

Question: *Who ran across the street?*   Answer: *I*

                                correct

Having run marathons, the mile-long race was no challenge.

Question: *Who has run marathons?*   Answer: *the mile-long race*

                        incorrect and needs revision

Having run marathons, I found the mile-long race no challenge.

EXERCISE 1 Detecting Dangling Modifiers

Write OK *for each correct sentence and* DM *to indicate those with dangling modifiers.*

1. _____ Many American students assume slavery could have been eliminated only through a violent struggle, having studied the Civil War.

2. _____ Heavily dependent on cheap labor to harvest cotton, Southern states seceded from the United States to maintain slavery.

3. _____ Costing 600,000 lives, many people needed to justify the sacrifices of the Civil War.

4. _____ Although devastating, books and movies portray the Civil War as necessary to end an evil system.

5. _____ Like the United States, slavery was a feature of Brazilian society for three centuries.

6. _____ Having received more slaves from Africa than any other nation, slave labor was an important element of the Brazilian economy.

7. _____ But unlike the United States, slavery was eliminated by the Brazilians without a major conflict.

8. _____ Forced to work in very dangerous conditions, slaves in Brazil had a very high death rate.

9. _____ Relying on fresh shipments of slaves from Africa, Brazil faced a crisis when the international slave trade was abolished in 1850.

10. _____ Confronted with increasing labor shortages, slaves were shipped from one region of Brazil to another.

11. _____ Inspired in part by America's abolition of slavery in 1863, slavery was opposed by many Brazilians.

12. _____ Brazilian abolitionists wanted to free the slaves, demanding reform.

13. _____ Needing slave labor, emancipation was blocked by the nation's wealthy coffee growers.

14. _____ Although resisted by many slave owners, the Brazilian government took steps to eradicate slavery.

15. _____ Unlike the United States, slavery was not abolished all at once in Brazil.

16. _____ Seeking to dismantle slavery in stages, children born to slaves after 1871 were declared free.

17. _____ Many coffee growers rebelled against the federal government, hoping to preserve slavery.

18. _____ Although it claimed several thousand lives, the conflict to end slavery in Brazil was far less devastating than the American Civil War.

19. _____ Having depended on slave labor to harvest cotton, the Southern economy faced a labor shortage after the Civil War.

20. _____ Benefiting from the world's increasing demand for rubber, the Brazilian economy was able to flourish despite the loss of slave labor.

EXERCISE 2 Detecting Dangling Modifiers

Write OK *for each correct sentence and* DM *to indicate those with dangling modifiers.*

1. _____ Born in Texas in 1908, Lyndon Baines Johnson became one of the most popular and most controversial American presidents.

2. _____ Johnson taught migrant schoolchildren in one of state's poorest regions, after graduating from Southwest Texas State Teachers College.

3. _____ Deeply moved by the poverty of his students, it became clear to Johnson that many people in the 1930s needed help.

4. _____ Learning that a Texas congressman had an opening for an assistant, Johnson saw an opportunity to further his career and help people in Texas.

5. _____ Inspired by President Roosevelt's New Deal programs, the chance to work in Washington appealed to Johnson.

6. _____ Quickly mastering the workings of government, it seemed to Johnson that the way to succeed in politics was to learn to make alliances to get bills passed.

7. _____ Elected to fill a vacant seat in the House of Representatives in 1937, Johnson soon developed a reputation for being hardworking and ambitious.

8. _____ Elected to the Senate in 1948, Johnson became the youngest majority leader in history.

9. _____ Realizing he would have to win Southern votes, Johnson accepted John F. Kennedy's offer to run as vice president.

10. _____ Balancing Kennedy's youth and Eastern image, Kennedy benefited from Johnson, who was popular with many Southerners.

11. _____ Overshadowed by Kennedy and his Ivy League advisers, Johnson felt ignored as vice president and considered leaving politics.

12. _____ Becoming president when John F. Kennedy was assassinated in Dallas, Johnson moved quickly to comfort a grieving nation.

13. _____ Reelected in 1964 in a major landslide, Johnson announced plans to build what he called the Great Society.

14. _____ Johnson signed bills to create job training programs, expand public housing, and provide childcare for working mothers, determined to reduce poverty.

15. _____ He secured enough congressional support to pass a voting rights act for African Americans, having been able to persuade Southern Democrats as well as Republican opponents.

16. _____ Advised to continue American support to South Vietnam, Johnson's decision to begin bombing North Vietnam increased the nation's role in Indochina.

17. _____ Sending additional troops to Vietnam in 1965, the commitment to prevent a Communist takeover of South Vietnam deepened.

18. _____ Costing billions of dollars and thousands of American lives, the war in Vietnam became controversial.

19. _____ Refusing to serve in what they saw as a bloody and meaningless conflict, Johnson was seen by many young people as a symbol of American imperialism.

20. _____ Unable to face the stress of office, Johnson decided not to run for re-election in 1968, ending one of the century's most tumultuous presidential administrations.

EXERCISE 3 Opening Sentences with Modifiers

Create a complete sentence by adding an independent clause to logically follow the opening modifying phrase. Test each sentence to make sure you avoid a dangling modifier. Make sure you create a complete sentence and not a fragment (see Chapter 14).

1. Popular with teenagers, _____

_____

2. Imported from France, _____

_____

3. Having worked all night, _____

_____

4. Damaged by last night's storm, _____

_____

5. Widely advertised on television, _____

_____

EXERCISE 4 Ending Sentences with Modifiers

Create a complete sentence by adding an independent clause to logically precede the modifying phrase. Test each sentence to make sure you avoid a dangling modifier. Make sure you create a complete sentence and not a fragment (see Chapter 14).

1. _____

_____, facing a massive lawsuit.

2. _____

_____, driving late at night with little sleep.

3. _____

_____, suffering from a serious knee injury.

4. _____

_____, unwilling to talk to reporters.

5. _____

_____, written by Edgar Allan Poe.

EXERCISE 5 Eliminating Dangling Modifiers

Rewrite each of the following sentences to eliminate dangling modifiers. Add needed words or phrases, but do not alter the basic meaning of the sentence.

1. Facing eviction, the landlord demanded police protection from angry tenants.

_____

_____

2. Opened just four years ago, city officials were dismayed that the stadium needed major repairs.

_____

_____

3. Having won eight games in a row, fans cheered when the coach appeared.

_____

_____

4. Heading north to avoid the storm, the passengers were informed by the captain that their arrival would be delayed.

_____

_____

5. *Gone with the Wind* has enthralled readers all over the world, having been translated into dozens of languages.

_____

_____

Misplaced Modifiers

Misplaced modifiers can occur anywhere in a sentence. Because they are often not set off by commas, they can be harder to detect:

I saw the quarterback who threw two touchdown passes *in the post office* yesterday.

The film won an Academy Award *which cost less than a million dollars to produce.*

Reading sentences out loud can help you detect misplaced modifiers, but even this may not help you avoid some of them. Because the ideas are clear in your mind, you may have a hard time recognizing the confusion your sentence creates. You know that you saw the quarterback in the post office, not that he threw two touchdown passes in the post office. You know that it was the film, not the award, that cost less than a million dollars. Readers, however, rely on the way your words appear on the page.

EXERCISE 6 Detecting Misplaced Modifiers

Write OK *for each correct sentence and* MM *for sentences containing a misplaced modifier.*

1. _____ One of the ideals of the Olympic Games is fostering peace through international athletic competition free of politics and ideology.

2. _____ The games, however, could not be fully shielded from world events, which often led to protests and cancellations.

3. _____ The first modern Olympics were held in Greece, where the ancient games were held in 1896.

4. _____ World War I canceled the 1916 games which claimed the lives of an entire generation of young athletes.

5. _____ The Olympic Games resumed after the war made more popular by the advent of radio and motion pictures.

6. _____ The 1932 games were held in Los Angeles, which desperately needed economic stimulation during the depression.

7. _____ Hitler used the 1936 Berlin games to showcase his nation's achievements eager to impress foreign visitors.

8. _____ In Berlin the Germans constructed a massive new stadium Hitler hoped to make the most impressive capital city in the world.

9. _____ The Nazis removed anti-Jewish signs that might temporarily offend foreign visitors.

10. _____ Hitler could not avoid controversy although attempting to be a gracious host.

11. _____ He was accused of shunning black athletes who refused to shake hands with the winners.

12. _____ The Nazi Olympics troubled many observers, who felt the games were exploited for propaganda purposes.

13. _____ Hitler's invasion of Poland started World War II and caused the cancellation of the Olympic Games three years later.

14. _____ The games flourished after the war still shadowed by politics and controversy.

15. _____ During the 1968 games in Mexico City two African American athletes raised their fists during an awards ceremony seen as a celebration of black power.

16. _____ Many Mexican students were beaten and shot by police seeking to use the games to bring attention to their antigovernment protests.

17. _____ Eleven Israeli athletes were murdered by Arab terrorists at the 1972 Munich games watched by millions around the world.

18. _____ President Carter pulled the United States out of the Moscow Olympics to protest the Soviet invasion of Afghanistan in 1980.

19. _____ Four years later when the games were held in Los Angeles, the Soviets, citing security reasons, refused to send athletes.

20. _____ In recent years, members of the International Olympic committee have been accused of taking bribes from representatives of cities hoping to host future games.

EXERCISE 7 Correcting Misplaced Modifiers

Rewrite each of the following sentences to eliminate misplaced modifiers. Add needed words or phrases, but do not alter the basic meaning of the sentence.

1. **The mayor tried to calm the anxious crowd speaking on television.**

   _____

   _____

2. **The paramedics who were badly injured rushed accident victims to the hospital.**

   _____

   _____

3. **The tourists requested Paris attorneys unfamiliar with French law.**

   _____

   _____

4. **The judge ordered psychiatric counseling for the defendant who feared the young woman might attempt suicide.**

   _____

   _____

5. We served lamb chops to our guests covered in mint sauce.

_____

_____

EXERCISE 8 Detecting Dangling and Misplaced Modifiers in Context

Underline dangling and misplaced modifiers in the following passage.

No other radio program had more impact on the American public than Orson Welles's famous "War of the Worlds" broadcast. Only twenty-three at the time, Welles's newly formed Mercury Theatre aired weekly radio productions of original and classic dramas. On October 30, 1938, an Americanized version of H. G. Wells's science fiction novel *The War of the Worlds* was aired by the Mercury Theatre, which described a Martian invasion.

Regular listeners understood the broadcast was fiction and sat back to enjoy the popular program. The play opened with the sounds of a dance band. Suddenly, the music was interrupted by a news report that astronomers on the surface of Mars had detected strange explosions. The broadcast returned to dance music. But soon the music was interrupted again with reports of a meteor crash in Grovers Mills, New Jersey. The broadcast then dispensed with music, and a dramatic stream of reports covered the rapidly unfolding events.

Equipped with eerie special effects, the strange scene in the New Jersey countryside was described by anxious reporters. The crater, listeners were told, was not caused by a meteor but by some strange spacecraft. A large, octopuslike creature emerged from the crater, presumably coming from Mars, and blasted onlookers with powerful death rays.

Regular listeners were gripped by this realistic-sounding drama. However, people who tuned in after the play started assumed the fictional news reports were genuine. New Jersey police stations were bombarded with phone calls from citizens asking about the invasion. Listeners in New Orleans and San Francisco called the police who had friends and relatives in New Jersey asking for news. Assuming the Martians would head toward New York, businesses closed. Bars and restaurants emptied as customers fled to rescue loved ones. Fearing attack, farmers on Long Island grabbed shotguns and stood guard.

The following day, stories about the broadcast made headlines across the country. Reports of accidental shootings and suicides were probably exaggerations, but many newspapers called for congressional hearings, angered that the new medium of radio had been misused. Criticized for creating a panic, Orson Welles reminded people that his show had been broadcast on the eve of Halloween, a day devoted to monsters and mischief.

Oddly enough, this was not the last time the mythic invasion was to cause controversy. In 1944 a Spanish version of the radio drama led listeners in Santiago to panic, believing that Chile was being invaded by Martians. Five years later, a broadcast of the play in Ecuador had a similar result. Angered by the false news of an alien invasion, the Quito radio station was attacked and burned to the ground by a mob.

EXERCISE 9 Using Modifiers

Insert the modifier into each sentence by placing it next to the word or words it describes.

1. Mary took Nancy to New York this summer.
   Insert: *who was born in Manhattan,* to refer to Mary

_____

_____

2. **The FBI closed the offices on Monday.**
   Insert: *which had been conducting an investigation for weeks,* **to refer to the FBI**

_____

_____

3. **The television show cost the network millions in lost advertising revenue.**
   Insert: *which suffered low ratings*

_____

_____

4. **Jean Shepherd's short-story collection** *In God We Trust: All Others Pay Cash* **was published in 1966.**
   Insert: *which later inspired the popular movie* **A Christmas Story**

_____

_____

5. **The missing girl was last seen by her mother.**
   Insert: *who is only three years old*

_____

_____

WORKING TOGETHER

Working with a group of students, revise this notice to eliminate dangling and misplaced modifiers.

Summer Parking Restrictions

This summer campus parking will be greatly limited because of major construction projects. Beginning June 1, students registered for summer classes will have to use orange parking passes. A map of campus parking lots can be found on the college website www.univtenn.edu for summer use. Faculty and administrators are only allowed to use the Lake Street parking lot. Cars will be towed by campus security guards not displaying orange parking passes on their visors.

EXERCISE 10 Cumulative Exercise

Revise each sentence for dangling or misplaced modifiers, fragments, and run-ons.

1. **Assisted by his grandson, the crowd surrounding the injured man as he emerged from the train.**

_____

_____

2. The police focused their entire investigation on Selena Anderson the FBI uncovered evidence implicating other suspects.

_____

_____

3. Shot entirely on location, critics praising the film for its realism.

_____

_____

4. Our company purchases paper products from National Office Supply but we order all other office products from Teldar.

_____

_____

5. We will have to take the bus cars are not allowed beyond this point.

_____

_____

GET THINKING
AND WRITING

CRITICAL THINKING

Do you want to own your own home? Why or why not? Do people who own a home feel different from those who rent? Do most people view owning a home as a major goal in life? Write a paragraph stating your views about owning a home.

WHAT HAVE YOU WRITTEN?

Underline the modifiers in each sentence. Are they properly placed? Are there any sentences that are confusing or could be interpreted in two ways?

WHAT HAVE YOU LEARNED?

Put an X next to each sentence with a dangling or misplaced modifier and OK next to each correct sentence.

1. _____ Reporting engine trouble, the control tower directed the pilot to make a forced landing.

2. _____ Operating in fifteen states, Coffee Express plans to become a national enterprise.

3. _____ Facing his accusers, the defendant insisted he would be acquitted.

4. _____ The cake was appreciated by everyone made of chocolate.

5. ____ Having failed two courses, the dean suggested Diana see a tutor.

6. ____ Although she never owned a pet, Nancy's mother left her entire estate to an animal shelter.

7. ____ The movie tells the story of a young woman coping with depression after the death of her lover in nineteenth-century Boston.

8. ____ Discovered only recently, historians are astounded by Lincoln's diary.

9. ____ Having grown up in Mexico, Nicki speaks excellent Spanish.

10. ____ Afraid of getting another speeding ticket, Sarah drove no faster than 55 mph on the expressway.

Answers appear on the following page.

GET WRITING

What makes a good leader? Describe a boss, teacher, coach, or politician you think demonstrates effective leadership skills.

Write a paragraph that uses examples and short narratives to support your point of view.

WRITING ON THE WEB

Using a search engine such as AltaVista, Yahoo!, or Google, enter terms such as *dangling modifiers* and *misplaced modifier* to locate current sites of interest.

1. Review some current online journals or newspapers to see how writers place modifying words and phrases in sentences.
2. Write a brief e-mail to a friend, then review it for dangling and misplaced modifiers and other errors.

POINTS TO REMEMBER

1. Modifiers are words or phrases that describe other words. To prevent confusion, they must be placed next to what they modify.

2. If sentences begin or end with a modifier, apply this simple test:

   Read the sentence, then turn the modifier into a question, asking who or what is being described:

   Question, Answer

   If the answer makes sense, the sentence is probably correct:

   > Born on Christmas, I never have a birthday party.
   > *Q: Who was born on Christmas?*   *A: I*

   > Correct

   If the sentence does not make sense, it probably contains a dangling modifier and needs revision:

   > Filmed in Iraq, critics praise the movie for its realism.
   > *Q: What was filmed in Iraq?*   *A: critics*

   > Incorrect

   Revisions:
   Filmed in Iraq, the movie was praised by critics for its realism.
   Critics praised the movie filmed in Iraq for its realism.

3. In revising papers, underline modifying words and phrases and circle the words or ideas they are supposed to modify to test for clear connections.

Answers to What Have You Learned? on Pages 256–257
1. X (see page 245), 2. OK, 3. OK, 4. X (see page 252), 5. X (see page 245), 6. OK, 7. X (see page 252), 8. X (see page 245), 9. OK, 10. OK

Understanding Parallelism

© Getty Images

What can the military do to protect the United States against terrorism? Should it focus on defending airports and public buildings or on tracking down terrorists overseas?

Write a paragraph that describes one or two things the military can do to make the country safer.

What Is Parallelism?

At first glance, the word *parallelism* may remind you of geometry. Some students find it abstract and confusing. But the concept is very simple: to make sentences easy to understand, pairs and lists of words have to *match;* they have to be all nouns, all adjectives, all adverbs, or all verbs in the same form. To be balanced, pairs and lists should be all phrases or clauses with matching word patterns. In most instances, we use parallelism without problem. When you write a shopping list, you automatically write in parallel form:

> We need *pens, pencils, paper, stamps,* and *envelopes.* [all nouns]

It is easy, however, to make errors when, instead of listing single nouns, you list phrases:

> The associate dean must approve faculty pay raises, schedule classes, order textbooks, and when the dean is unavailable take her place.

The last item, *when the dean is unavailable take her place,* does not match the other items in the list:

> The associate dean <u>must</u> . . . *approve* faculty pay raises
> . . . *schedule* classes
> . . . *order* textbooks
> . . . *when the dean* is unavailable take her place

Revised
The associate dean <u>must</u> *approve* faculty pay raises, *schedule* classes, *order* textbooks, and *take* the dean's place when she is unavailable.

Not Parallel	*Parallel*
Both *running* and *to swim* are good exercise.	Both *running* and *swimming* are good exercise.
We walked *slowly, quietly, and felt fear.*	We walked *slowly, quietly,* and *fearfully.*
Anger, doubting, and *depression* nagged him.	*Anger, doubt,* and *depression* nagged him.
Students should *read* carefully, *review* lecture notes, and *assignments* should be completed on time.	Students should *read* carefully, *review* lecture notes, and *complete* assignments on time.

WHAT DO YOU KNOW?

Label each sentence OK *for correct and* FP *for faulty parallelism.*

1. _____ The concert was loud, colorful, and many people attended.

2. _____ The film lacked a clear narrative, logical transitions, and the dialogue was unbelievable.

3. _____ The president's policy divided Congress, angered critics, and alienated voters.

4. _____ Taking care of the elderly and the education of children are important elements of our plan.

5. _____ She was unable to speak or sing and had to be replaced by her understudy at the last minute.

Answers appear on the following page.

WHAT ARE YOU TRYING TO SAY?

GET WRITING
AND REVISING

Most jobs require special skills, abilities, or aptitudes. Describe the job skills needed in the career you hope to pursue, or explain the abilities people needed—or lacked— in a job you had in the past.

_____

_____

_____

_____

_____

_____

_____

_____

_____

_____

_____

_____

_____

_____

_____

_____

_____

WHAT HAVE YOU WRITTEN?

Read your sentences out loud. Did you create sentences that contain pairs of words or phrases or lists? If so, are the items parallel—do they match each other?

Overcoming Parallelism Errors

Mistakes in parallelism are easy to make. If you are describing a close friend, for example, a number of ideas, words, or phrases may come to mind. They may be nouns, adjectives, or verbs:

bright   *caring*   *works well with children*   *teacher*

In putting these ideas together, make sure they are parallel:

Not Parallel
She is a teacher who is bright, caring, and works well with children.

Parallel
She is a bright, caring teacher who works well with children.
She is a teacher who is bright, caring, and good with children.

TESTING FOR PARALLELISM

The simplest way of determining if a sentence is parallel is to test each element to see if it matches the base sentence:

Example: The car is new, well maintained, and costs very little.

The car is *new.*
The car is *well maintained.*
The car is *costs very little.*

The last item does not match and should be revised:

The car is new, well maintained, and inexpensive.
The car is *new.*
The car is *well maintained.*
The car is *inexpensive.*

A TIP ON REVISING FAULTY PARALLELISM

Sometimes you may find it difficult to make all the items in a sentence match. You might not be able to think of a suitable noun form for an adjective. In making the sentence parallel, you may find yourself having to change a phrase you like or create something that sounds awkward. In some cases you may have simply been trying to get too many ideas in a single sentence.

It may be easier in some instances to break up an unparallel sentence. It is easier to make two short sentences parallel than one long one.

(continued)

> **Not Parallel**
> Example: The new dean will be responsible for scheduling new courses, expanding student services, upgrading the old computer labs, and most important, become a strong advocate for students.
>
> **Parallel**
> The new dean will be responsible for *scheduling* new courses, *expanding* student services, and *upgrading* the old computer labs. Most important, she must become a strong advocate for students.

EXERCISE 1 Detecting Faulty Parallelism

Write OK *by each correct sentence and* NP *by each sentence that is not parallel.*

1. _____ American football is exciting, fast paced, and can captivate fans.

2. _____ The origins of the game remain open to debate and controversial.

3. _____ Sports historians agree that American football includes the speed of soccer and the contact of rugby.

4. _____ In the early 1800s American college students played a running game that was often marked by violent confrontations and serious injuries often occurred.

5. _____ The games were more like gang fights, having few officials, limited rules, and excessive violence not being penalized.

6. _____ Harvard and Yale briefly banned these games, disturbed by the players' violence and fans behaving poorly.

7. _____ Rutgers played Princeton in 1869, both fielding teams of twenty-five men who could not run with the ball or use their hands.

8. _____ Following soccer rules, players advanced the ball down the field by kicking the ball or striking it with their heads.

9. _____ In 1874 McGill University was invited to play Harvard, and this historic game created the rules and set the tone for modern football.

10. _____ During practice Harvard students watched the Canadian players catch, hold, and to run with the ball.

11. _____ McGill students were playing rugby, a game Harvard players had never seen or played.

12. _____ To create a fair game, the teams decided on a compromise, using soccer rules in the first half and to follow rugby rules in the second half.

13. _____ Although awkward, confusing, and at times humorous, this game was very historic.

14. _____ Allowing soccer players to catch the ball and running down the field introduced elements that would be incorporated into a whole new game.

15. _____ Walter Camp wrote a book about football in 1891, limiting teams to eleven men and establishing the line of scrimmage.

16. _____ Early football games, however, remained violent and boredom.

17. _____ On offense, players formed a wedge and trying to plough through the defensive line.

18. _____ Resembling tug-of-war, these games saw little movement and touchdowns were few.

19. _____ In later years, coaches introduced new rules to the game to make it faster, less violent, and more exciting to watch.

20. _____ Knute Rockne energized the sport by emphasizing the forward pass, creating the sharply competitive and high-scoring game of modern football.

EXERCISE 2 Revising Sentences to Eliminate Faulty Parallelism

Rewrite each sentence to eliminate faulty parallelism. You may have to add words or invent phrases, but do not alter the meaning of the sentence. In some cases, you may create two sentences.

1. In the 1990s the Internet revolutionized business, education, the media, even a grandmother keeping in touch with her children.

   _____

   _____

2. Today, for instance, someone interested in restoring Model T's can easily and without a lot of expense connect with Model T enthusiasts all over the world.

   _____

   _____

3. A small entrepreneur can participate in the global economy without the cost of maintaining branch offices, mailing catalogs, or television commercials.

   _____

   _____

4. People who never thought they would use a computer now e-mail friends, search the web for recipes and childcare tips, buy airline tickets online, and tracking their stock portfolios.

   _____

   _____

   _____

5. No single person invented the Internet, but Robert E. Taylor played a role in designing the first networks and to overcome numerous obstacles.

   _____

   _____

   _____

6. While working for the Department of Defense in the late 1960s, Taylor explored ways to connect computer networks and making them work together.

   _____

   _____

   _____

7. At that time computers were like paper notebooks, so that whatever was entered into one could not be transferred to another without reentering the data, which was costly and took a lot of time.

_____

_____

_____

8. The military wanted to streamline and simplifying its procurement process.

_____

_____

_____

9. The government provided grants to corporations and universities to stimulate research into connecting computers, overcome incompatibility, and developing standards.

_____

_____

_____

10. When personal computers became affordable, it was only a matter of time before the Internet would link individuals to a worldwide network, revolutionize education and business, and entire subcultures would be created.

_____

_____

_____

EXERCISE 3 Revising Sentences to Eliminate Faulty Parallelism

Rewrite each sentence to eliminate faulty parallelism. You may have to add words or invent phrases, but do not alter the meaning of the sentence. In some cases, you may create two sentences.

1. In 1907 the Plaza Hotel opened in New York, featuring marble staircases, Irish linen, French crystal, and lace imported from Switzerland.

_____

_____

2. From its grand opening, the Fifth Avenue hotel was associated with the rich, the famous, the talented, and people known for being outrageous.

_____

_____

3. Alfred Vanderbilt, Lillian Russell, Diamond Jim Brady, and Mark Twain attended the opening and noting the hotel's brilliant lobby.

_____

_____

_____

4. A few months after the Plaza opened, Mrs. Patrick Campbell, a famed actress, lit a cigarette in the hotel's Palm Court, shocking the staff and angered guests who had never seen a woman smoke in public.

_____

_____

_____

5. In the 1920s F. Scott Fitzgerald and his wife, Zelda, were spotted frolicking and splash in the lobby fountain.

_____

_____

_____

6. In 1960 the Soviet leader Nikita Khrushchev made headlines and shocking diplomats when he stuck his tongue out at a jeering crowd that gathered while he waited for an elevator.

_____

_____

_____

7. When the Beatles made the Plaza their New York headquarters, the hotel staff had to protect the rock stars from prying reporters, zealous fans, and people hunting for souvenirs.

_____

_____

_____

8. When Cary Grant complained about the hotel's English muffins, the hotel changed its room service policy and providing guests with two full muffins instead of three slices.

_____

_____

9. Featured in movies like _North by Northwest, Plaza Suite, The Great Gatsby, Funny Girl, Arthur,_ and _Crocodile Dundee,_ the Plaza Hotel developed a reputation for style and becoming a New York monument.

_____

_____

10. Despite its historic associations, tasteful elegance, and attending to guests' needs, the Plaza Hotel has usually been granted only four of five possible stars by the famous Mobil guide.

_____

_____

EXERCISE 4 Writing Parallel Sentences

Complete each sentence by adding missing elements, making sure they create a matched pair or a list of matching words or phrases in order to be parallel.

1. To stay healthy, many people exercise regularly, avoid junk food, and _____

    _____.

2. Jogging, swimming, and _____ are good forms of exercise.

3. To be healthy, your meals should be balanced and _____.

4. You should also avoid environmental hazards such as secondhand smoke,

    asbestos, and _____.

5. Taking short naps, talking to friends, listening to soft music, and _____

    _____ can help decrease stress.

6. Getting enough sleep and _____ are important to

    maintain mental health and emotional _____.

7. Some people spend a great deal of time on expensive running shoes, costly

    health club memberships, and _____.

8. However, all you really need are a good pair of running shoes and

    _____ to get started.

9. Too many people attempt to do too much and become so sore and

    _____ they quit.

10. People who want to lose weight should set realistic goals, consult a physician

    before starting any radical diets, and _____

    _____.

WORKING TOGETHER

Working with a group of students, revise the following announcement to eliminate errors in parallelism. Notice how collaborative editing can help detect errors you may have missed.

Job Announcement

The Student Union is seeking a bright, hardworking undergraduate to serve as a special assistant to the union director. The ideal candidate will have a 3.0 GPA or better, good communications skills, and be able to organize clearly. Students with desktop publishing skills, sales ability, and having experience in working in a fast-paced environment are encouraged to apply. Applications can be picked up in U101 or downloading from the Union website www.studentunion.edu.

GET THINKING AND WRITING

CRITICAL THINKING

Write a list of tips to help high school students prepare for college. Try to create at least five recommendations.

WHAT HAVE YOU WRITTEN?

Review each item in your list for faulty parallelism.

GET WRITING

Should tapes made by terrorists be shown on television? Are they news or propaganda? Does showing these tapes inform the public or just help terrorists spread their message?

Write a short paragraph stating your opinion. Give examples of what you think should and should not be broadcast.

© CORBIS SYGMA

WHAT HAVE YOU LEARNED?

Label each sentence OK for correct or FP for faulty parallelism.

1. _____ The new mayor was colorful, energetic, and known for having a hot temper.

2. _____ The dessert had three layers: one filled with chocolate, one lined with pineapple slices, and one using strawberries for decoration.

3. _____ The Fourth of July celebration was subdued, having no fireworks, few picnics, and not a single parade.

4. _____ The circus performers were agile, highly trained, and they surprised us by being so articulate.

5. _____ The drought was responsible for destroying crops, creating fire hazards, and decimating cattle herds.

Answers appear on the following page.

WRITING ON THE WEB

Using a search engine such as AltaVista, Yahoo!, or Google, enter terms such as *faulty parallelism* and *writing parallel sentences* to locate current sites of interest.

1. Review some current online journals or newspapers to see how writers state ideas in parallel form.
2. Write a brief e-mail to a friend describing some recent activities or a person you have met. Review your sentences to see if pairs and lists of words and phrases are parallel.

POINTS TO REMEMBER

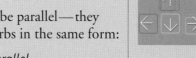

1. Words and phrases that appear as pairs or lists must be parallel—they must match and be nouns, adverbs, adjectives, or verbs in the same form:

Not Parallel	*Parallel*
Swimming and *to fish* are fun.	*Swimming* and *fishing* are fun.
She is *bright, witty,* and *has charm*.	She is *bright, witty,* and *charming*.
He must *design* the building, *establish* the budget, and *workers* must be hired.	He must *design* the building, *establish* the budget, and *hire* the workers.

2. You can discover errors in parallelism by testing each element in the pair or series with the rest of the sentence to see if it matches:

Whomever we hire will have to collect the mail, file reports, answer the phone, update the website, and accurate records must be maintained.

Whomever we hire will have to . . . *collect the mail*
file reports
answer the phone
update the website
accurate records must be
maintained

The last item does not match *will have to* and needs to be revised to be parallel with the other phrases in the list:

Whomever we hire will have to collect the mail, file reports, answer the phone, update the website, and *maintain accurate records*.

3. If you find it difficult to make a long or complicated sentence parallel, consider creating two sentences. In some instances, it is easier to write two short parallel lists than a single long one.

ANSWERS TO WHAT HAVE YOU LEARNED? ON PAGE 268
1. FP (see page 260), 2. FP (see page 260), 3. OK, 4. FP (see page 260), 5. OK

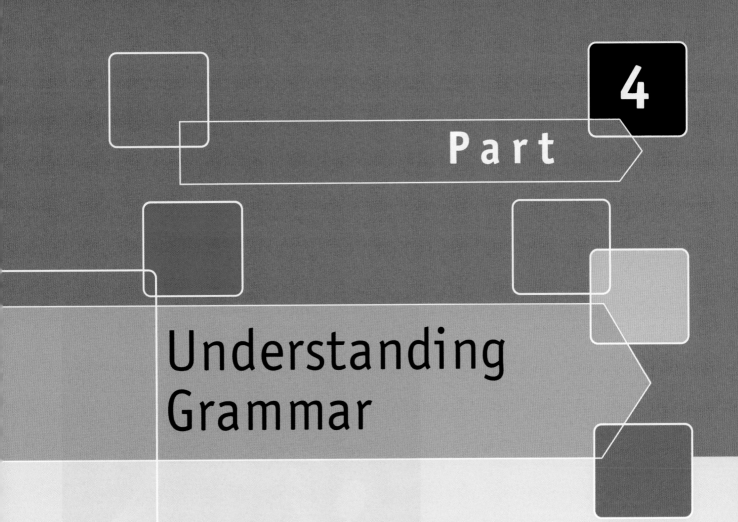

Part 4

Understanding Grammar

Subject-Verb Agreement

© Sandy Clark/Index Stock Imagery

What does this image mean to you? Is it just a picture of a girl in a costume, or does it show how attitudes about boys and girls have changed?

Write a paragraph describing what this picture represents to you.

What Is Subject-Verb Agreement?

The most important parts of any sentence are the *subject*—the actor or main idea—and the *verb*—a word or words that express action (*run, walk, argue*) or link the subject with other ideas (*is, are, was, were*). The subject and verb work together to state a *complete thought* and create a sentence:

Nancy *sells* insurance.   Nancy *is* smart.

To make sentences clear, it is important that subjects and verbs agree—that they match in number. *Singular subjects require singular verbs; plural subjects require plural verbs:*

Singular   **Plural**
The <u>boy</u> *walks* to school.   The <u>boys</u> *walk* to school.
The <u>bus</u> *was* late.   The <u>buses</u> *were* late.
The <u>memo</u> *is* on your desk.   The <u>memos</u> *are* on your desk.

In most cases you add an *s* or *es* to a noun to make it plural and add an *s* or *es* to a verb to make it singular.

Singular and plural verbs occur only in first and third person:

	Singular	**Plural**
First person:	I *am*	We *are*
Third person:	He *was*	They *were*

In second person, only the plural verb is used:

You *are* a person I can trust.   You *are* people I can trust.

WHAT DO YOU KNOW?

Select the correct verb in each sentence.

1. _____ The principal, backed by students and parents, (refuses/refuse) to cancel the prom.

2. _____ Fifteen days (don't/doesn't) give us enough time to finish the project.

3. _____ Where (is/are) the plan the students promised to send to the faculty committee?

4. _____ One of our students (works/work) at the mall.

5. _____ She (don't/doesn't) seem to understand the problem.

   Answers appear on the following page.

WHAT ARE YOU TRYING TO SAY?

Write a brief paragraph describing activities you and your family enjoy.

_____

_____

_____

_____

_____

_____

_____

_____

_____

_____

_____

_____

WHAT HAVE YOU WRITTEN?

Circle the subjects and underline the verbs in each sentence. Do the subjects and verbs match so that your sentences clearly identify which activities are singular and which are plural? Do your verbs show which things your family enjoys as a group and which are enjoyed by a single person?

Grammar Choices and Meaning

Matching subjects and verbs is not just a matter of avoiding a grammar mistake but of making your meaning clear. Changing a verb from singular to plural changes the meaning of a sentence:

Sentence	Meaning
Singular	
My accountant and adviser *is* coming.	*One person is both an accountant and an adviser.*
Plural	
My accountant and adviser *are* coming.	*The accountant and adviser are two individuals.*
Singular	
The desk and chair *is* on sale.	*The desk and chair is sold as one item.*
Plural	
The desk and chair *are* on sale.	*The desk and chair are sold separately.*

Singular
His drinking and driving *is*
unacceptable.

*One activity, indicating drunk
driving.*

Plural
His drinking and driving *are*
unacceptable.

*Two activities, indicating excessive
drinking and bad driving but not
necessarily drunk driving.*

Singular
Bacon and eggs *is* on the menu.

*Bacon and eggs served as a single
dish.*

Plural
Bacon and eggs *are* on the menu.

*The menu lists both bacon and egg
dishes.*

Before the Civil War, for example, the noun *United States* often appeared as a plural to emphasize the independence of each state. After the Civil War, in a desire to unite the country, writers began using *United States* as a singular noun.

EXERCISE 1 Choosing the Correct Verb

Write out the subject and correct verb in each sentence.

	Subject	Verb
1. The stock market (attracts/attract) speculators and investors.	_____	_____
2. A speculator (expects/expect) to reap a fortune with a fast deal or a hot tip.	_____	_____
3. Investors (plans/plan) to increase their wealth over time by researching the market.	_____	_____
4. Both speculators and investors (has/have) been known to achieve great wealth.	_____	_____
5. Investors (buy/buys) a variety of stocks.	_____	_____
6. A speculator, however, (is/are) likely to gamble everything on a single tip.	_____	_____
7. Speculators (rely/relies) on getting the odd bit of information about a buyout or a lawsuit.	_____	_____
8. Most people (has/have) no access to this kind of information.	_____	_____
9. A person saving for retirement (need/needs) to be careful about following a stock tip.	_____	_____
10. Too often tips (is/are) inaccurate or misleading.	_____	_____

Special Nouns and Pronouns

In most cases it is easy to tell whether a noun is singular or plural: most nouns add an *s* to become plural. But some nouns are misleading.

- Not all nouns add an *s* to become plural:

  deer   children   women   people

- Some nouns that end in *s* and look like plurals are singular:

  economics   mathematics   athletics   physics
  Mathematics *is* my toughest course.   Economics *demands* accurate data.

- Some nouns that may refer to one item are plural:

  pants   gloves   scissors   fireworks
  My scissors *are* dull.   *Are* these your gloves?

- Proper nouns that look plural are singular if they are names of companies, organizations, or titles of books, movies, television shows, or works of art:

  General Motors   *The Three Musketeers*   The Urban League
  General Motors *is* building a   *The Three Musketeers is*
  new engine.   funny.

- Units of time and amounts of money are generally singular:

  Twenty-five dollars *is* a lot for a T-shirt.   Two weeks *is* not enough time.

  They appear as plurals to indicate separate items:

  Three dollars *were* lying on the table.   My last weeks at camp *were* unbearable.

Group Nouns

Group nouns—nouns that describe something with more than one unit or member—can be singular or plural, depending on the meaning of the sentence.

COMMON GROUP NOUNS

audience	committee	faculty	number
board	company	family	public
class	crowd	jury	team

In most instances, group nouns are singular because they describe a group working together as a unit:

"Faculty Accepts School Board Offer"   [headline describing teachers acting as a group]

Group nouns are plural when they describe a group working independently:

"Faculty Protest School Board Offer"   [headline describing teachers
                                             acting individually]

Some group nouns are conventionally used as plurals because we think of them as
individuals rather than a single unit:

The Rolling Stones *are* releasing a new CD.   The Packers *play* the Bears on
                                                Sunday.

EXERCISE 2 **Choosing the Correct Verb with Special and Group Nouns**

Circle the correct verb in each sentence.

1. The United Nations (is/are) headquartered in New York City.

2. *Three Men and a Baby* (is/are) available on DVD.

3. The League of Women Voters (sponsor/sponsors) upcoming debates.

4. My trousers (is/are) ripped.

5. After six days of tense deliberations, the jury now (declares/declare) a
   verdict.

6. Our football team (plays/play) only five games on the road next season.

7. The Yankees (is/are) heading to the dugout.

8. Physics (is/are) challenging.

9. Naturally, you (plans/plan) to take a long vacation this summer,
   don't you?

10. The orchestra (travels/travel) by bus.

Hidden Subjects

In some sentences the subject is not easily spotted, and it is easy to make mistakes
in choosing the right verb.

- *Subjects followed by prepositional phrases:*

  Incorrect
  One of my oldest friends are visiting from New York.

  Correct
  One of my oldest friends *is* visiting from New York.

  [*Friends* is plural, but it is not the subject of the sentence; the subject is
  One, which is singular.]

  Incorrect
  Development of housing projects and public highways demand public
  support.

  Correct
  Development of housing projects and public highways demand*s* public
  support.

  [*Projects* and *highways* are plural, but the subject is *Development,* which is
  singular.]

Remember, the subject of a sentence does not appear in a prepositional phrase.

Make sure that you identify the key word of a subject and determine whether it is singular or plural:

The *price* of textbooks and school supplies *is* rising.   [singular]

The *prices* of gold *are* rising.   [plural]

Prepositions are words that express relationships between ideas, usually regarding time and place:

above	before	with	across
over	during	without	to
under	after	within	toward
below	since	from	of
around	like	near	off
past	except	like	along
against	inside	outside	among

- *Subjects followed by subordinate words and phrases.* In many sentences the subject is followed by words or phrases set off by commas. These additional words are subordinate—extra information that is not part of the main sentence. They should not be mistaken for compound subjects:

The teacher <u>and</u> the students *are* filing a complaint to the school board.
    [Plural *and* links *teacher* + *students* to form a compound subject.]
The teacher, supported by students, *is* filing a complaint with the school board.
    [Singular *is* and commas indicate students are subordinate and not part of the subject.]

- *Subjects following possessives.* It can be easy to choose the wrong verb if the subject follows a possessive noun:

Incorrect
The town's business leaders is debating the new bill.

Correct
The town's business leaders *are* debating the new bill.
    [The subject is not *town* but *leaders,* which is plural.]

Incorrect
The students' proposal fail to address the problem.

Correct
The students' proposal *fails* to address the problem.
    [The subject is not *students* but *proposal,* which is singular.]

POINT TO REMEMBER

The subject is never the word with the apostrophe but what follows it.

- *Inverted subjects and verbs.* In some sentences the usual subject-verb order is inverted or reversed, so the subject follows the verb:

Singular
Here *is* a <u>book</u> you will like.
There *is* a <u>letter</u> for you.
There *was* no <u>call</u> for you today.
Outside the city *lives* a <u>poor family</u>.

Plural
Here *are* the <u>books</u> you ordered.
There *are* several <u>letters</u> for you.
There *were* two <u>calls</u> for you today.
Outside the city *live* <u>the poor</u>.

EXERCISE 3 Choosing the Correct Verb with Hidden or Complex Subjects

Circle the correct verb in each sentence.

1. The creativity and originality of Hollywood filmmakers (has/have) excited both critics and fans around the world.
2. When (is/are) the coach and several players meeting with the dean to seek more funds?
3. The president, pressured by key senators, (is/are) going to address Congress.
4. There (is/are) no children attending the party.
5. Who (buys/buy) a car with cash these days?
6. After the blizzard, the unavailability of snowplows and trucks (was/were) frustrating.
7. Key supporters of the mayor (was/were) unwilling to believe the growing reports of corruption in city hall.
8. There (is/are) no plans for urban renewal or community development in the new budget.
9. Why (is/are) no reports available on your accident?
10. The new drug's effects (is/are) more powerful than expected.

"Either . . . Or" Subjects

More than one subject may appear in a sentence, but that does not automatically mean that the verb should be plural:

My aunt *and* my sister *are* taking me to the airport.   [aunt + sister = two people (plural)]
My aunt *or* my sister *is* taking me to the airport.   [aunt OR sister = one person (singular)]

Remember, the conjunctions *or* and *nor* mean "one or the other but not both."

- If both subjects are singular, the verb is singular:

Neither the teacher *nor* the principal *is* responsible.
Mathematics *or* physics *was* required.
My father *or* my brother *drives* us to school.

- If both subjects are plural, the verb is plural:

  Neither the teachers *nor* the parents *are* responsible.
  Mathematics books *or* physics lectures *were* helpful.
  Our fathers *or* our brothers *drive* us to school.

- If one subject is singular and one subject is plural, the subject closer to the verb determines whether it is singular or plural:

  Neither the teacher *nor* the parents *are* responsible.   [plural]
  A mathematics book *or* the physics lectures *are* helpful.   [plural]
  Our fathers *or* my brother *drives* us to school.   [singular]

With "either . . . or" sentences, it is important to focus on special and group nouns:

Neither the judge nor the jury *is* going to decide her ultimate fate.   [*"Jury"* is singular.]

The parents or the class *complains* about the new teacher.   [*"Class"* is singular.]

English or social studies *is* going to be taught online this fall.   [*"Social studies"* is singular.]

Indefinite Pronouns

Indefinite pronouns can be singular or plural, but most are singular.

INDEFINITE PRONOUNS

Singular Indefinite Pronouns

another	each	everything	nothing
anybody	either	neither	somebody
anyone	everybody	nobody	someone
anything	everyone	no one	something

<u>Anything</u> *is* possible.   <u>No one</u> *attends* those meetings.   <u>Someone</u> *is* coming.

Plural Indefinite Pronouns

both	few	many	several

<u>Both</u> *are* missing.   <u>Few</u> *are* available.   <u>Many</u> *are* called.

Indefinite Pronouns That Can Be Singular or Plural Depending on Meaning

all	any	more	most
none	some		

The children were in a bus crash. <u>Some</u> *were* injured.   [*Some* refers to *children.* (plural)]

Snow fell all night. <u>Some</u> *has* melted.   [*Some* refers to *snow.* (singular)]

Security is tight. But <u>more</u> *is* needed.   [*More* refers to *security.* (singular)]

Security guards are present. But <u>more</u> *are* needed.   [*More* refers to *guards.* (plural)]

EXERCISE 4 Choosing the Right Verb with "Either . . . Or" and Indefinite Pronouns

Circle the correct verb in each sentence.

1. Either the United States or a coalition of developing nations (is/are) going to organize a policy to reduce Third World debt.

2. Anyone concerned with eliminating poverty (has/have) to be concerned about the effect debt has on emerging nations.

3. Either business leaders or a skilled diplomat (is/are) needed to resolve the problem.

4. In the 1970s many (was/were) convinced that massive loans to poor countries would provide resources needed to reduce poverty and stimulate economic growth.

5. Few (was/were) able to predict that these loans would have a crippling effect on many poor countries.

6. Unfortunately, corruption or mismanagement (was/were) responsible for making poor use of the borrowed funds.

7. Some ventures failed, and many (was/were) barely profitable.

8. In Africa rapid population growth or AIDS (was/were) responsible for placing unexpected stress on already fragile economies.

9. Most (believes/believe) poor countries cannot repay the debts.

10. Leading economists or celebrities (has/have) brought public attention to the problem of Third World debt.

Relative Pronouns: *Who, Which,* and *That*

The words *who, which,* and *that* can be singular or plural, depending on the noun they replace:

Who

Sandy is a person who really *cares*.	[*Who* refers to "a person." (singular)]
They are people who really *care*.	[*Who* refers to "people." (plural)]

Which

He bought a bond, which *was* worthless.	[*Which* refers to "a bond." (singular)]
He bought bonds, which *were* worthless.	[*Which* refers to "bonds." (plural)]

That

She bought a car that *has* no engine.	[*That* refers to "a car." (singular)]
She bought cars that *have* no engines.	[*That* refers to "cars." (plural)]

It is important to locate the exact noun these words refer to in order to avoid making errors:

Incorrect

Vicki is among the athletes who trains off-season.	[*Who* refers to "athletes," not "Vicki."]

Correct

Vicki is among the athletes who *train* off-season.   [plural]

Incorrect

Terry or John is joining the students who is demonstrating.   [*Who* refers to "students," not "Terry or John."]

Correct

Terry or John is joining the students who *are* demonstrating.   [plural]

Incorrect

Listed in the newspapers is a story that reveal a scandal.   [*That* refers to "story," not "newspapers."]

Correct

Listed in the newspapers is a story that *reveals* a scandal.   [singular]

EXERCISE 5 Choosing the Right Verb with *Who, Which,* and *That*

Underline the correct verb in each sentence.

1. The cost of the books that (was/were) ordered last year has doubled.

2. Each of the students who (was/were) chosen by the dean for recognition attended the dinner.

3. Either Jane or Phil will join the teachers who (is/are) reviewing the budget.

4. We spent all our time shopping in stores that (was/were) crowded and overpriced.

5. Jenny's parents joined a committee that (meet/meets) every Friday evening.

6. The United Nations' hunger program that (was/were) so successful in Asia will be expanded next year.

7. Fixing the car cost $650, which (was/were) more than I made all week.

8. Did you see the three dollars that (was/were) left on the table?

9. Juan is one of those students who (is/are) heading to Florida on spring break.

10. I test drove each of the cars that (has/have) been recalled.

EXERCISE 6 Choosing the Right Verb

Underline the correct verb in each sentence.

1. Few people today (is/are) old enough to remember a quiz show called *Twenty-One* that changed television history and triggered a national scandal.

2. The lure of fame and money (was/were) to ruin the career of a rising academic.

3. Allegations by a previously unknown college student (was/were) to expose a scandal that led to congressional hearings and a national moral debate.

4. Herb Stempel was a twenty-nine-year-old college student when he wrote the producers who (was/were) selecting new contestants for *Twenty-One*.

5. Producers selected Stempel, whose photographic memory and knowledge of obscure topics (was/were) to astound viewers.

6. Week after week, millions of Americans (was/were) amazed at Stempel's ability to correctly answer tough questions.

7. Few viewers understood that many of the moments of high drama on the show (was/were) staged.

8. Before the shows, Stempel (was/were) coached by producers, who went over answers and told him when to pause and mop his brow to build tension.

9. Stempel appeared week after week and won a great sum of money, but producers and sponsors (was/were) disappointed by the show's ratings.

10. According to the producers, a more appealing contestant (was/were) needed.

11. Stempel, following instructions from producers, (was/were) told to take a dive, deliberately missing a simple question about his favorite movie.

12. The new winner, Charles Van Doren, (was/were) a handsome young Columbia University professor and son of the noted scholar Mark Van Doren.

13. Also coached on answers, Van Doren appeared week after week, becoming so popular that he (was/were) soon becoming a household name, his face appearing on the cover of *Time* magazine.

14. Seen as a genius, Van Doren was given a lucrative contract to appear on *The Today Show,* but Stempel (was/were) beginning to feel cheated and revealed that the game show was rigged.

15. Admitting before Congress his part in the scheme, Van Doren (was/were) disgraced, losing his television contract, resigning from Columbia, and dropping out of public life.

EXERCISE 7 Making Subjects and Verbs Agree

Complete each of the following sentences, making sure that the verb matches the subject. Write in the present tense—walk/walks, sing/sings, and so on.

1. **One of my neighbors** _____

_____

2. **Both my parents** _____

_____

3. **Either the attorneys or the judge** _____

_____

4. The price of these houses _____

_____

5. The governor, troubled by protests and demonstrations, _____

_____

GET THINKING AND WRITING

CRITICAL THINKING

Do you think public schools should require students to take a foreign language? Would the United States benefit from having more citizens who can speak German, Spanish, Japanese, or Arabic? Why or why not? Write a paragraph stating your opinion.

WHAT HAVE YOU WRITTEN?

1. _Select two sentences with singular verbs from your paragraph and write them below:_

_____

_____

   Read the sentences out loud. Have you identified the right word or words as the subject? Is the subject singular?

2. _Select two sentences with plural verbs and write them below:_

_____

_____

   Read the sentences out loud. Have you identified the right word or words as the subject? Is the subject plural?

3. _Edit your paragraph for fragments (see Chapter 14), comma splices (see Chapter 16), and run-ons (see Chapter 16)._

EXERCISE 8   Cumulative Exercise

Rewrite this passage to eliminate errors in subject-verb agreement, fragments, and run-ons.

Today many colleges offer courses through the Internet. The idea of broadcasting classes are not new, for decades, universities, colleges, and technical institutions has used television to teaching classes. Unlike educational television programs, Internet courses are interactive. Instructors can use chat rooms to hold virtual office hours and class discussions so that a student feel less isolated. Everyone in the class are able to post a paper on a computer bulletin board. Then the teacher or other students adds comments. Course websites with links containing text, audio, and video material. Because of the flexibility of the Internet. A last-minute change or instructions about an upcoming exam is able to be posted for students.

_____

_____

_____

_____

_____

_____

_____

_____

_____

_____

WORKING TOGETHER

Working with a group of students, read this letter and circle any errors in subject-verb agreement. Note how collaborative editing can help detect errors you may have missed on your own.

Dear Student:

The Student Services Committee are hosting a summer job seminar April 15-20. Any student who are interested in finding a job this summer will find this seminar valuable. United Dynamics are sponsoring this program and will be providing information to anyone who are looking for work. All meetings will be held at the Memorial Union, Upper Lounge. Members of the Student Services Committee is available for additional information beginning April 1. A representative or a recruiter from Smith, Watkins, Pierce, and Lang, a national temporary employment agency, meet with interested students Wednesday April 17 from 1:00 to 4:00 p.m. See the Student Union website for a complete schedule and last-minute updates.

© Key Color/Index Stock Imagery

GET WRITING

How were boys and girls raised in the past? Did giving boys and girls clear-cut roles limit their opportunities? Are today's children growing up with more options or less direction?

Write a paragraph about this picture. Does it imply that boys are socially programmed to be violent?

WHAT HAVE YOU LEARNED?

Select the correct verb in each sentence.

1. _____ Each of the children's mothers (expect/expects) a phone call.

2. _____ The farmworkers or the grower (needs/need) to get a lawyer to help with the negotiations.

3. _____ United Airlines (fly/flies) to Atlanta six times a day.

4. _____ Here (is/are) the winning lottery numbers.

5. _____ Where (is/are) the memos I sent last week?

Answers appear on the following page.

WRITING ON THE WEB

Using a search engine such as AltaVista, Yahoo!, or Google, enter terms such as *subject-verb agreement, verbs,* and *verb agreement* to locate current sites of interest.

1. Read online articles from magazines or newspapers and notice the number of group words such as *committee, jury,* or *Senate.*

2. Send an e-mail to a friend and make sure you choose the right verbs in sentences containing "either . . . or" and "which."

POINTS TO REMEMBER

1. Subjects and verb agree, or match, in number:

   Singular subjects take singular verbs:

   The boy *walks* to school.
   The bus *is* late.

   Plural subjects take plural verbs:

   The boys *walk* to school.
   The buses *are* late.

2. Verb choice affects meaning:

   The desk and chair *is* on sale.   [The items are sold as a set. (singular)]
   The desk and chair *are* on sale. [The items are sold separately. (plural)]

3. Group nouns, units of time and money, and some words that appear plural are singular:

   The jury *is* deliberating.
   Fifty dollars *is* not enough.

4. Some nouns that refer to a single item are plural:

   My scissors *are* dull.
   The fireworks *are* starting.

(continued)

POINTS TO REMEMBER *(continued)*

5. *Here* and *there* can precede singular or plural verbs depending on the subject:

   There *is* one girl who wants to join the team.
   Here *are* three girls who want to join the team.

6. The subject of a sentence never appears in a prepositional phrase:

   One of my friends *lives* in Brooklyn.   [*One* is the subject, not *friends*.]
   The prices of oil *are* rising.   [*Prices* is the subject, not *oil*.]

7. Nouns set off by commas following the subject are not part of the subject:

   The teacher, supported by students, *is* protesting. [singular]

8. The subject may follow a possessive:

   Tom's cars *are* brand new.   [*Cars* is the subject.]
   The children's playground *is* open.   [*Playground* is the subject.]

9. *Either . . . or* constructions can be singular or plural:

   If both subjects are singular, the verb is singular:

   Either my aunt or my sister *is* taking me to the airport.

   If both subjects are plural, the verb is plural:

   Either the boys or the girls *are* hosting the party.

   If one subject is singular and the other is plural, the subject closest to the verb determines whether it is singular or plural:

   Either the boy or the girls *are* hosting the party.
   Either the girls or the boy *is* hosting the party.

10. Some indefinite pronouns are singular:

another	each	everything	nothing
anybody	either	neither	somebody
anyone	everybody	nobody	someone
anything	everyone	no one	something

    Anything *is* possible.   Nothing *is* missing.

11. Some indefinite pronouns are plural:

both	few	many	several

    Both *are* missing.   Few *are* available.

12. Some indefinite pronouns can be singular or plural:

all	any	more	most
none	some		

    All the money *is* gone.   All the children *are* gone.

ANSWERS TO WHAT HAVE YOU LEARNED? ON PAGE 286
1. expects (see page 280), 2. needs (see page 280), 3. flies (see page 276), 4. are (see page 279),
5. are (see page 279)

20

Verb Tense, Mood, and Voice

© Annie Griffiths Belt/CORBIS

Did you attend daycare? Have you sent a child to daycare?

Consider your observations and experiences and those of others, then write a paragraph that compares good and bad daycare. Include details and use examples to support your views.

288

WHAT DO YOU KNOW?

Select the correct verb in each sentence.

1. _____ I (didn't/don't) work on Tuesdays.

2. _____ I (didn't/don't) work last Monday.

3. _____ She was born in Austin, which (is/was) the capital of Texas.

4. _____ If I (was/were) unemployed, I would be upset, too.

5. _____ Yesterday, I (drive/drove) home with a flat tire.

6. _____ She (sneak/sneaked) into the dorm after curfew last night.

7. _____ Let's (rise/raise) our glasses to congratulate Ted and Nancy!

8. _____ Don't (sit/set) there; the paint is still wet.

9. _____ She jogs and (swims/swam) to keep in shape.

10. _____ The children have (laid/lain) down for a nap.

Answers appear on the following page.

WHAT ARE YOU TRYING TO SAY?

GET WRITING
AND REVISING

Write a brief paragraph explaining an experience that taught you a lesson. How did a high school coach's lessons on discipline affect how you approach problems today? How did a car accident in high school influence the way you drive now? How did getting into credit card debt a few years ago change your buying habits?

_____

_____

_____

_____

_____

_____

_____

_____

_____

_____

_____

_____

_____

_____

_____

_____

WHAT HAVE YOU WRITTEN?

Read your paragraph out loud and underline the verbs. How did you use verbs to tell time? Is it clear what events or actions took place in the past, which ones began in the past and continue into the present, and which ones take place only in the present?

What Is Tense?

Tense refers to time. In addition to expressing action or linking the subject to other words, verbs tell the time. All actions, events, and conditions take place in time. To communicate effectively, we have to state time relationships accurately. A jury listening to witnesses of an auto accident would pay attention to the timing of events. Did the witness hear the horn before or after the car hit the pedestrian? Did the driver call 911 or her lawyer first? Were the police present at the time a witness claims she saw the driver throw away a liquor bottle? Timing is critical in many sentences. Explaining _when_ something happened can be just as important as telling readers _what_ happened.

Helping Verbs

Verb _tenses_ tell when events or actions occur. _**Helping verbs**_, also called _auxiliary verbs_, often appear with verbs to create tense. Common helping verbs are _be, do, have, can, could, may, might, must, shall, should, will_, and _would_.

Tenses

Tense	Use	Example
present	shows current and ongoing actions	I _drive_ to school.
simple past	shows actions that occurred in the past and do not continue into the present	I _drove_ to school last week.
future	shows future actions	I _will drive_ to school next week.
present perfect	shows actions that began in the past and concluded in the present	I _have_ just _driven_ to school.
past perfect	shows actions concluded in the past before another action occurred	I _had driven_ to school before the storm started on Monday.

Tense	Use	Example
future perfect	shows future actions preceding an action or event further in the future	I *will have driven* 5,000 miles by the time I graduate next May.
present progressive	shows ongoing action	I *am driving* to school.
past progressive	shows actions that were in progress in the past	I *was driving* my old Chevy to school in those days.
future progressive	shows ongoing future actions	Next year I *will be driving* to college.
present perfect progressive	shows actions that began in the past and continue in the present	I *have been driving* to school this winter.
past perfect progressive	shows actions in progress in the past before another past action	I *had been driving* to school until bus service resumed last fall.
future perfect progressive	shows future ongoing actions taking place before a future event	I *will have been driving* for years by the time bus service resumes in March.

This chart may seem complicated, but we use tense every day to express ourselves. Consider the difference in these responses to a question about a friend's health:

She *was* sick.   [past tense (indicates she has recovered from a past illness)]

She *is* sick.   [present tense (indicates she is currently ill)]

She *has been* sick.   [past perfect (indicates past illnesses that continue or an unsure recovery)]

She *will be* sick.   [future (indicates she will be ill in the future)]

We use perfect tenses to explain the differences between events in the recent past and distant past or between the near and far future:

She had won two Grammys when MTV asked her to host a show in 2002.
He will have twenty credits in history by the time he graduates next year.

PROGESSIVE TENSE

Some verbs express actions: *run, buy, sell, paint, create, drive*. Other verbs express conditions, emotions, relationships, or thoughts: *cost, believe, belong, contain, know, prefer, want*. These verbs don't generally use the progressive form:

Incorrect	Citizens of developing countries *are wanting* a higher standard of living.
Correct	Citizens of developing countries *want* a higher standard of living.

Regular and Irregular Verbs

Most verbs are called "regular" because they follow a regular, or standard, form to show tense changes. They add -*ed* to words ending with consonants and -*d* to words ending with an *e*:

Present	Past	Past Participle
walk	walked	walked
create	created	created
cap	capped	capped
develop	developed	developed
paint	painted	painted
rush	rushed	rushed
wash	washed	washed
xerox	xeroxed	xeroxed

VERB ENDING

The verb endings -*s* and -*ed* may be hard to hear when added to words that end in similar sounds. Some people don't pronounce these verb endings in speaking. Make sure to add them when you are writing.

Incorrect	They were *suppose* to give their presentation yesterday. She *learn* quickly.
Correct	They were *supposed* to give their presentation yesterday. She *learns* quickly.

Irregular verbs do not follow the -*ed* pattern.

- Some irregular verbs make no spelling change to indicate shifts in tense:

Present	Past	Past Participle
bet	bet	bet
cost	cost	cost
cut	cut	cut
fit	fit	fit
hit	hit	hit
hurt	hurt	hurt
put	put	put
quit	quit	quit
read	read	read
set	set	set
spread	spread	spread

- Most irregular verbs make a spelling change rather than adding -*ed*:

Present	Past	Past Participle
awake	awoke	awoken
be	was, were	been

Present	Past	Past Participle
bear	bore	borne (not *born*)
become	became	become
begin	began	begun
blow	blew	blown
break	broke	broken
bring	brought	brought
build	built	built
buy	bought	bought
catch	caught	caught
choose	chose	chosen
come	came	come
dive	dove (dived)	dived
do	did	done
draw	drew	drawn
drink	drank	drunk
drive	drove	driven
eat	ate	eaten
feed	fed	fed
feel	felt	felt
fight	fought	fought
fly	flew	flown
forget	forgot	forgotten
forgive	forgave	forgiven
freeze	froze	frozen
get	got	gotten
go	went	gone
grow	grew	grown
hang (objects)	hung	hung
hang (people)	hanged	hanged
have	had	had
hold	held	held
know	knew	known
lay (place)	laid	laid
lead	led	led
leave	left	left
lie (recline)	lay	lain
lose	lost	lost
make	made	made
mean	meant	meant
meet	met	met
pay	paid	paid
ride	rode	ridden
ring	rang	rung
rise	rose	risen
run	ran	run
say	said	said
see	saw	seen
seek	sought	sought

Present	Past	Past Participle
sell	sold	sold
shine	shone	shone
shoot	shot	shot
sing	sang	sung
sink	sank	sunk
sleep	slept	slept
sneak	sneaked	sneaked
	(not *snuck*)	
speak	spoke	spoken
spend	spent	spent
steal	stole	stolen
sting	stung	stung
strike	struck	struck
strive	strove	striven
swear	swore	sworn
sweep	swept	swept
swim	swam	swum
swing	swung	swung
take	took	taken
teach	taught	taught
tear	tore	torn
tell	told	told
think	thought	thought
throw	threw	thrown
understand	understood	understood
wake	woke	woken
weave	wove	woven
win	won	won
write	wrote	written

EXERCISE 1 Supplying the Right Verb

Complete the following sentences by supplying the correct verb form.

1. **Present**   I speak to youth groups.

   Past   I _____ to youth groups.

   Past participle   I have _____ to youth groups.

2. **Present**   I supply computers to schools.

   Past   I _____ computers to schools.

   Past participle   I have _____ computers to schools.

3. **Present**   They buy silk from China.

   Past   They _____ silk from China.

   Past participle   They have _____ silk from China.

4. **Present**   The clothes fit in my suitcase.

   Past   The clothes _____ in my suitcase.

Past participle   The clothes have _____ in my suitcase.

5. Present   Hope springs eternal.

    Past   Hope _____ eternal.

    Past participle   Hope has _____ eternal.

EXERCISE 2 Choosing the Correct Verb

Underline the correct verb form in each sentence.

1. During World War II the world oil supply (is/was) interrupted.

2. German U-boats (sinked/sank) oil tankers crossing the Atlantic.

3. Military and industrial needs (eat/ate) into Britain's limited oil supply.

4. Most English drivers (put/putted) their cars in storage for the duration of the war.

5. Even when convoys (begin/began) to successfully transport oil to Britain, the Allies (face/faced) problems.

6. Once they (invade/invaded) Europe, they would need fuel for tanks, planes, and trucks to succeed.

7. Engineers (design/designed) PLUTO — or Pipe Line Under The Ocean — to pump oil under the English Channel to France.

8. Cut off from imports, the Germans (bore/beared) even greater problems in securing fuel.

9. Scientists had (created/create) a process for converting coal to synthetic gasoline.

10. These efforts, however, (produce/produced) less fuel than needed, so that at war's end many German army vehicles had to be (tow/towed) by farm animals.

EXERCISE 3 Revising Tense Errors

Revise the tense errors in the following passage.

The summer of 1961 seen a great season for the New York Yankees. Two players, Roger Maris and Mickey Mantle, challenge Babe Ruth's record of hitting sixty home runs in a season. The 1927 record seem unbreakable. Despite a slow start that season, Maris soon begin hitting one home run after another, keeping pace with Mickey Mantle. Call the "M&M boys" by sportswriters, Maris and Mantle become national heroes.

As the summer wear on, and both players had hitted over forty home runs, attention grew. Even President Kennedy stop the nation's business to follow their progress. Not everyone is enthusiastic about their hitting. Many Ruth fans, including the baseball commissioner, do not want to saw the classic record breaked. Maris had only play with the Yankees one year, and many New York fans do not consider him worthy to replace Babe Ruth as the home run king. Because the 1961 season is eight games longer than the 1927 season, the baseball commissioner argued it would been unfair to Ruth if a player beated the record because he has extra games.

When Maris break the record during the extended season, he was honored for hitting sixty one home runs. But the record books placed an * after his name to indicate his season is longer than Ruth's. The * tarnish Maris's reputation. In 1991, six years after Maris die, the asterisk was remove from official records.

_____

_____

_____

_____

_____

_____

_____

_____

_____

_____

_____

_____

_____

_____

_____

Problem Verbs: *Lie/Lay, Rise/Raise, Set/Sit*

Some verbs are easily confused. Because they are spelled alike and express similar actions, they are commonly misused. In each pair, only one verb can take direct objects. The verbs *lay, raise,* and *set* take direct objects; *lie, rise,* and *sit* do not.

Lie/Lay

To lie means to rest or recline. You "lie down for nap" or "lie on a sofa." *To lay* means to put something down or set something into position. You "lay a book on a table" or "lay flooring."

Present	Past	Past Participle
lie	lay	lain
lay	laid	laid

To Lie
I love to lie on the beach.
She is lying under the umbrella.

To Lay
We lay ceramic tile using special glues.
They are laying the subfloor today.

Yesterday, I lay on the sofa all day.   Yesterday, we laid the kitchen tile.
I have lain in the sun all summer.   I have laid tile like that before.

Remember: Lie expresses an action done *by* someone or something:

Tom called 911, then *lay* on the sofa waiting for the paramedics.

Lay expresses action done *to* someone or something:

The paramedics *laid* Tom on the floor to administer CPR.

Rise/Raise

To rise means to get up or move up on your own. You "rise and shine" or "rise to the occasion." *To raise* means to lift something or grow something. You "raise a window" or "raise children."

Present	Past	Past Participle
rise	rose	risen
raise	raised	raised

To Rise
They rise every day at six.
He is rising to attention.
The children have risen from their naps.

He rose from the hot tub.

To Raise
Every morning they raise the flag.
He is raising wheat.
The merchants have raised prices again.
He raised his hand for help.

Remember: Rise can refer to objects as well as people:

The bread rises in the oven.   Oil prices are rising.

Set/Sit

To set means to put something in position or arrange in place. You "set down a glass" or "set down some notes." *Set* always takes a direct object. *To sit* means to assume a sitting position. You "sit in a chair" or "sit on a committee."

Present	Past	Past Participle
set	set	set
sit	sat	sat

To Set
The referee sets the ball on the goal line.
She is setting the table.
He set a new Olympic record.
They have set prices even lower.

To Sit
The player sits on the bench.
He is sitting at the table.
She sat in the airport all night.
Eric has sat on the federal bench for ten years.

EXERCISE 4 Choosing the Correct Verb

Underline the correct verb in each sentence.

1. The contractors (lay/laid) the plywood on my driveway.

2. Our prices are (rising/raising), but no one seems to be complaining.

3. Don't let the dogs (sit/set) in the sun without water.

4. The children's behavior (raised/rose) alarm in parents across the country.

5. We (rise/raise) the temperature slowly to prevent damaging the ovens.

6. They (set/sat) down guidelines for all future competitions.

7. We (had laid/had lain) in the snow for hours before help arrived.

8. They (had laid/had lain) the tiles in a random pattern.

9. (Sit/Set) the packages on the table.

10. We (have risen/have raised) the water level in the tanks.

Shifts in Tense

Events occur in time. In writing, it is important to avoid awkward or illogical shifts in time and write in a consistent tense:

Awkward

I *drove* to the beach and *see* Karen working out with Jim.
   past   present

Consistent

I *drove* to the beach and *saw* Karen working out with Jim.
   past   past

or

I *drive* to the beach and *see* Karen working out with Jim.
  present   present

You can change tenses to show a logical shift or change in time:

I *was born* in Chicago but *live* in Milwaukee. Next year I *will move* to New York.
  past   present   future

You can shift tense to distinguish between past events and subjects that are permanent or still operating:

I *worked* in Trenton, which *is* the capital of New Jersey.
  past   present

[Using the past tense *was* to refer to Trenton might lead readers to believe the city is no longer the state capital.]

Changing shifts in tense alters meaning:

Sandy *wrote* for the *Clarion*, which *is* the largest newspaper in the city. past present	[Meaning: Sandy once wrote for the largest newspaper in the city.]
Sandy *writes* for the *Clarion*, which *was* the largest paper in the city. present past	[Meaning: Sandy currently writes for a newspaper that used to be the city's largest.]
Sandy *wrote* for the Clarion, which *was* the largest paper in the city. past past	[Meaning: Sandy once wrote for a newspaper that is no longer the city's largest or has gone out of business.]

In writing about literature and film, you can relate the plot's events in either past or present tense, as long as you are consistent:

Present	*Past*
In *Death of a Salesman* the hero *is* frustrated by his lack of success. He *is* especially tormented by his son's rejection of his values. At sixty-three he *struggles* to make sense of a world he *cannot* control.	In *Death of a Salesman* the hero *was* frustrated by the lack of success. He *was* especially tormented by his son's rejection of his values. At sixty-three he *struggled* to make sense of a world he *could* not control.

One of the most common errors student writers make is beginning a passage in one tense, then shifting when there is no change in time:

I wake up and face another tough day on the job. The building site is getting busier, and the work is getting tougher. I walk to the corner and take the bus to Ben's house, who drives us to work. We stop for coffee, where Ben *broke* the news. He *told* me he *was* thinking of quitting. "I just can't take the stress anymore," he *said* softly. I look at him and realize how exhausted he is.

present

past
present

Revised — Present Tense

I wake up and face another tough day on the job. The building site is getting busier, and the work is getting tougher. I walk to the corner and take the bus to Ben's house, who drives us to work. We stop for coffee, where Ben *breaks* the news. He *tells* me he *is* thinking of quitting. "I just can't take the stress anymore," he *says* softly. I look at him and realize how exhausted he is.

Revised — Past Tense

I *woke* up and *faced* another tough day on the job. The building site *was* getting busier, and the work *was* getting tougher. I *walked* to the corner and *took* the bus to Ben's house, who *drove* us to work. We *stopped* for coffee, where Ben broke the news. He told me he was thinking of quitting. "I just can't take the stress anymore," he said softly. I *looked* at him and *realized* how exhausted he *was*.

Note: The best way to check your work for awkward shifts in tense is to read your essay out loud. It is often easier to hear than to see awkward shifts. Remember to shift tense only where there is a clear change in time.

WORKING TOGETHER

Revise this passage from a student essay to eliminate awkward and illogical shifts in tense. Note: *Some shifts in this passage logically distinguish between past events and current or ongoing conditions or situations.*

```
     I was born in Brooklyn and grew up in Long Island
where my parents live. I planned to become a contrac-
```

tor like my father and my two brothers, both of whom work for a company that installed and repairs swimming pools.

The summer after I graduated from high school, I work for a tree-trimming service in Lawrence. The job is tough. I had to climb trees, saw branches, even cut down whole trees. It was backbreaking work, and even with gloves and protective gear my hands and arms get cut and scraped. I get paid $18.50 an hour but was too exhausted on the weekends to spend much.

One day in August I fell from a tree and break my leg. Unable to work the rest of the summer, I watch TV and surf the Internet. To kill time I even start my own web page. Then it hit me, and I called my boss. I got the idea to have a website for the tree service, showing residents different types of trees, tree diseases, planting problems, and landscaping tips.

My boss ended up hiring me to create a bigger website that let people e-mail pictures of their landscaping problems for preliminary estimate. People like the idea of being able to use the Internet to send in a picture of a tree or some bushes rather than try to explain their problem on the phone. And it saved the company a lot of time and money.

Active and Passive Voice

English has two voices, active and passive. **Active voice** emphasizes the subject—who did the act. **Passive voice** emphasizes to whom or to what an act was done.

Active	*Passive*
The mayor vetoed the bill.	The bill was vetoed by the mayor.
The children greeted their parents.	The parents were greeted by their children.
Sidney selected the restaurant.	The restaurant was selected by Sidney.

Grammar Choices and Meaning

Active voice is generally preferred because it is direct, strong, and clear:

Active
Century 21 sold the house on the corner.
Karen painted the kitchen last night.
Judge Wilson authorized a wiretap.

Passive voice tends to reverse the order, emphasizing the object over the subject—sometimes creating a sentence that reports an action without naming a subject:

Passive
The house on the corner was sold by Century 21.
The kitchen was painted last night by Karen.
The wiretap was authorized.

Passive voice is used when the act is more significant than its cause:

Passive
The plane was refueled by Aviation Services.
My sister's wedding was delayed by rain.
The first baseman was hit by a line drive.

Police officers and other investigators are trained to use passive voice in writing reports to avoid jumping to conclusions. Since active voice makes a strong connection between subject and verb, it can lead writers to make assumptions. By writing in the passive voice, reporting can be made more objective. Facts are presented and events related without stressing cause and effect or assigning responsibility:

Passive
The office manager was found shot to death in his office. His partner was detained for questioning. Traces of gunpowder were found on his hands and clothing. Bloodstains matching the victim's blood type were found on his shirt sleeve.

However, passive voice is also used to *avoid* assigning responsibility:

Passive
Efforts to resuscitate him were made.
Complaints against the teachers were filed.
After the accident, photographs were taken.
Tests were performed on the engine.

In all these questions the "who" is missing. Who tried to resuscitate? Who filed complaints? Who took the photographs? Who performed tests?

EXERCISE 5 Identifying Active and Passive Voice

Write an A *next to sentences in active voice and* P *next to sentences in passive voice.*

1. _____ Erin showed us the new house.

2. _____ The car was examined thoroughly by the police.

3. _____ DNA results were made available to the press.

4. _____ We washed the dishes before we went to bed.

5. _____ My car was stolen last night.

6. _____ Thieves robbed the art museum during the night.

7. _____ The policy was widely rejected by voters.

8. _____ Several arrests were made.

9. _____ The plane landed safely.

10. _____ Students supported the new budget.

EXERCISE 6 Changing Passive to Active Voice

Rewrite these sentences to change them from passive to active voice. (Note: *In some cases you will have to invent a missing subject.*)

1. The contract was signed by Jason Andrews.

   _____

2. New dorms were constructed by the university.

   _____

3. The children were rushed to the hospital.

   _____

4. The drinks were served by the waiter.

   _____

5. The bridge was repaired.

   _____

Other Verb Problems

Could Have, Must Have, Should Have, Would Have

Because *have* and *of* sound alike in speaking, it is easy to mistakenly write "could *of*" instead of "could *have*." *Have* is used in verb phrases. *Of* is a preposition showing a relationship:

Have	Of
He could *have* bought a house.	The price *of* gas is rising.
She should *have* called by now.	He is the new chief *of* staff.
You must *have* gotten your bill by now.	Your bill *of* sale is ready.

EXERCISE 7 Revising Common Verb Problems

Rewrite incorrect sentences. Mark correct sentences OK.

1. We should of taken a cab to the airport.

   _____

2. She must have been the center of attention.

   _____

3. You should of never paid them in cash.

   _____

4. We would have come if only you could of called.

   _____

5. They should of been sued for breach of contract.

   _____

Double Negatives

Use only one negative to express a negative idea. Don't create **double negatives** using words like *hardly, scarcely, no, not,* or *never:*

Double Negative	*Correct*
I never have no money.	I never have any money.
We can't hardly wait for spring break.	We can hardly wait for spring break.
I didn't buy no concert tickets.	I didn't buy any concert tickets.

AVOIDING DOUBLE NEGATIVES

Double negatives are common in some languages and in some English dialects. If you are a native speaker of one of these languages or dialects, be careful to use only one negative word in each clause.

EXERCISE 8 Eliminating Double Negatives

Rewrite the following sentences to eliminate double negatives.

1. She didn't have no car insurance.

   _____

2. The School of Law never offered no paralegal courses.

   _____

3. The patients were so weak they could hardly take no steps.

   _____

4. The police never found no evidence of fraud.

   _____

5. Mary didn't scarcely have no time to play sports.

   _____

CRITICAL THINKING

Write a paragraph describing how your life plans have or have not changed over the years. What did you want to do as a child? What plans did you make in high school? What are your plans now? What would you like to do in the future?

GET THINKING
AND WRITING

WHAT HAVE YOU WRITTEN?

When you finish writing, review your use of tense, mood, and voice.

1. Write out one of your sentences stated in past tense:

   _____

   Have you used the proper verb to show past tense?

2. Write out one of your sentences stated in present tense:

   _____

   Does the verb state the present tense? Does it match the subject?

3. Have you avoided errors with verbs such as *lie* and *lay, raise* and *rise, set* and *sit*?

_____

4. Have you written *of* instead of *have* in *should have* or *would have*?

_____

Do you think it is better for a child to be brought up by a full-time parent rather than in day-care? Is this the ideal family situation, or is it just old-fashioned?

Write a paragraph stating your views. Support your points with examples.

© Royalty-Free/CORBIS

WHAT HAVE YOU LEARNED?

Select the right verb in each sentence:

1. _____ If I (was/were) the boss, I'd fire him immediately.

2. _____ The sun (rose/raised) over the clouds.

3. _____ We should (of/have) complained to the dean.

4. _____ I (rung/rang) the bell twice.

5. _____ Jose (struck/striked) out three times in last night's game.

6. ____ Karen worked in Chicago, which (is/was) the largest city in Illinois.

7. ____ Don't (lie/lay) anything on top of the printer.

8. ____ If we (set/sit) any longer we will miss the bus.

9. ____ They left us with hardly (any/no) money.

10. ____ She had (laid/lain) down for a nap when her son arrived.

Answers appear on the following page.

WRITING ON THE WEB

Using a search engine such as AltaVista, Yahoo!, or Google, enter terms such as *verb tense*, *past tense*, *past perfect tense*, *present progressive tense*, *irregular verbs*, *subjunctive*, and *passive voice* to locate current sites of interest.

1. Read online newspaper and magazine articles about an issue that interests you and notice how writers use tense to show shifts from past to present.
2. Write an e-mail to a friend about what you did last week. Choose verbs carefully to distinguish past events from ongoing ones.

POINTS TO REMEMBER

1. Explaining *when* something happens is as important as explaining *what* happens.
2. Regular verbs add *-d* or *-ed* to show past tense:

call	called
talk	talked
show	showed
want	wanted

3. Irregular verbs do not add *-d* or *-ed* to show past tense:

set	set
get	got
thrust	thrust
make	made

4. *Lie/lay, rise/raise,* and *set/sit* are often confused:

	To lie means "to rest or recline."	*To lay* means "to place."
present	lie *lie down*	lay *lay tile*
past	lay	laid
past participle	lain	laid

	To raise means "to lift."	*To rise* means "to get up."
present	raise *raise prices*	rise *Rise up!*
past	raised	rose
past participle	raised	risen

(continued)

POINTS TO REMEMBER *(continued)*

		To set means "to place."	*To sit* means "to recline."	
present	set	*set prices*	sit	*Sit down!*
past	set		sat	
past participle	set		sat	

5. Avoid awkward shifts in tense or time:

Awkward   We *drove* to the pier and *see* the whales.
Correct   We *drove* to the pier and *saw* the whales.

6. Avoid mistaking *of* for *have* in *should have* and *could have*:

I could *have* passed. *not* I could *of* passed.

7. Avoid double negatives:

I don't have any cash. *not* I don't have no cash.

ANSWERS TO WHAT HAVE YOU LEARNED? ON PAGES 304–305
1. were, 2. rose (see page 293), 3. have (see page 302), 4. rang (see page 293), 5. struck (see page 294),
6. is (see page 289), 7. lay (see page 296), 8. sit (see page 297), 9. any (page 303), 10. lain (see page 297)

Pronoun Reference, Agreement, and Case

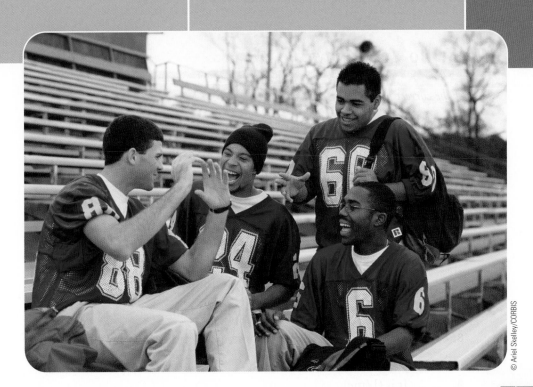

© Ariel Skelley/CORBIS

Do high school sports build character or distract students from their studies?

Write a paragraph describing the positive or negative impact of high school athletics. Support your views with examples.

What Are Pronouns?

Pronouns take the place of nouns. Without pronouns, your writing would be cumbersome:

> Nancy drove Nancy's new car home for the weekend. Nancy visited Nancy's parents. Nancy's parents were impressed with Nancy's new car, but Nancy's parents wondered if Nancy was spending too much of Nancy's salary on new purchases. Nancy's parents worried that Nancy's parents' daughter was not saving enough money.

Pronouns eliminate needless repetition:

> Nancy drove *her* new car home for the weekend. Nancy visited *her* parents. *They* were impressed with *her* new car, but *they* wondered if Nancy was spending too much of *her* salary on new purchases. *They* worried that *their* daughter was not saving enough money.

WHAT DO YOU KNOW?

Select the correct pronoun in each sentence.

1. _____ (He/him) and Nancy are driving to California this summer.

2. _____ Between you and (I/me), I think we need a new dean.

3. _____ Either Tina or Ann will lend me (their/her) car.

4. _____ Each of the girls has (their/her) dorm assignment.

5. _____ When I finally go to the top of the Eiffel Tower, all (I/you) could see was fog.

6. _____ The jury is making (its/their) decision as we speak.

7. _____ We are concerned about (him/his) driving.

8. _____ Please give (this/these) documents to someone (who/whom) you can trust.

9. _____ It is (I/me).

10. _____ Was it (he/him) who ran for help?

Answers appear on the following page.

GET *WRITING*
AND *REVISING*

WHAT ARE YOU TRYING TO SAY?

Summarize the plot of one of your favorite movies or television shows in a paragraph. Explain the main characters and events in the story.

_____

_____

_____

_____

_____

_____

_____

_____

_____

_____

_____

_____

_____

_____

WHAT HAVE YOU WRITTEN?

Underline all the pronouns in your paragraphs.

1. Can you circle the noun (antecedent) each pronoun represents?
2. Are plural nouns represented by plural pronouns? Are singular nouns represented by singular pronouns?
3. Are the pronouns in the right case? Do you use _I, we, he, she, they, it_ as subjects? Do you use _me, us, him, her, them_ as objects? Do you use _my, our, his, hers, their, its_ to show possession?

TYPES OF PRONOUNS

There are four types of pronouns: _personal, indefinite, relative,_ and _demonstrative._

Personal pronouns refer to people and have three forms, depending on how they are used in a sentence: _subjective, objective,_ and _possessive._

	Subjective		**Objective**		**Possessive**	
	Singular	Plural	Singular	Plural	Singular	Plural
1st person	I	we	me	us	my (mine)	our (ours)
2nd person	you	you	you	you	your (yours)	your (yours)
3rd person	he	they	him	them	his (his)	their (theirs)
	she		her		her (hers)	
	it		it		it (its)	

_He_ drove _their_ car to _our_ house, so _we_ paid _him._
They rented a cottage because _it_ was cheaper than _our_ time-share.

(continued)

ANSWERS TO WHAT DO YOU KNOW? ON PAGE 308
1. He (subject form needed),
2. me (object form needed), 3. her (one or the other but not both),
4. her (singular), 5. I (keep in first person), 6. its (singular), 7. his (possessive needed), 8. these (plural)/whom (object form needed), 9. I (subject form needed after "to be" verb),
10. he (subject form needed)

Relative pronouns introduce noun and adjective clauses:

who, whoever, whom, whose   which, whichever   that, what, whatever

I will work with *whoever* volunteers.
Tom was levied a thousand-dollar fine, *which* he refused to pay.

Demonstrative pronouns indicate the noun (antecedent):

this, that, these, those

That car is a lemon.
These books are on sale.

Indefinite pronouns refer to abstract persons or things:

Singular				Plural		Singular or Plural		
everyone	someone	anyone	no one	both	few	all	more	none
everybody	somebody	anybody	nobody	many		any	most	some
everything	something	anything	nothing					
each	another	either	neither					

Everyone should do his or her best.   *More* security is needed.
Both girls are attending summer school.   *More* security guards are needed.

Using Pronouns

To prevent confusion, pronouns have to be used with precision.

- Pronouns have to be clearly linked to **antecedents**—the nouns or other pronouns they represent.

    Unclear Reference
    The walls are covered with graffiti, and the hallways are cluttered with trash.
    They just don't care.
    [Whom does *they* refer to— residents, landlords, city inspectors?]

    Clear Reference
    Tenants cover the walls with graffiti and clutter the hallways with trash.
    They just don't care.
    [*They* refers to *tenants*.]

    Unclear Reference
    Sandy asked Erica to revise *her* report.
    [Whose report is it— Sandy's or Erica's?]

    Clear Reference
    Sandy sent *her* report to Erica for revision.
    Sandy reviewed Erica's report, then asked Erica to revise it.

- Pronouns have to agree with, or match, the antecedent in number:

    Incorrect
    Every student should bring *their* books to class.
    [*Student* is singular; *their* is plural.]

Singular
Every student should bring *his or her* books to class.
  [Singular *his or her* refers to singular *student*.]

Plural
The students should bring *their* books to class.
  [Plural *their* refers to plural *students*.]

- Pronouns have to agree or match in person:

Incorrect
We went up to the roof where *you* could see the Statue of Liberty.
  [Awkward shift between *we* (first person) and *you* (second person)]

Revised
We went up to the roof where *we* could see the Statue of Liberty.

- Pronouns have to be used in the right case:

Subjective
He took the money to the bank.

Objective
Maria gave *him* the bill.

Possessive
Juanita drove *his* car to the garage.

Reflexive
He did the work *himself*.

- Unnecessary pronouns should be eliminated:

Unnecessary Pronouns
George *he* should buy a new car.
The budget *it* makes no sense.
The teachers *they* are on strike.

Revised
George should buy a new car.
The budget makes no sense.
The teachers are on strike.

Pronoun Reference

To express yourself clearly, pronouns have to be used precisely. Because you know what you want to say, it is very easy to write sentences that make perfect sense to you but will leave your readers confused. The pronoun *he*, for example, can refer to any single male. It is easy to create sentences in which the word could refer to more than one person:

> Paul opened a limo service right after high school. *His* best friend, John, owned a cab service. *They* combined their forces and started Cream City Car Service. Business increased rapidly, but *he* soon found it hard to work with a partner.

Whom does the *he* in the last sentence refer to—Paul or John? Inserting the **antecedent,** the person's name in this case, eliminates confusion:

> Paul opened a limo service right after high school. *His* best friend, John, owned a cab service. *They* combined their forces and started Cream City Car Service. Business increased rapidly, but *John* soon found it hard to work with a partner.

Without a clear link between the pronoun (*I, we, you, he, she, they,* and *it*) and the antecedent or noun it represents, sentences can be misleading:

Confusing
The teachers met with the students to discuss their proposal.

Revised
The teachers met with the students to discuss the faculty proposal.
The students discussed their proposal at a meeting with teachers.

In order to correct reference errors, you may have to make only minor repairs to a sentence:

Unclear Reference
Jill gave Sylvia her keys.

Clear Reference
Jill gave her keys to Sylvia.

In other circumstances, you may have to reword the sentence to prevent confusion:

Unclear Reference
Jill gave Sylvia her keys.

Reworded
Jill returned Sylvia's keys.

EXERCISE 1 Eliminating Unclear Pronoun References

Revise the following sentences to eliminate unclear pronoun references. You may add words or change sentence structure.

1. Sara took Carla to her favorite restaurant in New Orleans.

   _____

   _____

2. John encouraged Sid to review his tax return for errors.

   _____

   _____

3. My cousin worked with Fred until he moved to San Diego.

   _____

   _____

4. The children asked their parents to change their clothes before they met with the principal.

   _____

   _____

5. **Armando's nephew told Mr. Mendoza his car needed new tires.**

_____

_____

USING *THEY* WITHOUT AN ANTECEDENT

The pronoun *they* is often used without a clear antecedent. In conversation, we frequently use *they* as an abstract reference to people with authority or power:

> "*They* put too much sex on violence on TV."
> "Can you believe what *they* are paying pro athletes these days?"
> "Why don't *they* fix this road?"

In writing, you should be more precise. Make sure every time *they* appears in your paper it is clearly linked to a specific plural noun. Replace unlinked *they*'s with concrete nouns:

> Networks put too much sex and violence on TV.
> Too much sex and violence appears on TV.

> Can you believe what owners are paying pro athletes these days?
> Can you believe what pro athletes are paid these days?

> Why doesn't the county fix this road?
> Why isn't this road fixed?

In editing papers, read them out loud. Pause when you see *they* and determine if it clearly refers to a noun. Revise sentences with unlinked *they*'s to eliminate confusion.

EXERCISE 2 Eliminate Unclear Uses of *They*

Rewrite the following sentences to eliminate unlinked uses of they. *You can revise the sentence to create a clear antecedent (noun) for* they *or eliminate the pronoun by supplying a noun.*

1. **The classrooms are dusty. The halls are marked by graffiti. The lockers are smashed. They just don't care about their school.**

_____

_____

2. **I don't like the way they advertise candy to children.**

_____

_____

3. **You would think they would take better care of fragile artwork.**

_____

_____

4. **Did you see *Sixty Minutes* last night? They showed how they use the Internet to steal people's credit card information.**

_____

_____

5. **When are they going to build cars with better engines?**

_____

_____

Pronoun Agreement

Just as singular subjects take singular verbs, singular nouns take singular pronouns:

teacher	he *or* she
school	it
Miss Landers	she
Eric	he
the quarterback	he
the nun	she
citizen	he *or* she

Miss Landers retired early because *she* wanted to move to California.
The school closed early on Monday, but *it* will open early on Tuesday.
The citizen plays an important role in shaping society. *He or she* votes.

Plural nouns take plural pronouns:

teachers	they
schools	they
the Landers	they
the quarterbacks	they
the nuns	they
citizens	they

The teachers retired early because *they* wanted to take advantage of the new pension.
The schools closed early on Monday, but *they* will open early on Tuesday.
Citizens play an important role in shaping society. *They* vote.

Singular and Plural Nouns and Pronouns

• Indefinite pronouns refer to no specific person, idea, or object and are always singular:

another	either	nobody	somebody
anybody	everybody	no one	someone
anyone	everyone	none	something
anything	everything	nothing	
each	neither	one	

Another boy is missing, and *he* is only six years old.
Somebody left *his* shoulder guards in the locker room.
Neither girl is going to get *her* paycheck on time.
Each citizen must cast *his or her* vote.

- Some nouns that end in *s* and look like plurals are singular:

economics   mathematics   athletics   physics

Mathematics is a tough course. *It* demands a lot of time.

- Some nouns that may refer to one item are plural:

pants   gloves   scissors   fireworks

My scissors are dull. *They* need sharpening.

- Proper nouns that look plural are singular if they are names of companies, organizations, or titles of books, movies, television shows, or works of art:

General Motors   *The Three Musketeers*   The League of Women Voters

I love *The Three Musketeers* because *it* is funny.

- Units of time and amounts of money are generally singular:

Two hundred dollars is not enough; *it* won't even pay for my plane ticket.

- They appear as plurals to indicate separate items:

Three dollars *were* lying on the table. *They* were brand new.

Avoiding Sexism

Because singular pronouns refer to only one sex or the other—*he* or *she*—it can be easy to create sentences that fail to include both males and females. It is acceptable, however, to use only *he* or *she* when writing about a single person or a group of people of the same sex:

Mitch has a cold, but *he* came to work this morning.
Each of the boys rode *his* bicycle to school.
Kelly is going to night school because *she* wants an associate degree.
Neither woman wanted to lose *her* place in line.

When writing about people in general, it is important to avoid sexist pronoun use:

Sexist
Every citizen must cast *his* vote.   [Aren't women citizens?]
A nurse must use *her* judgment.   [What about male nurses?]

Methods of Avoiding Sexism

- Provide both male and female singular pronouns:

Every citizen must cast *his or her* vote.

- Use plural antecedents:

  Citizens must cast *their* votes.
- Reword the sentence to eliminate the need for pronouns:

  Every citizen must vote.

USING *THEY* TO AVOID SEXISM

In speaking, people often use *they* rather than *he or she* to save time:

> Every student should do *their* best.
> Each employee is required to meet *their* supervisor before *they* can apply for a raise.
> A good teacher knows *their* students.

This agreement error is often accepted in speech, but writing requires more formal methods of eliminating sexism. If you find yourself using *they* to refer to a singular noun or pronoun, use these methods to both avoid sexism and an error in agreement.

1. Use plural nouns and pronouns to match *they:*

   > All *students* should do *their* best.
   > All *employees* are required to meet *their* supervisors before *they* can apply for raises.
   > Good *teachers* know *their* students.

2. Eliminate the need for pronouns:

   > A student should study hard.
   > Every employee must have approval from a supervisor to apply for a raise.
   > A good teacher knows students.

3. State as commands:

   > Employees— meet with your supervisor before applying for a raise.

EXERCISE 3 Selecting the Right Pronoun

Underline the right pronoun in each sentence.

1. Modern presidents often retire to build (his/their) libraries.
2. Previous chief executives, however, have made use of (his/their) skills in other government offices.
3. After leaving the White House, President Taft was nominated to the Supreme Court and became (their/its) chief justice.
4. Perhaps the most dogged former White House resident America ever had was (their/its) seventeenth president.
5. Andrew Johnson was Lincoln's vice president, and (he/they) became president in 1865.

6. Johnson's administration was marked by controversy over Reconstruction, and (it/he) reached a crisis in 1868 when he became the first president to be impeached.

7. Johnson survived impeachment because a single senator cast (his/their) vote in his favor.

8. Johnson completed his term, but (he/it) was marked by continued battles over policies dealing with the former Confederate states.

9. Johnson's troubled administration did make a lasting contribution to the nation's geography; (he/it) acquired Alaska from Russia.

10. After leaving the presidency, Johnson made three attempts to secure a political post before (he/it) returned to Washington as a senator from Tennessee.

Avoiding Shifts in Point of View

Pronouns express three persons:

	First	**Second**	**Third**
singular	I, me, my	you, you, your	he, him, his/she, her, her
plural	we, us, our	you, you, your	they, them, their

Avoid making illogical shifts when writing. Maintain a consistent point of view.

Shift
We went bird watching, but *you* couldn't even find a robin.
When *I* went to college, *you* couldn't go to law school part-time.

Revised

We went bird watching, but *we* couldn't even find a robin.	[consistent use of plural first person]
When *I* went to college, students couldn't go to law school part-time.	[use of *students* eliminates need for second pronoun]

EXERCISE 4 Eliminating Pronoun Shifts in Point of View

Revise the following sentences to eliminate illogical pronoun shifts in point of view.

1. When he moved to New York, you could find a nice apartment for three hundred dollars a month.

_____

_____

2. If one wants to succeed these days, you really should know computers.

_____

_____

3. We always thought he would be a star— you could tell by watching him rehearse.

_____

_____

4. I moved to Nevada, but the heat is more than you can tolerate.

_____

_____

5. We went to the beach to swim, but it was so cold you had to stay inside.

_____

_____

Using the Right Case

Nouns serve different functions in sentences. They can be subjects or objects, and they can be possessive. Pronouns appear in different forms to show how they function:

They gave _her_ car to _him_.
Subject   possessive   object

These different forms are called "cases."

PRONOUN CASES

	Subjective	Objective	Possessive	Reflexive/Intensive
singular	I	me	my, mine	myself
	you	you	you, yours	yourself
	he	him	his	himself
	she	her	her	herself
	it	it	its	itself
plural	we	us	our, ours	ourselves
	you	you	your, yours	yourselves
	they	them	their, theirs	themselves
singular or plural	who	whom	whose	

In most sentences we automatically use pronouns in the right case, telling our readers the role the pronoun plays:

Subjective pronouns serve the subject of a verb:

_We_ are driving to Florida on Monday.
This week _she_ is moving to New York.

Objective pronouns serve as objects:

The rental agency reserved a car for _us_.
Give _him_ the money.

Possessive pronouns demonstrate the pronoun owns something:

Our car is being repaired.
The garage lost _her_ car keys.

Note: Because these pronouns already indicate possession, no apostrophes are needed.

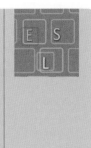

USING POSSESSIVE PRONOUNS

In English, possessive pronouns—*my, your, his, her, our, their*—must agree with the nouns they represent, not the words they modify.

Incorrect   The club members advertised *its* bake sale on TV.

Correct   The club members advertised *their* bake sale on TV.

The possessive pronoun *their* agrees with *club members,* not *bake sale.*

Reflexive pronouns refer to other pronouns:

We moved the furniture *ourselves.*

Intensive pronouns add emphasis:

I myself repaired the roof.

There are, however, some pronoun uses that can be confusing, including plurals, comparisons, and sentences using certain words.

Plural Constructions

Using a single pronoun as a subject or object is generally easy:

He gave the money to Paul.
Paul gave the money to *him.*

However, when pronouns are part of plural subjects and objects, many writers make mistakes:

Incorrect
Jane, Jordan, William, and *him* gave the money to Paul.
Paul gave the money to Jane, Jordan, William, and *he.*

Correct
Jane, Jordan, William, and *he* gave the money to Paul. [subjective case]
Paul gave the money to Jane, Jordan, William, and *him.* [objective case]

When editing, the quickest method of checking case is to simplify the sentence by eliminating the other nouns:

. . . *he* gave the money to Paul.
Paul gave the money to . . . *him.*

Between

Pronouns that serve as objects of prepositions use the objective case—*him, her, me, them.* Most constructions give writers few problems—to *him,* for *them,* with *her.* However, the preposition *between* is often misused:

Incorrect (Subjective Case)	Correct (Objective Case)
between you and *I*	between you and *me*
between you and *he*	between you and *him*
between you and *she*	between you and *her*
between *he* and *she*	between him and *her*
between *they* and the teachers	between *them* and the teachers

Although people often use the subjective case with *between* in speaking, the objective case is correct and should be used in writing.

Comparisons

Comparisons using *than* or *as* use the subjective case:

He is taller than *I*.	not	He is taller than *me*.
Nancy is smarter than *he*.	not	Nancy is smarter than *him*.

These constructions are confusing because the second verb is usually omitted. To test which pronoun to use, add the missing verb to see which pronoun sounds correct:

He is taller than *I am*.	not	He is taller than *me am*.
Nancy is smarter than *he is*.	not	Nancy is smarter than *him is*.

The Verb *To Be*

Subjective pronouns follow *to be* verbs:

It is *she* on the phone.	not	It is *her* on the phone.
It is *I*.	not	It is *me*.
Was it *they* in the car?	not	Was it *them* in the car?

Because we often use phrases like "It's me" or "Is that her talking?" when we talk, the correct forms can sound awkward. The subjective case is correct and should be used in writing.

If your sentences still sound awkward, rewrite them to alter the *to be–pronoun* form:

She is on the phone.
I am at the door.
Did *they* take the car?

Who and Whom

Who and *whom* are easily confused because they are generally used in questions and change the usual word pattern. *Who* is subjective and serves as the subject of a verb:

Who is at the door?	*Who* bought the car?	*Who* is going to summer school?

Whom is objective and serves as the object of a verb or a preposition:

Give the money to *whom*?	To *whom* it may concern.	For *whom* is this intended?

To help choose the right word, substitute *he* and *him*. If *he* sounds better, use *who*. If *him* sounds better, use *whom*.

(Who/whom) called?
(*He*/him) called.   [Use *who*. "Who called?"]

Take it from (whoever/whomever)
  can help.
(*He*/him) can help.   [Use *whoever*. "whoever can help"]

For (who/whom) are you looking?

For (he/him).   [Use *whom*. "for whom"]

This and *That*, *These* and *Those*

This and *that* are singular:

This book is overdue.   That boy is in trouble.   This is a fine day.

These and *those* are plural:

These books are overdue.   Those boys are in trouble.   These are fine days.

They and *Them*

They is subjective and used when subject to a verb:

They are leaving town on Monday.   You know *they* don't work on Sunday.

Them is objective and used as an object of prepositions or verbs:

Give the money to *them*.   We can't get *them* to work on Sunday.

UNNECESSARY PRONOUNS

Although in speaking people sometimes insert a pronoun directly after a noun, they are unnecessary and should be eliminated:

Unnecessary
Marsha *she* is going to retire early.
The children *they* won't listen.
The book *it* doesn't make sense.

Revised
Marsha is going to retire early.
The children won't listen.
The book doesn't make sense.

EXERCISE 5 Selecting the Right Pronoun Case

Select the right pronoun in each sentence.

1. Ted and (I/me) are going to the festival tomorrow.

2. The manager promised free tickets to Ted and (I/me) for helping them last year.

3. That gives (we/us) enough time to finish the job.

4. The faculty, the parents, and (he/him) will have to settle this issue.

5. The school board offered greater funding to the faculty and (him/he).

6. That is more work than (we/us) can handle.

7. She is offering more money to (we/us).

8. Ted, Frank, and (she/her) are leaving early to avoid the rush.

9. The airport limo was sent for Ted, Frank, and (she/her).

10. You know (he/him) and (I/me) went to the same grade school?

EXERCISE 6 Selecting the Right Pronoun

Select the right pronoun in each sentence.

1. Between (they/them) and (we/us) there is little desire for compromise.

2. Tom, Sissy, Eric, Lisa, and (I/me) are going to the library.

3. We could never afford (those/this) house.

4. The administration won't let (they/them) work on weekends.

5. (These/This) players are faster than (they/them).

6. Does Ted or (I/me) owe any money?

7. Give all the money either to Sue or to (he/him).

8. Don't let (she/her) work too hard.

9. It is (he/him) again.

10. We want to have a party for Nancy and (he/him) next week.

WORKING TOGETHER

Working with a group of students, revise the pronoun errors in the following e-mail:

```
New employees must submit pay forms to their super-
visors no later than May 1. If your supervisor does
not receive this form, they cannot request payment and
you will not receive you check on time. If you have
questions, please feel free to call Rick Terry, Janet
Sherman, or I. We are usually in our offices in the
afternoon. If you are unsure which supervisor you
should report to, call Frank Fallon's office or e-mail
he at frank.fallon@abc.com.

                                          Ted Matthews
```

EXERCISE 7 Cumulative Exercise

Rewrite each of the sentences for errors in pronoun use, subject-verb agreement, run-ons, and fragments.

1. Jim or me are working on the Fourth of July.

   _____

   _____

2. Having worked all summer, her was upset when bonuses were canceled.

   _____

   _____

3. The teachers and them discussed the new textbook it comes with free CDs.

   _____

   _____

4. Terry and him working all weekend.

   _____

   _____

5. They gave the job to we students but they never provided the supplies we needed.

   _____

   _____

CRITICAL THINKING

What is the toughest challenge you face at this point in the semester? Is it an upcoming exam or paper? Is it finding time to study or juggling work and school? Write a paragraph describing the challenge you face and how you plan to meet it.

GET THINKING AND WRITING

WHAT HAVE YOU WRITTEN?

1. Underline all the pronouns and circle their antecedents. Is there a clear link between the pronouns and the nouns or pronouns they represent?
   - Pay attention to uses of *they.*
2. Do nouns and pronouns agree in number? Do plural nouns have plural pronouns? Do singular nouns have singular pronouns?
   - Pay attention to nouns that look plural but are singular—*economics, committee, jury.*
   - Remember that indefinite pronouns like *each, everyone, anyone, someone,* and *somebody* are singular.
3. Review your use of case.
   - Use the subjective case in comparisons and with pronouns following *to be* verbs: "taller than I" or "It is I."
   - Use objective case with between: "between him and me."

WHAT HAVE YOU LEARNED?

Select the right pronoun in each sentence.

1. _____ You have to choose between Sally and (I / me).

2. _____ Jim Nash, Kelly Samson, and (I / me) were late.

3. _____ (This / These) plans of yours are very impressive.

4. _____ Is that Max and (she/her) in the lobby?

5. _____ Each student must bring (their/his or her) lab report to class.

6. _____ How will the new policy affect (we/us)?

7. _____ Give the door prize to (whomever/whoever) arrives first.

8. _____ (We/Us) boys will get a new gym next year.

9. _____ The school is telling the teachers, parents, and (we/us) to expect a change.

10. _____ You and (she/her) work too hard.

Answers appear on the following page.

Compare this picture with the one on page 307. Do you think playing sports affects high school girls differently than it does boys? Do they learn different lessons? Do they face more or less pressure than male athletes?

Write a short paragraph comparing male and female high school athletes.

© Randy Faris/CORBIS

WRITING ON THE WEB

Using a search engine such as AltaVista, Yahoo!, or Google, enter *pronoun, pronoun agreement, using pronouns,* and *pronoun cases* to locate current sites of interest.

Review e-mails you may have sent and look at your past use of pronouns. Can you locate errors in your writing? Which pronoun constructions have given you the most trouble in the past? Mark pages in this chapter for future reference.

POINTS TO REMEMBER

Pronouns have to be used with precision to prevent confusion.

1. Pronouns must clearly refer to a noun:

    Unclear Reference
    Sandy gave Vicki *her* keys.

    Clear Reference
    Sandy gave *her* keys to Vicki.

2. Pronouns and nouns match in number:

    Each girl took *her* car.   [singular]
    The *girls* took *their* cars.   [plural]

3. Pronouns use consistent point of view:

    Inconsistent
    When *one* visits New York, *you* have to dine at Sardis.
    When *I* work overtime, *it* gets boring.

    Consistent
    When *you* visit New York, *you* have to dine at Sardis.
    When *I* work overtime, *I* get bored.

4. Pronouns must appear in the right case:

    Subjective Case
    Who is at the door?
    She is smarter than I.
    It is I.
    Was that she on the phone?

    Objective Case
    To whom it may concern.
    Between you and me, the film is too long.

5. Pronouns directly following nouns they represent are unnecessary:

    Unnecessary
    The school *it* closed last week.
    Frank *he* works weekends.

    Revised
    The school closed last week.
    Frank works weekends.

ANSWERS TO WHAT HAVE YOU LEARNED? ON PAGES 323–324
1. me (see page 319), 2. I (see page 319), 3. These (see page 310), 4. she (see page 324), 5. his or her (see page 310), 6. us (see page 318), 7. whomever (see page 321), 8. We (see page 318), 9. us (see page 318), 10. she (see page 318)

22

Adjectives and Adverbs

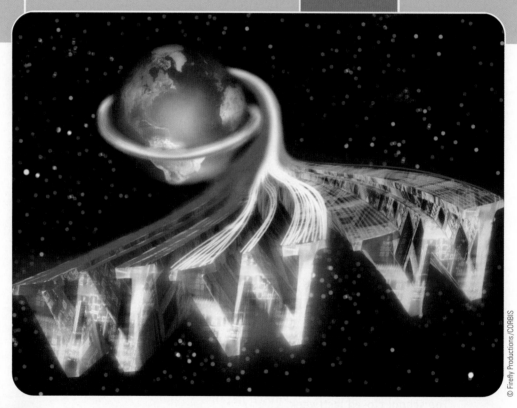

© Firefly Productions/CORBIS

GET WRITING

How has the Internet changed society? Does it make life easier, create jobs, and link people to information that can improve their lives? Or does it divide society into those with access and those without? Jobs are now posted on the Internet. Does this make it harder for some people to find employment?

Write a paragraph describing one or more positive or negative effects of the Internet. If you use the Internet, describe your online experiences.

What Are Adjectives and Adverbs?

The most important words in a sentence are the subject—the actor or main idea—and the verb, which connects the subject to actions or other words. Adjectives and adverbs add meaning to a basic sentence by telling us more about nouns and verbs.

Adjectives are words and phrases that describe nouns and pronouns:

a *red* hat   he was *smart*   a *restored antique* car

Adverbs are words and phrases that describe verbs, adjectives, and other adverbs. They generally end in *-ly:*

She walked *slowly.*   *hotly* debated   a *newly* restored antique car

Both add meaning to basic sentences:

Basic Sentence
Mary bought a car.

Basic Sentence Enhanced with Adjectives
Mary bought a *repainted used* car that was *affordable* and *easy to repair.*

Basic Sentence Enhanced with Adjectives and Adverbs
Mary *impulsively* bought a *recently* repainted used car that was affordable and *very* easy to repair.

WHAT DO YOU KNOW?

Identify the modifiers in each sentence by underlining adjectives and circling adverbs.

1. Recently discovered documents reveal the former governor accepted questionable campaign contributions from convicted criminals.

2. My favorite movie is *Curse of the Jade Scorpion* starring Woody Allen, who plays a humble insurance investigator who becomes a jewel thief after being hypnotized.

3. The Association of American Women in Small Business is holding its annual convention in San Diego in late December.

4. She drove carefully during the blizzard, slowly following the map Carrie gave her.

5. Laura Kensington was a noted forties singer whose carefully phrased versions of jazz classics made her a popular radio star.

6. Erik cautiously opened the dented lid of the just discovered trunk.

7. The pension board methodically investigates new stock issues before investing in new companies.

8. Vicki is seriously looking for a two-bedroom apartment near campus that is affordable and easy to clean.

9. The freshly waxed furniture looked brand new.

10. The office is so unbelievably old it has dial phones, typewriters, adding machines, and a 1930s mimeograph.

   Answers appear on the following page.

GET WRITING

AND REVISING

WHAT ARE YOU TRYING TO SAY?

Describe a recent movie or television program you found interesting. Explain what made it fascinating—the plot, the characters, the style, the theme?

_____

_____

_____

_____

_____

_____

_____

_____

_____

_____

_____

_____

_____

_____

WHAT HAVE YOU WRITTEN?

Read through your description and underline each adjective and circle each adverb. Notice how important modifiers are in expressing your ideas. If you eliminated the adjectives and adverbs, would your writing have the same effect? Would readers be able to appreciate your opinions or understand what you are trying to say?

Understanding Adjectives

Some words are clearly adjectives because they describe other words. They add information about nouns and pronouns, telling us about their age, shape, color, quality, quantity, or character:

new	round	red	rich	numerous
old	square	yellow	poor	many

recent   oval   tan   mediocre   few
classic   pear-shaped   purple   stable   single

Some adjectives are formed from nouns and verbs and have distinct endings.

Noun Form	Adjective	Verb Form	Adjective
South	Southern	slice	sliced
automobile	automotive	paint	painted
law	legal	choreograph	choreographed
medicine	medical	audit	audited

Past participles—past-tense verbs—are adjectives: *broken* window, *torn* shirt, *forgotten* keys, *frozen* pizza.

Other nouns and verbs appear as adjectives with no spelling change. You can tell they are adjectives only by context, their position in a sentence:

We bought *automobile* insurance.	Put that in the *paint* display.
I read a *law* book.	She liked the *choreography* director.
The aspirin is in the *medicine* cabinet.	There is going to be an *audit* review.

These words serve as adjectives because they add meaning to nouns:

What kind of insurance?	*automobile* insurance	Which display?	*paint* display
What kind of book?	*law* book	Which director?	*choreography* director
Which cabinet?	*medicine* cabinet	What kind of review?	*audit* review

ADJECTIVES AND PLURAL NOUNS

In many languages, such as Spanish, adjectives must agree with the nouns they modify. In English there is only one noun form for both singular and plural nouns.

Singular He wore an *old* suit.
Plural   He wore *old* suits.

EXERCISE 1 Identifying Adjectives

Underline the adjectives in each sentence.

1. One of the strangest disasters to hit an American city was the Boston Molasses Flood of 1919.

2. Shortly before noon on a warm January day, a large steel storage tank owned by the United States Alcohol Company suddenly exploded.

3. Within seconds over two million gallons of brown molasses gushed down the cobblestone streets of North Boston.

4. The eight-foot-high tide of molasses moved at thirty-five miles an hour, destroying everything in its path.

ANSWERS TO WHAT DO YOU KNOW? ON PAGES 327–328
1. adj.: discovered, former, questionable, campaign, convicted; adv.: Recently
2. adj.: favorite, *Jade,* humble, insurance, jewel
3. adj.: American, Small, annual, late
4. adv.: carefully, slowly
5. adj.: noted, forties, phrased, jazz, popular, radio; adv.: carefully
6. adj.: dented, discovered; adv.: cautiously, just
7. adj.: pension, new; adv.: methodically
8. adj.: two-bedroom, affordable, easy to clean; adv.: seriously
9. adj.: waxed, brand new; adv.: freshly
10. adj.: old, dial, adding, 1930s; adv.: unbelievably

5. A large truck was lifted up and driven through a wooden fence.

6. Sturdy buildings were knocked off their foundations like cardboard dollhouses.

7. Unable to outrun the oncoming flood, people and horses were buried by the sticky wave of molasses.

8. Rescue crews were hampered by the gooey muck that rose past their knees.

9. The final death toll reached twenty-one.

10. For decades local residents claimed that on hot summer days they could detect the telltale sweet odor of molasses.

EXERCISE 2 Using Adjectives

Add adjectives in each sentence.

1. I drove George's car, which was _____ and _____.

2. The _____ school was closed for _____ repairs.

3. We had lunch at a _____ restaurant, which was _____ and _____.

4. Her _____ speeches created _____ reactions from her _____ listeners.

5. The _____ apartment building was _____ and _____.

6. The _____ show was _____ and _____.

7. He was a _____ and _____ musician.

8. The job requires applicants who are _____, _____, and _____.

9. The _____ store is selling _____ clothing at _____ prices.

10. The school's _____ policy angered _____ students who were _____.

EXERCISE 3 Using Participles

Past participles are adjectives. Often in speaking, however, people drop the -ed endings and forget to add them in writing. In each sentence, underline the misused past participle and write out the correct adjective form.

1. It was so hot we drank ice tea all afternoon.   _____

2. We drove a rent car to Toronto.   _____

3. They served us mash potatoes and steam carrots.   _____

4. The salad has cheese and dice ham.   _____

5. Sara had to wear a borrow dress to the wedding.   _____

6. Those confuse policies wasted our funds.   _____

7. The date material is totally obsolete.   _____

8. It's the greatest thing since slice bread.   _____

9. She had coffee and a soft-boil egg. _____

10. Her reason arguments won over her critics. _____

COMMAS AND ADJECTIVES

Place a comma between two unrelated adjectives describing one noun or pronoun:

We saw a new, fascinating film.   They offered us a nutritious, inexpensive meal.

Do not place a comma between two related adjectives describing one noun or pronoun:

We saw a new Woody Allen film.   They offered us hot apple pie.

Apply this simple test to see if you need commas: Read the sentence aloud and place the word *and* between the two adjectives. If the sentence sounds OK, add a comma:

We saw a new *and* fascinating film. [sounds OK, add comma]

If the sentence sounds awkward, do not add a comma:

We saw a new *and* Woody Allen film. [sounds awkward, no comma needed]

ORDER OF MULTIPLE ADJECTIVES

When using two or more adjectives to modify the same noun, you must arrange them according to their meanings. Follow the order indicated below:

- Evaluation   charming, painful, valid
- Size   enormous, large, tiny
- Shape   rectangular, round, square
- Age   youthful, middle-aged, ancient
- Color   orange, blue, brown
- Nationality   Libyan, Chinese, Canadian
- Religion   Hindu, Catholic, Muslim
- Material   concrete, stone, adobe

Examples:
We rented rooms in a *charming old Spanish* castle.
A *tall young African* gentleman stood behind the pulpit.

Understanding Adverbs

Adverbs describe verbs, adjectives, and other adverbs. They usually add *-ly* to the adjective form:

adjective	+ *-ly*	=	adverb	adjective	+ *-ly*	=	adverb
careful	*-ly*		carefully	delicate	*-ly*		delicately
cautious	*-ly*		cautiously	soft	*-ly*		softly

adjective	+	-*ly*	=	adverb	adjective	+	-*ly*	=	adverb
hot		-*ly*		hotly	methodical		-*ly*		methodically
legal		-*ly*		legally	scientific		-*ly*		scientifically

Other adverbs do not end in -*ly*:

fast	hard	just	right	straight

EXERCISE 4 Identifying Adverbs

Underline the adverbs in each sentence.

1. Unlike football, basketball was developed by an undeniably creative individual.

2. This all-American game was actually invented by a Canadian-born minister, who was greatly concerned about young people and athletics.

3. Dr. James Naismith, who is largely unknown to today's fans, developed this quick-moving, fast-paced game.

4. While working as the athletic director of a YMCA, Naismith sought to overcome a routinely vexing problem.

5. During the winter young people became increasingly bored with indoor gymnastics.

6. Naismith wanted to invent a game people could play easily with little equipment.

7. Considering the limitations of most gyms, he carefully developed an indoor game using just one ball and a basket.

8. Today's NBA fans would find Naismith's game unbelievably crude.

9. The first basket was actually a peach basket carefully suspended above the court.

10. Someone had to stand patiently on a ladder to retrieve the ball every time a player made a basket.

EXERCISE 5 Using Adverbs

Add adverbs in each sentence.

1. She drove so _____ and _____, her parents _____ took away her car keys.

2. The mayor _____ decided the taxpayers had been treated _____ by the city council and _____ called for a special election.

3. The children were playing so _____, we _____ shut the windows.

4. The blizzard hit the city so _____, the mayor asked for federal support to _____ remove the snow.

5. The cities of the Southwest grew_____ following World War II because air-conditioning _____ made desert living bearable.

6. The championship team _____ entered the stadium and delighted the _____ screaming fans.

7. The ____ paced trial moved so _____ that many observers _____ debated if justice was being _____ administered.

8. The cast had to change costumes so _____, many broke buttons and tore sleeves.

9. The _____ structured tax law was so _____ difficult to understand that even _____ experienced accountants had trouble advising clients.

10. Although he took his medication _____, followed his _____ regulated diet _____, and exercised _____, his blood pressure remained _____ high.

Grammar Choices and Meaning

Because both adjectives and adverbs modify other words, they can be easily confused. Changing an adjective to an adverb changes meaning:

Form	Meaning
adjective + adjective fresh sliced bread	bread that is both fresh and sliced
adverb + adjective freshly sliced bread	bread (fresh or stale) that has just been sliced
adjective + adjective new waxed floor	a floor that is both new and waxed
adverb + adjective newly waxed floor	a floor (new or old) that has just been waxed
adjective + adjective great, expanded program	a program that is both great and expanded
adverb + adjective greatly expanded program	a program (of any quality) that has vastly expanded

Use adjectives and adverbs precisely in modifying verbs of sense—*see, hear, feel, smell, touch,* and *taste.*

Adjective: I feel poor after the accident.   [*Poor* modifies the noun *I,* suggesting the writer feels broke or financially distressed by the accident.]

Adverb: I feel poorly after the accident.   [*Poorly* modifies the verb *feel,* suggesting the writer is injured or in ill health following the accident.]

POINT TO REMEMBER

In speaking, people commonly use the shorter adjective form when an adverb is needed:

"Drive careful, now."	instead of	"Drive <u>carefully</u>, now."
"Do the tax work accurate."		"Do the tax work accurate<u>ly</u>."
"That's real good coffee."		"That is real<u>ly</u> good coffee."
"He drove real slow."		"He drove real<u>ly</u> slow<u>ly</u>."
"She acted crazy."		"She acted craz<u>ily</u>."

In writing, make sure you use adverbs (which often end in -*ly*) to modify verbs, adjectives, and other adverbs.

Good/Well, Bad/Badly

Two adjective/adverb pairs commonly confused are *good/well* and *bad/badly.*

Good *and* bad *are adjectives:*
You look good. [You appear attractive.]

I feel bad. [I am depressed or sad.]

Well *and* badly *are adverbs:*
You look well. [You appear healthy.]

I feel badly. [I have difficulty sensing touch.]

Good *and* bad *modify nouns and pronouns:*
<u>She</u> looked *good* despite her recent accident.
She had a *bad* <u>fracture</u> in her right arm.

Well *and* badly *modify verbs, adjectives, and other adverbs:*
She <u>walked</u> *well* despite injuring her leg.
Her right arm was *badly* <u>fractured</u>.

Good and *bad* and *well* and *badly* have special comparative and superlative forms:

Basic	**Comparative**	**Superlative**
good	better	best
bad	worse	worst
well	better	best
badly	worse	worst

That pasta was *good,* but the *best* pasta in town is served at Rocco's.
Your spare tire is *bad,* but mine is *worse.*
I sing *well,* but I have to admit he is *better.*
That is a *badly* designed house, but the *worst* designed structure in town is the bank.

EXERCISE 6 Using Adjectives and Adverbs

Select the correct adjective or adverb in each sentence.

1. The Yankees have a (good/well) pitching staff this year.

2. The Pirates are playing (good/well) this season.

3. The new stadium will offer (better/best) seating than the old stadium.

4. I visit ten or fifteen airports a year, and this is by far the (worse/worst) one.

5. The freshman class is (better/best) than the sophomore class in math and science.

6. You will do (good/well) on the exam if you don't get too anxious.

7. She sings (good/well) songs for a young audience.

8. I felt (bad/badly) about George losing his job.

9. The streets were so (bad/badly) paved, the city is suing the contractor.

10. They played so (bad/badly) even the most loyal fans walked out in the first quarter.

EXERCISE 7 Choosing Adjectives and Adverbs

Underline the correct modifier in each sentence. Remember that adjectives modify nouns and pronouns, and adverbs modify verbs, adjectives, and other adverbs.

1. The press has (frequent/frequently) used the term "crime of the century" to describe a (particular/particularly) infamous criminal act.

2. The nation was (deep/deeply) shocked in March 1932 when newspaper headlines and radio broadcasts announced that Charles Lindbergh Jr. had been taken from his crib.

3. Following instructions by the kidnapper, Lindbergh (ready/readily) paid the $50,000 ransom, but his son was not returned.

4. The (intense/intensely) search for the missing child took bizarre turns.

5. Al Capone offered to help find the Lindbergh baby, provided he was released from prison so he could use his (vast/vastly) underground network.

6. Two months later the (bad/badly) decomposed body of Charles Lindbergh Jr. was discovered less than two miles from the Lindbergh home.

7. In 1934 a man paid a New York gas station attendant with a ten-dollar bill authorities (quick/quickly) identified as ransom money.

8. Hauptmann maintained his innocence, but New Jersey's attorney general, who prosecuted the case, presented jurors with an (overwhelming/overwhelmingly) barrage of evidence.

9. Hauptmann was convicted and sentenced to death, and despite a new investigation ordered by the (new/newly) elected governor, he was executed in 1936.

10. The Lindbergh case remains controversial. In 1976 Anthony Hopkins played Hauptmann in a movie that depicted him as guilty; twenty years later, Stephen Rea portrayed Hauptmann as an innocent victim of circumstances in a movie (ironic/ironically) called *The Crime of the Century.*

Comparisons

Adjectives and adverbs are often used in comparing two things. There are three basic rules for showing comparisons:

1. Add *-er* for adjectives and adverbs with one syllable:

   Adjectives

Tom is *tall*.	Tom is *taller* than Jim.
The house is *old*.	The house is *older* than you think.
The street is *wet*.	The street is *wetter* than the sidewalk.

   Adverbs

He sang *loud*.	He sang *louder* than Bill.
She worked *hard*.	She worked *harder* than last week.
They drive *fast*.	They drive *faster* than they should.

2. Use *more* for adjectives with more than one syllable that do not end in *-y*:

The car is *expensive*.	The car is *more expensive* than I can afford.
He is *intelligent*.	He is *more intelligent*.

   Use *more* for adverbs, sometimes adding *-er* to the base form:

He spoke *boldly*.	She spoke *more boldly* than before.
He ran *fast*.	She ran *faster*.

3. Add *-ier* after dropping the *-y* for adjectives and adverbs ending in *-y*:

   Adjective

   The game is *easy*. The game is *easier* than you think.

   Adverb

   She felt *lucky*. She felt luckier than her sister.

EXERCISE 8 Using Adjectives and Adverbs in Comparisons

Write out the proper comparative form of each adjective and adverb, then use it in a sentence.

1. effective _____

   _____

2. lazy _____

   _____

3. rusty _____

   _____

4. loud _____

   _____

5. happy _____

   _____

6. icy _____

   _____

7. cold _____

   _____

8. costly _____

_____

9. fragile _____

_____

10. fascinating _____

_____

AVOIDING DOUBLE COMPARISONS

When speaking, some people use double comparisons:

> Sara is *more smarter* than Beth.
> This car is *more older* than mine.
> The final is *more harder* than the midterm.

Because both *more* and *-er* indicate something greater; only one is needed:

> Sara is *smarter* than Beth.
> This car is *older* than mine.
> The final is *harder* than the midterm.

Using Superlatives

Comparisons show a difference between two items:

> Tom is *older* than Sean.

To show differences between three or more items, use superlative forms:

> Tom is the *oldest* boy in class.

There are three basic rules for creating superlative adjectives and adverbs:

1. Add *-est* to adjectives and adverbs with one syllable:

Basic	Comparative	Superlative
hot	hotter	hottest
bold	bolder	boldest
fast	faster	fastest

2. Add *-iest* after dropping the *-y* in adjectives and adverbs that end in *-y:*

Basic	Comparative	Superlative
pretty	prettier	prettiest
easy	easier	easiest
silly	sillier	silliest

3. Use *most* for adjectives and adverbs with two or more syllables that do not end in *-y:*

Basic	Comparative	Superlative
exciting	more exciting	most exciting
relaxing	more relaxing	most relaxing
suitable	more suitable	most suitable

POINTS TO REMEMBER

Remember that superlatives—which usually end in *-est*—are used only when writing about three or more items. Many people mistakenly use superlatives instead of comparisons when writing about only two items:

Incorrect Use of Superlatives
Sara is the *eldest* of our two daughters.
In comparing New York and Chicago, New York is the *biggest*.

Correct Use of Comparison
Sara is the *elder* of our two daughters.
In comparing New York and Chicago, New York is *bigger*.

Do not use superlatives with absolute words such as *impossible, perfect, round, destroyed,* or *demolished.* These terms have no degree. If something is *impossible,* it means that it is not possible, not just difficult. If a building is *destroyed,* it is damaged beyond all repair. To say it is "completely destroyed" is repetitive, like saying someone is "completely dead."

Incorrect
The house was completely demolished.
The room was perfectly round.

Correct
The house was demolished.
The room was round.

EXERCISE 9 Eliminating Errors in Adjective and Adverb Use

Revise each of the following sentences to eliminate errors in using adjectives and adverbs.

1. Born to former slaves, Sarah Walker was orphaned at seven, married at fourteen, and widowed at twenty, enduring one of the worse upbringings possible.

   _____

   _____

2. She labored steady for twenty years as a laundress to support her daughter.

   _____

   _____

3. Her life radical changed when she invented a remarkably line of hair-care products for black women.

   _____

   _____

4. She sold her new developed products door-to-door, and eventual opened her own company.

   _____

   _____

5. Soon Sarah Walker's company was employing hundreds of newly workers.

   _____

   _____

6. Walker opened a beauty college to train black beauticians, when most black women were usual limited to working as cooks or maids.

   _____

   _____

7. Walker's rapid expanding enterprise also trained women to become sales agents and salon operators, allowing many black women to form independently businesses.

   _____

   _____

8. Soon dubbed Madame Walker, she became one of the most successfully women in America.

   _____

   _____

9. She became a respect figure in black society and was active involved in the civil rights movement.

   _____

   _____

10. High regarded by many politicians, Sarah Walker met with President Woodrow Wilson, urging him to make lynching a federal crime.

    _____

    _____

WORKING TOGETHER

Working with a group of students, review this e-mail for errors in adjective and adverb use. Underline mistakes and discuss corrections. Note how changing modifiers changes meaning.

Dear Sid:

I got your report last night. Please go over your figures careful. Are we really losing that much in the East Coast malls? I think your suggestions to increase sales are more better than those presented last month at the annually convention. Your report does make a clearly impression, especially about the Boston and Philadelphia stores. Boston is the best place of the two to expand. It seems cheap priced merchandise sells more better in Boston.

Your point about telemarketing and online sales catalogs makes a lot of sense. We have lagged behind the other department stores. It is totally impossible for us to compete unless we go after the high profitable Internet market.

See you next week in Chicago,

Perry Rand

_____

_____

_____

_____

_____

_____

_____

_____

_____

_____

_____

_____

_____

_____

GET THINKING
AND WRITING

CRITICAL THINKING

Write a paragraph describing how attending college has changed your life. Have you learned new skills, gained confidence, made new friends? Has attending college changed your personal life—forced you to work less or spend less time with family and friends? What are the positive and negative effects of college?

WHAT HAVE YOU WRITTEN?

Read your paragraphs, underlining each adjective and circling each adverb. Review the rules explained in this chapter. Have you used modifiers correctly?

WHAT HAVE YOU LEARNED?

Select the right adjective or adverb in each sentence.

1. _____ We drove over the (bad/badly) roads all night.

2. _____ We could not believe how (poor/poorly) maintained these roads were.

3. _____ The potholes only got (worse/worst) as we got closer to the camp-grounds.

4. _____ It was (impossible/totally impossible) to make the trip in less than two hours.

5. _____ Because we arrived late, we could not get assigned the (best/better) of the two campgrounds.

6. _____ The north site is (better/more better) than the old south site.

7. _____ We did manage to put up our (borrow/borrowed) tents before it got dark.

8. _____ A (sudden, powerful/sudden powerful) thunderstorm woke us up at midnight.

9. _____ Our (soak/soaked) tent began to leak.

10. _____ It got (much worse/much worser), so we slept in the SUV.

Answers appear on the following page.

GET WRITING

Can technology be overwhelming? Do you know anyone who is afraid of computers?

Write a paragraph describing people who seem locked out of the information age. Can they live without computers or the Internet, or are they losing opportunities and options?

WRITING ON THE WEB

Using a search engine such as AltaVista, Yahoo!, or Google, enter terms such as *adjective, adverb,* and *modifier* to locate current sites of interest.

ANSWERS TO WHAT HAVE YOU LEARNED? ON PAGES 340-341
1. bad (see page 328), 2. poorly (see page 331), 3. worse (see page 334), 4. impossible (see page 338), 5. better (see page 334), 6. better (see page 337), 7. borrowed (see page 327), 8. sudden, powerful (see page 331), 9. soaked (see page 327), 10. much worse (see page 337)

POINTS TO REMEMBER

1. Adjectives modify nouns and pronouns; adverbs modify verbs, adjectives, and other adverbs. *Note:* Use adjectives and adverbs carefully when modifying verbs like *see, hear, feel, smell, touch,* and *taste:*

    adjective: I see *good* coming from this.   [I predict good results.]
    adverb: I see *well*.   [I have good eyesight.]

2. Past participles are adjectives:

    a *rented* car   a *broken* window   *mashed* potatoes

    Note: When speaking, many people drop the *-ed* ending, but it should always be used in writing. Write "mashed potatoes," *not* "mash potatoes."

3. Most adverbs end in *-ly,* with some exceptions:

    hard   fast   right   just   straight

    Note: When speaking, many people commonly drop adverb endings, but they should always be used in writing. Write "drive carefully," not "drive careful."

4. Adjective and adverb use affects meaning:

    fresh sliced bread   = sliced bread that is fresh
    freshly sliced bread = bread (fresh or stale) that has just been sliced

5. *Good* and *bad* are adjectives that describe nouns and pronouns:

    I feel good. = I am healthy or happy.   I feel bad. = I am sad.

    Well and *badly* are adverbs that describe verbs, adjectives, or other adverbs:

    I feel well. = I have a good   I feel badly. = I have a poor
                          sense of touch.   sense of touch.

6. Use proper comparative form to discuss two items:

    Tom is *taller* than Barry.   My car is *more* expensive than hers.

    Note: Avoid using double comparisons—"more better."

7. Use proper superlative form to discuss three or more items:

    Tom is the *tallest* boy.   My car is the *most expensive*.

    Note: Avoid using superlatives to compare only two items—

    "eldest of my two girls."

(continued)

POINTS TO REMEMBER *(continued)*

8. Do not use superlatives with words like *impossible, destroyed, perfect, demolished, round:*

Incorrect	Correct
The house was completely destroyed.	The house was destroyed.
That is totally impossible.	That is impossible.
The room was perfectly round.	The room was round.

23

Using Prepositions

© Jutta Klee /CORBIS

GET WRITING

Do you think enough parents monitor what young children watch on TV?

Write a paragraph or develop a list of sentences stating guidelines parents should follow. How can you control what children watch when you are not at home?

344

What Are Prepositions?

Prepositions show relationships. They can express a geographical relationship— *above, below, inside*—a time relationship—*after, before, during*—or a connection between ideas or words—*with, without, for*. There are so many prepositions that you won't be able to remember all of them. But if you study a list, you will be able to recognize them when they appear in sentences:

about	at	beyond	in	out	toward
above	before	by	into	outside	under
across	behind	despite	inside	over	until
after	below	down	like	past	up
against	beneath	during	near	since	upon
along	beside	except	of	through	with
among	besides	for	off	throughout	within
around	between	from	on	to	without

Phrasal prepositions contain more than one word:

according to	because of	in case of
along with	by means of	in front of
apart from	by way of	in place of
as for	except for	in spite of
as to	in addition to	on account of

Prepositions often appear with nouns as their objects to create **prepositional phrases:**

above the counter	before the mail arrives	toward the park
after the game	behind the times	under the desk
against the grain	beside the freeway	without a clue
the cost of gas	the burden of debts	one of my classmates

UNNECESSARY PREPOSITIONS

Prepositions are not used before the following words:

- *today, tonight, tomorrow, yesterday*
- *here, there, home, downtown, uptown* after verbs showing motion
- *last* and *next* when they modify the object of a preposition

Incorrect
We leave *on* tomorrow.
They went *to* downtown.
He went *to* home last Friday.

Correct
We leave tomorrow.
They went downtown.
He went home last Friday.

We often create sentences that contain so many prepositional phrases they are hard to count:

> *During the game* fans *in the bleachers* tossed debris *on the field for the first time in the memory of parents in the area.* [seven prepositional phrases]

POINT TO REMEMBER

The subject of a clause never appears in a prepositional phrase:

One *of my friends* is sick.   [The subject is *one,* Not "*friends.*"]
The prices *of oil* are rising.   [The subject is *prices,* Not *oil.*]

To avoid errors in subject-verb agreement, make sure you do not mistake the object of a preposition for the subject. (*See Chapter 19*)

What Do You Know?

Circle the prepositions in each sentence.

1. Franklin Roosevelt was the first president to appear on television.

2. He gave a brief address at the opening of the World's Fair in 1939.

3. Grover Whalen, New York's official greeter, was in charge of the fair.

4. The 1939 fair was perhaps the most ambitious in history.

5. New Yorkers hoped the event would stimulate business during the depression.

6. Corporations designed unique displays and pavilions to create interest in their products.

7. On the brink of World War II, many nations staged elaborate cultural events to influence world opinion.

8. Despite the efforts by New York's flamboyant Mayor La Guardia and other celebrities, the World's Fair failed to attract enough tourists to pay for its extensive costs.

9. After Hitler invaded Poland in the fall of 1939, the mood of the fair changed.

10. In 1940, many of the national pavilions vanished as the countries that sponsored them fell to invasion and occupation.

    Answers appear on the following page.

AND REVISING

WHAT ARE YOU TRYING TO SAY?

Write a paragraph describing a rule or policy you would like to see changed. Explain your reasons why a college rule, a traffic law, a criminal statute, or a regulation in sports should be abolished or altered. Should the drinking age be changed? Should students have to take fewer classes to be considered full-time? Should your company's medical benefits be changed? Describe the problem the rule creates and explain how a change would provide a solution.

◄

WHAT HAVE YOU WRITTEN?

Underline the prepositions and prepositional phrases. Circle the subject of each sentence. Make sure subjects do not appear in prepositional phrases.

Incorrect
The problems <u>with</u> the rule *is* . . . [The subject is *problems*, not *rule*.]

Correct
The problems <u>with</u> the rule *are* . . . ◄

EXERCISE 1 Identifying Prepositions

Underline the preposition in each sentence.

1. Everyone was invited except Tim.

2. We must finish this by Monday.

3. We live in San Diego.

4. I took her to school.

5. The tornado swept through town.

6. That should be a secret among friends.

ANSWERS TO WHAT DO YOU KNOW? ON PAGE **346**
1. on; 2. at, of, in; 3. in, of;
4. in; 5. during; 6. in; 7. On, of;
8. Despite, by, for; 9. After, in, of, of; 10. In, of, to

7. We have tea at four.

8. He is running for city manager.

9. She was promoted to vice president.

10. They seem without hope.

EXERCISE 2 Identifying Prepositional Phrases

Underline the prepositional phrases in each sentence.

1. During the night road crews cleared debris left by the storm.

2. Despite rising costs, these cars remain popular with drivers under thirty.

3. Against his doctor's advice, Sam flew to Europe and biked through the mountains.

4. The passengers waited outside the terminal until the security guards searched through their baggage.

5. In the morning delivery trucks arrive from Madison with textbooks for the public schools.

6. I was so tired from running the marathon on Sunday that I slept until noon on Monday.

7. The dispute between the mayor and the city council stems from a long argument over property taxes.

8. Despite her best efforts, our office costs soared over budget, and we failed to get the shipment out on time.

9. We walked along the beach in the rain.

10. She drives past our house on her way to work in the morning.

EXERCISE 3 Identifying Subjects and Prepositional Phrases

Underline the subject of each clause twice and underline prepositional phrases once. Remember, subjects never appear in prepositional phrases.

1. Benito Juarez is one of the most important figures in Mexican history.

2. Born in a small village in the state of Oaxaca, Juarez was an orphan and runaway.

3. Despite many obstacles, Juarez graduated from a seminary.

4. Following his election as governor, Juarez developed programs to help the poor in Oaxaca.

5. During his term as governor Juarez initiated policies that brought him into conflict with powerful forces that began to align against him.

6. One of the most powerful leaders in Mexico at the time was Santa Anna, who exiled Juarez to New Orleans.

7. After liberals assumed power, they recalled Juarez from exile to become the minister of Justice.

8. In this position Juarez wrote a law that limited the power of military tribunals.

9. In 1857 he was elected chief justice of the Mexican Supreme Court.

10. After a year on the Supreme Court, Juarez assumed the presidency.

Commonly Confused Prepositions

We use most prepositions without a problem, automatically placing them in sentences to connect words and ideas. Some prepositions, however, are easily confused because their spellings or meanings are similar:

beside/besides
Beside means "next to":

> Walk *beside* me.

Besides means "in addition":

> *Besides* a skull fracture, he suffered a broken arm.

between/among
Between refers to two items:

> That should be settled *between* father and son.

Among refers to three or more items:

> That should be settled *among* players in the NBA.

due to/because
Due to should not be used in place of *because of:*

Incorrect
The flight was delayed *due to* thunderstorms.

Correct
The flight was delayed *because of* thunderstorms.

like/as
Like is a preposition and should be followed by a noun:

> It hit me *like* a *sledgehammer.*
> She ran *like* a *race horse.*

As is a conjunction and should be followed by a clause (a group of words with a subject and verb):

> It hit me *as I walked* under the bridge.
> She ran *as if she was chasing* a racehorse.

of
Of is not needed when other prepositions like *inside, outside,* and *off* appear:

I went inside the house.	*not*	I went inside *of* the house.
It fell off the table.	*not*	It fell off *of* the table.
She worked outside the law.	*not*	She worked outside *of* the law.

through/throughout

Through means "from one end to the other":

> We drove *through* Pittsburgh without hitting a red light.
> He went *through* high school with straight A's.

Throughout means "in every part":

> We drove *throughout* Pittsburgh looking for her lost dog.
> He went *throughout* the high school distributing flyers.

toward/towards

Both are correct:

> She walked *toward* the stage.
> She ran *towards* the audience.

IDIOMS WITH PREPOSITIONS

In English, certain nouns, verbs, and adjectives combine with prepositions to form idiomatic expressions:

Noun + Preposition	Verb + Preposition	Adjective + Preposition
criticism of	apologize for	different from
curiosity about	believe in	familiar with
dependence on	rely on	similar to

If you are unsure which preposition to use, refer to dictionaries like the *Longman Dictionary of American English* and the *Collins Cobuild English Language Dictionary.*

Locating Prepositions

Prepositions and prepositional phrases often serve as modifiers. They add extra information to a sentence. Like other adjectives and adverbs, they must be clearly linked to the words they describe to prevent confusion:

Confusing

We met the quarterback who scored the winning touchdown *in the supermarket.*
There is too much sex and violence viewed by children *on television.*
The crime wave angered voters, forcing the mayor to resign *on the South Side.*

Revised

When we were *in the supermarket,* we met the quarterback who scored the winning touchdown.
Children view too much sex and violence *on television.*
The crime wave angered voters *on the South Side,* forcing the mayor to resign.

EXERCISE 4 Eliminating Misplaced Prepositional Phrases

Rewrite the following sentences to eliminate confusion caused by misplaced prepositional phrases.

1. Tim was exhausted and passed out in the locker room by the marathon.

2. Mistrust can ruin a workplace among employees.

3. I want a sandwich for lunch without mustard.

4. She was the first student to get an athletic scholarship with disabilities.

5. We watched the children skating from the window on the lake.

6. I read the new book about terrorism on the bus.

7. The hikers took shelter from the sudden blizzard in a cave.

8. Because of the leaking roof tenants refused to pay rent on the top floor.

9. Tickets will be available for the midnight game at noon.

10. The children made so much noise that we had to close the window on the playground.

WORKING TOGETHER

Working with a group of students, revise this section of a student psychology paper to eliminate errors in preposition use.

Although it affects the lives of millions, schizophrenia is widely misunderstood. Many people outside of the medical profession think schizophrenics have a "split personality" as Jekyll and Hyde. The root *schiz* refers to a "split" but not a dual personality. It really means a patient is "split," or separated, of reality. Patients have difficulty functioning on society and often show poor social skills. Some hear voices and suffer from hallucinations. Beside these symptoms, patients may become extremely paranoid or agitated.

In recent years various medications have proved useful in helping schizophrenics lead more normal lives. There is no dispute among patients and doctors that the drugs are frequently effective. One of the main problems is that patients complain of side effects, such as lethargy and weight gain. Patients forget or refuse to take their drugs, and inside of a few days severe symptoms return.

Due to the fact that schizophrenia affects so many people, more research is needed to develop better drugs with fewer side effects.

_____

_____

_____

_____

_____

_____

_____

_____

_____

_____

_____

_____

_____

EXERCISE 5 Cumulative Exercise

Revise this passage to eliminate faulty parallelism, fragments, run-ons, and dangling or misplaced modifiers.

Expecting veterans to be tall, battle-scarred warriors, Audie Murphy struck the American public as an unlikely hero. Standing only five feet five inches and with a weight of only 112 pounds, the boyish twenty-year-old Texan had been thought unfit for combat. But having killed 241 enemy soldiers in seven bitter campaigns. Murphy emerged in 1945 as the most decorated soldier in American history. He appeared on the cover of *Life* magazine his smiling good looks fascinated the public. Impressed by the young man's charm, Audie Murphy was invited to Hollywood by Jimmy Cagney. Still recovering from war wounds, Murphy studied acting and working to soften his Texas accent. Murphy began appearing in movies and he wrote an autobiography of his war experiences. Having grown up in Texas and loving horses, producers saw Murphy as a natural for Westerns. But fame and having money troubled Murphy who feared fellow veterans might feel he was "cashing in" on his war record.

During the 1960s the unpopular war in Vietnam tarnished the image of war heroes and Murphy's film career faltered. Needing money, the public was dismayed when newspapers began linking Murphy with organized crime figures and gamblers. When he died in a plane crash in 1971, the media dismissed him as a relic of a bygone age and symbolizing old-fashioned values. Commenting on his friend's troubled last years and early death, cartoonist Bill Mauldin observed, "Long before his plane flew into a mountain, he was nibbled to death by ducks."

GET THINKING AND WRITING

CRITICAL THINKING

Write a paragraph describing your composing style at this point in the course. Do you write longhand or use a computer? Do you make outlines or plunge into writing? What prewriting methods do you use? What aspect of writing do you find the hardest? How could you improve the way you write?

WHAT HAVE YOU WRITTEN?

Read your paragraph out loud and examine it for logic and clarity. Do you avoid errors in sentence structure and preposition use?

1. Underline each preposition.
2. Do you avoid mistaking an object of a preposition for the subject in any sentences?
3. Do you make errors with easily confused prepositions such as *like* and *as* and *beside* and *besides*?

GET WRITING

© Network Productions/Index Stock Imagery

Do you think families spend too much time watching television? Would families benefit more by playing games, working on hobbies, or engaging in sports? Is watching television together a group activity?

Write a paragraph describing how families should spend their time together.

WRITING ON THE WEB

Using a search engine such as AltaVista, Yahoo!, or Google, enter terms such as *preposition, prepositional phrase, like and as,* and *beside and besides* to locate current sites of interest.

WHAT HAVE YOU LEARNED?

Circle the correct word in each sentence.

1. One of the most important automotive figures in Europe (was/were) André Citroën.

2. His influence on France was (as/like) Henry Ford's in America.

3. (Beside/Besides) building low-priced cars, Citroën helped introduce mass production techniques to French automaking.

4. (As/Like) Ford, Citroën believed cars should not just serve as luxury vehicles for the rich.

5. Low-priced cars and trucks, he thought, would revolutionize transport, freeing the public from bus and rail lines to travel (through/throughout) France when they wished.

6. (Inside/Inside of) a few years after their introduction, small two- and four-cylinder Citroëns became a common sight in Paris.

7. (Beside/Besides) using advertising, Citroën sponsored car expeditions to Africa and Asia to popularize his cars with drivers.

8. (Because of/due to) financial problems during the depression, Citroën was forced to declare bankruptcy and lost control over his car company.

9. On the streets of Paris, the vintage Citroën remains a common sight (as/like) a man with a beret.

10. (Among/Between) American tourists the cheap little cars became something of a joke (due to the fact that/because) the name Citroën sounds like *citron,* which is French for *lemon.*

Answers appear on the following page.

POINTS TO REMEMBER

1. Prepositions are words that show relationships between ideas:

Time	Location	Connection
before	above	with
after	under	without
during	inside	except

2. Prepositional phrases include a noun as a prepositional object:

The cost of *books.*   It's time for *fun.*   She was without *hope.*

(continued)

POINTS TO REMEMBER *(continued)*

3. The subject of a sentence is never the object of a preposition:

One of the players is injured.   [The subject is *One*, not *players*.]
Her choice of clothes is strange. [The subject is *choice*, not *clothes*.]

4. Use the correct preposition:

besides = in addition	Besides gas, we need oil.
beside = next to	Sit beside me.
between = two items	between mother and father
among = three or more	among the schoolchildren

Due to should not be used in place of *because of:*

The game was canceled *because of rain*.   not   The game was canceled *due to rain*.

Like is a preposition and should be followed by a noun:

She moved *like a dancer*.

As is a conjunction and should be followed by a clause:

She moved *as the dancers took the stage*.

Of is not needed with other prepositions like *inside, outside, off:*

inside the house   *not*   inside *of* the house

through = from one end to the other

We drove *through* the Holland Tunnel.

throughout = in every part

Repairs were made *throughout* the Holland tunnel.

toward/towards   Both are correct.

5. When using a preposition to modify other words, place it next to the word or words it modifies to prevent confusion.

Confusing
I met the quarterback who sued the NFL *in the airport*.

Correct
In the airport I met the quarterback who sued the NFL.

Part

Using Punctuation and Mechanics

Using Commas and Semicolons

© Bill Varie/CORBIS

GET WRITING

Many people now work at home. For some it means being more productive and having more free time because they don't spend hours commuting. They save money on parking and daycare. Others find working at home means a loss of privacy because they feel tied to their work twenty-four hours a day.

Write a paragraph explaining why you would or would not like to work at home.

What Are Commas and Semicolons?

Commas [,] and semicolons [;] are two of the most common, and often misused, marks of punctuation. Because they function like road signs, directing the way we read sentences, they are very important.

WHAT DO YOU KNOW?

Insert commas and semicolons where needed in the following sentences.

1. Anyone who wants to lose weight must have concentration willpower and energy.

2. My brother who wants to quit smoking has tried the patch hypnosis and psychotherapy.

3. The August 14 2003 blackout that affected New York New Jersey Ohio Michigan Connecticut and Ontario demonstrated defects in the power grid and it may have shown terrorists a way to cripple our economy.

4. Children no matter how young should be taught about the dangers of drugs.

5. First let me explain why I am here.

6. Madison the capital of Wisconsin is nicknamed "Mad City" by college students.

7. Toronto is the largest city in Ontario Montreal is the largest city in Quebec.

8. Her brother works in San Antonio her sister works in Tallahassee.

9. The film symposium included Martin Scorcese a director Robert Evans a producer Robert De Niro an actor and Jack Valenti a former industry spokesperson.

10. Because parking is limited we are asking students to carpool.

   Answers appear on the following page.

WHAT ARE YOU TRYING TO SAY?

Write a paragraph describing a place you go to when you want to be alone.

GET WRITING
AND REVISING

_____

_____

_____

_____

_____

_____

_____

_____

_____

_____

_____

_____

_____

_____

_____

WHAT HAVE YOU WRITTEN?

Circle the commas and semicolons that appear in your paragraph.

1. Can you provide a reason for inserting each comma?
2. Do you insert commas almost on reflex, without thought?
3. Do you sometimes think you miss needed commas or put them where they don't belong?
4. Do you know if any of your commas should be semicolons?

ANSWERS TO WHAT DO YOU KNOW? ON PAGE 359

1. Anyone who wants to lose weight must have concentration, willpower, and energy.
2. My brother, who wants to quit smoking, has tried the patch, hypnosis, and psychotherapy.
3. The August 14, 2003, blackout that affected New York, New Jersey, Ohio, Michigan, Connecticut, and Ontario demonstrated defects in the power grid, and it may have shown terrorists a way to cripple our economy.
4. Children, no matter how young, should be taught about the dangers of drugs.
5. First, let me explain why I am here.
6. Madison, the capital of Wisconsin, is nicknamed "Mad City" by college students.
7. Toronto is the largest city in Ontario; Montreal is the largest city in Quebec.
8. Her brother works in San Antonio; her sister works in Tallahassee.
9. The film symposium included Martin Scorcese, a director; Robert Evans, a producer; Robert De Niro, an actor; and Jack Valenti, a former industry spokesperson.
10. Because parking is limited, we are asking students to carpool.

Comma ,

In speaking, we pause to separate ideas or create emphasis. In writing, we use commas to signal pauses and shifts in our flow of words. Commas are the most common mark of punctuation used within sentences. By habit you may automatically insert the proper commas just as you remember to capitalize a person's name or place a period at the end of a sentence. No doubt, however, there are some places where you forget to use commas or wonder if the comma you added is needed at all.

Commas work like hooks to attach additional ideas to a basic sentence:

Inez won a scholarship.

After two years of hard work, Inez, *who speaks three languages,* won a scholarship, *which impressed her friends.*

Read this sentence aloud and notice the pauses you instinctively make to signal shifts in the flow of ideas.

Comma mistakes, like spelling errors, can seem like minor flaws, but they weaken your writing and make your ideas difficult to follow. Remember, when you are writing you are taking your readers on a journey. If you use commas correctly, they will be able to follow your train of thought without getting lost. Consider how commas change the meaning of these sentences:

The president says Congress will raise taxes.
The president, says Congress, will raise taxes.

Let's drink Brandy.
Let's drink, Brandy.

We need ice cream, sugar, a lemon soda, and cups.
We need ice, cream, sugar, a lemon, soda, and cups.

Planning to leave Georgia, Blake bought a car.
Planning to leave, Georgia Blake bought a car.

The best way to master comma use is to first review all the rules, then concentrate on the ones you do not understand or find confusing.

Comma Uses

Commas have ten basic uses.

1. **Use commas with *and, or, yet, but,* or *so* to join independent clauses to create compound sentences and avoid run-ons (see pages 212–216 and 229–230).**

    When you join two independent clauses (simple sentences), use a comma and the appropriate coordinating conjunction:

    Chinatown is a popular tourist attraction, <u>and</u> it serves as an important cultural center.

    We must develop new energy sources, <u>or</u> we will remain dependent on foreign oil.

    His movies won praise from critics, <u>yet</u> they failed at the box office.

    The blizzard knocked out power lines, <u>but</u> the hospital never lost electricity.

    Students are demanding more parking, <u>so</u> we expanded the lot behind the gym.

    Note: In informal writing, some writers omit commas in very short compound sentences:

    I drove but she walked.   She sings and he dances.

POINT TO REMEMBER

Use commas with *and, or, yet, but,* or *so* only to join two independent clauses, not pairs of words or phrases:

Unnecessary Commas
We like cake, and ice cream.

Rising prices of fossil fuels, and environmental concerns sparked interest in solar power.

Ted worked overtime throughout the summer, and now works full-time this semester.

Correct
We like cake and ice cream.

Rising prices of fossil fuels and environmental concerns sparked interest in solar power.

Ted worked overtime throughout the summer and now works full-time this semester.

To see if you need a comma with *and, or, yet, but* or *so,* apply this test:

1. Place a period just before the coordinating conjunction.
2. If there is a complete sentence on the left and the right, add the comma. If placing a period creates a fragment, omit the comma.

2. **Use a comma after a dependent clause that opens a complex sentence.**

> Because the parade was canceled, we decided to go to the shore.
> While he waited for the bus, Tom made business calls on his cell phone.
> After she graduated from law school, Lenore moved back to Chicago.

If the dependent clause follows the independent clause, the comma is usually deleted:

> We decided to go to the shore because the parade was canceled.
> Tom made business calls on his cell phone while he waited for the bus.
> Lenore moved back to Chicago after she graduated from law school.

3. **Use a comma after a long phrase or an introductory word.**

To prevent confusion, commas should usually follow phrases of three or more words that open sentences.

A short opening phrase may not require a comma to prevent confusion:

> After breakfast we are going to the natural history museum.

Longer phrases should be set off with commas to prevent confusion and signal the shift in ideas:

After breakfast with the new students and guest faculty, we are going to the natural history museum.

Introductory words such as interjections or transitions are set off with commas to prevent confusion and dramatize a shift in ideas:

Yes, I am cashing your check today.

Accordingly, we must demand more money.

No, we cannot afford a new car.

Of course, you are a welcome guest.

EXERCISE 1 Compound and Complex Sentences

Insert commas where needed in these compound and complex sentences. Note that some sentences are correct and do not need any changes.

1. The Statue of Liberty is a symbol of American freedom and it commemorates French-American friendship.

2. The idea for a great statue celebrating American freedom did not originate in the United States but in France.

3. Edouard de Laboulaye was a French historian and he was a great admirer of American democracy.

4. He proposed that France present America with a colossal statue and suggested the United States provide the location and the pedestal.

5. Frederic-Auguste Bartholdi designed the statue and he selected the site in New York Harbor.

6. The statue was completed in France and it was presented to the U.S. minister to France on July 4, 1884.

7. After Congress approved use of Bedloe Island construction on the pedestal began.

8. Because the statue was too large to be transported intact it was disassembled and shipped across the Atlantic in 214 packing cases.

9. The 225-ton statue took a year to erect and it was completed in 1886 to celebrate America's Centennial.

10. Although the statue is immediately recognized by Americans few citizens know that its official name is "Liberty Enlightening the World."

4. Use commas to separate words, phrases, and clauses in a series:

Words
We purchased computer paper, ink, pens, and pencils.
We sang, danced, and acted all summer.

Note: Some writers omit the final comma before the conjunction:

We purchased computer paper, ink, pens and pencils.

But most editors recommend adding the final comma to prevent confusion:

We need ice cream, sugar, chocolate and mint cookies.

[Do you need (bars of) chocolate and mint cookies or cookies made with mint and chocolate?]

Phrases

We purchased computer paper, ordered fax supplies, and photocopied the records.

We sang carefully, danced precisely, and acted flawlessly all summer.

Clauses

We purchased computer paper, Sarah ordered fax supplies, and Tim photocopied the records.

We sang opera carefully, the girls danced precisely, and the boys acted flawlessly all summer.

Note: If clauses contain commas, separate them with semicolons (see pages 370–371).

EXERCISE 2 Commas in Series

Add commas where needed to set off elements in a series.

1. Throughout history people came across large bones fossils and teeth.

2. The word *dinosaur* did not enter the English language until 1841, when Robert Owen coined the term from Greek words meaning "terrible" and "lizard."

3. Before Owen, people thought these strange bones were evidence of extinct dragons giant birds or mythical beasts.

4. Scientists discovered more dinosaur remains in the western United States Australia and Africa.

5. At first, researchers believed all dinosaurs were cold blooded because they resembled modern reptiles, such as alligators crocodiles and lizards.

6. In the 1950s, however, some scientists speculated that dinosaurs may have been warm blooded because of the rich blood supply evident in their bone structure the form of their cells and their projecting plates which may have been used for cooling.

7. Dinosaurs dominated the planet for millions of years, living on grass small plants and other wildlife.

8. Although some dinosaurs weighed several tons were eighty feet long and had tremendous endurance they had very small brains.

9. The extinction of dinosaurs remains a puzzle with some scientists blaming the Ice Age others blaming changes in their food supply and some blaming a comet or asteroid.

10. Researchers think an asteroid may have struck the earth which caused massive dust clouds to blot off sunlight alter the climate and kill the plants dinosaurs depended on for survival.

5. **Use commas to set off nonrestrictive or parenthetical words or phrases.**

You might notice a phrase such as *who is my friend* set off with commas in one sentence, then see the same phrase without commas in another sentence. A word or phrase is or is not set off with commas depending on whether it is nonrestrictive or restrictive. When a word or words only describe or add extra information about a noun, they are **nonrestrictive** and set off with commas. Nonrestrictive words are parenthetical and can be taken out of the sentence without changing the meaning of the noun they describe. If the words limit or define the noun, they are **restrictive** and *not* set off with commas. Restrictive words tells us more about a general or abstract noun like *anyone, someone, student, person,* or *parent*:

Anyone *who drives more than two hours a day* . . .
Someone *who donates blood regularly* . . .
The student *who developed the school web site* . . .
Any person *who drinks and drives* . . .
Each parent *with a child in my class* . . .

These phrases limit or define the subject. Without them the nouns lose much of their meaning. These restrictive phrases are part of the noun and therefore are not set off with commas. These same words could be nonrestrictive and set off with commas if they followed more specific nouns:

Nancy Sims, *who drives more than two hours a day,* . . .
My father, *who donated blood regularly,* . . .
Ted Greene, *who developed the school web site,* . . .

In each case the phrase only adds extra information about a clearly defined noun. Removing the phrase from the sentence does not change the meaning of the noun.

Nonrestrictive	**Restrictive**
Adds extra information about a noun Commas needed	Defines or limits the noun No commas
My mother, who wants to lose weight, should exercise. [*My mother* can only refer to one person. *Who wants to lose weight* only adds extra information about her.]	Anyone who wants to lose weight should exercise. [*Anyone* refers to any person. *Who wants to lose weight* defines which person should exercise.]
Ted Hughes, who won an Olympic medal, will coach. [*Ted Hughes* clearly defines the noun, so his winning a medal only adds extra details about him.]	The teacher who won an Olympic medal will coach. [*who won an Olympic medal* defines which teacher will coach.]

EXERCISE 3 Restrictive and Nonrestrictive elements

Insert commas where needed to set off nonrestrictive phrases and clauses. Remember, no commas are needed if the phrase or clause defines, or IDs, the noun.

1. In 1962 the United States which was the leading Western power during the Cold War nearly went to war with the Soviet Union.
2. Cuba which had become a communist country in 1959 was supported by the Soviet Union.
3. President Kennedy who wanted the country to take a strong stand against communism had permitted a group of Cuban exiles to attack Cuba.
4. The raid which became known as the Bay of Pigs failed.
5. Fidel Castro who feared an American invasion sought protection from the Soviet Union.
6. Cuba only ninety miles off the Florida coast gave the Soviets a valuable base to conduct surveillance against the United States.
7. The Soviets secretly shipped missiles that could carry nuclear warheads to Cuba.
8. When President Kennedy was shown photographs of missiles being installed in Cuba he and his brother who was attorney general sensed America was being threatened.
9. Although some generals suggested the United States launch a massive air strike the president who feared starting a nuclear war ordered a blockade to stop Soviet ships from bringing weapons into Cuba.
10. After days of tense negotiations Khrushchev the Soviet leader agreed to remove the nuclear missiles from Cuba ending the greatest crisis of the cold war.

POINT TO REMEMBER

To determine whether a phrase or clause is restrictive or nonrestrictive, just think of the term "ID." If the phrase or clause, identifies, or IDs, the noun, it is *restrictive* and should not be set off with commas:

> Will the student who missed the test see me after class.
> > Which student? *the student who missed the test*
> > The phrase *who missed the test* IDs which student, so no commas.

If the phrase or clause does not ID the noun but only adds extra information, it is *nonrestrictive* and should be set off with commas:

> Will Sam, who missed the test, see me after class.
> > Which student? *Sam*
> > The phrase *who missed the test* only adds extra information about *Sam,* who is defined by his name, so add commas.

If the phrase or clause IDs the noun—no commas.
If the phrase or clause is extra—add commas.

6. Use commas to set off contrasted elements.

To prevent confusion and highlight contrast, set off words and phrases with commas to signal abrupt or important shifts in a sentence:

The teachers, not the students, argue the tests are too difficult.
This president, unlike all his predecessors, is making the environment a priority.

7. **Use commas after interjections, words used in direct address, and around direct quotations.**

    Hey, get a life.
    Paul, help Sandy with the mail.
    George said, "Welcome to the disaster," to everyone arriving at the party.

8. **Use commas to separate city and state or city and country, items in dates, and every three numerals 1,000 and above:**

    I used to work in Rockford, Illinois, until I was transferred to Paris, France.

    Note: A comma goes after the state or country if followed by other words.

    She was born on July 7, 1986, and graduated high school in May 2004.

    Note: A comma goes after the date if followed by other words. No comma is needed if only month and year are given.

    The new bridge will cost the state $52,250,000.

    Note: A comma separates every three numerals.

9. **Use commas to set off absolute phrases.**
    Absolute phrases are groups of words that are not grammatically connected to other parts of sentences. To prevent confusion, they are attached to the main sentence with a comma:

    Her car unable to operate in deep snow, Sarah borrowed Tim's Jeep.
    Wilson raced down the field and caught the ball on one knee, his heart pounding.

10. **Use commas where needed to prevent confusion or add emphasis.**
    Writers add commas to create pauses or signal shifts in the flow of words to prevent readers from becoming confused:

    Confusing
    Whenever they hunted people ran for cover.
    To Sally Madison was a good place to live.
    To help feed the hungry Jim donated bread.

    Improved
    Whenever they hunted, people ran for cover.
    To Sally, Madison was a good place to live.
    To help feed the hungry, Jim donated bread.

    Note: Reading sentences out loud can help you spot sentences that need commas to prevent confusion.

Writers often use commas for special effect to emphasize words, phrases, and ideas. Because readers pause when they see a comma, it forces them to slow down and pay additional attention to a word or phrase:

Without Comma   *With Comma for Emphasis*
Today I quit smoking.   Today, I quit smoking.

EXERCISE 4 Comma Use

Insert commas where needed in each sentence.

1. Louis Pasteur a noted French chemist first discovered antibiotics.

2. He observed that certain bacteria killed anthrax a deadly disease.

3. Around 1900 Rudolf von Emmerich a German bacteriologist isolated pyocyanase which had the ability to kill cholera and diphtheria germs.

4. It was an interesting discovery but it worked only in the test tube.

5. In the 1920s the British scientist Sir Alexander Fleming discovered lysozyme a substance found in human tears that had powerful antibiotic properties.

6. Lysozyme however killed only harmless bacteria and it could not be concentrated to affect disease-producing germs.

7. In 1928 Fleming accidentally discovered penicillin and he demonstrated its antibiotic properties in a series of experiments against a range of germs.

8. Fleming however never conducted animal or human tests.

9. During World War II two British scientists conducted further tests on penicillin helping put Fleming's discovery to practical use.

10. Introduced in the last stages of the war the new drug proved effective in treating infected wounds saving thousands of lives.

EXERCISE 5 Comma Use

Insert commas where needed in each sentence.

1. Aaron Burr America's third vice president was born in Newark New Jersey on February 6 1756.

2. After attending the College of New Jersey now Princeton University Burr joined the Continental Army in 1775 rising to the rank of lieutenant colonel.

3. Burr entered politics and he was elected to the U.S. Senate in 1791.

4. Burr's leadership in the old Republican party brought him into bitter conflict with Alexander Hamilton a leading figure in the Federalist party.

5. In 1800 Burr became Thomas Jefferson's vice president which brought him into greater conflict with political foes.

6. In 1804 he failed to secure renomination as vice president and lost a bid to become governor of New York largely because of Hamilton's opposition.

7. Angered by Hamilton's attacks Burr challenged Hamilton to a duel.

8. Burr and Hamilton met in Weehawken New Jersey on July 11 1804.

9. Burr shot and killed Hamilton ending one of the most bitter personal feuds in American politics.

10. Burr's victory however came at great personal cost because many considered him a murderer and he was widely discredited for killing one of the country's founding fathers.

Avoiding Unnecessary Commas

Because commas have so many uses, we sometimes place them where they are not needed. After reviewing all the rules, you may find yourself putting commas where they don't belong.

GUIDE TO ELIMINATING UNNECESSARY COMMAS

1. Don't put a comma between a subject and verb unless setting off nonrestrictive elements or a series:

   Incorrect: The old, car was stolen.
   Correct: The car, which was old, was stolen.

2. Don't use commas to separate prepositional phrases from what they modify:

   Incorrect: The van, in the driveway, needs new tires.
   Correct: The van in the driveway needs new tires.

3. Don't use commas to separate two items in a compound verb:

   Incorrect: They sang, and danced at the party.
   Correct: They sang and danced at the party.

4. Don't put commas around titles:

   Incorrect: The film opens with, "Love Me Tender," and shots of Elvis.
   Correct: The film opens with "Love Me Tender" and shots of Elvis.

5. Don't put commas after a series unless it ends a clause that has to be set off from the rest of the sentence:

   Incorrect: They donated computers, printers, and telephones, to our office.
   Correct: They donated computers, printers, and telephones, and we provided office space.

6. Don't set off a dependent clause with a comma when it ends a sentence:

   Incorrect: The game was canceled, because the referees went on strike.
   Correct: The game was canceled because the referees went on strike.

   Note: A comma is needed if a dependent clause opens the sentence:

   Because the referees went on strike, the game was canceled.

EXERCISE 6 Comma Use

Correct comma use in the following passage, adding missing commas where needed and deleting unnecessary commas.

The suburbs, exploded after World War II. In 1944 only 114000 houses were built in America. By 1950 over 1700000 new houses were built. Veterans most of whom were eligible for low-interest loans through the GI Bill created a massive market for single-family homes. Developers built neighborhoods subdivisions and entire new communities. Orchards farms wheat fields orange groves dairies and forests were bull-dozed to build streets, and houses. In less than ten years more than 9000000 Americans left the cities for the new housing developments which offered young couples a chance to live in their own homes. To the parents, of the baby-boom, generation, suburbs offered security space and recreation they could not find in congested, city neighborhoods. Anyone in the fifties who planned to stay in the city to raise a family was considered old-fashioned or eccentric.

_____

_____

_____

_____

_____

_____

_____

_____

_____

_____

_____

_____

Semicolon ;

You can think of semicolons as capitalized commas. They are used to connect larger items—clauses and complex items in a list.

Semicolons have two uses:

1. **Use semicolons to join independent clauses when *and, or, yet, but,* or *so* are not present:**

   We drove to San Francisco; Jean and Bill flew.
   Olympia is the capital of Washington; Salem is the capital of Oregon.

   Note: Remember to use semicolons even when you use words such as *nevertheless, moreover,* and *however:*

They barely had time to rehearse; however, opening night was a
success.
The lead has a commanding stage presence; moreover, she has a
remarkable voice.

2. **Use semicolons to separate items in a series that contains commas.**

Normally we use commas to separate items in a list:

We need paper, pens, ink, and computer discs.

However, if items in the list contain commas, it is difficult to tell which
commas are separating items and which commas are separating elements
within a single item:

The governor will meet with Vicki Shimi, the mayor of Bayview, Sandy
Bert, the new city manager, the district attorney, Peter Plesmid, and
Al Leone, an engineering consultant.

How many people will the governor meet? Is Vicki Shimi the mayor of
Bayview or are Vicki Shimi and the mayor two different people? To prevent
confusion, semicolons are inserted to separate items in the series:

The governor will meet with Vicki Shimi, the mayor of Bayview; Sandy
Bert, the new city manager; the district attorney; Peter Plesmid; and
Al Leone, an engineering consultant.

The governor will meet with five people:

1. *Vicki Shimi, the mayor of Bayview*
2. *Sandy Bert, the new city manager*
3. *the district attorney*
4. *Peter Plesmid*
5. *Al Leone, an engineering consultant*

EXERCISE 7 Understanding Semicolons

Underline the items in each list and enter the number in the right column.

1. The clinic needs plasma, a blood product; Motrin, an analgesic;
   bandages; first-aid supplies; and antibiotics.   # _____

2. The auto show featured a Stanley Steamer; a 1920 Model T;
   a Kubelwagen, a military version of the Volkswagen; a
   WWII jeep; a Hummer; a '57 Thunderbird; a Prism, a
   solar-powered car; a new Buick; and a hydrogen-powered
   test vehicle.   # _____

3. The wedding party consisted of Cheryl, Heather's cousin;
   Dave Draper; Tony Prito, Dave's brother-in-law; Tony's nephew;
   Mindy Weiss, a fashion model; Chris, a photographer; and
   Heather's best friend.   # _____

4. A number of campus facilities need repairs, especially
   Felber Hall, a science lab; the business library; Riley Hall;
   the math center; Matthews Hall, the tutoring center; and
   the main dorm.   # _____

5. The alumni fund-raiser attracted a former senator;
   Nancy Price, the former ambassador to Greece; Paige Brooks,
   a U.S. attorney; Westbrook Sims; a screenwriter;
   Lorne Michaels, producer of *Saturday Night Live;* and
   William Stone, former mayor of Seattle.   # _____

EXERCISE 8 Comma and Semicolon Use

Insert commas and semicolons where needed in each sentence.

1. The Marx brothers were born in New York City and were known by their stage names: Chico born Leonard Harpo born Arthur Groucho born Julius and Zeppo born Herbert.

2. The brothers studied music and they began a show business career touring vaudeville houses with their aunt and mother calling themselves the Six Musical Mascots.

3. The brothers appeared on their own as the Four Nightingales later they changed the name of their act to simply the Marx Brothers.

4. Their wild stage antics and funny sight gags made the Marx Brothers popular soon Hollywood took notice.

5. Their early films including *Animal Crackers Horse Feathers* and *Duck Soup* won praise from fans and critics.

6. Though only thirty-four Zeppo Marx decided to retire in 1935 the remaining three brothers continued making movies.

7. The late 1930s was a period of continuing success for the Marx brothers films such as *A Night at the Opera A Day at the Races* and *Room Service* became comedy classics.

8. Each brother had a distinct stage persona they hardly seemed related.

9. Groucho smoked cigars had a large false moustache and made sarcastic jokes Chico talked with an Italian accent and played the piano Harpo never spoke wore a trench coat played the harp and chased women.

10. Few Marx Brothers fans realize there was a fifth Marx brother Gummo Marx nicknamed after his rubber overshoes did not pursue a career in show business.

WORKING TOGETHER

Working with a group of students, edit this e-mail and add commas and semicolons where needed. Note how adding correct punctuation makes the message easier to read.

Dear Sandi:

I read the report about the December 15 2003 and March 15 2004 power outages that affected the Pike Street Plant the Fall River Warehouse and our sales offices.

I think you are correct in assuming we will have to spend at least $1250000 to upgrade our control systems. Although all our facilities have emergency generators any power shortage causes extensive delays in data processing manufacturing and communications.

We have studied the municipal systems in Trenton New Jersey El Paso Texas and Bozeman Montana. I suggest we incorporate the control systems used by these cities. These systems are also widely used in major industries including Ford a car company IBM a computer firm and Nike an athletic shoe manufacturer.

Sandi it's important to present your proposal in person at the budget meeting on May 12. Hope to see you there.

Maria Sanchez

CRITICAL THINKING

Write one or more paragraphs about the most challenging course you are taking this semester. Which is your hardest course and why? Describe the problems you face, how you try to overcome them, the way other students seem to cope, and what you will have to do to successfully complete the course.

GET THINKING AND WRITING

WHAT HAVE YOU WRITTEN?

Review your writing for comma and semicolon use and other errors. Read your paragraphs out loud. Does this help you discover comma errors, misspelled words, fragments, and awkward phrases?

Do you enjoy working with other people? If you worked at home, would you miss the social interaction?

Write a paragraph that describes past coworkers or explains the kind of people you hope to work with in the future.

© Myrleen Cate/Index Stock Imagery

WRITING ON THE WEB

Using a search engine such as AltaVista, Yahoo!, or Google, enter terms such as *commas, semicolons, using commas, comma drills, comma rules, understanding commas,* and *punctuation* to locate current sites of interest.

WHAT HAVE YOU LEARNED?

Insert commas and semicolons where needed in the following sentences.

1. On September 1 1939 Hitler invaded Poland launching a war in Europe that would last six years and kill millions.

2. I am willing to sell my Firebird for $17500 but you must pay with cash money order or certified check.

3. This morning unlike most mornings I took the bus to work.

4. The teacher who gets the most votes will be placed on the school board.

5. We flew to Berlin then rented a car to tour Frankfurt Bonn Dusseldorf and Hamburg.

6. We import cocoa beans wood carvings and oil from Nigeria.

7. Because oil prices are difficult to predict trucking companies have problems guaranteeing future rate schedules.

8. Historians consider Abraham Lincoln who led the country during the Civil War Franklin Roosevelt who carried the nation through the depression and World War II and Woodrow Wilson president during World War I as some of our greatest leaders.

9. Well we will have to lower prices to compete with discount malls or we may have to close one of our downtown stores.

10. High school students report math gives them the most problems college students state writing poses the greatest challenges.

Answers appear on the following page.

POINTS TO REMEMBER

Commas are used for ten reasons:

1. Use commas with *and, or, yet, but,* or *so* to join independent clauses to create compound sentences and avoid run-ons:

   I went to the fair, but Margaret drove to the beach.

2. Use a comma after a dependent clause that opens a complex sentence:

   Before the game began, the coach spoke to her players.

3. Use a comma after a long phrase or introductory word:

   Having waited in the rain for hours, I caught a cold.
   Furthermore, I caught a cold waiting in the rain.

4. Use commas to separate words, phrases, and clauses in a series:

   She bought a battered, rusted, and windowless Model A Ford.
   They dug wells, planted crops, and erected new silos.

5. Use commas to set off nonrestrictive or parenthetical words or phrases:

   Sid, who lives in Chicago, should know a lot about Illinois politics.
   Anyone who lives in Chicago should know a lot about Illinois politics.

6. Use commas to set off contrasted elements:

   Children, not parents, should make this decision.

7. Use commas after interjections, words used in direct address, and around direct quotations:

   Nancy, can you work this Saturday?
   Wait, you forgot your keys.
   Rick said, "We must pay cash," every time we wanted to buy something.

8. Use commas to separate city and state or city and country, items in dates, and every three numerals 1,000 and above.

   He moved to Topeka, Kansas, on October 15, 2003, and bought a $125,000 house.

9. Use commas to set off absolute phrases:

   Their plane grounded by fog, the passengers became restless.

(continued)

POINTS TO REMEMBER *(continued)*

10. Use commas where needed to prevent confusion or add emphasis:

    Every time I drive, home is my final destination.
    This morning, we play to win.

Semicolons are used for two reasons:

1. Use semicolons to join independent clauses when *and, or, yet, but,* or *so* are not present:

    We walked to school; they took a limo.

2. Use semicolons to separate items in a series that contains commas:

    I asked Frank, the field manager; Candace, the sales representative; Karla, our attorney; and Erica, the city manager, to attend the budget meeting.

ANSWERS TO WHAT HAVE YOU LEARNED? ON PAGES 374–375

1. On September 1, 1939, Hitler invaded Poland, launching a war in Europe that would last six years and kill millions.
2. I am willing to sell my Firebird for $17,500, but you must pay with cash, money order, or certified check.
3. This morning, unlike most mornings, I took the bus to work.
4. The teacher who gets the most votes will be placed on the school board.
5. We flew to Berlin, then rented a car to tour Frankfurt, Bonn, Dusseldorf, and Hamburg.
6. We import cocoa beans, wood carvings, and oil from Nigeria.
7. Because oil prices are difficult to predict, trucking companies have problems guaranteeing future rate schedules.
8. Historians consider Abraham Lincoln, who led the country during the Civil War; Franklin Roosevelt, who carried the nation through the depression and World War II; and Woodrow Wilson, president during World War I, as some of our greatest leaders.
9. Well, we will have to lower prices to compete with discount malls, or we may have to close one of our downtown stores.
10. High school students report math gives them the most problems; college students state writing poses the greatest challenges.

Using Other Marks of
Punctuation

Do people always have a right to protest in a democracy? Should protests ever be banned?

Write a paragraph explaining your view and support it with examples.

What Are the Other Marks of Punctuation?

Writers use punctuation to show when they are quoting other people, presenting parenthetical ideas, posing a question, or creating a contraction. Most students know when to use a question mark or an exclamation point. Other punctuation marks, however, can be confusing, so they are worth looking at in detail.

WHAT DO YOU KNOW?

Add apostrophes, quotation marks, italics, parentheses, question marks, colons, and exclamation points where needed in the following sentences.

1. Erika shouted, Run immediately to the exits now as soon as she spotted the fire.

2. The new car $32,500 with taxes was more than we could afford.

3. The team needs new equipment helmets, shoulder pads, and shoes.

4. Dont they realize that The Cask of Amontillado is one of Poes greatest short stories.

5. I saw the episode Terrorists at Our Doorstep on Sixty Minutes last Sunday.

6. Why wont they give you your money back.

7. There is a sale on mens coats, but they only have 38s and 40s left.

8. The band toured the major cities of Europe London, Berlin, Paris, Madrid, and Rome.

9. Pauls daughter took a plane, but his two boys drove the familys car.

10. The telephone is near the womens room.

   Answers appear on the following page.

GET WRITING
AND REVISING

WHAT ARE YOU TRYING TO SAY?

Many critics argue that television shows, movies, and music videos present negative images of women and minorities. Do you agree with this viewpoint? Why or why not? Write a paragraph stating your views and provide examples to support your opinion.

_____

_____

_____

_____

_____

_____

_____

_____

_____

_____

_____

_____

WHAT HAVE YOU WRITTEN?

Review the punctuation in your paragraph and circle items you think are wrong.

ANSWERS TO WHAT DO YOU KNOW? ON PAGE 378

1. Erika shouted, "Run immediately to the exits now!" as soon as she spotted the fire.
2. The new car ($32,500 with taxes) was more than we could afford.
3. The team needs new equipment: helmets, shoulder pads, and shoes.
4. Don't they realize that "The Cask of Amontillado" is one of Poe's greatest short stories?
5. I saw the episode "Terrorists at Our Doorstep" on _Sixty Minutes_ last Sunday.
6. Why won't they give you your money back?
7. There is a sale on men's coats, but they only have 38's and 40's left.
8. The band toured the major cities of Europe: London, Berlin, Paris, Madrid, and Rome.
9. Paul's daughter took a plane, but his two boys drove the family's car.
10. The telephone is near the women's room.

Apostrophe '

Apostrophes are used for three reasons.

1. _Apostrophes indicate possession._ The standard way of showing possession, that someone or something owns something else, is to add an apostrophe and an -s:

Noun	Erica's car broke down.
Acronym	NASA's new space vehicle will launch on Monday.
Indefinite pronoun	Someone's car has its lights on.
Endings of _s, x,_ or _z_ sound	Phyllis' car is stalled. [or _Phyllis's_]

   Note: Apostrophes are deleted from geographical names:

Pikes Peak	Taylors Meadows	Warners Pond

   Note: Apostrophes may or may not appear in possessive names of businesses or organizations:

Marshall Field's	Sears	Tigers Stadium	Sean's Pub

   Follow the spelling used on signs, stationery, and business cards.

   Because we also add an -s to make many words plural, apostrophes have to be placed carefully to show whether the noun is singular or plural:

Singular	Plural
a boy's hat	the boys' hats
my girl's bicycle	my girls' bicycles
her brother's car	her brothers' car (two or more brothers own one car)
a child's toy	children's toys*
the woman's book	women's books*

*Because *children* and *women* already indicate plurals, the apostrophe is placed before the -*s*.

Compound nouns can indicate joint or individual possession. Ted and Nancy, for example, could own and share one car, share the use of several vehicles, or own separate cars they drive individually. The placement of apostrophes indicates what you mean:

Ted and Nancy's car	[Ted and Nancy both own one car.]
Ted and Nancy's cars	[Ted and Nancy both own several vehicles.]
Ted's and Nancy's cars	[Ted and Nancy individually own cars.]

2. *Apostrophes signal missing letters and numbers in contractions.* In speaking we often shorten and combine words, so that we say "don't" for "do not" and "could've" for "could have." We also shorten numbers, particularly years, so that we talk about "the Spirit of '76" or refer to a car as a "'99 Mustang." Apostrophes indicate that letters or numerals have been eliminated:

shell = an outer casing	she'll = she will
well = source of water	we'll = we will
cant = trite opinions	can't = cannot

Note: Only one apostrophe is used, even if more than one letter is omitted.

Apostrophes are placed over the missing letter or letters, not where the words are joined:

do not = don't   *not*   do'nt

Deleted numbers are indicated with a single apostrophe:

The stock market crashed back in '29.
She won the gold medal in the '88 Olympics.
I am restoring his '67 VW.

3. *Apostrophes indicate plurals of letters, numbers, or symbols.* Words do not need apostrophes to indicate plurals. An added -*s* or other spelling changes indicate that a noun has been made plural. However, because adding an -*s* could lead to confusion when dealing with individual letters, numbers, or symbols, apostrophes are used to create plurals:

I got all B's last semester and A's this semester.
Do we have any size 7's or 8's left?
We can sell all the 2003's at half price.

Note: Apostrophes are optional in referring to decades, but be consistent:

Inconsistent

She went to high school in the 1990's but loved the music of the
1960s.

Consistent

She went to high school in the 1990's but loved the music of the
1960's.

or

She went to high school in the 1990s but loved the music of the 1960s.

Note: Common abbreviations such as *TV* and *UFO* do not need apostrophes
to indicate plurals:

We bought new TVs and several DVDs.

POINT TO REMEMBER

it's = contraction of "it is"
  It's raining.
  I know it's going to be a long day.
its = possessive of "it"
  My car won't start. Its battery is dead.
  The house lost its roof in the storm.

In editing, use this test to see if you need an apostrophe:

1. Read the sentence out loud, substituting *it is* for *its* or *it's.*
2. If the sentence sounds OK, use *it's:*
     It is going to be hot.
     It's going to be hot.
3. If the sentence sounds awkward, use *its:*
     I like *it is* style.
     I like its style.

EXERCISE 1 Using Apostrophes to Show Possession

Use apostrophes to create possessive forms of nouns.

1. a car belonging to one girl   _____

2. photographs belonging to the people   _____

3. the short stories of Kate Chopin   _____

4. a park operated by the city   _____

5. evidence collected by the FBI   _____

6. books owned by my mother-in-law   _____

7. pictures drawn by children   _____

8. characters created by Dickens   _____

9. a boat owned by two men   _____

10. a car owned by Karl and Hedda Muller _____

EXERCISE 2 Using Apostrophes to Show Contractions

Use apostrophes to create contractions of each pair of words.

1. you are _____

2. I am _____

3. would not _____

4. who is _____

5. should not _____

6. does not _____

7. he will _____

8. they are _____

9. could have _____

10. have not _____

EXERCISE 3 Using Apostrophes

Revise this essay, adding apostrophes where needed.

On October 1, 1910, an explosion wracked the *Los Angeles Times* offices. The buildings second floor collapsed, crushing employees working below. Despite the fire departments rescue attempts, twenty-one people were killed and dozens injured.

Another bomb exploded in the home of the newspapers owner. A third bomb was discovered in the home of the Merchants and Manufacturers Associations secretary. This bomb did not explode, and police officers analysis traced its dynamite to James McNamara, a member of the Typographical Union. He was the brother of Joseph McNamara, the International Union of Bridge and Structural Workers secretary-treasurer.

To many people the bombing of the citys largest newspaper and the murder of twenty-one workers was an act of sheer terrorism, an attack against journalism and free speech. Members of the nations growing labor movement, however, believed the brothers arrest was unfair. They insisted the MacNamaras had been framed to undermine the publics support for unions. The countrys largest union organization, the American Federation of Labor, hired Americas most famous lawyer, Clarence Darrow, to defend the brothers.

Darrow agreed to take the MacNamaras case. But the brothers supporters were soon disappointed by the famed attorneys actions. Darrow understood investigators efforts had assembled a considerable amount of evidence against the brothers. Convinced his clients trial would only result in convictions and probable death sentences, Darrow persuaded the brothers to confess in exchange for prison sentences. James McNamara admitted to the judge he had planted a bomb in an alley next to the building, hoping only to scare the newspapers employees. He had no idea his bombs explosion would ignite a fatal fire. The states attorney accepted this confession and approved of the judges decision to sentence James McNamara to life in prison. Although no direct evidence connected James brother to the bombing, he received fifteen years.

Quotation Marks " "

Quotation marks—always used in pairs—enclose direct quotations, titles of short works, and highlighted words.

- **For direct quotations**
  When you copy word for word what someone has said or written, enclose the statement in quotation marks:

    Martin Luther King said, "I have a dream."

  Note: The final mark of punctuation precedes the final quotation mark, unless it does not appear in the original text:

    Did Martin Luther King say, "I have a dream"?

  Remember: Set off identifying phrases with commas:

    Shelly insisted, "We cannot win unless we practice."
    "We cannot win," Shelly insisted, "unless we practice."
    "We cannot win unless we practice," Shelly insisted.

  Note: Commas are not used if the quotation is blended into the sentence:

    They exploited the "cheaper by the dozen" technique to save a fortune.

  Quotations within quotations are indicated by use of single quotation marks:

    Shelly said, "I was only ten when I heard Martin Luther King proclaim, 'I have a dream.'"

  Long quotations are indented and not placed in quotation marks:

    During the depression, many cities and states had little or no money to pay employees:

    > Milwaukee and other cities began paying public employees with promissory notes because they did not have funds to issue standard paychecks. One town in Nebraska paid its sheriff in chickens donated by local farmers who could not afford to feed them and could find no buyers to sell them to. A village in Vermont paid teachers with obsolete library books. (Smith 10)

  Final commas are placed inside quotation marks:

    The letter stated, "The college will lower fees," but few students believed it.

  Colons and semicolons are placed outside quotation marks:

    The letter stated, "The college will lower fees"; few students believed it.

  Indirect quotations do not require quotation marks:

    Martin Luther King said that he had a dream.

- **For titles of short works**

  The titles of poems, short stories, chapters, essays, songs, episodes of television shows, and any named section of a longer work are placed in quotation marks. (Longer works are underlined or placed in italics.)

  > Did you read "When Are We Going to Mars?" in *Time* this week?

  Note: Do not capitalize articles, prepositions, or coordinating conjunctions (*and, or, yet, but, so*) unless they are the first or last words.

  Quotation marks and italics (or underlining) distinguish between shorter and longer works with the same title. Many anthologies and albums have title works. Quotation marks and italics indicate whether you are referring to a song or an entire album:

  > Her new CD *Wind at My Back* has only two good songs: "Daybreak" and "Wind at My Back."

- **To highlight words**

  Words are placed in quotation marks to draw extra attention:

  > I still don't know what "traffic abatement" is supposed to mean.
  > This is the fifth time this month Martha has "been sick" when we needed her.

EXERCISE 4 Quotation Marks and Apostrophes

Add quotation marks and apostrophes where needed.

1. Mayor Hughes proclaimed during his speech, I won't raise taxes.
2. Patrick Henry is famous for saying that he had but one life to give to his country.
3. George Orwell began his famous novel with the sentence, It was a bright cold day in April and the clocks were striking thirteen.
4. He sang a lot of early Sinatra numbers like Ive Got You Under My Skin and Ill Never Smile Again.
5. Did you read Paul Masons article Coping with Depression?
6. Ted told us he is going to summer school.
7. Last night the president stated, Whenever I feel confused, I remember the words of Abraham Lincoln, who said, Listen to the angels of your better nature.
8. Forming a New Nation is the first chapter in our history book.
9. I plan to retire after next season, Terry Wilson announced to her coach, noting, NBC has offered me a job covering womens tennis.
10. Toms only eight, but he memorized The Gettysburg Address in less than an hour.

EXERCISE 5 Direct Quotations

Add quotation marks, commas, and apostrophes where needed to indicate direct quotations, quotations within quotations, and titles of short works.

You know Tom said I really like our English class.

I know Vicki responded. I really enjoy the stories we have been reading this semester. Which one is your favorite?

Let me think. I guess I really liked all the Poe stories Tom said, tapping his book. I really like The Pit and the Pendulum and The Tell-Tale Heart. What about you? What is your favorite so far?

Bartleby the Scrivener. I just loved that story Vicki laughed. I just love the way Bartleby keeps saying I would prefer not to every time his boss asks him to do something.

I would prefer not to Tom repeated flatly. You know there is a movie version with Crispin Glover and David Paymer?

Really? Vicki said. I'd love to see that!

_____

_____

_____

_____

_____

_____

_____

_____

_____

_____

_____

_____

_____

Colon :

Colons are placed after independent clauses to introduce elements and separate items in numerals, ratios, titles, and time references:

Lists The coach demanded three things from his players: loyalty, devotion, and teamwork.

Note: Colons are placed only after independent clauses to introduce lists:

Incorrect
We need: paper, pens, pencils, and ink.

Correct

We need school supplies: paper, pens, pencils, and ink.

Phrases	The coach demanded one quality above all others: attention to detail.
Time references	The game started at 12:05 p.m.
Ratio	We have a 10:1 advantage.
Title and subtitle	Kathy Frank's new book is called *Arthur Miller: Playwright and Philosopher*.
After salutations in business letter	Dear Ms. Smith:
Scripture reference	Romans 12:1–5
Introduction of block quotations	Catherine Henley argues the loss of rain forests will have serious consequences for the planet and the quality of life in the future:

> It is obvious that the continual erosion of rain forests will increase global warming by decreasing a major producer of the planet's oxygen-generating ability. Cutting down trees will cause more mudslides, more flooding, and more water pollution.

Parentheses ( )

Parentheses set off nonessential details and explanations and enclose letters and numbers used for enumeration:

Nonessential detail	The Senate committee (originally headed by Warner and Kennedy) will submit a special report to the White House.
First-time use of acronym	The Federal Aviation Administration (FAA) has new security policies.
Enumeration	The report stated we must (1) improve tutoring services, (2) provide additional housing, and (3) increase funding of bilingual classes.

Brackets [ ]

Brackets set off interpolations or clarifications in quotations and replace parentheses within parentheses.

Sometimes quotations taken out of context can be confusing because readers may misunderstand a word or reference. A quotation using the word "Roosevelt" in a biography of Theodore Roosevelt would be clear in context. But if you use this quotation in a paper, readers could easily assume you're referring to Franklin, not Theodore, Roosevelt. If you have to add clarifications or corrections, place them in brackets:

Interpolations to prevent confusion	Eric Hartman observed, "I think [Theodore] Roosevelt was the greatest president."
	Time noted, "President Bush told Frank Bush [no relation] that he agreed with his tax policies."
	The ambassador stated, "We will give them [the Iraqi National Congress] all the help they need."
Corrections	Kaleem Hughes called 911, saying, "Come quick. We have hundreds of people [35–50 according to the FAA report] trapped in the terminal."
Parentheses within parentheses	The Senate committee (originally headed by Warner and Kennedy [both running for reelection this year]) will submit a special report to the White House.

Dash —

Dashes mark a break in thought, set off a parenthetical element for emphasis, and set off an introduction to a series.

Sudden break in thought	Ted was angry after his car was stolen— who wouldn't be?
Parenthetical element	The studio— which faced bankruptcy— desperately needed a hit movie.
Introduction	They had everything needed to succeed— ideas, money, marketing, and cutting-edge technology.

Note: Create dashes by a continuous line or hit your hyphen key twice. No spaces separate dashes from the word they connect.

Hyphen -

A hyphen is a short line used to separate or join words and other items.

- Use hyphens to break words:

    We saw her on tele-
    vision last night.

    Note: Only break words between syllables.

- Use hyphens to connect words to create adjectives:

    We made a last-ditch attempt to score a touchdown.

Do *not* use hyphens with adverbs ending in *-ly:*

We issued a quickly drafted statement to the press.

- Use hyphens to connect words forming numbers:

   The firm owes nearly thirty-eight million dollars in back taxes.

- Use hyphens after some prefixes:

   His self-diagnosis was misleading.

- Use hyphens between combinations of numbers and words:

   She drove a 2.5-ton truck.

Ellipsis . . .

An ellipsis, composed of three spaced periods [. . .], indicates that words have been deleted from quoted material.

Original Text
The mayor said, "Our city, which is one of the country's most progressive, deserves a high-tech light-rail system."

With Ellipsis
The mayor said, "Our city . . . deserves a high-tech light-rail system."

Note: Delete only minor ideas or details—never change the basic meaning of a sentence by deleting key words. Don't eliminate a negative word like "not" to create a positive statement or remove qualifying words:

Original
We must, only as a last resort, consider legalizing drugs.

Incorrect Use of Ellipsis
He said, "We must . . . consider legalizing drugs."

Note: When deleting words at the end of a sentence, add a period before the ellipsis:

The governor said, "I agree we need a new rail system. . . ."

Note: An ellipsis is not used if words are deleted at the opening of a quotation:

The mayor said that "the city deserves a high-tech light-rail system."

Note: If deleting words will create a grammar mistake, insert corrections with brackets:

Original
"Poe, Emerson, and Whitman were among our greatest writers."

With Ellipsis
"Poe . . . [was] among our greatest writers."

Slash /

Slashes separate words when both apply and show line breaks when quoting poetry:

> The student should study his/her lessons.
> Her poem read in part, "We hope / We dream / We pray."

Question Mark ?

Question marks are placed after direct questions and to note questionable items:

> Did Adrian Carsini attend the auction?
> Did you read, "Can We Defeat Hunger?" in *Newsweek* last week?

Note: Question marks that appear in the original title are placed within quotation marks. If the title does not ask a question, the question mark is placed outside the quotation marks:

> Did you read "The Raven"?

Question marks in parentheses are used to indicate that the writer questions the accuracy of a fact, number, idea, or quotation:

> The children claimed they waited two hours (?) for help to arrive.

Exclamation Point !

Exclamation points are placed at the end of emphatic statements:

> Help!
> We owe over ten million dollars!

Note: Exclamation points should be used as special effects. They lose their impact if used too often.

Period .

Periods are used after sentences, in abbreviations, and as decimals:

> I bought a car.
> We gave the car to Ms. Chavez, who starts working for Dr. Gomez on Jan. 15.
> The book sells for $29.95 in hardcover and $12.95 in paper.

When an abbreviation ends a sentence, only one period is used. Widely used abbreviations such as FBI, CIA, ABC, BBC, and UCLA do not require periods.

EXERCISE 6 Punctuation

Add missing punctuation in each sentence.

1. The receipt is stamped Jan 15 1005 a.m.

2. The childrens museum will close early because its going to snow.

3. The school offers students three key services tutoring, housing, and guidance.

4. The Lottery is still my favorite short story

5. Can you help me

6. I cant be in two places at the same time.

7. Frank Kennedy no relation to the president helped design NASAs first rockets

8. To save money we have to accomplish three goals 1 lower travel costs, 2 cancel unnecessary magazine subscriptions and 3 cut down on cell phone use.

9. Ted and Nancy car is the only one on the island.

10. He made a lastminute effort to study for the exams.

WORKING TOGETHER

Working with a group of students, correct the punctuation in the following announcement.

New Payroll Procedure

To prevent confusion we have established a new payroll policy. Employees pay slips must be filed by 400 every Fri in person or sent by e-mail no later than 600 pm Thurs in order to receive a check the following week. Its too difficult for us to hand-process separate checks. If you want to use payroll deduction for your childs daycare fee, just check the box at the bottom of the form. Remember to provide your child children with insurance coverage, fill out the State Insurance Profile SIP and give it to Ms Green by Mar. 30.

EXERCISE 7 Cumulative Exercise for Punctuation and Coordination and Subordination

Rewrite this passage to correct errors in punctuation and reduce awkward and repetitive phrasing through coordination and subordination. You may have to reword some sentences, adding or deleting phrases. If you have difficulty revising some of the sentences, review pages 212–216.

On St Patrick's Day 1930 ground was broken on the Empire State Building in New York City. The date was chosen to bring the project good luck. The builders were facing an awesome challenge. They were constructing the tallest building in the world. The building was conceived during the Roaring Twenties. Construction did not start until 1930. This was the time of the Great Depression. Thousands of businesses in New York had closed. Few people needed new office space. The Empire State Building thrived. It became a prestigious address. It also became one of Manhattans top tourist attractions. The building was made famous when millions of moviegoers around the world saw King Kong mount it's summit. In 1945 an army bomber became lost in fog. It smashed into the building. It struck the 79th floor. It caused a fire. The building was damaged. It was quickly repaired. There are now taller buildings. Few are as well known as the Empire State Building.

_____

_____

_____

_____

_____

_____

_____

_____

_____

_____

_____

_____

CRITICAL THINKING

*GET THINKING
AND WRITING*

How do you define poverty? Is an urban family with a car, TV, and VCR poor if they cannot afford vacations, new clothes, or expensive meals? Would you consider Amish farmers, who choose to live without modern conveniences or cars, poor? Is being poor a matter of income, a matter of living simply, or a matter of wanting more than you can afford? Write a paragraph explaining your definition of poverty.

GET WRITING

This WWII poster warned Americans to remain silent. Does this suggest that speech can be unpatriotic? Do you think during a war on terrorism people should be careful about what they say?

Write a paragraph stating your opinion. Can we have free speech and security?

SILENCE
MEANS SECURITY

© CORBIS

WRITING ON THE WEB

Using a search engine such as AltaVista, Yahoo!, or Google, enter terms such as *colons, slashes, brackets, parentheses, ellipsis, question marks, exclamation points, punctuation, understanding punctuation, using punctuation,* and *punctuation rules* to locate current sites of interest.

WHAT HAVE YOU LEARNED?

Add apostrophes, quotation marks, italics, parentheses, question marks, colons, and exclamation points where needed in the following sentences.

1. Karen and Adrians car is a 04 BMW.

2. Its on sale for less than twenty one thousand dollars.

3. We will meet at 1030 Mon morning.

4. Tom screamed, Call 911, now.

5. Her Newsweek article Why Are We in Iraq makes a lot of sense.

6. The boys department has moved to the third floor.

7. The Rolls Royce $175,000 with tax was a major investment for Ms Columbo.

8. Give Tim a call, or hell demand a refund.

9. The mens department has plenty of 38s and 40s you might like.

10. Dont let my dog scare you. Shes just scared.

   Answers appear on the following page.

POINTS TO REMEMBER

1. Apostrophes show possession:

Erica's car	NASA's rocket	someone's hat

   Ted and Nancy's cars.   [mutual ownership]
   Ted's and Nancy's cars.   [individual ownership]

   Apostrophes indicate missing letters or numbers:

   Didn't you sell the '67 Thunderbird?
   its = possessive of it   it's = it is

   Apostrophes indicate plurals of letters, numbers, or symbols:

   She got all A's this year.   Get the W-2's at the payroll office.

2. Quotation marks enclose direct quotations, titles of short works, and highlighted words:

   He said, "I'll be there."   Can you sing "Blue   Is he "sick"
                                 Eyes"?   again?

3. Colons are placed after independent clauses to introduce elements and separate items in numerals, titles, ratios, and time references:

   We need supplies: gas, oil, and spark plugs.   It is now 10:17 a.m.

4. Parentheses set off nonessential details and explanations and enclose letters and numbers used for enumeration:

   We got an apartment ($950 a month) because our state loan application (SLA) had not been approved for three reasons: (1) we needed more references, (2) we needed a bigger down payment, and (3) we owed too much on credit cards.

5. Brackets set off interpolations or clarifications in quotations and replace parentheses within parentheses:

   Time notes, "Frank Bush [no relation to the president] will work for the White House next fall."

   (continued)

POINTS TO REMEMBER *(continued)*

6. Dashes mark breaks in thought, set off parenthetical elements, and set off introductions to series:

   She expected help— wouldn't you?

7. Hyphens separate and join words and other items:

   He wrote a fast-paced soundtrack for the action film.
   You still owe twenty-eight dollars.

8. An ellipsis indicates words have been deleted from a direct quotation:

   The senator stated, "Our country . . . needs new leadership."

9. Question marks are placed within quotation marks if they appear in the original title or quotation:

   Her article is called "Can Anyone Lose Weight?"

   Question marks are placed outside quotation marks if they are not part of the original:

   Did you read "The Gold Bug"?

ANSWERS TO WHAT HAVE YOU LEARNED? ON PAGES 392–393

1. Karen and Adrian's car is a '04 BMW.
2. It's on sale for less than twenty-one thousand dollars.
3. We will meet at 10:30 Mon. morning.
4. Tom screamed, "Call 911, now!"
5. Her *Newsweek* article "Why Are We in Iraq?" makes a lot of sense.
6. The boys' department has moved to the third floor.
7. The Rolls Royce ($175,000 with tax) was a major investment for Ms. Columbo.
8. Give Tim a call, or he'll demand a refund.
9. The men's department has plenty of 38's and 40's you might like.
10. Don't let my dog scare you. She's just scared.

Using Capitalization

© AP Photo/Gregory Smith

Do you think smoking should be banned in all public places, including bars and restaurants? Given the cost of smoking-related illnesses, does the government have the right to restrict smoking? Do smokers have any rights?

Write a paragraph stating your views on smoking in public.

What Is Capitalization?

Capital letters are used to begin sentences, indicate special meanings, and prevent confusion.

Words are capitalized to indicate proper nouns and prevent confusion. The word *catholic* means universal; *Catholic* refers to a specific religion. The word *mosaic* describes decorations or paintings made from tiny inlaid pieces of tile or other material, but *Mosaic* refers to the Biblical figure Moses, as in *Mosaic laws*. A *mustang* is a wild horse; a *Mustang* is the brand name of a Ford car. The word *Earth* refers to the planet we live on, while *earth* means soil.

Capitalizing words changes their meaning:

Sue loves modern poetry.	[indicates an interest in current literature]
Sue loves Modern Poetry.	[indicates she likes a specific poetry class]
We flew African airlines.	[indicates several different airlines in Africa]
We flew African Airlines.	[indicates a single company called African Airlines]
Will banks cash my check?	[indicates financial institutions]
Will Banks cash my check?	[indicates someone named Banks]

WHAT DO YOU KNOW?

Underline the letters in each sentence that should be capitalized.

1. At the beginning of the civil war the south achieved its initial goal of establishing the confederate states of america.

2. Relief efforts by the united nations were hampered by floods, civil war, and poor communications.

3. Gina tucci was born in brooklyn but grew up in a jersey suburb.

4. This semester i am taking english, american history, a music class, and professor andrews' introduction to abnormal psychology.

5. We took a united airlines flight to new orleans, known as the crescent city.

   Answers appear on the following page.

GET WRITING
AND REVISING

WHAT ARE YOU TRYING TO SAY?

Write a shopping list of common items you buy—food, clothing, office supplies, or CDs.

_____

_____

_____

_____

_____

_____

_____

_____

_____

_____

_____

WHAT HAVE YOU WRITTEN?

Review your list for capitalization. Did you capitalize proper nouns, such as names of stores or product brand names? Review the rules on the following pages, then edit your list.

ANSWERS TO WHAT DO YOU KNOW? ON PAGE 396

1. At the beginning of the Civil War the South achieved its initial goal of establishing the Confederate States of America.
2. Relief efforts by the United Nations were hampered by floods, civil war, and poor communications.
3. Gina Tucci was born in Brooklyn but grew up in a Jersey suburb.
4. This semester I am taking English, American history, a music class, and Professor Andrews' Introduction to Abnormal Psychology.
5. We took a United Airlines flight to New Orleans, known as the Crescent City.

Rules for Capitalization

There are a dozen main rules for capitalizing words. At first the list may seem overwhelming, but if you remember a simple guideline, you can avoid most problems: *Capitalize words that refer to something specific or special — proper names or specific places or things.*

1. Capitalize the first word of every sentence:

    We studied all weekend.

2. Capitalize the first word in direct quotations:

    Felix said, "The school should buy new computers."

3. Capitalize the first word and all important words in titles of articles, books, plays, movies, television shows, seminars, and courses:

"Terrorism Today"	*Gone With the Wind*	*Death of a Salesman*
The Way We Were	*Sixty Minutes*	Urban Planning II

4. Capitalize the names of nationalities, languages, races, religions, deities, and sacred terms:

    Many Germans speak English.   The Koran is the basic text in Islam.

I bought a French poodle.

She was the city's first African American mayor.

5. Capitalize the days of the week, months of the year, and holidays:

We celebrate Flag Day every June 14.

Some people celebrate Christmas in January.

The test scheduled for Monday is canceled.

We observed Passover with her parents.

Note: The seasons of the year are not capitalized:

We loved the spring fashions.

Last winter was mild.

6. Capitalize special historical events, documents, and eras:

Battle of the Bulge
World War II
Magna Carta

Declaration of Independence
Middle Ages
Russian Revolution

7. Capitalize names of planets, continents, nations, states, provinces, counties, towns and cities, mountains, lakes, rivers, and other geographical features:

Mars	North America	Canada	Ontario
Toronto	Mount Everest	Lake Michigan	Mississippi
the Badlands	Great Plains	Amazon	Kuwait

8. Capitalize *north, south, east,* and *west* when they refer to geographical regions:

The convention will be held in the Southwest.
He has an Eastern accent.
He raised castle in the West.

Note: Do not capitalize *north, south, east,* and *west* when used as directions:

We drove north for almost an hour.
The farm is southwest of Rockford.

9. Capitalize brand names:

Coca-Cola   Ford Thunderbird   Cross pen

Note: Some common brand names like *Kleenex, Xerox,* and *Coke* sometimes appear in lowercase.

10. Capitalize names of specific corporations, organizations, institutions, and buildings:

This engine was developed by General Motors.
After high school he attended Carroll College.
The event was sponsored by the Chicago Urban League.
We visited the site of the former World Trade Center.

11. Capitalize abbreviations, acronyms, or shortened forms of capitalized words when used as proper nouns:

FBI	CIA	NOW	ERA
IRA	JFK	LAX	NBC
UN	AT&T	VT	OPEC

12. Capitalize people's names and nicknames:

Barbara Roth   Timmy Arnold

Note: Capitalize professional titles when used with proper names:

Doctor Ryan suggested I see an eye doctor.
Three deans supported Dean Manning's proposal.
Our college president once worked for President Carter.
This report must be seen by the president.
(The word *president* is often capitalized to refer to the president of the United States.)

Note: Capitalize words like *father, mother, brother, aunt, cousin,* and *uncle* only when used with or in place of proper names:

My mother and I went to see Uncle Al.
After the game, I took Mother to meet my uncle.

POINT TO REMEMBER

The rules of capitalization sometimes vary. Some publications always capitalize *president* when it refers to the president of the United States; other publications do not. *African American* is always capitalized, but editors vary whether blacks should be capitalized. Some writers capitalize *a.m.* and *p.m.*, while others do not.
    Follow the standard used in your discipline or career and be consistent.

EXERCISE 1 **Capitalization**

Underline letters that should be capitalized.

1. Most cities in the world have emerged naturally, often growing up around a river, such as the nile, the rhine, or the mississippi.

2. On the other hand, brazil made a striking departure in the 1950s, creating an entirely new city in an uninhabited region.

3. The coastal city of rio de janeiro served as brazil's capital for generations.

4. Although known for its striking mountains and beaches, rio had little open land, limiting the city's potential growth.

5. As the economy expanded after wwii, government agencies and corporations needed more office space.

6. In addition, the national government wanted to exploit the rich resources of brazil's undeveloped interior.

7. During the administration of president juscelino kubitschek, planning began on the new capital to be called brasilia.

8. To emphasize the futuristic aspect of the city, the brazilian urban planner lucio costa created a city layout that resembled a jet airliner.

9. The fuselage of the plane contains government offices, while apartment buildings form the plane's wings.

10. The plaza of the three powers and the presidential residence called the palace of the dawn form the nose of the airliner.

11. The famous architect oscar niemeyer designed brasilia's major buildings.

12. The city is surrounded on three sides by an artificial lake, created by damming the paraná river.

13. On april 21, 1960, brasilia was officially dedicated by the brazilian government.

14. The city is home to the university of brasilia, the national theater, parks, a stadium, and a zoo.

15. Highways and rail lines link brasilia with rio de janeiro, são paulo, and other major brazilian cities.

16. Moving the capitol to brasilia forced thousands of civil servants to move, freeing up office and apartment space in crowded rio.

17. Although the strikingly modern city was considered an architectural marvel, many federal employees did not appreciate the actions of president kubitschek.

18. Some complained, "it's like living in a world's fair exhibit."

19. In the early years, the city was deserted on weekends as workers flew back to rio to enjoy the old city's famous beaches and nightlife.

20. Gradually brasilia developed a character of its own, and its population rapidly swelled to nearly two million by the end of the century.

EXERCISE 2 Capitalization

Underline letters that should be capitalized.

1. The aztecs took their name from azatlan, a mythical homeland in northern mexico.

2. When the toltec civilization collapsed around 1100 AD, various peoples moved into mexico's central plateau and occupied the land around lake texcoco.

3. Arriving late, the aztecs were forced into the unoccupied marshes on the western side of lake texcoco.

4. Settling on a single island of dry land in the swamp, the aztecs were dominated by powerful neighbors who forced them to pay tributes.

5. Although poor and greatly outnumbered, the aztecs gradually built a great empire.

6. Within two hundred years the aztecs developed a superior civilization and established the city of tenochtitlán on the site of modern mexico city.

7. Over the years, the aztecs built bridges to connect their island city to surrounding dry land and drained marshes to create productive gardens.

8. Causeways and canals formed a highly effective transportation system, which helped tenochtitlán become an important market city.

9. From their small island, the aztecs expanded their influence, conquering other peoples and creating an empire that reached the border of guatemala.

10. The aztecs created a highly structured society divided into three classes: slaves, commoners, and nobles.

11. They developed writing and created a calendar based on an earlier mayan date-keeping system.

12. The aztecs worshipped numerous gods, including the moon goddess coyolxauhqui, the rain god tlaloc, and the sun god uitzilopochtli.

13. The spanish explorer hernan cortés arrived in tenochtitlan in 1519.

14. Amazed by the city's architecture and network of canals, the european visitors called the city the venice of the new world.

15. At first, the aztec king montezuma ii welcomed cortés, thinking him to be the god quetzalcoatl.

16. But cortés's arrival spelled the end of the aztec empire.

17. Armed with superior weapons and aligning himself with rebellious tribes, cortés was able to defeat montezuma's army.

18. The europeans also brought smallpox and other diseases, which devastated the aztecs, who had no immunity to these foreign germs.

19. Today a million aztecs, mostly poor farmers, live on the fringes of mexico city.

20. The mexican government honors the aztecs by using many of their symbols on government emblems and paper money.

EXERCISE 3 Capitalization

Underline letters that require capitalization.

Today we are accustomed to television networks battling for ratings. During sweeps weeks, networks broadcast their most popular or controversial programs. Networks have been known to wage intense bidding wars to land a late-night tv host, news anchor, or sitcom to secure larger audiences and higher advertising revenue. In the early 1990s, nbc, for example, hoped to keep both letterman and leno after johnny carson retired from hosting the long-running *tonight show*. After a number of meetings, letterman decided to move to cbs. Such rivalry was not unknown in other media. In the pre-tv era, newspapers fought bitter and costly circulation wars. In chicago, newspaper distributors were often attacked and their papers burned by rival publishers. In britain the circulation battles were less violent but no less intense. Newspapers offered subscribers premium items such as free encyclopedias or special editions of dickens's most popular books. Often clever londoners would sign up with one newspaper to get a premium item, then cancel and subscribe to a rival paper to receive yet another free gift.

WORKING TOGETHER

Work with a group of students to determine the definition of each word. What difference does capitalization make? You may use a dictionary to check your answers.

1. China _____

china _____

2. tide _____

Tide _____

3. NOW _____

now _____

4. Corvette _____

corvette _____

5. democratic _____

Democratic _____

6. new deal _____

New Deal _____

7. Dodgers _____

dodgers _____

8. bull moose _____

Bull Moose _____

9. Acre _____

acre _____

10. mars _____

Mars _____

GET THINKING AND WRITING

CRITICAL THINKING

Write a paragraph describing what you did on a recent weekend.

WHAT HAVE YOU WRITTEN?

Review your writing for capitalization. Did you remember to capitalize proper nouns — names of people, products, stores, movies, restaurants, or bands?

IMPROVING YOUR WRITING

Review drafts of upcoming papers, past assignments, and writing exercises in this book for capitalization. Can you find errors you have made? Note rules that apply to areas you have found confusing.

© RNT Productions/CORBIS

GET WRITING

Write a paragraph describing what you do to stay in shape. Do you wish you had more time to work out? Do you find dieting a challenge? If you could change anything in your lifestyle to improve your health, what would it be?

WRITING ON THE WEB

Using a search engine such as AltaVista, Yahoo!, or Google, enter terms such as *capitalization rules,* *using capitals,* and *proper nouns* to locate current sites of interest.

WHAT HAVE YOU LEARNED?

Underline letters in each sentence that should be capitalized.

1. According to the fbi, internet fraud is a growing problem.

2. Mayors from large cities met with president Bush seeking federal aid to fight crime.

3. The lecture by dr. westin was sponsored by the american academy of social historians.

4. We had to ford the rock creek river to reach the boy scout camp.

5. She taught english and history in high school before getting a job at alverno college.

Answers appear on the following page.

POINTS TO REMEMBER

1. Capitalize the first word in each sentence and direct quotation.
2. Capitalize first and important words in titles of books, articles, movies, and works of art.
3. Capitalize names of nationalities, languages, races, and religions.
4. Capitalize days of the weeks, months, holidays, historical events, documents, and eras.
5. Capitalize proper names and nicknames of people, places, products, organizations, and institutions.
6. Capitalize abbreviations such as *FBI* and *NAACP.*
7. Capitalize titles only when they precede a name or are used in place of a name: "I took Mother to see Dr. Grant."
8. Do not capitalize seasons such as *spring* and *fall.*
9. Do not capitalize *north, south, east,* and *west* when used as directions.

ANSWERS TO WHAT HAVE YOU LEARNED? ON PAGE 403
1. According to the FBI, Internet fraud is a growing problem.
2. Mayors from large cities met with President Bush seeking federal aid to fight crime.
3. The lecture by Dr. Westin was sponsored by the American Academy of Social Historians.
4. We had to ford the Rock Creek River to reach the Boy Scout camp.
5. She taught English and history in high school before getting a job at Alverno College.

Correcting Spelling Errors

© Tom Grill/CORBIS

GET WRITING

What will increase your chances of graduating? Do you need to improve your computer skills, devote more time to school, or develop better study habits?

Write three sentences that state three specific things you would like to change. Read your sentences carefully, proofreading them for errors and revising word choices to make sure they clearly express what you want to say. ◄

Spelling influences the way readers look at your writing. Consider the impression this letter makes:

```
Dear Ms. Ling:

This semmester I will be graduting from Stanton Commu-
nity College with an assocate degree in marketing. In
addition to studing business law, advertizing, sales
management, and economics, I served as an intern at
Lockwood and Goldman. As my resumme shows, I was a
specal asistant to Grace Lockwood and help desin web-
sites, cataloge pages, and two radio commercals.

Given my education and experience, I belief I would
be an asset to you're firm. I would apprecate having
the oppurtunity to meet with you at your convenince.
I can be reached at (504) 555-7878.

Sincerly,

Carlo Colfield
```

All the student's education and hard work are overshadowed by spelling errors, which make the writer appear careless and uneducated. Not every reader can detect a dangling modifier or faulty parallelism, but almost everyone can identify a misspelled word.

Some people have a photographic memory and need only see a word once to remember its exact spelling. Others, even highly educated professional writers, have difficulty with spelling. If English is your second language or if you frequently misspell words, make spelling a priority. It can be the easiest, most dramatic way to improve your writing and your grades. Make sure you reserve enough time in the writing process to edit papers to correct spelling mistakes.

WHAT DO YOU KNOW?

Underline the misspelled or misused words in each sentence.

1. The commitee reported to the Common Counsel yesterday.

2. This will cost more then the financal planner suggested.

3. I am not familar with any of the sophmores this year.

4. Her advise was quit irrevlent.

5. We are to dependant on foriegn oil.

6. This is beccoming a problem.

7. I belief you are write about that.

8. This arguement has to be settled by a carring person.

9. Its tough if you don't have alot of money to loose.

10. I past the final exam.

Answers appear on the following page.

WHAT ARE YOU TRYING TO SAY?

GET WRITING
AND REVISING

Write one or more paragraphs that compare how college differs from high school. You may focus on teachers, courses, grading, or student attitudes. Include one or more examples.

_____

_____

_____

_____

_____

_____

_____

_____

_____

_____

_____

_____

_____

WHAT HAVE YOU WRITTEN?

Review what you have written and check with a dictionary to see if you have misspelled any words.

1. Review assignments you have written in this or any other course for spelling errors. Do you see any patterns, any words you repeatedly misspell?

2. List any words you find confusing or have doubts about:

_____   _____

_____   _____

_____   _____

_____   _____

_____   _____

ANSWERS TO WHAT DO YOU KNOW? ON PAGES 406–407:
1. committee, Council; 2. than, financial; 3. familiar, sophomores; 4. advice, quite, irrelevant; 5. too, dependent, foreign; 6. becoming; 7. believe, right; 8. argument, caring; 9. It's, a lot, lose; 10. passed.

STEPS TO IMPROVING SPELLING

1. Make spelling a priority, especially in editing your papers.
2. Look up new words in a dictionary for correct spelling and meaning. Write them out a few times to help you memorize them.
3. Study the glossaries in your textbooks to master new terms.
4. Review lists of commonly misspelled words (pages 456–457) and commonly confused words (pages 453–456).
5. Create a list of words you have trouble with. Keep copies of the list next to your computer and in your notebook. Each week try to memorize three or four of these words. Update your list by adding new terms you encounter.
6. Read your writing out loud when editing. Some spelling errors are easier to hear than see.
7. Remember, *i* before *e* except after *c* or when it sounds like *a* as in *neighbor* and *weigh*:

i before *e*

achieve	field	niece	shield
brief	grievance	piece	yield

except after *c*

ceiling	deceive	perceive	receipt

or when it sounds like *a*

eight	freight	rein	vein

Exceptions: *either, height, leisure, seize, weird*

8. Review rules for adding word endings (pages 412–414).
9. Learn to use computer spellcheck programs and understand their limitations. Although such programs can easily spot typos and commonly misspelled words, not every program will alert you to confusing *there* for *their* or *affect* for *effect*. (See pages 453–456.)
10. If you are a poor speller, eliminating spelling errors is the fastest and easiest way to improve your grades.

Commonly Misspelled Words

There are many words we commonly misspell. They may be foreign words, contain silent letters, or have unusual letter combinations. Often we misspell words because in daily speech we slur and fail to pronounce every letter:

Incorrect	*Correct*
goverment	govern<u>m</u>ent
suppose (past tense)	suppose<u>d</u>
ice tea	ice<u>d</u> tea

FORTY COMMONLY MISSPELLED WORDS

absence	belief	generous	mortgage
achieve	benefit	grammar	necessary
acquire	challenge	guard	obvious
address	committee	height	opinion
among	control	heroes	parallel
analyze	decision	identity	persuade
argument	dying	label	possess
athletic	embarrass	license	privilege
beautiful	enough	marriage	separate
becoming	familiar	material	vacuum

See pages 456–457 for the complete list.

EXERCISE 1 Commonly Misspelled Words

Underline the correctly spelled word in each pair.

1. yield/yield
2. albumn/album
3. sincerely/sincerly
4. noticable/noticeable
5. libary/library
6. fulfill/fulfil
7. equiptment/equipment
8. fourty/forty
9. surprize/surprise
10. similar/similiar

Commonly Confused Words

In addition to easily misspelled words, there are easily confused words. The word we put on the page is correctly spelled, but it is the wrong word and has a different meaning than we intend. Many words look and sound alike but have clearly different meanings:

all together	acting in unity or in the same location	"The children stood *all together*."
altogether	totally	"The repairs will be $75 *altogether*."
any one	a single person, idea, or item	"*Any one* of the rooms is open."
anyone	anybody	"Can *anyone* help us?"
conscious	awake or aware	"The patient is *conscious*."

conscience	moral sensibility	"Let your *conscience* be your guide."
desert	an empty expanse of land	"There is no water in the *desert*."
dessert	an after-dinner treat	"Can we have cake for *dessert*?"

Using the wrong word not only creates a spelling error but creates confusion, often resulting in a statement that means something very different from what you intend:

Let's *adopt* the Tennessee pollution standards.	[Let's *accept* Tennessee's standards.]
Let's *adapt* the Tennessee pollution standards.	[Let's *change* Tennessee's standards.]
She made an *explicit* call for action.	[She made a *clear, blatant* call for action.]
She made an *implicit* call for action.	[She made an *implied, subtle* call for action.]
Personal e-mail is being examined.	[*Private or intimate* e-mail is being examined.]
Personnel e-mail is being examined.	[*Employee* e-mail or e-mail *about employees* is being examined.]

TEN MOST COMMONLY CONFUSED WORD GROUPS

accept/except

| accept | to take | "Please *accept* my apology." |
| except | but/to exclude | "Everyone *except* Tom attended." |

affect/effect

| affect | to change or influence | "Will this *affect* my grade?" |
| effect | a result | "What *effect* did the drug have?" |

farther/further

| farther | geographic distance | "The farm is ten miles *farther* on." |
| further | in addition | "*Further* negotiations proved useless." |

hear/here

| hear | to listen | "Did you *hear* her new song?" |
| here | a place or direction | "Put it over *here*." |

its/it's

| its | possessive of *it* | "My car won't start. *Its* battery died." |
| it's | "it is" | "Looks like *it's* going to rain." |

lay/lie

| lay | to put or place | "*Lay* the boxes on the table." |
| lie | to recline | "*Lie* down. You look tired." |

(continued)

principal/principle		
principal	main/school leader	"Oil is the *principal* product of Kuwait."
principle	basic law	"This violates all ethical *principles*."
than/then		
than	used in comparisons	"Bill is taller *than* Tom."
then	refers to time	"He took the test, *then* went home."
there/their/they're		
there	direction/a place	"*There* he goes." "Put it *there*."
their	possessive of *they*	"*Their* car won't start."
they're	"they are"	"*They're* taking the bus home."
to/too/two		
to	preposition/infinitive	"Walk *to* school." "He likes *to* dance."
too	excessive/in addition	"It's *too* hot." "I want to go, *too*."
two	a number	"The dress costs *two* hundred dollars."

See pages 453–456 for a complete list.

EXERCISE 2 Commonly Confused Words

Underline and correct misspelled words in each sentence.

1. Its going to be difficult to except an out-of-state check.

2. The president's speech made illusions to the New Deal.

3. My broker gave me advise about investing.

4. Our students don't have excess to the Internet.

5. These medications may effect your ability to drive.

6. We toured the construction sight.

7. All my school cloths are in the dryer.

8. Your welcome to use there cottage this summer.

9. Don't work to hard.

10. The evening was cool and quite .

EXERCISE 3 Commonly Misspelled and Confused Words

Underline each misspelled or misused word and write the correct spelling over it.

In June 1942, a German U-boat surfaced of Long Island. Four secrete agents paddled ashore in a rubber boat, equipted with demolition supplies and over $80,000 in American money to fiance a rain of terror designed to last two years.

The men had been carefully chosen. Through born in Germany, all four had lived in the United States before the war. One had even served in the U.S. Army and become an American citizen. There instructions were to destroy the New York water supply, war factories, rail links, bridges, and canals. They also planed to terrorize the civilan population by setting of bombs in crowded deparment stores.

The leader of the team, however, had no intention of carryng out there mission. After the war, George Dasch would right that he had become disilusioned with Nazism and had no desire to harm his adapted country. The team buried their gear and took a train to New York City.

A few days latter a second team of agents landed in Florida with similiar plans. The eight Nazis fanned out across the county, but few seemed committed to there cause. Instead of spreading terror, they spent there time shopping, buying new cloths, visiting old girlfriends, and causally telling German Americans about there recent arival from Germany.

George Dasch traveled to Washington and surrendered to the FBI and made a full confession. Within two weeks all eight men were under arrest. The Nazis were tried in secret miltary courts. Dasch and another man who coperatted with the FBI were given long prison terms. The other six were executed.

Forming Plurals

Words change their spelling to indicate when they are plural. Most nouns simply add an -s:

Singular	Plural
book	books
car	cars
boy	boys
generator	generators
ornithologist	ornithologists

However, many nouns use different spellings to indicate plurals. In order to avoid making spelling errors, it is important to understand which words require more than an added -s to become plural:

- For words ending in s, ss, x, z, sh, or ch, add -es:

Singular	Plural
miss	misses
church	churches
wish	wishes
fox	foxes
fizz	fizzes

- For words ending in an o preceded by a vowel, add -s:

Singular	Plural
radio	radios
studio	studios
curio	curios

zoo	zoos
rodeo	rodeos

- For words ending in an *o* preceded by a consonant, add *-es:*

Singular	*Plural*
hero	heroes
zero	zeroes
echo	echoes
tomato	tomatoes
veto	vetoes

Exceptions

Singular	*Plural*
grotto	grottos
motto	mottos
photo	photos
solo	solos
piano	pianos

- For words ending in *f* or *fe,* change the *f* to *v* and add *-es:*

Singular	*Plural*
shelf	shelves
wife	wives
half	halves
wolf	wolves
thief	thieves

Exceptions

Singular	*Plural*
safe	safes
roof	roofs
proof	proofs
chief	chiefs

- For words ending in *y* preceded by a consonant, change the *y* to *i* and add *-es:*

Singular	*Plural*
city	cities
story	stories
flurry	flurries
baby	babies
celebrity	celebrities

- For some words, the plural form is irregular:

Singular	*Plural*
tooth	teeth
child	children
mouse	mice
person	people
woman	women

- For some words the singular and plural spelling are the same:

Singular	Plural
deer	deer
fish	fish
sheep	sheep
series	series

- For Greek and Latin nouns, there are special spellings:

Singular	Plural
memorandum	memoranda
datum	data
thesis	theses
alumnus	alumni
analysis	analyses

- For compound nouns—made up of two or more words—make the needed change to the main word. For compound nouns written as one word, make the ending plural:

Singular	Plural
stepchild	stepchildren
bookshelf	bookshelves
girlfriend	girlfriends

Exceptions

Singular	Plural
passerby	passersby

For compound nouns that appear as separate words or connected by hyphens, make the main word plural:

Singular	Plural
body shop	body shops
beer tap	beer taps
water tank	water tanks
brother-in-law	brothers-in-law
man-of-the-year	men-of-the-year

EXERCISE 4 Creating Plurals

Write out the correct plural form of each noun.

1. knife _____

2. fork _____

3. deer _____

4. loss _____

5. child _____

6. chapter _____

7. century _____

8. cactus   _____

9. index   _____

10. stereo   _____

EXERCISE 5 Creating Plurals

Rewrite each sentence, changing all singular nouns to plurals.

1. The boy drove the new car.

_____

2. My sister-in-law planned the wedding for the family.

_____

3. Oil taken from grain can provide useful medicine.

_____

4. The snow flurry made the street slippery.

_____

5. The fox, wolf, and dog have been vaccinated.

_____

EXERCISE 6 Plural Spellings

Correct errors in plurals in each sentence.

1. The childrens loved the rodeos, the circuss, and the zooes.

_____

2. Today, sports heros seem more interested in money than their fans.

_____

3. My brother-in-laws must pay taxs in two states because their companys do business in both New York and New Jersey.

_____

_____

4. The vet examined the calfs and colts.

_____

5. Two people lost their lifes in the accident.

_____

Adding Endings

In most instances suffixes or word endings follow simple rules to indicate past tense or to create an adjective or adverb.

Past-Tense Spellings

Most verbs are called "regular" because one simply adds *-ed* or *-d* if the word ends with an *e:*

Regular Verbs

Present	*Past*
walk	walked
integrate	integrated
create	created
type	typed
paint	painted

- If a verb ends in *y,* change the *y* to *i* + *-ed:*

cry	cried
spy	spied
try	tried

- If a one-syllable verb ends in a consonant preceded by a vowel, double the last letter + *-ed:*

pin	pinned
plan	planned
drip	dripped
stop	stopped
grab	grabbed

Other verbs, called "irregular," have different spellings to indicate past tense:

Irregular Verbs

Present	*Past*
teach	taught
sing	sang
write	wrote
swim	swam
buy	bought

See pages 292–293 for a complete list.

Spelling Other Endings

Endings are added to words to create adjectives, adverbs, or nouns:

sad (adjective)	*sadly* (adverb)	*sadness* (noun)
create (verb)	*creative* (adjective)	*creatively* (adverb)
motivate (verb)	*motivation* (noun)	*motivated* (adjective)
happy (adjective)	*happily* (adverb)	*happiness* (noun)

- For words ending with a silent *e,* drop the *e* if the ending begins with a vowel:

arrive	+ -al	= arrival
come	+ -ing	= coming
fame	+ -ous	= famous
create	+ -ion	= creation

Examples of exceptions to this rule are *mileage* and *dyeing.*

- For words ending with a silent *e,* retain the *e* if the ending begins with a consonant:

      elope   + -ment = elopement
      safe   + -ty   = safety
      like   + -ness = likeness
      complete + -ly   = completely

- Double the last consonant of one-syllable words if the ending begins with a vowel:

      rob + -ing = robbing
      spot + -ed = spotted
      spin + -ing = spinning

- Double the last consonant of words accented on the last syllable if the ending begins with a vowel:

      refer   + -ing = referring
      admit   + -ed = admitted
      technical + -ly   = technically

Note: Prefixes do not change the spelling of base words. When you add letters before a word, no letters are dropped or added:

    un- + natural = unnatural   dis- + able   = disable
    pre- + judge   = prejudge   il- + legal   = illegal
    im- + moral   = immoral   de- + mobilize = demobilize

EXERCISE 7 Past-Tense Spellings

Write the correct past-tense form of each verb.

1. drive _____

2. talk _____

3. speak _____

4. defend _____

5. negotiate _____

6. strike _____

7. wash _____

8. press _____

9. build _____

10. boil _____

EXERCISE 8 Past-Tense Spellings

Change the verbs in each sentence to past tense.

1. **We take the bus to school.**

_____

2. They only eat and drink what the doctor suggests.

_____

3. We meet at the library.

_____

4. We choose the courses we want.

_____

5. They sing all night.

_____

EXERCISE 9 Adding Endings

Combine the following words and endings.

1. like   +   -able   _____

2. sorrow   +   -full   _____

3. respect   +   -fully   _____

4. intensify   +   -ing   _____

5. defy   +   -ence   _____

6. force   +   -ing   _____

7. begin   +   -ing   _____

8. profit   +   -able   _____

9. notice   +   -ing   _____

10. debate   +   -able   _____

EXERCISE 10 Identifying and Correcting Misspelled Words

Underline misspelled and misused words and write the correct spelling above them.

Early on the morning of June 30, 1908, a strange light filed the sky over a remote part of Siberia. A streak of fire raced across the treetops and vanished suddenlly over the horizon, followed by a massive explosion. Seven hundred reindeer grazing in a clearing were instantlly vaporized. Over 60 million trees were flattend in a circle larger then halve of Rhode Island. A giant fireball rose into the sky, visible for hundreds of miles. Seismographs in America and Europe registered the impact of the blast. A grate fire swept the region for weeks, burning over 700 squre miles of forest. Thousands of tons of ash boilled into the atmosphere, creating wierd sunsets seen all over the world.

Preoccupied by revolutionarries and a recent war with Japan, the Russian government did not bother too investigate an event in an isolated part of its vast empire. In the late 1930s scientists photographed the region, still devastated from the blast. Strangeley, no crater could be found. Whatever fell to earth, weather a comet or meteor, must have broken apart before impact.

After World War II, researchers estimated that the blast was one thousand to two thousand times more powerful then the atomic bomb that destroyed Hiroshima. Further studys reveald genetic mutations in plant life and blood abnormalities in local residents. These findings led some theoriests to speculate the Earth had been hit by a nuclear weapon from another planet or visited by a UFO. Scientists, however, are convinced the event was a totaly nautral phenomonen.

EXERCISE 11 Cumulative Exercise

Rewrite these paragraphs, correcting spelling errors and eliminating fragments and run-ons.

Henry M. Robert is best remembered as the creator of *Robert's Rules of Order*. Almost every club, organization, and public meeting in the United States. Uses this nineteenth-century manual. Henry Robert was not a debator, politican, teacher, or attorny. He was an engineer working for the U.S. Army. Although his military duties carried him across the county on various construction projects, Robert was active in a number of organizations. He was once asked to head a meeting but he became frustrated because he found few guidlines for conducting an orderly discussion.

Robert studied existing manuals but he found them sketchy and incomplete. Robert began to set forth his own rules and he started to write a book. In the winter of 1874 ice in Lake Michigan delayed sheduled construction and Robert had ample time too work on his book. Robert's wife, who was active in several organizations herself. Helped him in setting forth rules and proceedures.

The first printing was only for four thousand copies but the volumn had profound influence. Professors, ministers, business leaders, and social organizations were eager to have rules that were fare and unbiased. Within a few years, Roberts revised his book, adding new sections each time. Hundreds of people rote too him, asking questions about parliamentery practices. In 1915, a thorouhly revised edition, was printed. By that time over half a million copies had been sold. Since Robert's death in 1923, his book has become the stadard book guiding how people in all walks of live conduct meetings and make decisions.

_____

_____

_____

_____

_____

_____

_____

_____

_____

_____

_____

_____

_____

_____

_____

_____

_____

_____

_____

_____

WORKING TOGETHER

Working with a group of students, review this résumé for spelling errors. Have each member underline misspelled words, then work as a group. Note how collaborative editing can help detect errors you may have missed on your own. Refer to a dictionary if you have questions.

ROBIN LIEBERMAN
311 East 55th Street
New York, NY 10022
(212) 555-0909
rlieberman@aol.com

GOAL	Editoral Assistant and Researcher
OVERVIEW	Two years experence editing both on line and hard-copy journals. Skiled at working with writers and editers. Proven ability to meet deadlines and working within bugets.
EXPERINCE 2005–	*Editor,* ActionDotCom One of three editors producing online entertainment journal recieving over 75,000 hits weakly.

- Edited all movie, theater, and resturant reviews.
- Wrote and edited "Manhattan on the Move" column, reprinted in *Style Now.*
- Worked as senior fact checker for investgative reports.

2003–2005	*Assistant Editor, Dining Out* Edited restaurant reviews, travell articles for magazine with 50,000 circulation.

- Assisted marketing manger in developing new sales campagn.

EDUCATION   Manhattan Community College
                Associate Degree in Communications, 2004
                Completed courses in journalism, gaphic design, writing
                and editing, marketing, business accounting, and mass
                communications.

                • 3.75 GPA
                • Worked on student literary magazine and yearbook
                • Atended National Convention of Student Editors,
                  2003, 2004

AFFLIATIONS   National Assocation of Student Journalists

REFERENCES   Avialable on request

CRITICAL THINKING

GET THINKING
AND WRITING

After graduation you are offered two jobs. One pays a small salary but offers great opportunities for advancement and is in a career you enjoy. The other job pays twice as much but requires extensive overtime doing boring and repetitive tasks. Write a paragraph explaining which job you would choose and why.

WHAT HAVE YOU WRITTEN?

When you complete your writing, review it for spelling errors.

© Paul Barton/CORBIS

GET WRITING

What are your most important skills, experiences, or qualities that you think will impress employers when you look for a job?

Write three sentences, each providing a reason why someone should hire you. Read your sentences carefully, proofreading them for errors and revising word choices to make sure they clearly express what you want to say.

WRITING ON THE WEB

Using a search engine such as AltaVista, Yahoo!, or Google, enter terms such as *spelling, improving spelling, spelling rules,* and *using spellcheck* to locate current sites of interest.

WHAT HAVE YOU LEARNED?

Underline and correct the misspelled or misused words in each sentence.

1. We only had fourty dollars when we left Los Angeles.

2. Its never to late too start.

3. Two mens are waiting in are office.

4. He seems so hoplessy lost.

5. Her room mate wants to hold a surprise party.

6. The company was severly mismanaged.

7. We cannot start filming untill the knew camera technigue is perfected.

8. We will meat at the resturant next Tuesday at three.

9. The new song has a familiar, old-fashion rythym.

10. Why can't we serve ordnary, every day coffee instead of these expensive imported blends?

   Check a dictionary to make sure you have successfully identified and corrected all twenty errors.

POINTS TO REMEMBER

1. Edit your papers carefully for commonly misspelled words such as *library, yield, opinion, opportunity,* and *separate.* (See list on pages 456–457.)
2. Edit your papers carefully for commonly confused words such as *anyone* and *any one* or *implicit* and *explicit.* (See list on pages 453–456.)
3. Remember, *i* before *e* except after *c* or when it sounds like *a* in *neighbor* and *weigh.*

   achieve   ceiling   freight
   Exceptions: *either, height, leisure, seize*

4. Follow the guidelines for creating plurals:
   For words ending in *s, ss, x, z, sh,* or *ch,* add *-es:*

   misses   boxes   churches

   For words ending in *o* preceded by a vowel, add *-s.*
   For words ending in *o* preceded by a consonant, add *-es.*

   zoos   radios   heroes   zeroes
   Exceptions: *mottos, photos, pianos, solos*

(continued)

POINTS TO REMEMBER *(continued)*

For words ending in *f* or *fe*, change the *f* to *v* and add *-es:*

shelves   halves   thieves
Exceptions: *safes, roofs, proofs, chiefs*

For some words the plural form is irregular:

teeth   children   people

Some words have no plural spelling:

sheep   fish   series

Greek and Latin nouns have special plural spellings:

memoranda   data   theses

For compound nouns, make the needed change to the main word:

bookshelves   stepchildren   boyfriends

For compound nouns that appear as separate words, change the
main word:

brothers-in-law   beer taps   water tanks

5. Follow guidelines for creating past-tense endings.
   For regular verbs, add *-ed* or *-d* if the word ends in *e:*

   walked   created   painted

   For verbs ending in *y*, change the *y* to *i* + *-ed:*

   cried   spied   tried

   For a one-syllable verb ending with a consonant preceded by a vowel,
   double the last letter + *-ed:*

   pinned   stopped   grabbed

   Some verbs have irregular past-tense forms:

   taught   sang   swam

6. Follow guidelines for adding suffixes:
   For words ending with a silent *e*, drop the *e* if the ending begins with a
   vowel:

   arrival   coming   creation

   For words ending with a silent *e*, keep the *e* if the ending begins with a
   consonant:

   safety   likeness   completely

   Double the last consonant of one-syllable words if the ending begins
   with a vowel:

   robbing   spotted   spinning

   Double the last consonant of words accented on the last syllable if the
   ending begins with a vowel:

   referring   admitted   technically

7. Make and review lists of words you commonly misspell.
8. Always budget enough time in the writing process to edit your papers for
   spelling errors.

IMPROVING SPELLING

Review writing exercises you have completed in this book and papers you have written in this or other courses for errors in spelling. List each word. Add words that you frequently misspell or are unsure of. Check a dictionary and carefully write out each word correctly. Add definitions to words that are easily confused, such as *conscious* and *conscience* or *then* and *than*.

1._____

2._____

3._____

4._____

5._____

6._____

7._____

8._____

9._____

10._____

11. _____

12. _____

13. _____

14. _____

15. _____

16. _____

17. _____

18. _____

19. _____

20. _____

Handbook

A Writer's Guide to Overcoming Common Errors

Basic Sentence Structure

A sentence is a group of words that contains a subject and verb and states a complete thought.

Phrases and Clauses

Phrases are groups of related words that form parts of a sentence:

| After the game | Ted and Carlos | are willing to help distribute | decorations for the party. |

Clauses consist of related words that contain both a subject and a verb:

- **Independent clauses** contain a subject and verb and express a complete thought. They are sentences:

    I waited for the bus.   It began to rain.

- **Dependent clauses** contain a subject and verb but do *not* express a complete thought. They are not sentences:

    While I waited for the bus

    Dependent clauses have to be connected to an independent clause to create a sentence that expresses a complete thought:

    While I waited for the bus, it began to rain.

Types of Sentences

Sentence types are determined by the number and kind of clauses they contain.
A **simple sentence** consists of a single independent clause:

Jim sings.
Jim and Nancy sing and dance at the newly opened El Morocco.
Seeking to reenter show business, Jim and Nancy sing and dance at the newly opened El Morocco, located at 55th and Second Avenue.

A **compound sentence** contains two or more independent clauses but no dependent clauses:

Jim studied dance at Columbia; Nancy studied music at Julliard.
   [two independent clauses joined by a semicolon]

Jim wants to stay in New York, but Nancy longs to move to California.
   [two independent clauses joined with a comma and coordinating conjunction]

A **complex sentence** contains one independent clause and one or more dependent clauses:

Jim and Nancy are studying drama because they want to act on Broadway.
Because they want to act on Broadway, *Jim and Nancy are studying drama*.
   [When a dependent clause begins a complex sentence, it is set off with a comma.]

A **compound-complex sentence** contains at least two independent clauses and one or more dependent clauses:

Jim and Nancy perform Sinatra classics, and they often dress in forties clothing *because the El Morocco draws an older crowd.*

Because the El Morocco draws an older crowd, Jim and Nancy perform Sinatra classics, and they often dress in forties clothing.

PARTS OF SPEECH

Nouns	name persons, places, things or ideas: *teacher, attic, Italy, book, liberty*
Pronouns	take the place of nouns: *he, she, they, it, this, that, what, which, hers, their*
Verbs	express action: *buy, sell, run, walk, create, think, feel, wonder, hope, dream*
	link ideas: *is, are, was, were*
Adjectives	add information about nouns or pronouns: a *red* car, a *bright* idea, a *lost* cause
Adverbs	add information about verbs: drove *recklessly,* sell *quickly, angrily* denounced
	add information about adjectives: *very* old teacher, *sadly* dejected leader
	add information about other adverbs: *rather* hesitantly remarked
Prepositions	link nouns and pronouns, expressing relationships between related words: *in* the house, *around* the corner, *between* the acts, *through* the evening
Conjunctions	link related parts of a sentence: **Coordinating conjunctions** link parts of equal value: *and, or, yet, but, so* He went to college, *and* she got a job. **Subordinating conjunctions** link dependent or less important parts: *When* he went to college, she got a job.
Interjections	express emotion or feeling that is not part of the basic sentence and are set off with commas or used with exclamation points: *Oh,* he's leaving? *Wow!*

(continued)

Words can function as different parts of speech:

> I bought more *paint* [noun].
> I am going to *paint* [verb] the bedroom.
> Those supplies are stored in the *paint* [adjective] room.

Parts of speech can be single words or phrases, groups of related words that work together:

> Tom and his entire staff [noun phrase]
> wrote and edited [verb phrase]
> throughout the night [prepositional phrase].

Sentence Errors

Fragments

Fragments are incomplete sentences. They lack a subject, a complete verb, or fail to express a complete thought:

Subject Missing
Worked all night. [Who worked *all night*?]

Revised
He worked all night.

Verb Missing
Juan the new building. [What was Juan doing?]

Revised
Juan designed the new building.

Incomplete Verb
Juan designing the new building. [*-ing* verbs cannot stand alone.]

Revised
Juan is designing the new building.

Incomplete Thought
Although Juan designed the building. [It has a subject and verb but fails to express a whole idea.]

Revised
Juan designed the building.

or

Although Juan designed the building, he did not receive any recognition.

Correcting Fragments
There are two ways of correcting fragments.

1. Turn the fragment into a complete sentence by making sure it expresses a complete thought:

   Fragments
   Yale being the center for this research
   Based on public opinion surveys
   The mayor designated

Revised
Yale is the center for this research. [complete verb added]
The new study is based on public opinion surveys. [subject and verb added]
The mayor designated Sandy Gomez to head the commission. [words added to express a complete thought]

2. Attach the fragment to a sentence to state a complete thought. (Often fragments occur when you write quickly and break off part of a sentence.)

Fragments
He bought a car. *While living in Florida.*
Constructed in 1873. The old church needs major repairs.

Revised
He bought a car while living in Florida.
Constructed in 1873, the old church needs major repairs.

POINT TO REMEMBER

Reading out loud can help identify fragments. Ask yourself, "Does this statement express a complete thought?"

Run-ons

Fused Sentences

Fused sentences lack the punctuation needed to join two independent clauses. The two independent clauses are *fused,* or joined, without a comma or semicolon:

Travis entered the contest he won first prize

Revised
Travis entered the contest; he won first prize.

Nancy speaks Spanish but she has trouble reading it.

Revised
Nancy speaks Spanish, but she has trouble reading it.

Comma Splices

Comma splices are compound sentences where a comma is used instead of a semicolon:

My sister lives in Chicago, my brother lives in New York.

Revised
My sister lives in Chicago; my brother lives in New York.

The lake is frozen solid, it is safe to drive on.

Revised
The lake is frozen solid; it is safe to drive on.

Identifying Run-ons

To identify run-ons, do two things:

1. Read the sentence carefully. Determine if it is a compound sentence. Ask yourself if you can divide the sentence into two or more independent clauses (simple sentences).

Sam entered college but dropped out after six months.

Sam entered college . . . [independent clause (simple sentence)]
dropped out after six months. [not a sentence]
[not a compound sentence]

Nancy graduated in May but she signed up for summer courses.

Nancy graduated in May . . .   [independent clause (simple sentence)]
she signed up for summer courses. [independent clause (simple
sentence)]
[compound sentence]

2. If you have two complete sentences, determine if they should be joined. Is there a logical relationship between them? What is the best way of connecting them? Independent clauses can be joined with a comma and *and, or, yet, but, so,* or with a semicolon.

Nancy graduated in May, but she signed up for summer courses.

But indicates a contrast between two ideas. Inserting the missing comma quickly repairs this run-on.

Repairing Run-ons: Minor Repairs

A fused sentence or comma splice may need only a minor repair. Sometimes in writing quickly we mistakenly use a comma when a semicolon is needed:

The Senate likes the president's budget, the House still has questions.

Revised
The Senate likes the president's budget; the House still has questions.

In other cases we may forget a comma or drop one of the coordinating conjunctions:

The Senate likes the president's budget but the House still has questions.

Senators approve of the budget, they want to meet with the president's staff.

Revised
The Senate likes the president's budget, but the House still has questions.

Senators approve of the budget, and they want to meet with the president's staff.

Repairing Run-ons: Major Repairs

Some run-ons require major repairs. Sometimes we create run-ons when our ideas are not clearly stated or fully thought out:

Truman was president at the end of the war and the United States dropped the atomic bomb.

Adding the needed comma eliminates a mechanical error but leaves the sentence awkward and unclear:

Truman was president at the end of the war, and the United States dropped the atomic bomb.

Repairing this kind of run-on requires critical thinking. A compound sentence joins two complete thoughts, and there should be a clear relationship between them. It may be better to revise the entire sentence, changing it from a compound to a complex sentence:

Revised
Truman was president at the end of the war when the United States dropped the atomic bomb.

In some instances you may find it easier to break the run-on into two simple sentences, especially if there is no strong relationship between the main ideas:

Swansea is a port city in Wales that was severely bombed in World War II and Dylan Thomas was born there in 1914.

Revised
Swansea is a port city in Wales that was severely bombed in World War II. Dylan Thomas was born there in 1914.

POINT TO REMEMBER

A compound sentence should join independent clauses that state ideas of equal importance. Avoid using an independent clause to state a minor detail that could be contained in a dependent clause or a phrase:

Awkward

My brother lives in Boston, and he is an architect.

Revised

My brother, who lives in Boston, is an architect.
My brother in Boston is an architect.

Modifiers

Dangling Modifiers

Modifiers that serve as introductions must describe what follows the comma. When they do not, they "dangle" so that it is unclear what they modify:

Grounded by fog, airport officials ordered passengers to deplane.
  [Were airport officials *grounded by fog*?]

Revised
Grounded by fog, the passengers were ordered by airport officials to deplane.
Airport officials ordered passengers to deplane the aircraft grounded by fog.

STRATEGY TO DETECT DANGLING MODIFIERS

Sentences with opening modifiers set off by commas fit this pattern:

    Modifier, main sentence

To make sure the sentence is correct, use the following test:

(continued)

1. Read the sentence, then turn the modifier into a question, asking who or what in the main sentence is performing the action:

   question, answer

2. What follows the comma forms the answer. If the answer is appropriate, the construction is correct:

   Hastily constructed, the bridge deteriorated in less than a year.

   > Question: What was *hastily constructed*?
   > Answer: the bridge
   > This sentence is <u>correct</u>.

   Suspected of insanity, the defense attorney asked that her client be examined by psychiatrists.

   > Question: Who was *suspected of insanity*?
   > Answer: the defense attorney
   > This sentence is <u>incorrect</u>.

   > Revised: Suspecting her client to be insane, the defense attorney asked that he be examined by psychiatrists.

Misplaced Modifiers

Place modifying words, phrases, and clauses as near as possible to the words they describe:

Confusing
Scientists developed new chips for laptop computers *that cost less than fifty cents*.

> [Do laptop computers cost *less than fifty cents*?]

Revised
Scientists developed laptop computer chips that cost less than fifty cents.

Faulty Parallelism

When you create pairs or lists, the words or phrases must match—they have to be all nouns, all adjectives, all adverbs, or all verbs in the same form:

Nancy is *bright, creative,* and *funny.* [adjectives]
Mary writes *clearly, directly,* and *forcefully.* [adverbs]
Reading and *calculating* are critical skills for my students. [gerunds]
She should *lose* weight, *stop* smoking, and *limit* her intake of alcohol.
   [verbs matching with *should*]

The following sentences are not parallel:

The concert was loud, colorful, and many people attended.
   [*Many people attended* does not match with the adjectives *loud* and *colorful*.]
John failed to take notes, refused to attend class, and his final exam is unreadable.
   [*His final exam is* does not match the verb phrases *failed to take* and *refused to attend*.]

Quitting smoking and daily exercise are important.
[*Quitting,* a gerund, does not match with *daily exercise.*]

Revised

The concert was *loud, colorful,* and *well attended.* [all adjectives]
John *failed* to take notes, *refused* to attend class, and *wrote* an almost unreadable final exam. [all verbs]
Quitting smoking and *exercising* daily are important.
[both gerunds or *-ing* nouns]

Strategies for Detecting and Revising Faulty Parallelism

Apply this simple test to any sentences that include pairs or lists of words or phrases to make sure they are parallel:

1. Read the sentence and locate the pair or list.
2. Make sure each item matches the format of the basic sentence by testing each item.

Example

Students should read directions carefully, write down assignments accurately, and take notes.

Students should read directions.
Students should write down assignments accurately.
Students should take notes.

[Each item matches *Students should . . .*]
This sentence is <u>parallel</u>.

Computer experts will have to make more precise predictions in the future to reduce waste, create more accurate budgets, and public support must be maintained.

Computer experts will have to make more precise . . .
Computer experts will have to create more accurate . . .
Computer experts will have to public support must be . . .

[The last item does not link with *will have to.*]
This sentence is <u>not parallel</u>.

A TIP ON PARALLELISM

In many cases it is difficult to revise long sentences that are not parallel:

To build her company, Shireen Naboti is a careful planner, skilled supervisor, recruits talent carefully, monitors quality control, and is a lobbyist for legal reform.

If you have trouble making all the elements match, it may be simpler to break it up into two or even three separate sentences:

To build her company, Shireen Naboti is a careful planner, skilled supervisor, and lobbyist for legal reform. In addition, she recruits talent carefully and monitors quality control.

(continued)

The first sentence contains the noun phrases; the second consists of the two verb phrases. It is easier to create two short parallel lists than one long one.

Verbs

Subject-Verb Agreement

Singular subjects require singular verbs:

> The <u>boy</u> *walks* to school.
> Your <u>bill</u> *is* overdue.

Plural subjects require plural verbs:

> The <u>boys</u> *walk* to school.
> Your <u>bills</u> *are* overdue.

Changing a verb from singular to plural changes the meaning of a sentence:

Singular

The desk and chair *is* on sale.   [The desk and chair is sold as one item.]

Plural

The desk and chair *are* on sale.   [The desk and chair are sold separately.]

RULES

- Not all nouns add an *s* to become plural:

  The deer run across the road.   The women play cards.

- Some nouns that end in *s* and look like plurals are singular:

  Mathematics *is* my toughest course.   Economics *demands* accurate data.

- Some nouns that may refer to one item are plural:

  My scissors *are* dull.   *Are* these your gloves?

- Proper nouns that look plural are singular if they are names of companies, organizations, or titles of books, movies, television shows, or works of art:

  General Motors *is* building   *The Three Musketeers is* funny.
  a new engine.

- Units of time and amounts of money are generally singular:

  Twenty-five dollars *is* a lot for   Two weeks *is* not enough time.
  a T-shirt.

  They appear as plurals to indicate separate items:

  Three dollars *were* lying on   My last weeks at camp *were*
  the table.   unbearable.

  (continued)

- Group nouns—*audience, board, class, committee, jury, number, team,* and so on—are singular when they describe a group working together:

  "Faculty Accepts School Board Offer"   [headline describing teachers acting as a group]

  "Faculty Protest School Board Offer"   [headline describing teachers acting individually]

- Verbs in "either . . . or" sentences can be singular or plural. If both subjects are singular, the verb is singular:

  Either the <u>father</u> or the <u>mother</u> *is* required to appear in court.

  If both subjects are plural, the verb is plural:

  Either the <u>parents</u> or the <u>attorneys</u> *are* required to appear in court.

  If one subject is plural and one is singular, the subject closer to the verb determines whether it is singular or plural:

  Either the parent or the <u>attorneys</u> *are* required to appear in court.
  Either the parents or the <u>attorney</u> *is* required to appear in court.

- Indefinite pronouns can be singular or plural.

  Singular indefinite pronouns:

another	each	everything	nothing
anybody	either	neither	somebody
anyone	everybody	nobody	someone

  Anything is possible   *Someone* is coming.

  Plural indefinite pronouns:

both	few	many	several

  Both are here.   *Many* are missing.

  Indefinite pronouns that can be singular or plural:

all	some	more	most

  Snow fell last night, but <u>most</u> *has* melted.   [*Most* refers to the singular "snow."]

  Passengers were injured, but <u>most</u> *have* recovered.   [*Most* refers to plural "passengers."]

Verb Tense

Regular Verbs

Most verbs show tense changes by adding *-ed* to words ending with consonants and *-d* to words ending with an *e:*

Present	Past	Past Participle
walk	walked	walked
create	created	created
cap	capped	capped

Irregular Verbs

Irregular verbs do not follow the *-ed* pattern.

Some irregular verbs make no spelling change to indicate shifts in tense:

Present	Past	Past Participle
cost	cost	cost
cut	cut	cut
fit	fit	fit
hit	hit	hit
hurt	hurt	hurt
put	put	put

Most irregular verbs make a spelling change rather than adding *-ed:*

Present	Past	Past Participle
arise	arose	arisen
awake	awoke	awoken
be	was, were	been
bear	bore	borne (not *born*)
become	became	become
break	broke	broken
bring	brought	brought
build	built	built
choose	chose	chosen
come	came	come
dive	dove (dived)	dived
do	did	done
draw	drew	drawn
eat	ate	eaten
feed	fed	fed
fly	flew	flown
forgive	forgave	forgiven
freeze	froze	frozen
get	got	gotten
grow	grew	grown
hang (objects)	hung	hung
hang (people)	hanged	hanged
have	had	had
lay (place)	laid	laid
lead	led	led
leave	left	left
lie (recline)	lay	lain
lose	lost	lost
make	made	made
mean	meant	meant
meet	met	met
pay	paid	paid
ride	rode	ridden
ring	rang	rung
rise	rose	risen
run	ran	run
say	said	said

Present	Past	Past Participle
see	saw	seen
sell	sold	sold
shake	shook	shaken
shine	shone	shone
shoot	shot	shot
sing	sang	sung
sink	sank	sunk
sleep	slept	slept
sneak	sneaked (not *snuck*)	sneaked
speak	spoke	spoken
spend	spent	spent
steal	stole	stolen
sting	stung	stung
strike	struck	struck
swim	swam	swum
swing	swung	swung
take	took	taken
teach	taught	taught
think	thought	thought
throw	threw	thrown
understand	understood	understood
wake	woke	woken
write	wrote	written

Problem Verbs: Lie/Lay, Rise/Raise, Set/Sit

Lie/Lay

To lie = to rest or recline: "lie down for nap"

To lay = to put something down or place into position: "lay a book on a table"

Present	Past	Past Participle
lie	lay	lain
lay	laid	laid

Remember: *Lie* expresses action done *by* someone or something:

Tom called 911, then *lay* on the sofa waiting for the paramedics.

Lay expresses action done *to* someone or something:

The paramedics *laid* Tom on the floor to administer CPR.

Rise/Raise

To rise = to get up or move up on your own: "rise and shine" or "rise to the occasion."

To raise = to lift or grow something: "raise a window" or "raise children."

Present	Past	Past Participle
rise	rose	risen
raise	raised	raised

Remember: *Rise* can refer to objects as well as people:

The bread rises in the oven.   Oil prices are rising.

Set/Sit

To set = to put something in position or arrange in place: "set down a glass" or "set down some notes." *Set* always takes a direct object.

To sit = to assume a sitting position: "sit in a chair" or "sit on a committee"

Present	Past	Past Participle
set	set	set
sit	sat	sat

Shifts in Tense

Avoid awkward or illogical shifts in time and write in a consistent tense:

Awkward
I *drove* to the beach and *see* Karen working out with Jim.
   past   present

Consistent
I *drove* to the beach and *saw* Karen working out with Jim.
   past   past

or

I *drive* to the beach and *see* Karen working out with Jim.
  present   present

Change tenses to show a logical change in time:

I *was born* in Chicago but *live* in Milwaukee. Next year I *will move* to New York.
  past   present   future

Change tense to distinguish between past events and subjects that are permanent or still operating:

He *was born* in Trenton, which *is* the capital of New Jersey.

Pronouns

Reference

Pronouns should clearly refer to specific antecedents. Avoid unclear references.

- Make sure pronouns are clearly linked to **antecedents**—the nouns or other pronouns they represent. Avoid constructions in which a pronoun could refer to more than one noun or pronoun:

  Unclear
  Nancy was with Sharon when *she* got the news.
    [Who received the news— Nancy or Sharon?]

  Revised
  When Sharon received the news, *she* was with Nancy.

- Replace pronouns with nouns for clearer references:

  Unclear
  The teachers explained to the students why *they* couldn't attend the ceremony.
  [Who cannot attend the ceremony— teachers or students?]

  Revised
  The teachers explained to the students why *faculty* couldn't attend the ceremony.
  The teachers explained to the students why *children* couldn't attend the ceremony.

- State "*either . . . or*" constructions carefully.

  Either George or Jim can lend you *their* key.
  [George and Jim share one key.]

  Either George or Jim can lend you *his* key.
  [Both George and Jim have keys.]

  Either George or Anna can lend you *a* key.
  [avoids need for *his or her*]

- Avoid unclear references with *this, that, it, which,* and *such*:

  Unclear
  Many people think that diets are the only way to lose weight. *This* is wrong.

  Revised
  Many people mistakenly think that diets are the only way to lose weight.

- Avoid unnecessary pronouns after nouns:

  Unnecessary
  Thomas Jefferson *he* wrote the Declaration of Independence.

  Revised
  Thomas Jefferson wrote the Declaration of Independence.

- Avoid awkward use of *you. You* is acceptable for directly addressing readers. Avoid making awkward shifts in general statements:

  Awkward
  Freeway congestion can give you stress.

  Revised
  Freeway congestion can be stressful.

Agreement

- Pronouns agree in number and gender with antecedents:

  Bill took *his* time.   *Nancy* rode *her* bicycle.   The *children* called *their* mother.

- Compound nouns require plural pronouns:

Both the *students and the teachers* argue that *their* views are not heard.
Tom and Nancy announced *they* plan to move to Colorado next year.

- Collective nouns use singular or plural pronouns:

  Singular
  The *cast* played *its* last performance.
     [The cast acts as one unit.]

  Plural
  The *cast* had trouble remembering *their* lines.
     [Cast members act independently.]

- *Either . . . or* constructions can be singular or plural. If both nouns are singular, the pronoun is singular:

  Either the city council *or* the county board will present *its* budget.
     [Only one group will present a budget.]

  If both nouns are plural, the pronoun is plural:

  The board members or *the city attorneys* will present *their* report.
     [In both instances, several individuals present a report.]

  If one noun is singular and the other is plural, the pronoun agrees with the nearer noun:

  Either the teacher or students will present *their* findings to the principal.

  Place the plural noun last to avoid awkward statements or having to represent both genders with *he and she, his or her,* or *him and her.*
- Pronouns should maintain the same person or point of view in a sentence, avoiding awkward shifts:

  Awkward Shift
  To save money, *consumers* should monitor *their* [third person] use of credit cards to avoid getting in over *your* [second person] head in debt.

  Revised
  To save money, *consumers* should monitor *their* use of credit cards to avoid getting in over *their* heads in debt.

- Indefinite pronouns. In speaking, people often use the plural pronouns *they, them,* and *their* to include both males and females. In formal writing, make sure singular indefinite pronouns agree with singular pronouns:

  Singular

anybody	everybody	nobody	somebody
anyone	everyone	no one	someone
either	neither	each	one

  Anybody can bring *his or her* tax return in for review.
  Everybody is required to do the test *himself or herself.*

  Plural
  If *many* are unable to attend the orientation, make sure to call *them.*

Indefinite pronouns like *some* may be singular or plural depending on context:

Singular
Some of the ice is losing *its* brilliance.

Plural
Some of the children are missing *their* coats.

AVOID SEXISM IN PRONOUN USE

Singular nouns and many indefinite pronouns refer to individuals who may be male or female. Trying to include both men and women, however, often creates awkward constructions:

If a student has a problem, *he or she* should contact *his or her* adviser.

In editing your writing, try these strategies to eliminate both sexism and awkward pronoun use:

• Use plurals:

If students have problems, *they* should contact *their* advisors.

• Revise the sentence to limit or eliminate the need for pronouns:

Students with problems should contact advisers.
Advisers assist students with problems.

Adjectives and Adverbs

• Understand differences between adjectives and adverbs:

She gave us *freshly sliced* peaches.
[The adverb *freshly* modifies the adjective *sliced,* meaning that the peaches, whatever their freshness, have just been sliced.]

She gave us *fresh sliced* peaches.
[The adjectives *fresh* and *sliced* both describe the noun *peaches,* meaning the peaches are both fresh and sliced.]

• Review sentences to select the most effective adjectives and adverbs. Adjectives and adverbs add meaning. Avoid vague modifiers:

Vague
The concert hall was *totally inappropriate* for our group.

Revised
The concert hall was *too informal* for our group.
The concert hall was *too large* for our group.

• Use adverbs with verbs:

Incorrect
Drive *careful.* [adjective]

Revised
Drive *carefully.*

- Avoid unnecessary adjectives and adverbs:

   Unnecessary
   We drove down the *old, winding, potholed, dirt* road.

   Revised
   We drove down the *winding, potholed* road.

- Use *good* and *well,* and *bad* and *badly* accurately. *Good* and *bad* are adjectives and modify nouns and pronouns:

   The cookies taste *good.* [*Good* modifies the noun *cookies.*]
   The wine is *bad.* [*Bad* modifies the noun *wine.*]

   Well and *badly* are adverbs and modify verbs, adjectives, adverbs:

   She sings *well.* [*Well* modifies the verb *sings.*]
   He paid for *badly* needed repairs. [*Badly* modifies the adjective *needed.*]

Comma ,

- Use commas with *and, or, yet, but,* or *so* to join independent clauses to create compound sentences and avoid run-ons:

   Chinatown is a popular tourist attraction, <u>and</u> it serves as an important cultural center.

- Use a comma after a dependent clause that opens a complex sentence:

   Because the parade was canceled, we decided to go to the shore.

   If the dependent clause follows the independent clause, the comma is usually deleted:

   We decided to go to the shore because the parade was canceled.

- Use a comma after a long phrase or an introductory word:

   After breakfast with the new students and guest faculty, we are going to the museum.
   Yes, I am cashing your check today.

- Use commas to separate words, phrases, and clauses in a series:

   Words
   We purchased computer paper, ink, pens, and pencils.

   Phrases
   We purchased computer paper, ordered fax supplies, and photocopied the records.

   Clauses
   We purchased computer paper, Sarah ordered fax supplies, and Tim photocopied the records.

   If clauses contain commas, separate them with semicolons (see page 371).

- Use commas to set off nonrestrictive or parenthetical words or phrases. *Nonrestrictive* words or phrases describe or add extra information about a noun and are set off with commas:

  George Wilson, who loves football, can't wait for the Superbowl.

  Restrictive words or phrases limit or restrict the meaning of abstract nouns and are not set off with commas:

  Anyone who loves football can't wait for the Superbowl.

- Use commas to set off contrasted elements:

  The teachers, not the students, argue the tests are too difficult.

- Use commas after interjections, words used in direct address, and around direct quotations:

  Hey, get a life.
  Paul, help Sandy with the mail.
  George said, "Welcome to the disaster," to everyone arriving at the party.

- Use commas to separate city and state or city and country, items in dates, and every three numerals 1,000 and above:

  I used to work in Rockford, Illinois, until I was transferred to Paris, France.
    [A comma goes after the state or country if followed by other words.]
  She was born on July 7, 1986, and graduated high school in May 2004.
    [A comma goes after the date if followed by other words. No comma needed if only month and year are given.]

  The new bridge will cost the state 52,250,000 dollars.

- Use commas to set off absolute phrases:

  Her car unable to operate in deep snow, Sarah borrowed Tim's Jeep.
  Wilson raced down the field and caught the ball on one knee, his heart pounding.

- Use commas where needed to prevent confusion or add emphasis:

  Confusing
  Whenever they hunted people ran for cover.
  To Sally Madison was a good place to live.
  To help feed the hungry Jim donated bread.

  Improved
  Whenever they hunted, people ran for cover.
  To Sally, Madison was a good place to live.
  To help feed the hungry, Jim donated bread.

  Reading sentences out loud can help you spot sentences that need commas to prevent confusion.

GUIDE TO ELIMINATING UNNECESSARY COMMAS

1. Don't put a comma between a subject and verb unless setting off nonrestrictive elements or a series:

   Incorrect
   The old, car was stolen.

   Correct
   The car, which was old, was stolen.

2. Don't use commas to separate prepositional phrases from what they modify:

   Incorrect
   The van, in the driveway, needs new tires.

   Correct
   The van in the driveway needs new tires.

3. Don't use commas to separate two items in a compound verb:

   Incorrect
   They sang, and danced at the party.

   Correct
   They sang and danced at the party.

4. Don't put commas around titles:

   Incorrect
   The film opens with, "Love Me Tender," and shots of Elvis.

   Correct
   The film opens with "Love Me Tender" and shots of Elvis.

5. Don't put commas after a series unless it ends a clause that has to be set off from the rest of the sentence:

   Incorrect
   They donated computers, printers, and telephones, to our office.

   Correct
   They donated computers, printers, and telephones, and we provided office space.

6. Don't set off a dependent clause with a comma when it ends a sentence:

   Incorrect
   The game was canceled, because the referees went on strike.

   Correct
   The game was canceled because the referees went on strike.

   A comma is needed if a dependent clause opens the sentence:

   Because the referees went on strike, the game was canceled.

Semicolon ;

Semicolons have two uses.

1. Use semicolons to join independent clauses when *and, or, yet, but,* or *so* are not present:

   Olympia is the capital of Washington; Salem is the capital of Oregon.

   Remember to use semicolons even when you use words such as *nevertheless, moreover,* and *however:*

   They barely had time to rehearse; however, opening night was a success.

2. Use semicolons to separate items in a series that contain commas:

   The governor will meet with Vicki Shimi, the mayor of Bayview; Sandy Bert, the new city manager; the district attorney; Peter Plesmid; and Al Leone, an engineering consultant.

Apostrophe '

Apostrophes are used for three reasons:

1. Apostrophes indicate possession:

Noun	Erica's car broke down.
Acronym	NASA's new space vehicle will launch on Monday.
Indefinite pronoun	Someone's car has its lights on.
Endings of *s, x,* or *z* sound	Phyllis' car is stalled. [or *Phyllis's*]

   Apostrophes are deleted from geographical names:

Pikes Peak	Taylors Meadows	Warners Pond

   Apostrophes may or may not appear in possessive names of businesses or organizations:

Marshall Field's	Sears	Tigers Stadium	Sean's Pub

   Follow the spelling used on signs, stationery, and business cards.

2. Apostrophes signal missing letters and numbers in contractions:

   Ted can't restore my '67 VW.

3. Apostrophes indicate plurals of letters, numbers, or symbols:

   I got all B's last semester and A's this semester.
   Do we have any size 7's or 8's left?
   We can sell all the 2003's at half price.

   Apostrophes are optional in referring to decades, but be consistent:

She went to high school in the 1990's but loved the music
of the 1960's.

or

She went to high school in the 1990s but loved the music
of the 1960s.

Common abbreviations such as *TV* and *UFO* do not need apostrophes to indicate plurals:

We bought new TVs and several DVDs.

POINT TO REMEMBER

it's   =   contraction of "it is"

   It's raining.

its   =   possessive of "it"

   My car won't start. Its battery is dead.

Quotation Marks " "

Quotation marks—always used in pairs—enclose direct quotations, titles of short
works, and highlighted words:

- For direct quotations:

   Martin Luther King said, "I have a dream."

   The final mark of punctuation precedes the final quotation mark, unless it
   does not appear in the original text:

   Did Martin Luther King say, "I have a dream"?

Set off identifying phrases with commas:

   Shelly insisted, "We cannot win unless we practice."
   "We cannot win," Shelly insisted, "unless we practice."
   "We cannot win unless we practice," Shelly insisted.

Commas are not used if the quotation is blended into the sentence:

   They exploited the "cheaper by the dozen" technique to save a fortune.

Quotations within quotations are indicated by use of single quotation marks:

   Shelly said, "I was only ten when I heard Martin Luther King proclaim,
   'I have a dream.'"

Final commas are placed inside quotation marks:

   The letter stated, "The college will lower fees," but few students
   believed it.

Colons and semicolons are placed outside quotation marks:

> The letter stated, "The college will lower fees"; few students believed it.

Indirect quotations do not require quotation marks:

> Martin Luther King said that he had a dream.

- For titles of short works
  Titles of short works—poems, stories, articles, and songs—are placed in quotation marks:

  > Did you read "When Are We Going to Mars?" in *Time* this week?

  Do not capitalize articles, prepositions, or coordinating conjunctions (*and, or, yet, but, so*) unless they are the first or last words. (Longer works—books, films, magazines, and albums—are underlined or placed in italics.)
- To highlight words
  Highlighted words are placed in quotation marks to draw extra attention:

  > I still don't know what "traffic abatement" is supposed to mean.
  > This is the fifth time this month Martha has "been sick" when we needed her.

Colon :

Colons are placed after independent clauses to introduce elements and separate items in numerals, ratios, titles, and time references:

> The coach demanded three things from his players: loyalty, devotion, and teamwork.
> The coach demanded one quality above all others: attention to detail.
> The coach says the team has a 3:1 advantage.
> I am reading *Arthur Miller: Playwright of the Century.*
> The play started at 8:15.

Parentheses ( )

Parentheses set off nonessential details and explanations and enclose letters and numbers used for enumeration:

> The Senate committee (originally headed by Warner) will submit a report to the White House.
> The Federal Aviation Administration (FAA) has new security policies.
> The report stated we must (1) improve services, (2) provide housing, and (3) increase funding.

Brackets [ ]

Brackets set off interpolations or clarifications in quotations and replace parentheses within parentheses:

Eric Hartman observed, "I think [Theodore] Roosevelt was the greatest president."

Time noted, "President Bush told Frank Bush [no relation] that he agreed with his tax policies."

The ambassador stated, "We will give them [the Iraqi National Congress] all the help they need."

Dash —

Dashes mark a break in thought, set off a parenthetical element for emphasis, and set off an introduction to a series:

Ted was angry after his car was stolen— who wouldn't be?

The movie studio— which faced bankruptcy— desperately needed a hit.

They had everything needed to succeed— ideas, money, marketing, and cutting edge technology.

Hyphen -

A hyphen is a short line used to separate or join words and other items.

- Use hyphens to break words:

    We saw her on tele-
    vision last night.

    Only break words between syllables.

- Use hyphens to connect words to create adjectives:

    We made a last-ditch attempt to score a touchdown.

    Do *not* use hyphens with adverbs ending in *-ly:*

    We issued a quickly drafted statement to the press.

- Use hyphens to connect words forming numbers:

    The firm owes nearly thirty-eight million dollars in back taxes.

- Use hyphens after some prefixes:

    His self-diagnosis was misleading.

- Use hyphens between combinations of numbers and words:

    She drove a 2.5-ton truck.

Ellipsis . . .

An ellipsis, three spaced periods [. . .], indicates words are deleted from quoted material:

Original Text
The mayor said, "Our city, which is one of the country's most progressive, deserves a high-tech light-rail system."

With Ellipsis
The mayor said, "Our city . . . deserves a high-tech light-rail system."

Delete only minor ideas or details—never change the basic meaning of a sentence by deleting key words. Don't eliminate a negative word like "not" to create a positive statement or remove qualifying words:

Original
We must, only as a last resort, consider legalizing drugs.

Incorrect
He said, "We must . . . consider legalizing drugs."

When deleting words at the end of a sentence, add a period before the ellipsis:

The governor said, "I agree we need a new rail system. . . ."

An ellipsis is not used if words are deleted at the opening of a quotation:

The mayor said "the city deserves a high-tech light-rail system."

If deleting words will create a grammar mistake, insert corrections with brackets:

Original
"Poe, Emerson, and Whitman were among our greatest writers."

With Ellipsis
"Poe . . . [was] among our greatest writers."

Slash /

Slashes separate words when both apply and show line breaks when quoting poetry:

The student should study his/her lessons.
Her poem read in part, "We hope / We dream / We pray."

Question Mark ?

Question marks are placed after direct questions and to note questionable items:

Did Adrian Carsini attend the auction?
Did you read "Can We Defeat Hunger?" in *Newsweek* last week?

Question marks that appear in the original title are placed within quotation marks. If the title does not ask a question, the question mark is placed outside the quotation marks:

Did you read "The Raven"?

Question marks in parentheses are used to indicate that the writer questions the accuracy of a fact, number, idea, or quotation:

The children claimed they waited two hours (?) for help to arrive.

Exclamation Point !

Exclamation points are placed at the end of emphatic statements:

Help!
We owe her over ten million dollars!

Exclamation points should be used as special effects. They lose their impact if overused.

Period .

Periods are used after sentences, in abbreviations, and as decimals:

I bought a car.
We gave the car to Ms. Chavez who starts working for Dr. Gomez on Jan. 15.
The book sells for $29.95 in hardcover and $12.95 in paper.

When an abbreviation ends a sentence, only one period is used.

Common abbreviations such as FBI, CIA, ABC, BBC, and UCLA do not require periods.

Capitalization

- Capitalize the first word of every sentence:

    We studied all weekend.

- Capitalize the first word in direct quotations:

    Felix said, "The school should buy new computers."

- Capitalize the first word and all important words in titles of articles, books, plays, movies, television shows, seminars, and courses:

    "Terrorism Today"   *Gone with the Wind*   *Death of a Salesman*

- Capitalize the names of nationalities, languages, races, religions, deities, and sacred terms:

    Many Germans speak English.
    The Koran is the basic text in Islam.

- Capitalize the days of the week, months of the year, and holidays:

    We celebrate Flag Day every June 14.
    The test scheduled for Monday is canceled.
    Some people celebrate Christmas in January.
    We observed Passover with her parents.

    The seasons of the year are not capitalized:

    We loved the spring fashions.   Last winter was mild.

- Capitalize special historical events, documents, and eras:

    Battle of the Bulge   Declaration of Independence

- Capitalize names of planets, continents, nations, states, provinces, counties, towns and cities, mountains, lakes, rivers, and other geographic features:

    Mars   North America   Canada   Ontario

- Capitalize *north, south, east,* and *west* when they refer to geographic regions:

    The convention will be held in the Southwest.

    Do not capitalize *north, south, east,* and *west* when used as directions:

    The farm is southwest of Rockford.

- Capitalize brand names:

    Coca-Cola   Ford Thunderbird   Cross pen

    Some brand names like *Kleenex, Xerox,* and *Coke* appear in lowercase.
- Capitalize names of specific corporations, organizations, institutions, and buildings:

    This engine was developed by General Motors.
    After high school he attended Carroll College.
    We visited the site of the former World Trade Center.

- Capitalize abbreviations, acronyms, or shortened forms of capitalized words when used as proper nouns:

    FBI   CIA   NOW   ERA
    IRA   JFK   LAX   NBC

- Capitalize people's names and nicknames:

    Barbara Roth   Timmy Arnold

Capitalize professional titles when used with proper names:

    Last week Doctor Ryan suggested I see an eye doctor.
    Our college president once worked for President Carter.
    This report must be seen by the president.
    [The word *president* is often capitalized to refer to the president of the United States.]

Capitalize words like *father, mother, brother, aunt, cousin,* and *uncle* only when used with or in place of proper names:

    My mother and I went to see Uncle Al.
    After the game, I took Mother to meet my uncle.

POINT TO REMEMBER

A few capitalization rules vary. *African American* is always capitalized, but editors vary whether *blacks* should be capitalized. Some writers capitalize *a.m.* and *p.m.,* while others do not. Follow the standard used in your discipline or career and be consistent.

Spelling

Commonly Confused Words

accept	to take	Do you *accept* checks?
except	but/to exclude	Everyone *except* Joe went home.
adapt	to change	We will *adapt* the army helicopter for civilian use.
adopt	to take possession of	They want to *adopt* a child.
adverse	unfavorable	*Adverse* publicity ruined his reputation.
averse	opposed to	I was *averse* to buying a new car.
advice	a noun	Take my *advice*.
advise	a verb	Let me *advise* you.
affect	to influence	Will this *affect* my grade?
effect	a result	What is the *effect* of the drug?
all ready	prepared	We were *all ready* for the trip.
already	by a certain time	You are *already* approved.
allusion	a reference	She made a biblical *allusion*.
illusion	imaginary vision	The mirage was an optical *illusion*.
all together	unity	The teachers stood *all together*.
altogether	totally	*Altogether,* that will cost $50.
among	relationship of three or more	This outfit is popular *among* college students.
between	relationship of two	This was a dispute *between* Kim and Nancy.
amount	for items that are measured	A small *amount* of oil has leaked.
number	for items that are counted	A large *number* of cars are stalled.
any one	a person, idea, item	*Any one* of the books will do.
anyone	anybody	Can *anyone* help me?
brake	to halt/a stopping	Can you fix the *brakes?*
break	an interruption	Take a coffee *break*.
	to destroy	Don't *break* the window.
capital	money	She needs venture *capital*.
	government center	Trenton is the *capital* of New Jersey.

capitol	legislative building	He toured the U.S. *Capitol.*
cite	to note or refer to	He *cited* several figures in his speech.
site	a location	We inspected the *site* of the crash.
sight	a view, ability to see	The *sight* from the hill was tremendous.
complement	to complete	The jet had a full *complement* of spare parts.
compliment	express praise, a gift	The host paid us a nice *compliment.*
conscience	moral sensibility	He was a prisoner of *conscience.*
conscious	aware of/awake	Is he *conscious* of these debts? Is the patient *conscious?*
continual	now and again	We have *continual* financial problems.
continuous	uninterrupted	The brain needs a *continuous* supply of blood.
council	a group	A student *council* will meet Tuesday.
counsel	to advise/advisor	He sought legal *counsel.*
discreet	tactful	He made a *discreet* hint.
discrete	separate/distinct	The war had three *discrete* phases.
elicit	evoke/persuade	His hateful remarks will *elicit* protest.
illicit	illegal	Her use of *illicit* drugs ruined her career.
emigrate	to leave a country	They tried to *emigrate* from Germany.
immigrate	to enter a country	They were allowed to *immigrate* to America.
eminent	famous	She was an *eminent* eye specialist.
imminent	impending	Disaster was *imminent.*
everyday	ordinary	Wear *everyday* clothes to the party.
every day	daily	We exercise *every day.*
farther	distance	How much *farther* is it?
further	in addition	He demanded *further* investigation.
fewer	for items counted	There are *fewer* security guards this year.
less	for items measured	There is *less* security this year.

good	an adjective	She has *good* eyesight.
well	an adverb	She sees *well*.
hear	to listen	Can you *hear* the music?
here	a place/direction	Put the table *here*.
imply	to suggest	The president *implied* he might raise taxes.
infer	to interpret	The reporters *inferred* from his comments that the president might raise taxes.
its	possessive of *it*	The car won't start because *its* battery is dead.
it's	contraction of *it is*	*It's* snowing.
lay	to put/to place	*Lay* the books on my desk.
lie	to rest	*Lie* down for a nap.
loose	not tight	He has a *loose* belt or *loose* change.
lose	to misplace	Don't *lose* your keys.
moral	dealing with values	She made a *moral* decision to report the crime.
morale	mood	After the loss, the team's *morale* fell.
passed	successfully completed	She *passed* the test.
past	history	That was in my *past*.
personal	private/intimate	She left a *personal* note.
personnel	employees	Send your resume to the *personnel* office.
plain	simple/open space	She wore a *plain* dress.
plane	airplane/geometric form	They took a *plane* to Chicago.
precede	to go before	A film will *precede* the lecture.
proceed	go forward	Let the parade *proceed*.
principal	main/school leader	Oil is the *principal* product of Kuwait.
principle	basic law	I understand the *principle* of law.
raise	to lift	*Raise* the window!
rise	to get up	*Rise* and shine!
right	direction/correct	Turn *right*. That's *right*.
rite	a ritual	She was given last *rites*.

write	to inscribe	They *write* essays every week.
stationary	unmoving	The disabled train remained *stationary*.
stationery	writing paper	The hotel *stationery* was edged in gold.
than	used to compare	I am taller *than* Helen.
then	concerning time	We *then* headed to class.
their	possessive of *they*	*Their* car is stalled.
there	direction/place	Put the chair over *there*.
they're	contraction of *they are*	*They're* coming to dinner.
there're	contraction of *there are*	*There're* two seats left.
to	preposition/infinitive	I went *to* school *to* study law.
too	in excess/also	It was *too* cold to swim.
two	a number	We bought *two* computers.
wear	concerns clothes/ damage	We *wear* our shoes until they *wear* out.
where	a place in question	*Where* is the post office?
weather	climatic conditions	*Weather* forecasts predict rain.
whether	alternatives/no matter what	You must register, *whether* or not you want to audit the class.
who's	contraction of *who is*	*Who's* on first?
whose	possessive of *who*	*Whose* book is that?

Commonly Misspelled Words

absence	analyze	beautiful	column	definite
accept	annual	becoming	coming	deliberate
accident	anonymous	beginning	commitment	dependent
accommodate	apparent	belief	committee	description
accumulate	appreciate	believe	competition	difficult
achieve	approach	benefit	completely	disappear
achievement	arctic	breakfast	complexion	disappoint
acquaint	argument	business	conceive	discipline
acquire	article	calendar	consistent	discuss
across	assassination	candidate	continually	dominant
address	assistance	career	control	dying
advertisement	athletic	carrying	controversial	efficient
adolescence	attention	celebrate	criticism	eighth
a lot	attitude	cemetery	curious	eligible
amateur	basically	challenge	dealt	embarrass
analysis	basis	characteristic	decision	enough

environment	identity	mortgage	publicly	stereotype
equipment	identically	necessary	qualify	straight
essential	immediately	ninety	quality	strict
exaggerate	importance	noticeable	quantity	studying
excellent	incidental	obligation	query	success
existence	independence	obvious	quiet	summary
experience	influence	occasionally	quizzes	surprise
explanation	intelligence	occupation	realize	synonymous
extremely	interest	occurred	recede	technique
fallacy	interpret	omit	receive	temperament
familiar	interrupt	operate	reception	tenable
fantasy	involvement	opinion	recognition	tendency
fascination	irrelevant	opportunity	recommend	thorough
favorite	irresistible	oppose	refer	thought
February	irresponsible	optimism	regulation	throughout
feminine	judgment	ordinarily	relation	tomorrow
field	judicial	original	religious	tragedy
finally	judicious	paid	remember	tremendous
foreign	knowledge	pamphlet	repetition	truly
forgotten	label	parallel	responsible	unfortunate
forty	laboratory	particularly	restaurant	uniform
fourth	language	perform	rhythm	unique
frequent	leisure	permanent	ridicule	until
friend	libel	permission	roommate	unusual
frighten	library	persistent	sacrifice	useful
fulfill	license	persuade	safety	using
fundamental	lightning	persuasion	scene	usually
further	loneliness	philosophy	schedule	vacillate
generally	luxury	physical	seize	vacillation
generous	lying	playwright	separate	vacuum
government	magazine	politician	sergeant	valuable
gradually	maintenance	positive	severely	various
grammar	maneuver	possession	significance	vengeance
grateful	marriage	possible	significant	villain
guarantee	martial	precede	similar	violence
guard	material	preference	simplify	vulnerable
guidance	mathematics	prejudice	sincerely	weird
happiness	meant	presence	situation	whole
height	mechanical	primitive	skillfully	writing
heroes	medieval	probably	sociology	yield
holocaust	mere	procedure	sophisticated	
huge	miniature	prominent	sophomore	
humorous	mischief	psychic	special	
hypocrite	misspell	psychology	specimen	

Add other words you often misspell:

_____

_____

_____

_____

_____

_____

_____

_____

_____

_____

_____

_____

_____

_____

_____

_____

Two Hundred Topics for College Writing

best friends	AIDS	outsourcing jobs	steroids
gangs	cults	labor unions	binge drinking
fad diets	lawsuits	married priests	single parents
job interviews	sweatshops	night clubs	summer jobs
athletes as role	chat rooms	gas prices	animal testing
models	drunk drivers	car repairs	life after death
bad habits	school prayer	plea bargaining	Hollywood
child support	commercials	banks	school choice
NBA salaries	student housing	lying	hate speech
doctors	wearing fur	fast food	suburbs
terrorism	work ethic	cable TV	public schools
military	eating disorders	fatherhood	birth control
spending	insanity defense	racism	credit cards
solar power	Internet	study skills	funerals
right to die	voting	immigration	toughest course
best teacher	adoption	the Olympics	working out
car insurance	celebrity justice	cell phones	Social Security
health clubs	favorite movie	property taxes	talk shows
shopping malls	teen eating habits	bilingual	heating bills
fashion models	cable TV bills	education	drug testing
hobbies	minimum wage	world hunger	aging population
foreign aid	the president	slavery	summer jobs
airport security	health insurance	reparations	stereotypes
cruise ships	images of women	worst boss	car prices
blind dates	taking the bus	binge drinking	affirmative action
exploring Mars	discrimination	the pope	moving
being "in"	TV moms	college	animal rights
used cars	the Superbowl	instructors	living wills
Osama bin	pensions	cyberspace	marriage vows
Laden	welfare reform	best restaurant	reading
democracy	the UN	profanity in	grandparents
being religious	being downsized	public	plastic surgery
freeways	favorite singer	reporters	passion
televised trials	prenatal care	your mayor	dreams
sitcoms	workaholics	Wall Street	family values
cheating	cable news	shopping till you	hospitals
today's comics	parties	drop	best jobs
drug prevention	reality TV	overcoming	stalking
ethnic	school loans	depression	gay marriage
stereotypes	women in	fraternities and	NFL
lotteries	combat	sororities	public schools
euthanasia	secondhand	racial profiling	pets
goal for this year	smoke	casinos	divorce
SAT	spring break	prisons	domestic
daycare	drinking age	family values	violence
taxes	coffee bars	online dating	Iraq

gay bashing
MTV
Islam
sex on television
hip-hop
glass ceiling
remembering
   9/11
gun control
the homeless
soap operas
learning English

being in debt
relationships
dorm life
person you
   admire
surveillance
   cameras
sexual
   harassment
Letterman or
   Leno
rape shield laws

world hunger
right to privacy
Internet
   pornography
biological
   weapons
downloading
   music
teaching
   methods
coping with
   illness

sexist or racist
   jokes
definition of
   success
drug busts
final exams
raising boys
   and girls

Odd-Numbered and Partial-Paragraph Answers to the Exercises in Chapters 3–27

CHAPTER 3

Exercise 1

1. Home is where the heart is.

3. Change comes hard in America, but it comes constantly.

Exercise 2

1. d

3. a

5. d

Exercise 3

Answers vary.

Exercise 4

Answers vary.

Exercise 5

I loved Toms River, New Jersey. We lived only a few miles from the shore, and I often spent summer afternoons sailing in the bay or walking on the beach. I enjoyed my high school because I had a lot of friends and participated in a lot of activities. I played softball and football.

My father was transferred to Minneapolis my junior year. I hated leaving my school and friends but thought I would be able to adjust. I found the move harder to deal with than I thought. Instead of living in a colonial house on a half-acre lot, we moved into a downtown loft. It was spacious, offered a wonderful view, and had both a swimming pool and a health club. As big as our two-floor loft was, it began to feel like a submarine. I missed the feel of wind and fresh air. . . .

Exercise 6

I love my sister, but often Sharon drives me crazy. Just last week I faced a crisis. I had to drive to school to take a makeup exam before my math teacher had to file her midterm grades. I got dressed, packed up my books, and raced downstairs to my car only to discover I had a flat tire. I raced upstairs and woke Sharon, who was still sleeping.

"Sharon, I need to borrow your car," I blurted out.

"Why," she asked, upset that I disturbed her.

"My car has a flat."

"So, this is your day off."

"I know, but I have to make up an exam today."

"Go tomorrow after work," she said. . . .

CHAPTER 4

Exercise 1

Answers vary.

Exercise 2

1. b, c, e

3. a, b, e

5. a, c, d

Exercise 3

Answers vary.

Exercise 4

Answers vary.

Exercise 5

Answers vary.

CHAPTER 5

Exercise 1

State Street is marked by poverty, decay, and empty buildings.

Exercise 2

Answers vary.

Exercise 3

Answers vary.

Exercise 4

Answers vary.

Exercise 5

Answers vary.

CHAPTER 6

Exercise 1

Answers vary.

Exercise 2

When I first arrived in Bellingham . . .

After checking in . . .

It was not until after . . .

Exercise 3

Answers vary.

Exercise 4

Answers vary.

CHAPTER 7

Exercise 1

1. Gentrification, the process of turning slums into upscale neighborhoods, is changing cities across America.

3. The final example is hypothetical.

Exercise 2

Answers vary.

Exercise 3

Answers vary.

Exercise 4

Answers vary.

CHAPTER 8

Exercise 1

Answers vary.

Exercise 2

Answers vary.

Exercise 3

Answers vary.

CHAPTER 9

Exercise 1

1. X

3. C

5. P

7. P

9. P

Exercise 2

1. Atlas Industries closed its National Avenue plant in 1999.

Exercise 3

1. The closing of the Atlas plant crippled the local economy, especially on the city's south side.

Exercise 4

Answers vary.

CHAPTER 10

Exercise 1

introduction
description of building

    <u>Tremont was a great place to grow up.</u> My sisters and I loved our large apartment with its wide balconies, spacious living room, and big bedrooms. Our building did not have elevators, and we lived on the third floor. We did not care, because we enjoyed playing dolls on the wide, carpeted steps.

transition and topic sentence
description of neighborhood

    <u>Living in Tremont was like living in a small town.</u> We could walk to school and to Brucker Park where we played on the monkey bars and slides. After school we bought candy at the corner store or caught a matinee at the Knickerbocker, an elaborate old theater with crushed velvet seats and gold moldings. On summer evenings we played on the stoop while neighborhood dads played catch with their sons and

details

nervous moms helped toddlers pedal their tricycles down the crooked pavement. Although we lived in New York City, it felt like a small town where people knew their neighbors, cared for friends, and watched out for each other's children.

transition

    <u>All this changed when I was eight years old.</u> Every family on our block, in fact every family in the neighborhood, got "the letter." We had to move.

contrast

The city had condemned whole blocks of Tremont. Our spacious apartment buildings, cute stores, and candy shops were considered "blighted." Tremont was

details

described as being "old," "decayed," "distressed," and "a slum." . . .

Exercise 2

Answers vary.

Exercise 3

Answers vary.

CHAPTER 11

Exercise 1

Answers vary.

CHAPTER 12

Exercise 1

1. principal
3. Whether
5. who's
7. emigrated
9. allusions

Exercise 2

archaic	old	*lucrative*	profitable
discriminate	differentiate	*patron*	customer or donor
homicide	killing of one person by another	*topical*	current

Exercise 3

Answers vary.

Exercise 4

1. In July 1976 an employee of a cotton warehouse in Nzara, Sudan, suddenly suffered shock and died from uncontrollable hemorrhages.
3. The disease raced through the village, infecting and killing the people of Nzara.
5. Not understanding the deadly nature of the disease, hospital doctors and nurses contracted the disease as they examined patients.
7. Suddenly the epidemic ended when the virus ran out of healthy people it could infect.
9. Medical experts saw the outbreak as greatly significant because it suggested that science had not conquered infectious disease.

Exercise 5

1. Throughout World War II, Stalin pressured Churchill and Roosevelt to open the Second Front by invading Europe.
3. Affirmative action policies that once energized the administration to employ more minorities have been ignored to reduce costs.
5. Until our insurance problem is fixed, don't let anyone from the sales department use company cars.

Exercise 6

Answers vary.

CHAPTER 13

Exercise 1

1. Chicago Fire
3. Illinois
5. fires (plural)
7. firestorm
9. Over 250 men, women, and children (plural)

Exercise 2

1. F. Scott Fitzgerald
3. he (pronoun)
5. Fitzgerald
7. novel
9. It (pronoun)

Exercise 3

1. guesswork
3. experts
5. calculations
7. studies
9. oil deposits

Exercise 4

1. people (subject) in the country, of thieves, in black masks, into houses
3. About five years ago, group (subject), of criminals, in California
5. ATMs (subject), to any banking network
7. customers (subject)
9. After a month, of complaints, the criminals (subject), to the mall owners

Exercise 5

Answers vary.

Exercise 6

1. discovered
3. gripped
5. mounted
7. discovered
9. closed

Exercise 7

1. are
3. could (helping verb) carry
5. was
7. could (helping verb) operate
9. would (helping verb) change

Exercise 8

Answers vary.

Exercise 9

1. laser (subject), stands (verb)
3. beam (subject), diffuses (verb)
5. geographers and mapmakers (subject), use (verb)
7. weapons (subject), could (helping verb), disable (verb), disrupt (verb)
9. loss of key satellites (subject), could (helping verb), ruin (verb)

CHAPTER 14

Exercise 1

1. OK

3. OK

5. F

7. F

9. F

Exercise 2

1. Few people realize Harlem was originally designed to be an exclusive white community.

3. Developers cleared Harlem's pastures and small farms to build blocks of luxury townhouses featuring elevators and servants' quarters.

5. OK

7. OK

9. OK

Exercise 3

1. Although computers have revolutionized writing and publishing, some historians are concerned about the effect technology will have on written records.

3. In addition, literary scholars have been able to view various drafts of a play or poem, allowing them to see how a writer like Ibsen or Poe worked.

5. Journalists also wonder if computers will make it easier for political and business leaders to alter records.

7. OK

9. On the other hand, computers and the Internet allow today's researchers to examine documents held by libraries around the world.

Exercise 4

Howard Hughes was born in Texas in 1905, the son of a wealthy industrialist. At nineteen Hughes inherited his father's lucrative tool company. Fascinated with movies from an early age, Hughes moved to Hollywood. At first, the Hollywood establishment dismissed the young millionaire as a starstruck amateur. His first movie was so bad that Hughes refused to release it. But in 1927 his film *Wings* won an Academy Award for Best Picture. Eager to pursue his passion for flying, Hughes wanted to make a film about World War I pilots. Sparing no expense, Hughes began filming *Hell's Angels*. He bought so many aircraft for battle scenes, his studio had more planes than many European air forces. . . .

Exercise 5

Long before people could communicate using the Internet, telephones, or the telegraph, they saw the need

to relay information quickly. Without electricity
all messages had to be delivered by coach or runner.
During the French Revolution, a young engineer proposed a signaling system to connect Paris and Lille
using semaphores. Claude Chappe, who received backing
from the government, worked with his brother to con-
struct a series of towers five to ten miles apart. The
towers were equipped with two telescopes and two long
wooden arms that could be set in forty-nine different
positions, each signaling a letter or symbol. Letter
by letter, the operator in one tower set the wooden
arms to send a message to the operator in the next
tower who watched through a telescope. . . .

CHAPTER 15

Exercise 1

Answers vary.

Exercise 2

1. Lee De Forest developed the sound-on-film technique, and it revolutionized the film industry.
3. Immigrant stars with heavy accents seemed laughable playing cowboys and cops, and their careers were ruined.
5. Hollywood's English-language films lost foreign markets, and dubbing techniques had to be created.

Exercise 3

Answers vary.

Exercise 4

Answers vary.

Exercise 5

Answers vary.

Exercise 6

1. I loved taking carriage rides in Central Park when I lived in New York.
   When I lived in New York, I loved taking carriage rides in Central Park.
3. Many children still delight in old-fashioned puppet shows although people are accustomed to watching television.
   Although people are accustomed to watching television, many children still delight in old-fashioned puppet shows.
5. Although he completed only four major plays, Chekhov is considered one of the world's greatest dramatists.
   Chekhov is considered one of the world's greatest dramatists although he completed only four major plays.

Exercise 7

1. Marcus Garvey, who was born in Jamaica, became one of the most inspiring and controversial black leaders in the United States.

3. Because Garvey's philosophy stressed black nationalism, black pride, and black entrepreneurship, many African Americans found his message uplifting.

5. The UNIA was unlike other black organizations at the time because it was international in scope.

7. Many people saw Garvey, who wore flashy uniforms and held marches, as a simple-minded buffoon leading ignorant people into wasted efforts and lost causes.

9. Garvey's opponents, who supported the government's prosecution of Garvey for mail fraud, also urged that the UNIA be disbanded.

Exercise 8

Answers vary.

CHAPTER 16

Exercise 1

1. OK
3. CS
5. F
7. CS
9. F

Exercise 2

<u>Today's college students are accustomed to using notebook computers they are smaller and lighter than their parents' old portable typewriters.</u> These slim models bear no relation to their ancestors. <u>The first generation of computers were massive contraptions they filled entire rooms.</u> They used thousands of vacuum tubes, which tended to burn out quickly. <u>To keep the computers running people had to run up and down aisles, they pushed shopping carts full of replacement tubes.</u> Because of their size, computers had limited military value. . . .

Exercise 3

Answers vary.

Exercise 4

Answers vary.

Exercise 5

1. Recovering alcoholics sometimes call themselves Friends of Bill W.; he was a founder of Alcoholics Anonymous.

3. He tried to remain sober and focus on rebuilding his career, but the temptation to drink often overwhelmed him.

5. To keep himself from drinking he knew he needed to talk to someone, and he began calling churches listed in a hotel directory.

7. Wilson was put in touch with Dr. Robert Smith; he was a prominent physician whose life and career had been nearly destroyed by drinking.

9. They shared the guilt about broken promises to their wives; they knew how alcohol affected their judgment, their character, and their health.

Exercise 6

"Quota quickies" were some of the worst movies ever made, but they served a purpose. In the 1930s members of Parliament became concerned about the number of American motion pictures playing in British cinemas. To combat the Americanization of British society and stimulate the lagging British film industry, the government imposed a quota; it demanded that a certain percentage of films shown in Britain had to be made in Britain.

American studios did not want to limit the number of films they showed in England. Hollywood executives hit on a plan that would maintain their share of the British market. Instead of lowering the number of American films they showed in Britain to meet the quota, they increased the number of British films. American studios hastily set up British film companies, hired British writers and directors, and made a series of low-budget English movies. They did not want to spend money on stars, **so** they hired London stage actors looking for extra pay. . . .

CHAPTER 17

Exercise 1

1. DM
3. DM
5. DM
7. DM
9. OK
11. DM
13. DM
15. DM
17. DM
19. OK

Exercise 2

1. OK
3. DM
5. DM
7. OK
9. DM

11. OK
13. OK
15. DM
17. DM
19. DM

Exercise 3

Answers vary.

Exercise 4

Answers vary.

Exercise 5

1. The landlord demanded police protection from angry tenants facing eviction.
3. Having won eight games in a row, the coach was cheered by fans when he appeared.
5. Having been translated into dozens of languages, *Gone With the Wind* has enthralled readers all over the world.

Exercise 6

1. OK
3. MM
5. MM
7. MM
9. MM
11. MM
13. OK
15. MM
17. OK
19. OK

Exercise 7

1. Speaking on television, the mayor tried to calm the anxious crowd.
3. The tourists, unfamiliar with French law, requested Paris attorneys.
5. We served lamb chops covered in mint sauce to our guests.

Exercise 8

No other radio program had more impact on the American public than Orson Welles's famous "War of the Worlds" broadcast. <u>Only twenty-three at the time</u>, Welles's newly formed Mercury Theatre aired weekly radio productions of original and classic dramas. On October 30, 1938, an Americanized version of H. G. Wells's science fiction novel *The War of the Worlds* was aired by the Mercury Theatre, <u>which described a Martian invasion</u>.

Regular listeners understood the broadcast was fiction and sat back to enjoy the popular program. The play opened with the sounds of a dance band.

Suddenly, the music was interrupted by a news report that astronomers <u>on the surface of Mars</u> had detected strange explosions. The broadcast returned to dance music. But soon the music was interrupted again with reports of a meteor crash in Grovers Mills, New Jersey. The broadcast then dispensed with music, and a dramatic stream of reports covered the rapidly unfolding events.

    <u>Equipped with eerie special effects</u>, the strange scene in the New Jersey countryside was described by anxious reporters. The crater, listeners were told, was not caused by a meteor but by some strange space-craft. A large, octopuslike creature emerged from the crater, <u>presumably coming from Mars</u>, and blasted onlookers with powerful death rays. . . .

Exercise 9

1. Mary, who was born in Manhattan, took Nancy to New York this summer.

3. The television show, which suffered low ratings, cost the network millions in lost advertising revenue.

5. The missing girl, who is only three years old, was last seen by her mother.

Exercise 10

Answers vary.

CHAPTER 18

Exercise 1

1. NP
3. OK
5. NP
7. OK
9. OK
11. OK
13. OK
15. OK
17. NP
19. OK

Exercise 2

1. In the 1990s the Internet revolutionized business, education, the media, even family life.

3. A small entrepreneur can participate in the global economy without the cost of maintaining branch offices, mailing catalogs, or airing television commercials.

5. No single person invented the Internet, but Robert E. Taylor played a role in designing the first networks and overcoming numerous obstacles.

7. At that time computers were like paper notebooks, so that whatever was entered into one could not be transferred to another without reentering the data, which was costly and time consuming.

9. The government provided grants to corporations and universities to stimulate research into connecting computers, overcoming incompatibility, and developing standards.

Exercise 3

1. In 1907 the Plaza Hotel opened in New York, featuring marble staircases, Irish linen, French crystal, and Swiss lace.

3. Alfred Vanderbilt, Lillian Russell, Diamond Jim Brady, and Mark Twain attended the opening and noted the hotel's brilliant lobby.

5. In the 1920s F. Scott Fitzgerald and his wife, Zelda, were spotted frolicking and splashing in the lobby fountain.

7. When the Beatles made the Plaza their New York headquarters, the hotel staff had to protect the rock stars from prying reporters, zealous fans, and souvenir hunters.

9. Featured in movies like *North by Northwest, Plaza Suite, The Great Gatsby, Funny Girl, Arthur,* and *Crocodile Dundee,* the Plaza Hotel developed a reputation for style and became a New York monument.

Exercise 4

Answers vary.

CHAPTER 19

Exercise 1

1. stock market/attracts
3. Investors/plan
5. Investors/buy
7. Speculators/rely
9. person/needs

Exercise 2

1. is
3. sponsors
5. declares
7. are
9. plan

Exercise 3

1. have
3. is
5. buys
7. were
9. are

Exercise 4

1. is
3. is

5. were
7. were
9. believe

Exercise 5

1. were
3. are
5. meets
7. was
9. are

Exercise 6

1. are
3. were
5. was
7. were
9. were
11. was
13. was
15. was

Exercise 7

Answers vary.

Exercise 8

```
Today many colleges offer courses through the Inter-
net. The idea of broadcasting classes is not new. For
decades, universities, colleges, and technical insti-
tutions have used television to teach classes. Unlike
educational television programs, Internet courses are
interactive. Instructors can use chat rooms to hold
virtual office hours and class discussions so that a
student feels less isolated. . . .
```

CHAPTER 20

Exercise 1

1. Present   I speak to youth groups.
    Past   I <u>spoke</u> to youth groups.
    Past participle   I have <u>spoken</u> to youth groups.
3. Present   They buy silk from China.
    Past   They <u>bought</u> silk from China.
    Past participle   They have <u>bought</u> silk from China.
5. Present   Hope springs eternal.
    Past   Hope <u>sprang</u> eternal.
    Past participle   Hope has <u>sprung</u> eternal.

Exercise 2

1. was
3. ate

5. began, faced
7. designed
9. created

Exercise 3

      The summer of 1961 <u>saw</u> a great season for the New York Yankees. Two players, Roger Maris and Mickey Mantle, <u>challenged</u> Babe Ruth's record of hitting sixty home runs in a season. The 1927 record <u>seemed</u> unbreakable. Despite a slow start that season, Maris soon <u>began</u> hitting one home run after another, keeping pace with Mickey Mantle. <u>Called</u> the "M&M boys" by sportswriters, Maris and Mantle <u>became</u> national heroes.

      As the summer <u>wore</u> on, and both players had <u>hit</u> over forty home runs, attention grew. Even President Kennedy <u>stopped</u> the nation's business to follow their progress. Not everyone <u>was</u> enthusiastic about their hitting. Many Ruth fans, including the baseball commissioner, <u>did</u> not want to <u>see</u> the classic record <u>broken</u>. . . .

Exercise 4

1. laid
3. sit
5. raise
7. had lain
9. Set

Exercise 5

1. A
3. P
5. P
7. P
9. A

Exercise 6

1. Jason Andrews signed the contract.
3. Paramedics rushed the children to the hospital.
5. The county repaired the bridge.

Exercise 7

1. We should have taken a cab to the airport.
3. You should have never paid them in cash.
5. They should have been sued for breach of contract.

Exercise 8

1. She didn't have any car insurance.
3. The School of Law never offered paralegal courses.
5. Mary scarcely had time to play sports.

CHAPTER 21

Exercise 1

1. Sara went to her favorite New Orleans restaurant, taking Carla as her guest.

3. Until he moved to San Diego, my cousin worked with Fred.

5. Armando's nephew told Mr. Mendoza, "My car needs new tires."

Exercise 2

1. The classrooms are dusty. The halls are marked by graffiti. The lockers are smashed. Students just don't care about their school.

3. You would think a museum would take better care of fragile artwork.

5. When are manufacturers going to build cars with better engines?

Exercise 3

1. their

3. its

5. he

7. his

9. it

Exercise 4

1. When he moved to New York, a nice apartment cost three hundred dollars a month.

3. We always thought he would be a star—we could tell by watching him rehearse.

5. We went to the beach to swim, but it was so cold we had to stay inside.

Exercise 5

1. I

3. us

5. him

7. us

9. her

Exercise 6

1. them

3. this

5. These/they

7. him

9. he

Exercise 7

1. Jim or I am working on the Fourth of July.

3. The teachers and they discussed the new textbook; it comes with free CDs.

5. They gave the job to us students, but they never provided the supplies we needed.

CHAPTER 22

Exercise 1

1. strangest, American
3. brown, cobblestone
5. large, wooden
7. oncoming, sticky
9. final

Exercise 2

Answers vary.

Exercise 3

1. iced
3. mashed
5. borrowed
7. dated
9. boiled

Exercise 4

1. creatively
3. largely, quickly, fast
5. increasingly
7. carefully
9. carefully

Exercise 5

Answers vary.

Exercise 6

1. good
3. better
5. better
7. good
9. badly

Exercise 7

1. frequently/particularly
3. readily
5. vast
7. quickly
9. newly

Exercise 8

1. more effective
3. rustier
5. happier
7. colder
9. more fragile

Exercise 9

1. Born to former slaves, Sarah Walker was orphaned at seven, married at fourteen, and widowed at twenty, enduring one of the worst upbringings possible.
3. Her life radically changed when she invented a remarkable line of hair-care products for black women.
5. Soon Sarah Walker's company was employing hundreds of new workers.
7. Walker's rapidly expanding enterprise also trained women to become sales agents and salon operators, allowing many black women to form independent businesses.
9. She became a respected figure in black society and was actively involved in the civil rights movement.

CHAPTER 23

Exercise 1

1. except
3. in
5. through
7. at
9. to

Exercise 2

1. During the night, by the storm
3. Against his doctor's advice, to Europe, through the mountains
5. In the morning, from Madison, with textbooks, for the public schools
7. between the mayor and the city council, from a long argument, over property taxes
9. along the beach, in the rain

Exercise 3

1. <u>Benito Juarez</u> is one <u>of the most important figures in Mexican history</u>.
3. <u>Despite many obstacles</u>, <u>Juarez</u> graduated <u>from a seminary</u>.
5. <u>During his term</u> as governor <u>Juarez</u> initiated policies that brought him <u>into conflict</u> <u>with powerful forces</u> that began to align <u>against him</u>.
7. After liberals assumed power, <u>they</u> recalled Juarez <u>from exile</u> to become the <u>minister of justice</u>.
9. <u>In 1857</u> <u>he</u> was elected chief justice <u>of the Mexican Supreme Court</u>.

Exercise 4

1. Tim was exhausted by the marathon and passed out in the locker room.
3. I want a sandwich without mustard for lunch.
5. From the window we watched the children skating on the lake.
7. The hikers took shelter in a cave from the sudden blizzard.
9. Tickets for the midnight game will be available at noon.

Exercise 5

```
Expecting veterans to be tall, battle-scarred war-
riors, the American public found Audie Murphy an
```

unlikely hero. Standing only five feet five inches
and weighing only 112 pounds, the boyish twenty-year-
old Texan had been thought unfit for combat. But having killed 241 enemy soldiers in seven bitter campaigns, Murphy emerged in 1945 as the most decorated
soldier in American history. He appeared on the cover
of *Life* magazine, and his smiling good looks fascinated the public. Impressed by the young man's charm,
Jimmy Cagney invited Audie Murphy to Hollywood. Still
recovering from war wounds, Murphy studied acting
and worked to soften his Texas accent. Murphy began
appearing in movies, and he wrote an autobiography of
his war experiences. . . .

CHAPTER 24

Exercise 1

1. The Statue of Liberty is a symbol of American freedom, and it commemorates French-American friendship.

3. Edouard de Laboulaye was a French historian, and he was a great admirer of American democracy.

5. Frederic-Auguste Bartholdi designed the statue, and he selected the site in New York Harbor.

7. After Congress approved use of Bedloe Island, construction on the pedestal began.

9. The 225-ton statue took a year to erect, and it was completed in 1886 to celebrate America's centennial.

Exercise 2

1. Throughout history people came across large bones, fossils, and teeth.

3. Before Owen, people thought these strange bones were evidence of extinct dragons, giant birds, or mythical beasts.

5. At first, researchers believed all dinosaurs were cold blooded because they resembled modern reptiles, such as alligators, crocodiles, and lizards.

7. Dinosaurs dominated the planet for millions of years, living on grass, small plants, and other wildlife.

9. The extinction of dinosaurs remains a puzzle, with some scientists blaming the Ice Age, others blaming changes in their food supply, and some blaming a comet or asteroid.

Exercise 3

1. In 1962 the United States, which was the leading Western power during the Cold War, nearly went to war with the Soviet Union.

3. President Kennedy, who wanted the country to take a strong stand against communism, had permitted a group of Cuban exiles to attack Cuba.

5. Fidel Castro, who feared an American invasion, sought protection from the Soviet Union.

7. The Soviets secretly shipped missiles that could carry nuclear warheads to Cuba.

9. Although some generals suggested the United States launch a massive air strike, the president, who feared starting a nuclear war, ordered a blockade to stop Soviet ships from bringing weapons into Cuba.

Exercise 4

1. Louis Pasteur, a noted French chemist, first discovered antibiotics.

3. Around 1900, Rudolf von Emmerich, a German bacteriologist, isolated pyocyanase, which had the ability to kill cholera and diphtheria germs.

5. In the 1920s, the British scientist Sir Alexander Fleming discovered lysozyme, a substance found in human tears that had powerful antibiotic properties.

7. In 1928 Fleming accidentally discovered penicillin, and he demonstrated its antibiotic properties in a series of experiments against a range of germs.

9. During World War II, two British scientists conducted further tests on penicillin, helping put Fleming's discovery to practical use.

Exercise 5

1. Aaron Burr, America's third vice president, was born in Newark, New Jersey, on February 6, 1756.

3. Burr entered politics, and he was elected to the U.S. Senate in 1791.

5. In 1800 Burr became Thomas Jefferson's vice president, which brought him into greater conflict with political foes.

7. Angered by Hamilton's attacks, Burr challenged Hamilton to a duel.

9. Burr shot and killed Hamilton, ending one of the most bitter personal feuds in American politics.

Exercise 6

The suburbs exploded after World War II. In 1944 only 114,000 houses were built in America. By 1950 over 1,700,000 new houses were built. Veterans, most of whom were eligible for low-interest loans through the GI Bill, created a massive market for single-family homes. Developers built neighborhoods, subdivisions, and entire new communities. Orchards, farms, wheat fields, orange groves, dairies, and forests were bulldozed to build streets and houses. . . .

Exercise 7

1. plasma, Motrin, bandages, first-aid supplies, antibiotics   5

3. Cheryl, Dave Draper, Tony Prito, Tony's nephew, Mindy Weiss, Chris, Heather's best friend   7

5. a former senator, Nancy Price, Paige Brooks, Westbrook Sims, a screenwriter, Lorne Michaels, William Stone   7

Exercise 8

1. The Marx brothers were born in New York City and were known by their stage names: Chico, born Leonard; Harpo, born Arthur; Groucho, born Julius; and Zeppo, born Herbert.

3. The brothers appeared on their own as the Four Nightingales; later, they changed the name of their act to simply the "Marx Brothers."

5. Their early films, including *Animal Crackers, Horse Feathers,* and *Duck Soup,* won praise from fans and critics.

7. The late 1930s was a period of continuing success for the Marx brothers; films such as *A Night at the Opera, A Day at the Races,* and *Room Service* became comedy classics.

9. Groucho smoked cigars, had a large false moustache, and made sarcastic jokes; Chico talked with an Italian accent and played the piano; Harpo never spoke, wore a trench coat, played the harp, and chased women.

CHAPTER 25

Exercise 1

1. a girl's car
3. Kate Chopin's short stories
5. the FBI's evidence
7. children's pictures
9. two men's boat

Exercise 2

1. you're
3. wouldn't
5. shouldn't
7. he'll
9. could've

Exercise 3

On October 1, 1910, an explosion wracked the *Los Angeles Times*' offices. The building's second floor collapsed, crushing employees working below. Despite the fire department's rescue attempts, twenty-one people were killed and dozens injured.

Another bomb exploded in the home of the newspaper's owner. A third bomb was discovered in the home of the Merchants' and Manufacturers' Association's secretary. This bomb did not explode, and police officers' analysis traced its dynamite to James McNamara, a member of the Typographical Union. He was the brother of Joseph McNamara, the International Union of Bridge and Structural Workers' secretary-treasurer.

To many people the bombing of the city's largest newspaper and the murder of twenty-one workers was an act of sheer terrorism, an attack against journalism and free speech. Members of the nation's growing labor movement, however, believed the brothers' arrest was unfair. They insisted the McNamaras had been framed to undermine the public's support for unions. The country's largest union organization, the American Federation of Labor, hired America's

most famous lawyer, Clarence Darrow, to defend the
brothers. . . .

Exercise 4

1. Mayor Hughes proclaimed during his speech, "I won't raise taxes."

3. George Orwell began his famous novel with the sentence, "It was a bright cold day in April and the clocks were striking thirteen."

5. Did you read Paul Mason's article "Coping with Depression"?

7. Last night the president stated, "Whenever I feel confused, I remember the words of Abraham Lincoln, who said, 'Listen to the angels of your better nature.'"

9. "I plan to retire after next season," Terry Wilson announced to her coach, noting, "NBC has offered me a job covering women's tennis."

Exercise 5

"You know," Tom said, "I really like our English class."

"I know," Vicki responded. "I really enjoy the stories we have been reading this semester. Which one is your favorite?"

"Let me think. I guess I really liked all the Poe stories," Tom said, tapping his book. "I really like 'The Pit and the Pendulum' and 'The Tell-Tale Heart.' What about you? What is your favorite so far?" . . .

Exercise 6

1. The receipt is stamped Jan. 15. 10:05 a.m.

3. The school offers students three key services: tutoring, housing, and guidance.

5. Can you help me?

7. Frank Kennedy [no relation to the president] helped design NASA's first rockets.

9. Ted and Nancy's car is the only one on the island.

Exercise 7

On St. Patrick's Day 1930 ground was broken on the Empire State Building in New York City. The date was chosen to bring the project good luck. The builders were facing an awesome challenge—constructing the tallest building in the world. The building was conceived during the Roaring Twenties, but construction did not start until 1930. This was the time of the Great Depression. Thousands of businesses in New York had closed, and few people needed new office space. But the Empire State Building thrived, becoming a prestigious address. . . .

CHAPTER 26

Exercise 1

1. Most cities in the world have emerged naturally, often growing up around a river, such as the Nile, the Rhine, or the Mississippi.
3. The coastal city of Rio de Janeiro served as Brazil's capital for generations.
5. As the economy expanded after WWII, government agencies and corporations needed more office space.
7. During the administration of President Juscelino Kubitschek, planning began on the new capital to be called Brasilia.
9. The fuselage of the plane contains government offices, while apartment buildings form the plane's wings.
11. The famous architect Oscar Niemeyer designed Brasilia's major buildings.
13. On April 21, 1960, Brasilia was officially dedicated by the Brazilian government.
15. Highways and rail lines link Brasilia with Rio de Janeiro, São Paulo, and other major Brazilian cities.
17. Although the strikingly modern city was considered an architectural marvel, many federal employees did not appreciate the actions of President Kubitschek.
19. In the early years, the city was deserted on weekends as workers flew back to Rio to enjoy the old city's famous beaches and nightlife.

Exercise 2

1. The Aztecs took their name from Azatlan, a mythical homeland in northern Mexico.
3. Arriving late, the Aztecs were forced into the unoccupied marshes on the western side of Lake Texcoco.
5. Although poor and greatly outnumbered, the Aztecs gradually built a great empire.
7. Over the years, the Aztecs built bridges to connect their island city to surrounding dry land and drained marshes to create productive gardens.
9. From their small island, the Aztecs expanded their influence, conquering other peoples and creating an empire that reached the border of Guatemala.
11. They developed writing and created a calendar based on an earlier Mayan date-keeping system.
13. The Spanish explorer Hernan Cortés arrived in Tenochtitlan in 1519.
15. At first, the Aztec king Montezuma II welcomed Cortés, thinking him to be the god Quetzalcoatl.
17. Armed with superior weapons and aligning himself with rebellious tribes, Cortés was able to defeat Montezuma's army.
19. Today a million Aztecs, mostly poor farmers, live on the fringes of Mexico City.

Exercise 3

Today we are accustomed to television networks battling for ratings. During sweeps weeks, networks broadcast their most popular or controversial programs. Networks have been known to wage intense bidding wars to land a late-night TV host, news anchor, or sitcom to secure larger audiences and higher advertising revenue. In the early 1990s, NBC, for example, hoped to keep both Letterman and Leno after Johnny Carson retired from hosting the long-running *Tonight Show.* After a number of meetings, Letterman decided to move to CBS. . . .

CHAPTER 27

Exercise 1

1. yield

3. sincerely

5. library

7. equipment

9. surprise

Exercise 2

1. Its [It's] going to be difficult to except [accept] an out-of-state check.

3. My broker gave me advise [advice] about investing.

5. These medications may effect [affect] your ability to drive.

7. All my school cloths [clothes] are in the dryer.

9. Don't work to [too] hard.

Exercise 3

In June 1942, a German U-boat surfaced of [off] Long Island. Four secrete [secret] agents paddled ashore in a rubber boat, equipted [equipped] with demolition supplies and over $80,000 in American money to fiance [finance] a rain [reign] of terror designed to last two years.

The men had been carefully chosen. Through [Though] born in Germany, all four had lived in the United States before the war. One had even served in the U.S. Army and become an American citizen. There [Their] instructions were to destroy the New York water supply, war factories, rail links, bridges, and canals. They also planed [planned] to terrorize the civilan [civilian] population by setting of [off] bombs in crowded deparment [department] stores.

The leader of the team, however, had no intention of carryng [carrying] out there [their] mission. After the war, George Dasch would right [write] that he had become disilusioned [disillusioned] with Nazism and had no desire to harm his adapted [adopted] country. The team buried their gear and took a train to New York City.

Exercise 4

1. knives

3. deer

5. children

7. centuries

9. indexes

Exercise 5

1. The boys drove the new cars.

3. Oils taken from grain can provide useful medicines.

5. The foxes, wolves, and dogs have been vaccinated.

Exercise 6

1. The children loved the rodeos, the circuses, and the zoos.

3. My brothers-in-law must pay taxes in two states because their companies do business in both New York and New Jersey.

5. Two people lost their lives in the accident.

Exercise 7

1. drove

3. spoke

5. negotiated

7. washed

9. built

Exercise 8

1. We took the bus to school.

3. We met at the library.

5. They sang all night.

Exercise 9

1. likeable

3. respectfully

5. defiance

7. beginning

9. noticing

Exercise 10

Early on the morning of June 30, 1908, a strange light _filed_ [filled] the sky over a remote part of Siberia. A streak of fire raced across the treetops and vanished _suddenlly_ [suddenly] over the horizon, followed by a massive explosion. Seven hundred reindeer grazing in a clearing were _instantlly_ [instantly] vaporized. Over 60 million trees were _flattend_ [flattened] in a circle larger _then_ [than] _halve_ [half] of Rhode Island. A giant fireball rose into the sky, visible for hundreds of miles. Seismographs in America and Europe registered the impact of the blast. A _grate_ [great] fire swept the region for

weeks, burning over 700 <u>squre</u> [square] miles of forest. Thousands of tons of ash <u>boilled</u> [boiled] into
the atmosphere, creating <u>wierd</u> [weird] sunsets seen
all over the world.

Preoccupied by <u>revolutionarries</u> [revolutionaries]
and a recent war with Japan, the Russian government
did not bother <u>too</u> [to] investigate an event in an
isolated part of its vast empire. In the late 1930s
scientists photographed the region, still devastated
from the blast. <u>Strangeley</u> [Strangely], no crater
could be found. Whatever fell to earth, <u>weather</u>
[whether] a comet or meteor, must have broken apart
before impact. . . .

Exercise 11

Henry M. Robert is best remembered as the creator
of *Robert's Rules of Order*. Almost every club, organization, and public meeting in the United States
uses this nineteenth-century manual. Henry Robert was
not a debater, politician, teacher, or attorney. He
was an engineer working for the U.S. Army. Although
his military duties carried him across the country on
various construction projects, Robert was active in a
number of organizations. He was once asked to head a
meeting, but he became frustrated because he found
few guidelines for conducting an orderly discussion.

Robert studied existing manuals, but he found
them sketchy and incomplete. Robert began to set
forth his own rules, and he started to write a book.
In the winter of 1874 ice in Lake Michigan delayed
scheduled construction, and Robert had ample time to
work on his book. . . .

Credits

Photo Credits

2: ©Photodisc Green/Getty Images; **8:** ©Eric Kamp/Index Stock Imagery; **10:** ©David Chen/Index Stock Imagery; **21:** ©Jim Starr/Index Stock Imagery; **24:** ©Ed Lallo/Index Stock Imagery; **38:** ©Tim Lynch/Index Stock Imagery; **40:** ©Lonnie Duka/Index Stock Imagery; **53:** ©Mary Ellen Mark; **55:** ©Reuters/CORBIS; **71:** ©Gabe Palmer/CORBIS; **73:** ©Images.com/CORBIS; **92:** ©Yellow Dog Productions/Getty Images; **93:** ©Ed Andrieski-Pool/Getty Images; **110:** ©Elwin Williamson/Index Stock Imagery; **112:** ©Jon Feingersh/CORBIS; **127:** ©Bettmann/CORBIS; **128:** ©Zefa Visual Media/Index Stock Imagery; **143:** ©Najlah Feanny/CORBIS SABA; **145:** ©Julie Dennis/Index Stock Imagery; **152:** ©Images.com/CORBIS; **154:** ©Stephen Derr/Getty Images; **165:** ©Nancy Kaszerman/ZUMA/CORBIS; **168:** ©Canstock Images Inc./Index Stock Imagery; **180:** ©Piotr Powietrzynski/Index Stock Imagery; **182:** ©Mark Segal/Index Stock Imagery; **197:** ©Omni Photo Communications Inc./Index Stock Imagery; **198:** ©Doug Mazell/Index Stock Imagery; **209:** ©Carol Guenzi Agents/Index Stock Imagery; **210:** ©Ewing Galloway/Index Stock Imagery; **226:** ©Ed Kashi/IPN/AURORA; **228:** ©Tom Grill/CORBIS; **242:** ©Bill Keefrey/Index Stock Imagery; **244:** ©Aneal Vohra/Index Stock Imagery; **257:** ©Reuters/CORBIS; **259:** ©Getty Images; **268:** ©CORBIS SYGMA; **272:** ©Sandy Clark/Index Stock Imagery; **285:** ©Key Color/Index Stock Imagery; **288:** ©Annie Griffiths Belt/CORBIS; **304:** ©Royalty-Free/CORBIS; **307:** ©Ariel Skelley/CORBIS; **324:** ©Randy Farls/CORBIS; **326:** ©Firefly Productions/CORBIS; **341:** ©Royalty-Free/CORBIS; **344:** Jutta Klee/CORBIS; **354:** ©Network Productions/Index Stock Imagery; **358:** ©Bill Varie/CORBIS; **374:** ©Myrleen Cate/Index Stock Imagery; **377:** ©REUTERS/Peter Morgan/Landov; **392:** ©CORBIS; **395:** ©AP Photo/Gregory Smith; **403:** ©RNT Productions/CORBIS; **405:** ©Tom Grill/CORBIS; **421:** ©Paul Barton/CORBIS; *Working Together* icon: ©Photodisc/Getty Images

Text Credits

82: "Tickets to Nowhere" by Andy Rooney used by permission of Tribune Media Services; **85:** "The Fender Bender" by Ramon T. Perez is reprinted with permission from the publisher of *Diary of an Undocumented Immigrant* (Houston: Arte Publico Press, Univ. of Houston, 1991); **102:** "The Company Man" by Ellen Goodman, © 1976, The Washington Post Writers Group. Reprinted with permission; **105:** "Odd Enders" by Larry Orenstein used by permission of the author; **122:** "Neat People vs. Sloppy People" by Suzanne Britt reprinted by permission of the author; **135:** "Why We Crave Horror Movies" by Stephen King. Copyright © Stephen King. All rights reserved. Originally appeared in *Playboy* (1982). Reprinted with permission; **138:** "I Refuse to Live in Fear" by Diana Bletter used by permission of the author.

Index